Dahlia Scheindlin
The Crooked Timber of Democracy in Israel

Democracy in Times of Upheaval

Series Editor
Matt Qvortrup, Coventry University

Volume 7

Dahlia Scheindlin

The Crooked Timber of Democracy in Israel

Promise Unfulfilled

DE GRUYTER

ISBN 978-3-11-079645-2
e-ISBN (PDF) 978-3-11-079658-2
e-ISBN (EPUB) 978-3-11-079667-4
ISSN 2701-147X
e-ISSN 2701-1488

Library of Congress Control Number: 2023937996

Bibliographic information published by the Deutsche Nationalbibliothek
The Deutsche Nationalbibliothek lists this publication in the Deutsche Nationalbibliografie; detailed bibliographic data are available on the Internet at http://dnb.dnb.de.

© 2023 Walter de Gruyter GmbH, Berlin/Boston
Cover image: tzahiV / iStock / Getty Images Plus
Printing and binding: CPI books GmbH, Leck

www.degruyter.com

For my family

Acknowledgments

It would be impossible to name all the people who truly deserve my gratitude. Tragically, space limitations prevent me from giving elaborate, personalized descriptions of each person's contribution.

Friends and colleagues, your time, patience, knowledge and sometimes daily support have been invaluable. I would like to thank Rafi Barzilay, Yael Berda, Dan Chyutin, Dan Ephron, Amir Fuchs, Gilad Halpern, Tania Hary, Riva Hocherman, Dina Kraft, Anshel Pfeffer, Adam Shinar, Esther Solomon, Yael Sternhell, Shibley Telhami, Nancy Updike, Dov Waxman (and the Nazarian Center at UCLA for hosting me as a non-resident visiting scholar). I am particularly grateful to those who invested precious time reading and commenting on chapters: Omar Dajani, David Kretzmer, Yehezkel Lein, Frances Raday, Meron Rapoport, Shira Robinson, Gershon Shafir, Noam Sheizaf, Limor Yehuda. Akin Ajayi read the whole thing! I am grateful to Noam Lehmann for research assistance for Sections II and III. All remaining errors, of course, are my responsibility alone.

Matt Qvortrup encouraged me to publish this with De Gruyter. No less important, he has been my academic champion, and an invaluable friend, for years.

My deep thanks to Thanassis Cambanis and to Michael Wahid Hanna for bringing me to Century International, where I developed many of the ideas and initial research for this book. It was a great privilege to work with Eamon Kircher-Allen, a pitch-perfect editor, on this book and at Century. My sincere thanks to Gerhard Boomgaarden, Michaela Göbels and Antonia Mittelbach of De Gruyter, for giving this project a home.

I owe the most to my family. Janice Meyerson gave me a gift that cannot be matched, volunteering her formidable professional skills to copyedit the entire book, at a breakneck pace, out of pure, selfless support. My father, Raymond Scheindlin, provided advice, analytic and intellectual feedback, and much-needed moral support, now and always.

I am very lucky to have Stanley Friedman in my life, a critical thinker about Israel, and pretty much everything else. My mother, Shira Scheindlin, has granted both material and non-material support, for this book and for life, with the love of a mother. Dov, Kat, Zeke, Lila—you keep my spirits alive.

https://doi.org/10.1515/9783110796582-001

Contents

Section I
Introduction

On election night in Israel in November 2022, overjoyed supporters of the militant, ultranationalist Jewish Power Party filled a hall with chants of "Death to terrorists!" The slogan was a sanitized version of the original "Death to Arabs!" popular on the far right, and every Israeli heard its echoes.

"We ask for complete separation between those who are loyal to the state of Israel . . . and those who undermine its existence," party leader Itamar Ben-Gvir told the triumphant crowd. "We must become the owners of our state once again!"[1]

Benjamin Netanyahu, as the leader of the Likud Party, returned to power after the 2022 elections, to begin his sixth term and fifteenth cumulative year as leader. At the time, Netanyahu was standing trial in three different corruption cases.

Jewish Power and its political allies had run in a unified list that won third place, and joined Israel's new governing coalition along with two ultra-Orthodox parties. The new government declared the exclusive right of the Jewish people to all territory west of the Jordan River (the Land of Israel). It also began to rebuild Jewish settlements in the West Bank and to ensure Israel's permanent control over Palestinians, who lacked both civil rights and political representation. Coalition partners proposed changing Israeli laws to permit discrimination by providers of goods and services. The government floated plans to shut down the Israeli Public Broadcasting Corporation, and to levy punitive taxes on civil society organizations critical of the government. It also passed a law to deport Arab Palestinian citizens convicted of terrorism.

International newspapers published editorials warning that Israel could become an "illiberal democracy."[2] Outgoing prime minister Yair Lapid said that the imminent new government "is not committed to democracy, is not committed to the rule of law."[3]

Israelis who supported the parties of the coalition knew what they were voting for. The Religious Zionism Party, which included Ben-Gvir's faction, had campaigned on a detailed program for political takeover of the judiciary, calling its plan "Law and Justice," like the name of the populist party of Poland that had undermined judicial independence for years.[4] Three of the winning parties openly hoped to deepen the grip of religion over public and private life, entrench higher status for Jews in Israel above Arab Palestinian citizens, and legitimize gender and LGBTQ discrimination. All of them opposed Palestinian self-determination. And all four coalition parties were fiercely loyal to Netanyahu, supporting legal changes that could elide his corruption cases.

https://doi.org/10.1515/9783110796582-002

But after the elections, the government's sweeping plans to weaken the judiciary unleashed a tectonic social crisis. Just days after being sworn in, in the first week of 2023, the government announced proposals for near-total executive takeover of the Supreme Court, judicial appointments, and other reforms. The plans would have eviscerated the judiciary, leaving hardly any structural constraints on executive power, beyond elections.

Israelis panicked. Masses of people believed the country was about to be unrecognizably transformed into an undemocratic regime, following the fate of Hungary, Poland, and Turkey. By mid-January 2023, demonstrations of 20,000 protesters in Tel Aviv had exploded into 200,000 people or more, throughout the country, and the protests became a weekly ritual. The noise in these crowds could be deafening —too loud to hear speeches. The hand-lettered signs were carnivalesque, but one chant unified them all: it was a single word, called out in syllables to the rhythm of young Israelis beating drums, blocking traffic junctions on Saturday nights: "De! Mo! Cra! Cy!"

The protests against judicial overhaul reached a peak when the main labor union answered the call for a general strike, demonstrators shut down highways, and military reservists threatened to not report for training. Economists warned of long-term financial damage. Three months after the government was formed, Netanyahu paused the legislation. It looked like Israeli citizens' devotion to democracy had brought the government to its knees.

Most of this book was written prior to the great national quest to save democracy in 2023. The current events have unleashed an unprecedented collective conversation about the meaning of democracy in Israel. But for this conversation to succeed, it needs to acknowledge that the roots of Israel's democratic problems reach far further back. This book argues that the unresolved democratic dilemmas that appear to be tearing the country apart date back to Israel's founding, and earlier. From its start as a Jewish national movement in the late nineteenth century, Israel has had a complicated, sometimes tortured relationship with democracy. Modern Israel has always treated democracy with ambiguity and sometimes suspicion. It has adopted democracy in compromised and partial ways, making some progress at some times while backsliding precipitously at others. Democracy in Israel should never have been taken for granted.

The dramatic events that unfolded as I finished writing this book lent new urgency to its message, but they did not change the history it recounts, nor did they even require major changes to the book's conclusions. Citizens who brought the country to a standstill in the name of democracy in 2023 should be commended —but they should never have waited so long. The current crisis is not an aberration. It is fundamentally a culmination of Israel's troubled historic relationship with democracy.

I do not consider this book to be a radical critique. In Israel, criticism of democracy is commonplace and has accelerated in the decade prior to this project. Israelis have long taken outward pride in Israel's boisterous democratic competition and culture of debate, especially in contrast to the grim state of democracy in the rest of the Middle East. But from roughly 2019, surveys showed that the proportion of Israelis who feel optimistic about the future of their democracy fell below half and has remained a minority.[5]

While I was working on this book, the worries about democracy in Israel bubbled up in daily conversations—whether I was talking to the proverbial taxi driver (he raised it), a former politician, or a seatmate on a plane. It was surprising to discover how cynically—and reflexively—Jewish Israelis reacted when the issue of Israeli democracy came up, sometimes quipping, "What democracy?" It would not have been surprising to hear these reactions from Palestinians living under various forms of undemocratic Israeli control in the West Bank, Gaza, or East Jerusalem—or even from Arab Palestinian citizens of Israel. But the reaction kept coming from Jews, including some with a right-wing background.

Where did the skepticism start? In June 2019, the Israel Democracy Institute seismographs registered a sharp drop in optimism about the future of democracy. This turn toward pessimism was apparently the result of the failure of the April 2019 elections to yield a new government, which forced the country into fresh elections. Such electoral paralysis had never happened before, but continued for three additional election cycles—five in total—within just a few years.

But it wasn't just an electoral crisis. For years, democratic values and institutions had been under attack, including from the political leadership. On the day in May 2019 that Israel called the second election, I published a report chronicling what had become an onslaught on democratic values, including threats to the judiciary, over the previous decade.[6] The report included findings of several democracy indexes and other political analysts who had been tracking illiberal trends. These trends included the legislature advancing bills that more or less openly targeted minorities—including Arab citizens—as well as left-wingers and civil society. The legislature also passed a law deepening exclusive, triumphalist Jewish nationalism; laws targeting the funding sources of certain nongovernmental organizations (NGOs); and laws to suppress certain kinds of civic political protest. Israel's Knesset also passed a law to legalize settlements built on private property belonging to Palestinians. The government advanced annexation and sought to permanently prevent Palestinian self-determination.

When citizens challenged these laws in the Supreme Court, the ruling political parties and their supporters unleashed an avalanche of insults against the Court, which became a full-blown attack accompanied by policy and legislative proposals to weaken the judicial branch, accelerating from 2015.[7] Politicians and influential media figures issued screeds accusing the state bureaucracy, the media, and academia of acting like a "deep state."

Of course, some Israelis were concerned about democracy much earlier. Israel's Zionist left wing had argued for decades that the occupation of the Palestinian territories represented the gravest threat to Israeli democracy. In this view, ongoing occupation would inexorably lead to a single state, in which Jews would lose their demographic majority to Palestinians. At that point, based on the principle of majority rule, Israel could not be both democratic and Jewish. There was also a deeper critique that the undemocratic occupation practice would bleed into democratic culture within Israel, a warning made famous by Yeshayahu Leibowitz, and adopted by many in Israel's anti-occupation community. This critique held that undemocratic occupation practices employ a colonial mentality that corrodes Israel's own society, culture, and politics.[8]

However, most Israeli Jews either do not see a contradiction between democracy and the ongoing occupation, or else they are resigned to compromising on democracy. In a 2014 Peace Index survey, 90 percent of Israelis said that democracy was "important" or "very important."[9] Since a majority of Israelis do not actively oppose the occupation, most of these respondents apparently do not view the two issues as connected; or they consider the occupation to be an unfortunate, if remote, flaw in an otherwise decent democracy. Aside from returning the Sinai Peninsula for a peace treaty with Egypt decades ago and withdrawing settlements from Gaza, Israel's grip over the territories grows only deeper, with some qualified adjustments. And in recent decades, Israelis have increasingly elected parties committed to expanding this control.

To be sure, the peace process that could have ended Israeli control over Palestinians has been a protracted and traumatic failure, and the Palestinian political leadership shares some of the blame. But Israel has also actively expanded settlements and many other forms of control, both visible and less visible, over Palestinian areas since 1967.[10] Many Israelis now believe—or hope—that Israel's control, no matter how undemocratic, is irreversible.

But the historical analysis in this book ventures much further back. In the early decades of statehood, most Palestinian Arab citizens lived under military rule and experienced nothing like democracy. Between 1948 and 1950, when Israel was establishing its legal foundations, the country failed to adopt a formal written constitution or a bill of rights—a failure that it has never truly remedied. Israel's institutionalized undemocratic practices, such as ruling civilians under a military regime for nearly twenty years, began shortly after independent Israel took over from the colonial British Mandate, and retained its practices. Some of these same practices would later be applied to the areas occupied in 1967, and continue to the present. The roots of Israel's compromised democratic culture predate even

1948. The early Zionist ideologies that drove the movement for statehood included but did not prioritize democracy. The pre-state Zionist institutions, successful as they were for proto-state-building, adopted formalistic democratic mechanisms of parliamentary politics, to be sure. But deeper democratic values were often sacrificed in practice. Modern-day protesters longing for Israel's past will make little democratic progress if they are unable to see what was wrong from the start.

Why This Book and Why This Structure

While I have always felt committed to democracy during my life in Israel over twenty-five years, it was my alarm over the increasingly politically driven attacks on the judiciary in the late 2010s that led me to trace the origins of those attacks. I questioned why a swath of Israelis, particularly on the right side of Israel's political map in these years, seemed to harbor a visceral loathing for the law and legal institutions. This line of inquiry opened complex problems that forced me to journey backward. It turned out that the rush of energy focused on eviscerating the judiciary in 2022 and 2023 reflected a convergence of interests of different groups within Israel, and some of these interests dated back to early Zionism. In 2023, the political right wing has taken the lead on antidemocratic policies; historically, the parties known roughly as the historical Left have been no less responsible. But the left–right divide is not exhaustive; in fact, a range of political constituencies that make up Israel today have resisted democratic norms over time, making common cause with one another.

Who laid such weak foundations? Who led the charge for advancing democratic values? How, and at what price? Where did the skeptics and setbacks to democracy come from? Who said one thing and did another, and where, exactly, are the gaps between Israel's treasured democratic image and its actions?

The search took me backward through time; but for readers, I will start from the beginning. I review early Zionist thinking not to provide another book about Zionism but to find out how Israel's founders envisioned the governance, society, and institutions of the future state. In the period after Israeli independence, I look at the aborted constitutional efforts and how this missing vision has affected Israeli law, norms, politics, and governance. By the same logic, I address how democracy is affected by conflict. This is not a book specifically about war, peace, or the Israeli–Arab and Israeli–Palestinian conflicts; but I incorporate them through the prism of their considerable impact on democracy in Israel.

The story of democracy anywhere can include everything, it seems, from law and constitution, parties and elections, governance and civil society, civil liberties and human rights, media, culture, public engagement, and even international relations. Societies change over time, and each of these aspects evolves. Israel is also a country of extremes: in certain phases in history, it behaved very undemocratically; at other times, the country appeared to move in a democratic direction; and in other phases, it rolled itself back. Sometimes Israel did both of these at once, while almost always seeking to craft a democratic image and obfuscate violations. If the narrative becomes entangled within all these threads, I ask the reader's forgiveness in advance.

I do not seek to categorize Israel once and for all as a democracy or not—an artificial binary divide that does not suit the topic. Nor do I search for a new label (though I discuss labels briefly below, to situate the portrait within current debates), or compete with quantitative democracy indexes to provide a numerical grade—though I try to draw on these very valuable tools. My aim is to chronicle the aspects and trajectory of democracy, analyze how Israel is or is not democratic, and dispel what I view as unhelpful myths or frameworks of analysis that I believe have misled understandings of Israel for too long.

Just What Is Democracy?

Painting a democratic portrait of Israel or any country requires some outline of the picture. How does a country fill in the democratic lines and markers? Which colors are used? And which parts are never completed? Those questions can be answered only by establishing the basic markers.

Of course, democracy cannot be captured in a short introduction. Some have concluded that democracy, in general, is an elusive ideal—a process, more than a destination.[11] Instead of delving into democratic theory, the following basic observations guide the book: certain core values of democracy are ancient and enduring over time and are nonnegotiable. From the eighteenth century, representative democracy and the modern republic emerged alongside the growing force of liberalism in the West. Democracy became an emerging ideal and a global currency over the twentieth century, including over Israel's formative prestate decades, and particularly following World War II. A slowdown of the late twentieth century and particularly the backlash in the early decades of the twenty-first century have led to debates over "illiberal democracy." But the rights and freedoms that have emerged from liberalism still give meaning to the procedures and governance of democracy. Democracy without them is a promise unfulfilled.

Ancient Values

Both theorists and politicians have used the word "democracy" in ways that have changed substantially over centuries, and even over the course of the last century. Many references to democracy in the early twentieth century do not reflect the way the term is used today. What we call "democracy" today was called "republic" in the eighteenth century. As I work through this book's chronology, which unfolds from the late nineteenth century, I seek to contextualize what democracy meant, at different points, to those using the term and shaping the history of Israel.

But the historical changes need not obscure the common threads that do exist, particularly a continuity of values, if not institutions.

For example, Athenian democracy would be almost unrecognizable compared with that of modern democratic countries, in terms of how it was practiced and who was allowed to participate. Citizens governed themselves directly, taking on personal roles, and thus literally governed themselves; but famously few residents were included as citizens.

However, the Athenian governance was grounded in its then-innovative notions of equality. The system aimed to provide equal weight for all citizens in governance. Herodotus referred to *isonomia, isêgoria,* and *isokratia*—equality of law, speech, and power, respectively—as the system called *demokratia,* meaning "rule by the people."[12] Voluntarism and participation distinguished Athens from its rival city-states, or tyrannical regimes; Herodotus linked these qualities to social commitment and resilience.[13] Athens allowed its citizens relative freedom in their personal lives and much of their economic activity, provided they followed the law.[14]

The underlying ideas of equality among the citizens before the law—equality of speech and influence, individual freedoms, voluntarism, and citizen participation—were incipient values that informed this small and ancient society. These principles of the ancient democratic experiment remain relevant in contemporary definitions of democracy.

In the late eighteenth century, the new institutional form of governance by the people began to emerge. The great shifts of the Enlightenment, the French and American Revolutions, and the emergence of liberalism changed the sources of the state's authority, as well as the purpose of the state itself. Monarchies had ruled with absolute power and divine right, with the will of God known only to them, but Enlightenment thinkers established the capacity of all individuals for rational thinking and reason. If, as John Locke argued, all people were equal and free, they must consent to be governed, under laws known to all. The purpose of the state was to protect individual rights, particularly property; but freedom itself meant liberation from arbitrary power.[15]

When America's constitutional authors wrote the Federalist Papers, "democracy" still referred to "a small number of citizens, who assemble and administer the government in person."[16] The republic, by contrast, was a "scheme of representation" for Madison, consistent with John Stuart Mill's notion that the ideal government is elected by the people in order to act as representatives of the people's will.[17]

Liberalism was spreading in the Anglo-American and European world in the mid-nineteenth century, recognizing the value, and therefore the rights, of individuals, particularly the middle class.[18] Critically, liberalism was not necessarily or inherently connected to popular governance at the time. Nevertheless, liberalism and republicanism—the protection of individuals by a government selected by the people to represent them and for the common good—form the layers of modern citizenship. Civil rights became the means to protect individuals, while political rights established participation in representative governance.[19]

The framers of emerging notions of a democratic republic during the late eighteenth and nineteenth centuries recognized that the new danger lay in the power of the state itself, which could be used to oppress the people, just like monarchs. The answer was for the state to voluntarily limit its own power. As Eugene Rostow wrote in his 1962 book *The Sovereign Prerogative*, "The freedom and dignity of man can be assured only by imposing severe and enforceable limitations upon the freedom of the state... . Man can be free [and] political processes can in truth be democratic only when, and only because, the state is not free."[20] Immanuel Kant, writing in 1784, observed that the "crooked timber of humanity" required flawed people to be constrained by justice and sanctions in order for everyone else to be free; at the level of the state, he later wrote that "the republican constitution is the only one which is compatible with the rights of human beings."[21]

That constitution, for the Federalist authors, embraced Montesquieu's doctrine of separation of powers. The constitution was to represent the will of the people in a fundamental way, and a fully independent judiciary was to interpret the constitution. The judiciary should "prefer" the constitution over any statute that violated its values. The constitution would lay out the structures to purposely limit the power of any one body in governance.[22]

Thus, by the late eighteenth century, ideas about democracy had taken the basic form of representative government selected by the people and expected to be accountable to their interests: protection of individual rights and freedoms; and voluntary limits on the power of the elected representatives through institutional constraints on state power.

And it wasn't only the governing institutions that distributed power. In the 1830s, Alexis de Tocqueville, deeply concerned with the threat of a tyrannical majority, was also interested in mitigating influences on state power by the public itself. He was struck by American civic associations that, he believed, prevented both rampant individualism and the runaway power of the government. His observations about these associations convinced him that freedom of association and expression among citizens was part of the backbone of democracy.[23] Tocqueville concluded that for the public, knowing how to associate was "the mother of all knowledge since the success of all others depends on it."[24] The institutions of government must be made accountable to the public by demands from citizens outside of government, through their public activities. Democracy theorist Robert Dahl captured the requirement for genuine competition of power throughout institutions and society as a necessary feature for democratic governance, using the term "polyarchy."[25]

By the twentieth century, the pillars of liberal democracy were clear. Authority flowed from the people, and citizens enjoyed equality, protection of individual rights, and representative government. The state was expected to decentralize power, adopt limitations on itself, subject the executive to the popular vote, and be accountable to engaged citizens between elections. Civil society and freedom of speech and association were essential for citizens to check government power. In 1997, Fareed Zakaria asserted that democracy in the West over the past century actually meant *"liberal* democracy."[26]

It is ironic that universal suffrage emerged as a sine qua non of democratic governance, yet lagged severely, even in more democratic countries of the nineteenth and twentieth centuries.[27] The United States only guaranteed effective equal voting rights to Black Americans in the 1960s, nearly a century after the Fifteenth Amendment, which was supposed to give Black men the right to vote. Switzerland did not give women the right to vote in federal elections until 1971. Thus, universal suffrage was not taken for granted at mid-century; but today, it is impossible to consider democracy without it.

In the mid-twentieth century, the context for legitimate elections in democracy was further developed: polls had to be free, fair, and regular; electoral authorities needed to be accountable to voters; and incumbents had to transfer power peacefully if they lost. Liberal elements of democracy—civil liberties such as physical protection of life and property, freedom of religion, speech, press, association, and political activity—required institutional structures to protect them. These, too, became conditions of democracy.[28]

These basic contours of democracy in the twentieth century provide the basis of quantitative, measurable, and comparable indexes that emerged from approximately the 1970s.

In 1973, Freedom House began publishing its annual index, called "Freedom in the World." In 1978, its fifth year, the social scientist Raymond Gastil, writing for

Freedom House, observed a "democratic revolution," in which a growing number of states provided "equal treatment before the law; protection against arbitrary government; right of representation of all adult individuals in the formation of laws; majority rule and the secret ballot; free access to knowledge and open discussion of issues of public policy; and right of freedom of choice—in work, residence, religion, and even in right of resignation."[29]

It was increasingly clear that the two elements—liberal rights and political representation—were deeply intertwined. Gastil wrote:

> *Civil liberties* are the rights of the individual against the state, rights to free expression, to a fair trial; they are what most of us mean by freedom. *Political rights* are legal rights to play a part in determining who governs or what the laws of the community are. The two kinds of rights are interdependent: civil liberties without political rights are apt to be lost, and political rights without civil rights are meaningless.[30]

This and other systematic indexes were a breakthrough for standardizing the variables that make up democracy. The establishment of several such tools indicated that the meaning of democracy was converging around these ideas. Other indexes include the Economist Intelligence Unit's Democracy Index; and the Global State of Democracy Index, by International IDEA (Institute for Democracy and Electoral Assistance).[31] All these focus on electoral integrity, governance, civil liberties, institutional accountability, and social participation. They include subcategories ranging from freedom of expression to judicial independence. Specific questions vary: the Economist's Democracy Index includes literacy rates and separation of religion and state, for example.[32] But the differences are often technical rather than substantive. This book refers to the broad parameters included in the indexes mentioned here, reflecting the evolution of democracy in the twentieth century, as the prism for reviewing Israel's past and present.

It is worth noting that there have been efforts over the years to establish additional requirements to democracy that have not been as widely incorporated. During World War II, for example, Franklin D. Roosevelt argued passionately for what he considered a "Second Bill of Rights," linking basic material stability with freedom itself.[33] Yet, while minimum economic and social welfare standards have been taken up by individual states and international conventions, they are not a universal measure of democracy.

Also in the twentieth century, numerous countries emerged from the fall of empires with pluralistic societies, including multiple ethnic, national, language, and religious groups. Some democracies experimented with power-sharing systems, which Arend Lijphart called "consociational," using mechanisms that guaranteed meaningful representation and power for the different groups in society, such as an executive veto or a guaranteed position, fixed proportions in branches of government representing ethnic groups, and regional autonomy.[34] Some formal consociational arrangements have failed to provide stable governance, or may be prohibitively complex. As such, power-sharing based on identity is not a measure of democracy but represents an attempt to contain social competition through institutions, rather than confrontations. These additional aspects are relevant to Israel but are not included as an actual indicator of democracy.

The Current Global Context: Backlash against Democracy

The story of democracy in Israel or anywhere cannot be told in isolation from the global context at the time of writing. Just as this book argues that Israel's democratic crisis had deep roots in its own history, my analysis at this time—and Israel's specific developments at present—is influenced by the global context.

Democracy in the twenty-first century is experiencing a backlash. But the backlash itself is not new.

The number of democracies grew significantly around the world from the mid-nineteenth century to the early twenty-first, the historical context of Zionism and the modern state of Israel. Samuel Huntington, a foremost scholar of global democratic trends, identified "waves" and "reverse waves" throughout that time. His definitions and methodology have drawn criticism, but the basic trends he identified remain a valuable indicator. From 1828 to 1926, Huntington counted thirty-three democratic countries. In the second wave, 1943–62, he counted fifty-two democracies. In 1991, Huntington posited that the world was amid a third wave that had started in 1974, during which about sixty-five countries were democratic. Each rise was met with reversals, complicating the ability to count growth; but by his third wave, the number of democratizing countries was seven times larger than those countries reversing.[35]

In 1997, Fareed Zakaria counted 118 democracies among 193 countries in the world.[36] Zakaria observed that the next reverse wave was characterized by a "coming apart" of constitutional liberalism and democracy—the former representing a structure placing limits on state power and guaranteeing individual rights, while "democracy" referred to states with popularly and fairly elected governments; the political theorist Larry Diamond observed the same distinction, finding that there were significantly more "formal" than "liberal" democracies.[37] Zakaria found that the number of democratically elected governments that failed to become liberal democracies was growing. These illiberal democracies were found to be consolidating executive power and suppressing opposition; they placed restrictions on freedom of speech and assembly, or pressure on media, and violated human rights.[38]

By the twenty-first century, the trend had become full-blown. If Zakaria had largely observed illiberalism among transitioning or young electoral democracies, by the 2010s, backsliding was happening in "unmistakably developed" countries, according to political scientist Matt Qvortrup, including "established polyarchies."[39] The new backlash was characterized by populism, with a distinctive political style depicting a struggle between the people and the entrenched elite, often in "apocalyptic" terms, as per Jan-Werner Mueller, one of the leading observers of this phenomenon.[40] Such strongmen leaders could represent the historical Left or Right, but they shared illiberal and often nationalist outlooks and policies, from Donald Trump to leaders in the Philippines, Poland, Brazil, India, and, this book argues, Israel. It was Hungary's Viktor Orbán who popularized the term "illiberal democracy" in the twenty-first century and who has generated a flurry of justifiable alarm about the decline of liberal democracy (examined at greater length in Section VI). The approach of this book sides with Gastil and Freedom House in the 1970s, viewing civil liberties and political rights as intertwined and interdependent; without one, the other is lost or meaningless. By this logic, I share Mueller's critique of the term "illiberal democracy," which ends up legitimizing a category, rather than critiquing the problem. For Mueller, "[t]hese political rights are not just about liberalism (or the rule of law); they are constitutive of democracy as such."[41]

Where Did Israel Fit In?

It is not always easy to locate Israel within these trends because Israel is often left out of comparative academic literature, partly because it is considered uniquely complex or unique in general.[42] In popular treatment, but also in much Western and Israeli scholarship, democracy in Israel is taken for granted, mostly due to its boisterous and too-regular elections, universal suffrage, and largely independent press.[43]

This approach has always been flawed. First, the presumption of democracy is grounded in a focus on Israeli citizens; for any text written after 1967, this analysis neglected the reality that Israel directly controlled millions of noncitizens in the Occupied Territories. In 1967, Israel had about 2.7 million citizens and governed some 1 million noncitizens living in what had recently become the Occupied Territories; today, Israel's population is over 9.7 million, and it controls, directly or indirectly, over 5 million Palestinians in the West Bank, Gaza, and East Jerusalem through various undemocratic mechanisms.

But Israel's democratic deficits existed prior to the occupation, though only a relatively small group of scholars have chronicled this aspect. In the late 1970s, Israeli sociologist Jonathan Shapira broke new ground, focusing on the concentration of power in the hands of a single-party-dominated ruling elite in the pre-state era and in Israel's early years; he was considered a pioneer but was also resented for "tainting" the image of the founding decades.[44] In the 1980s, Bernard Avishai, in *The Tragedy of Zionism*, challenged the health of democracy in Israel in its first four decades, as democratic qualities foundered under pressure from both the legacy of Labor Zionism and newly emerging undemocratic trends. The political philosopher Avishai Margalit responded with puzzlement that anyone would expect Israel to become a liberal democracy, which was hardly central to the hodgepodge of ideologies at the core of Zionism.[45]

Law scholar Menachem Mautner has argued that liberalism itself was imported into the Yishuv during the British Mandate years (1922–48), part of the "Anglification" of the legal system—sparking resistance among Jews seeking to establish Hebraic law based on Judaic sources. Mautner concludes that, throughout Israeli history, it was the legal establishment—specifically, the Supreme Court—that became the main "agent" of liberal values in Israel's political culture.[46]

In the 1990s, Israeli scholars further critiqued and sought to characterize Israel's system. In 1997, Israeli sociologist Sammy Smooha found that Israel was best characterized as an "ethnic democracy," in which Jews, the majority, hold most of the control over institutions and resources. Ethnic democracy was "located somewhere in the democratic section of the democracy-non-democracy continuum," in Smooha's words.[47] Asad Ghanem, Nadim Rouhana, and Oren Yiftachel responded that "ethnic democracy" was a contradiction; they viewed Israel as an "ethnocracy."[48] The historian Alan Dowty argued that they held Israel to a higher democratic standard than other countries.[49] Looking specifically at Israel's policies in its earliest decades and the military-occupation-like regime within Israel prior to 1967, the historian Shira Robinson in 2013 described Israel as a "liberal settler state."[50]

All the while, most examinations continued to distinguish between what is often called "Israel proper," and the Occupied Territories. All the international indexes separate the two regimes for analysis; and Israel's own Israel Democracy Index, published by the Israeli Democracy Institute since 2003, does not assess the occupation regime. In this book, when evaluating democratic practice in Israel, I have chosen to consider all people and territory under Israeli control. This is not an arbitrary decision—I believe that the historical analysis of Israeli policy demonstrates that the control of the land and population of the Occupied Territories is inseparable from Israeli governance and society.

Including the occupation complicates democratic inquiries. One of the most successful approaches is Gal Ariely's 2021 book, *Israel's Regime Untangled: Between Democracy and Apartheid*. The author takes a comprehensive approach toward time, space, and types of Israeli governance. Gershon Shafir and Yoav Peled also avoided a quantitative democratic measure or label, considering Israel's trajectory through the prism of citizenship instead.[51]

Nonacademic literature, from op-eds to the writings of student activists and NGOs, tends to reduce the question of democracy to the occupation: Does occupation negate democracy, or is occupation an unfortunate flaw in an otherwise robust democracy? This is a limiting analytical framework because it encourages the misleading perception that the problem with democracy began, and could end, with occupation. Worse, allowing the occupation to categorically negate democracy ignores the ways in which Israel *is* democratic, proving its own capacity to be so. The picture I have found while working on this book is more complicated but also simple: Israel is democratic enough to know just how undemocratic it is.

How the Book Is Organized

The attempt to paint a comprehensive (if incomplete) picture of democracy in Israel raised an immediate dilemma between a thematic versus a chronological structure. I have chosen the mostly chronological approach for the overall structure because I believe that the story changes in coherent ways over time, each phase laying the groundwork for democratic improvement or deterioration in the next stage. Yet not every relevant democratic development fits perfectly into the chronological breakdown. As such, at times in this book, I describe specific events in the "wrong" historical phase, if I think that they are more relevant to the main themes represented in that era.

The story can be messy. As I was writing, rather than envisioning a straight line, I often pictured a tree with roots representing different directions, along with the trunk and a tangle of branches; I ask which parts flourish, or wither, and when and why. The "crooked timber" of the title is borrowed from Immanuel Kant: "Out of the crooked timber of humanity no straight thing was ever made."[52] But the rendering was made popular by Isaiah Berlin, who argued that Kant accepted humanity's flaws and that the struggle for perfection (utopia) was both wrong and dangerous. Democracy, too, is not perfect anywhere, but the process of improvement matters.

The historical story begins with the early Zionists who dreamed up and eventually founded the modern state (Section II).

The next sections cover Israel's history as an independent state. The landmarks of this book are democratic turning points, sometimes coinciding with wars and sometimes not. Therefore, Section III covers the phase after independence, 1948–66, when Israel had its least democratic form of governance, with statist and party-driven control over society and a military regime governing a segment of its own citizens. The announcement of the end of the military government over Israeli Arab citizens marks the end of this phase, though the regime of colonial-era laws governing these citizens lingered until 1968.

Section IV covers a span of twenty-five years, 1967–92, which I have come to view as Israel's democratic adolescence. At the start of that phase, Israel appeared poised to make democratic progress by ending its military regime over its citizens. During this period, there are examples of growing judicial oversight of the government and spontaneous citizen action to express political discontent—forces that set the stage for Israel's first transition of power. At the same time, however, Israel conquered major new territory and established a new occupation. Nevertheless, from 1977, some of the democratizing and liberalizing trends became more established—even as the occupation deepened alongside them.

Section V spans 1992–2009, when Israel passed watershed human rights legislation that symbolized an acceleration of liberalizing trends in law, social norms, and even progress toward peace with the Palestinians. I argue that the confluence of liberalization and significant steps toward a peace process is not a coincidence. Israel also expressed progressive tendencies during this time; yet the breakdown of the peace process and the resurgence of violent conflict, set the stage for the next phase of democratic erosion, overlapping with nascent populist illiberal trends in other countries, within Israel's specific context.

Section VI takes us from 2009 to the present and begins with a full-blown nationalist leadership driving a populist, illiberal agenda that tapped and leveraged accelerating antidemocratic global trends in local garb. The new movement skillfully exploited Israel's oldest conflicts and democratic vulnerabilities to pull Israel toward a new undemocratic phase of its history.

It should be clear that this is not a story of linear progress toward democracy, or a consistent high grade, followed by a plunge. The roots of Israel's democratic problems were there from the start.

Analytic but Not Unbiased

Over the twenty-five years that I've lived in Israel, my thinking has been shaped by an extremely lucky perch as a political consultant and then as a political analyst and commentator. These roles offered greater access to the political world than I sometimes wished to see, in the sense of not wishing to know how sausage is made.

In passing conversations, people tend to get excited when they hear about my experiences with politicians, but my specific job—listening to people as a public-opinion researcher—is still far more exciting to me. I have been listening for twenty-four years, ever since I was hired to support the American campaign gurus advising an Israeli political campaign in 1999, though all I brought to the job was two degrees in comparative religion and a passion for social issues and conflict resolution. My mentor, the Washington-based international pollster Stan Greenberg, must have thought that religious studies gave me an aptitude for (or, at least, an interest in) how people think—while I thought that it was a leap to hire a humanities student for a statistics-based professional track. Nevertheless, he did hire me, and he taught me everything.

Twenty-four years and nine Israeli campaigns later (there have been twelve in that time—I skipped a few), I have worked for Israeli political parties in the center and, more often, on the left—this is a disclosure. I believed that these parties were committed to advancing peace and democracy, and a book about democracy is no place to avoid transparency about my own priorities. I have aimed to keep my bias for democracy separate from my investigation of specific episodes in Israeli history, with no presumption that one side or political force was naturally better (or worse) than the other. Some of the analysis belies my own professional and voting history.

Of necessity, I have tried to draw a distinction between flaws that can truly appear in any democracy—such as certain forms of de facto discrimination—and structural failures or victories of democracy. If I considered every kind of democratic flaw, Israel truly would be held to a higher standard and—even worse—the book would never end.

Ultimately, I came to think of this book as a biography of democracy; as in any life, there can be an arc, but there are also fits and starts, progress, backsliding, contradictions, and hypocrisies. Death is not, I hope, the inevitable outcome, as it is in life. But there is another apt biological metaphor. If one thing seems clear at present, it's that democracy in Israel is not well. The right diagnosis is key to any treatment, and the wrong diagnosis will make the medicine ineffective, at best. The myth of a celebrated democracy—plucky, boisterous, or any other saccharine adjective—needs to be laid to rest by anyone who truly cares about the country and the people it rules.

Section II
Pre-State Zionism and the Tangled Roots of Democracy: Late Nineteenth Century to 1947

A simple story about Israel's Zionist roots holds that the European basis of the movement provided the democratic foundations, which were later eroded by the realities of the undemocratic Middle East and the influx of immigrants from countries without a democratic tradition, either from Arab countries or from the Soviet Union.

But the European democratic roots of pre-state Zionist ideas and institutions were themselves tangled, fragmented, and partial. The "Europe" of early Zionism was no monolith then, any more than it is now. The political traditions of Eastern Europe differed vastly from those of the Anglo-American Western liberal tradition. And the most influential movements and competing streams within Zionist ideology emerged from the East.

This section follows the place of democracy in the early stages and streams of Zionist ideology, through institution-building, and the role of democratic ideals in winning international legitimacy.

Nineteenth-century nationalism was a force for self-determination and liberation, linked to popular sovereignty and majority rule. For Zionists, nationalism offered an answer to persecution. The earliest Zionists appreciated the liberation but were cautious regarding majority rule, since they were a minority everywhere. Early Zionists would adopt certain parliamentary democratic organizational practices for movement-building, but Labor Zionism, which came to dominate the movement, developed a statist, Jewish-nationalist ethos for Zionist institution-building. Democracy became increasingly important for establishing international legitimacy and was incorporated into the international terms for statehood. Those European builders and dreamers of the state would ultimately redefine democracy to fit Zionism first—sacrificing the pillars and legs of the edifice along the way.

https://doi.org/10.1515/9783110796582-003

Chapter 1: European Context of Early Zionism

Zionism emerged from the two sociocultural poles of European Jewish life in the late nineteenth century: the urbanized, cosmopolitan polyglot Jews populating the cafés of Berlin, Vienna, and Odessa, in a century of liberalism, represented one side of Jewish life;[1] and throughout the Pale of Jewish Settlement, stretching through parts of modern-day Poland, Lithuania, Belarus, Ukraine, and Russia, were the shtetls. Here Jews lived in insular, self-organized, and traditional communities, which were increasingly under the threat of violent pogroms.

In the 1880s, clusters of Jewish activists emerging from the shtetl began settling in Ottoman Palestine. The following decade, Theodor Herzl, an intense, ambitious Jewish journalist who, in other circumstances, might have ended up (in the words of a biographer) "a fanatical demi-intellectual, whiling away his days in cafés, scribbling feverishly in a diary," instead became the intellectual and organizational founder of modern Zionism.[2]

The geographic and social boundaries between the two worlds—the cosmopolitan Jews and the insular traditionalists—could be fluid. Young Jews from the small communities then under the Russian Empire—like David Gruen, better known as David Ben-Gurion—would seek their fortunes in the cities. The urbane Jewish intellectual Theodor Herzl would realize the power of the Jewish masses in the Pale for creating a movement.

These two early drivers of modern Zionism were of different generations, but they shared the urgent aim of protecting Jewish lives and communities from persecution. They were influenced by different political currents: Marxism and socialism formed the revolutionary backdrop for the "young and scruffy" activists from Eastern Europe.[3] But for Herzl and his Jewish intellectual circles, nineteenth-century liberalism held tremendous promise throughout the century—and yet its failure to protect the Jews drove their anxiety and the urgency of his task. In a way, the nascent interest in Zionism reflected the failures of liberalism and the promise of socialism among European Jews seeking to fend off disaster.

Herzl Preferred Aristocracy

For Herzl in 1890s France, democracy was a matter of "the masses," and he was worried about them. Herzl witnessed anti-Semitism rising in the cosmopolitan cultures of both Paris and Vienna; he wrote that the Dreyfus affair galvanized him, but he was at least as concerned about Karl Lueger's victory in Vienna's 1895 elections. Herzl came to associate democracy with mob rule, in which regular people voted democratically for anti-Semites.[4] Nineteenth-century Europe was supposed to be emancipated, rational, and liberal, but as Herzl's close friend Max Nordau understood, this same environment hosted "a new kind of political Jew-hatred, an anti-Jewishness no longer derived from the old religious prejudices but grounded in the new liberal atmosphere, which was supposed to cure the traditional hatred of the Jews."[5]

In *The Jewish State*, an 1896 pamphlet, Herzl confronted the danger as his faith in the promise of equality withered.

> No one can deny the gravity of the situation of the Jews... . *[T]heir equality before the law, granted by statute, has become practically a dead letter.* They are debarred from filling even moderately high positions, either in the army, or in any public or private capacity. And attempts are made to thrust them out of business... . Attacks in Parliaments, in assemblies, in the press, in the pulpit, in the street ... become daily more numerous.[6] [emphasis mine]

Yet Herzl rejected the posture of powerless victim: "But this is not to be an attempt to make out a doleful category of Jewish hardships. I do not intend to arouse sympathetic emotions," he wrote, which would be a "futile and undignified proceeding."[7]

Nordau surmised that there was a cultural lag between evolving values and practice: "Jews were emancipated in Europe not from an inner necessity, but in imitation of a political fashion; not because the people had decided from their hearts to stretch out a brotherly hand."[8] Instead of fostering tolerance, popular representation gave free expression to enduring Jew-hatred. Nordau believed that, in England, the Jewish Emancipation reflected values that were deeper and more genuine than on the Continent. In England, these values were written into the law, and he believed that these laws were a true expression of social norms.[9]

Compounding Herzl's gloomy mood toward democratic practices, he feared that factional struggles among Jews would destroy the Zionist project from within. He wrote that the proto-state-building institutions must *not* be democratic, in the sense of holding debates and votes, which would "ruin the cause from the outset," and he called democracy "political nonsense."[10]

Instead, Herzl imagined an aristocratic republic and thought that the best way to achieve it was to lobby tirelessly with elite power brokers of the world. Herzl eventually concluded that global leaders would not be convinced by arguments alone and that a mass movement was necessary to amplify the efforts. But he "remained strongly committed to authoritarian leadership from above," as historian Alan Dowty writes, "even though circumstances forced him to modify it in practice."[11]

Still, when the first World Zionist Congress (WZC) was held in 1897, the social forces favored a parliamentary democratic mechanism for establishing the movement. The traditional structure of European Jewish communities had no central-ized authority; participation in the congress was voluntary, and consensus-building was the only option. The adoption of a parliamentary system was considered the cornerstone for Israel's future legislature. But it was a compromise for Herzl. Dowty writes: "Herzl was not the founder of Israeli democracy; he was only com-ing to terms with a reality that he could not have changed anyway."[12]

According to one argument, Jews were suited to parliamentary culture. Jewish shtetl life and community organization rested on political bargaining, consensus-building, power-sharing, voluntarism, and elections—all qualities that made it amenable to democracy. But that same Jewish culture of governance had idiosyn-crasies, as well. Dowty cites an "anthropological portrait" drawn by other scholars from contemporary sources:

> The actual mechanics of election vary widely, but a constant feature is the campaigning in-separable from all elections, the forming of factions, the influencing of the humble members by the city bosses... . There is little order and more talking than listening... . Majority rule is followed but not accepted. The minority may concede momentary victory but the issue is not considered settled... . "Every Jew has his own *Shulhan Aruch*," they say, meaning his own in-terpretation of the Law.[13]

These Jewish community organizational practices were also oriented toward insu-larity. The very glue that kept the struggling Jewish minority communities tightly bound provided "little guidance or experience in encompassing groups who were not a part of this community."[14] The system was not designed to incorporate outsiders.

Still, it is ironic to consider Dowty's argument that traditional Jewish shtetl life in the Pale was a substantive basis for procedural democracy, while European lib-eralism alongside expansion of the franchise had yielded to anti-Semitism and a xenophobic backlash. Chaim Weizmann viewed the emerging Zionist sentiment as no less than a democratic wave. "In the depths of the masses an impulse awoke, vague, groping, unformulated, for Jewish self-liberation," he wrote in his autobiography. The urge was "revolutionary and democratic." Weizmann viewed the Russian Jewish awakening as a revolt not only against the czar's persecution of the Jews but also as a revolt against the traditional Jewish leaders who claimed to represent the community. This double revolution "was, in short, the birth of modern Zionism."[15] Weizmann also participated in a smaller sort of rebellion, as part of a nascent opposition within Herzl's movement, called the "democratic faction."[16]

Chapter 2: Three Visions of Zionism

Of the numerous ideological factions and streams within modern Jewish national-ism, three of them—the socialist-oriented, secular Labor Zionism, Revisionist Zion-ism, and religious Zionism—left the most prominent mark on the independent state after 1948. These Zionist movements continue to shape Israel's ideological di-lemmas as an independent state, and in the present time; therefore this chapter focuses on the origins of the three influential streams, rather than a full review of Zionism in general. The streams were led, respectively, by David Ben-Gurion, who represented Labor Zionism; Vladimir (Ze'ev) Jabotinsky, the founder of Revi-sionist Zionism; and Rabbi Isaac Herzog (father of Israel's sixth president and grandfather of its eleventh) and Rabbi Abraham Isaac Hacohen Kook, who were among the most influential figures of early religious Zionism.

The British took control over the areas now known as Mandatory Palestine from the Ottoman Empire, including Cisjordan (the lands between the Jordan River and the Mediterranean) and Transjordan (today's Jordan), during World War I. In 1917, the British issued the Balfour Declaration, which promised a Jewish national home in Palestine. The Allied powers decided to establish an international mandate at the San Remo conference of 1920, and the League of Nations approved the British Mandate in 1922; by that time, the British had already determined that Transjordan was closed to Jewish immigration.[17] The Jewish community in Pales-tine was known as the Yishuv; each of the Zionist streams described here sought to shape its emerging contours.

Ben-Gurion: Socialist, Statist, and Zionist Above All

David Ben-Gurion was the unrivaled workhorse of both the Zionist movement and the institutions of the future state. He laid the tracks for social organization and political life that would dominate the state before independence and for decades afterward. His socialist-oriented Labor Zionist movement, spearheaded by what became the Mapai Party, ruled the most powerful proto-state Zionist institutions of the early twentieth century.

Ben-Gurion's thinking about democracy in the pre-state era can be character-ized broadly as piecemeal, secondary, and instrumental. Ben-Gurion certainly en-visioned democratic systems of governance in a future state. But democracy was neither his core ideology nor his favored political strategy. Section III, analyzing the first decades of statehood, shows that Ben-Gurion unsentimentally cut corners on democratic institutions, practice, and values for the sake of state-building, and he presided over the least democratic era in Israel's postindependence history.

Ben-Gurion was born David Gruen in 1886 in Plonsk, in the Russian Empire (now Poland). Though educated in a religious seminary, by age fourteen he was already a Zionist activist enthralled by socialism. Gruen moved to Warsaw at eighteen and soon started a local chapter of the socialist Zionist group Po'alei Zion ("Workers of Zion").[18] He and his closest Zionist friends, Berl Katznelson and Yitzhak Tabenkin—three key figures within Labor Zionism—were steeped in Marxism and socialism.[19]

Ben-Gurion traveled to Palestine early in the new century, and then left to study law in Istanbul. During World War I, he spent three years in New York, where he studied the political system, befriended a Supreme Court judge, pondered capitalism, and studied the Constitution.[20]

But Ben-Gurion clung to his socialist roots for the organizing principle of pre-state Jewish settlement. In 1919, his movement merged with other labor Zionist parties to form the Ahdut Ha'avodah Party. Although by the 1920s, the Soviet regime was already hostile to Zionism, and Ben-Gurion would come to loathe communism, he favored certain organizational aspects of the regime, including the "extreme centralization" of communism in Russia and a planned, top-down economy.[21] The Histadrut was founded in 1920 by recent Jewish immigrants in Palestine, initially as a non-party-aligned trade union. Ben-Gurion was elected to the Histadrut's secretariat in 1921, and became the dominant force for the next fifteen years.[22] He wrote the Histadrut's constitution and established a holding company for the main industries of the Yishuv, Hevrat Ovdim, making the organization both a supreme contractor and the representative of the workers.[23]

Under Ben-Gurion's leadership, the Histadrut was to become one of the most powerful institutions shaping politics and society in the Yishuv and, later, in the independent state. The Histadrut was intended to supply labor, wages, and all needs of the workers. It also became perhaps the most party-aligned pre-state institution, eventually almost indistinguishable from Ben-Gurion's party (in its evolving iterations). Despite the complex relationship with the Soviet Union, Ben-Gurion visited there in 1923, still enthralled with the October Revolution and scouring for ideas on how to build society.[24] He was also strategic, projecting sympathetic attitudes toward the Soviet Union when it was politically expedient, and later making overtures to the Communist Party in the Yishuv when he wished to curry favor with the Soviet Union.

It was during his visit to the Soviet Union that Ben-Gurion marked the first known instance of the word *mamlakhtiyut* in his diary, possibly striving to translate the Russian term for "kingdom-like" or "state-like."[25] Ben-Gurion embraced the word to describe top-down efforts to unify the patchwork of disparate Jewish communities, languages, and culture, to instill loyalty to a new (future) state, and to strengthen the case for self-determination. Later, the concept of *mamlakhtiyut* would be associated with statism, or "etatism," though the legal historian Nir Kedar views the concept more favorably as a republican civic-minded ethos. Critics, even within his own party, charged that the concept became a coercive ideology that violated the voluntary spirit of the early Labor Zionist movement, or even a "cult of the military."[26]

Ben-Gurion may have envisioned democratic governing institutions based on multiparty elections and a parliamentary system. But his institutional vision for the Histadrut was rather less democratic. He spoke of a "dictatorship of the Hebrew laborer" and a Zionist dictatorship. Historian Tom Segev holds that "what he really meant was a dictatorship of his party and the Histadrut" to take charge of "all areas of life."[27] Critics accused Ben-Gurion of intolerance and authoritarian rule. More than his intellectual output, the evolution of Zionist institutions (examined in Chapter 3) provides an apt representation of Ben-Gurion's state-building legacy.

For Ben-Gurion, democracy might have been a useful mechanism for choosing the leaders of institutions, but his was an instrumental, rather than a principled, commitment at this time. Some have portrayed his Zionism and socialism as evenly matched, but Zionism clearly won out.[28] When faced with economic threats to the growth of a Jewish economy in the late 1920s, Ben-Gurion favored pragmatic compromises, allowing the parallel development of private enterprise; support for a planned and private sector would eventually place his party to the right of the pure socialist parties, or in Israel's political center, based on the understanding of ideological terms at the time.[29] Nir Kedar's biography of Ben-Gurion offers the strongest argument that Ben-Gurion was ideologically committed to democracy; but notably, Kedar's analysis begins after independence.[30] Even after independence, the following chapters find that Ben-Gurion unsentimentally sacrificed democratic aspects for Zionist aims. Ultimately, Ben-Gurion's singular focus was building Jewish society, economy, political leverage, and Jewish statehood in Palestine.

Jabotinsky: Liberal Democracy and Ultranationalism

The biggest ideological challenge to Ben-Gurion's Labor Zionism was the Revisionist movement—even before the Revisionists carried serious political weight. Ze'ev Jabotinsky, the formidable and sometimes sentimental intellectual who founded the movement, left a complex legacy that sometimes seems irreconcilable with itself. Jabotinsky led an ultranationalist, militant movement that sparked violent, even terrorist, fringe groups in later years and that some viewed as fascist. Yet Jabotinsky went significantly further than the early Zionist thinkers with his elaborate and eloquent commitment to liberal values and a liberal democratic constitutional order. His views toward Arabs in a future state seemed contradictory. What was he?

Much of Jabotinsky's legacy has focused on his maximalist nationalism. He demanded a Jewish state on both sides of the Jordan and was an early commander of the Haganah, the pre-state Jewish defense militia; a breakaway group later became the underground Etzel militia.[31] Members of his Betar youth movement demonstrated at the Western Wall in 1929, followed by the deadly riots in which Arabs killed more than 130 Jews (about half of them in the infamous Hebron rampage).[32] Late in his life, Jabotinsky considered favorable precedents for mass migration or even transfer of Arabs; but in general, he had firmly rejected it.[33]

In 1910, Jabotinsky declared liberalism to be dead and saw "no foundation for the classical liberal humanist view."[34] His galvanizing moment was not the Dreyfus trial but the atrocities of the 1903 Kishinev pogrom (then in Russia; today, Moldova), which killed dozens of Jews, horrifying and galvanizing Jews around the world.[35] The massacre convinced Jabotinsky that only force could guarantee justice. "Stupid is the person who believes in his neighbor," he wrote, "good and loving as the neighbor may be. Justice exists only for those whose fists and stubbornness make it possible for them to realize it."[36]

Yet Jabotinsky remained committed to liberalism in his political thinking. He advocated separation of religion and state and supplied a stream of articles and talks addressing the meaning of democracy.[37] Jabotinsky placed a primacy on individual rights and freedom—a sharp contrast to Labor Zionism's collectivist ethos.

Regarding Arabs in a future state, Jabotinsky did not obfuscate but directly addressed the question. He advocated freedom and protection of minorities and saw individual sovereignty, freedom of expression, and opposition, including the right to criticize government, as litmus tests dividing democracies from "their opposite." Jabotinsky was indignant that democracy was commonly reduced to majority rule, "for unexplainable reasons."[38] Most striking is his vision of total equality for Arabs or other non-Jews of a future state:

> If we were to have a Jewish majority in Eretz Israel ... we would create here a situation of total, absolute, and complete equal rights, with no exceptions: whether Jew, Arab, Armenian, or German, there is no difference before the law; all paths are open before him.... . Complete equal rights would be granted not only to citizens as individuals but *also to languages and nations.*[39] [emphasis mine]

To elaborate on these rights in practice, Jabotinsky read from a draft constitution, quipping that it might seem idle to draft a constitution when statehood was far off —ironic, considering that seven decades after statehood, Israel still does not have one.[40] The constitution stipulated equal rights for all citizens of any "race, creed, language, or class," including in "all sectors" of public life; and guaranteed vice-executive positions for whichever "ethno-community" did not occupy the top spot, even at the level of prime minister, to be mirrored at local or municipal levels. The scholar Arye Naor even interprets his approach as supporting a form of binationalism in practice, something that Jabotinsky himself would surely have rejected. But he proudly asserted his role in developing a program of "national rights for all nationalities living in the same state."[41]

Jabotinsky was thus one of the only influential figures in Zionism to consider power-sharing governance between majority and minority groups. However, the entire idea was conditioned on Jews becoming a majority: "Palestine can be promoted to independent statehood only after the formation of the Jewish majority," he wrote, underlining "after."[42] Jabotinsky's Revisionists became the forerunner of Herut (Liberty), the party of Menachem Begin—later to form the core of the Likud Party.

Ben-Gurion and Jabotinsky were bitter rivals and traded Nazi-fascist accusations. The divisions were principled and deep; Jabotinsky preferred a confrontational rather than an accommodationist approach toward the British Mandate authorities and fundamentally opposed the agrarian, collectivist socialism of Labor Zionism. Jabotinsky broke with the Zionist Executive in 1923, and the Revisionists established their own labor union in 1934.[43]

But Segev posits that they were not as far apart as they appeared. "Jabotinsky was not a fascist any more than Ben-Gurion was a Marxist. Ben-Gurion was no less nationalist or militarist than Jabotinsky."[44] Both prized the achievement of a Jewish state above all else. In 1935, Ben-Gurion and Jabotinsky held a détente in London, and their correspondence around the meetings reflected a surprisingly emotional breakthrough of mutual appreciation.[45] The two men reached a partial agreement to reintegrate their movements; but Ben-Gurion's party voted against it, and the Revisionists broke with the Zionist Organization.

Jabotinsky may not have been a fascist, and his constitutional vision was far-reaching in terms of power-sharing within a liberal democratic order. But ultimately, it was the hardline nationalism of Jabotinsky's movements that rallied followers at the time, as well as a militant approach that could go too far even for him, whether through revenge attacks on innocent victims, or when a militia group challenged political authority. The ultranationalism and territorial expansionism formed the ideological core of successor political parties that would, in later years, come to dominate Israel's political system.

But in the pre-state era and in the early decades of statehood, it was Ben-Gurion's Labor Zionist movement that won out in the competition between them. Socialism and collectivism became the dominant ethos of the emerging pre-state institutions, a romanticized ideal even if subordinated to pragmatic institutional and economic practice. Liberal ideas were disdained as bourgeois indulgence, and Jabotinsky's political heirs felt politically persecuted—and, to some extent, they were. But Herut retained its commitment to liberal values, along with the factions that formed the Likud Party in 1973. Jabotinsky's elaborate thinking about democratic values generated renewed interest decades later, particularly after Likud's populist illiberal turn in the twenty-first century (the subject of Section VI). The change alienated many traditional Likud figures and supporters, prompting a revival of interest in the liberal-democratic side of Jabotinsky's legacy.

Religious Zionism: God, Then State

After Labor Zionism and Revisionism, a third defining influence on the future of Israeli democracy came from Orthodox religious Jews. For the Orthodox communities, Zionism created a deep theological dilemma and, ultimately, enduring political dilemmas. In the early twentieth century, the communities known today as ultra-Orthodox (Haredim) and religious Zionists—each with its own subdivisions —were less clearly distinguished; their attitudes toward Zionism would become a major element distinguishing them.

The ultra-Orthodox groups that unified under the Agudath Israel organization in the early twentieth century broadly rejected the idea of Jewish statehood. They believed that only the Messiah could establish the Kingdom of Israel, while modern nationalism was a secular, profane notion. Zionism therefore preempted the work of God, a form of idolatry. Agudath Israel broke from the Zionist Yishuv in the 1920s, protesting women's voting rights in the first election for the pre-state body representing Jews of the Yishuv, an early iteration of the (eponymous) Knesset.[46] Jacob Israel de Haan, a Dutch Jewish journalist who moved to Palestine and became a prominent representative of Agudath Israel, advocated so prominently against Zionist aspirations that he was assassinated, apparently under orders from the Haganah. His strange legacy includes being the first internecine political assassination, as well as an openly homosexual ultra-Orthodox icon.[47] As seen later in this section, Agudah ultimately agreed to conditional and instrumental cooperation with the state, while a small fringe element maintained an anti-Zionist position over the years.[48]

By contrast, the partial accommodation of religious Zionists, both "pragmatic" and "principled," has been deeply fraught, leaving open a constant challenge to the sources of state authority over time.[49] Rabbi Abraham Isaac Hacohen Kook was among the prominent figures to adapt his understanding of Zionism to the Orthodox worldview. He had migrated to Jaffa in 1904 from Lithuania, and in 1921 helped establish the institution of the chief rabbinate under the British Mandate, an adaptation of the religious courts governing each faith community under the Ottoman Empire, known as the millet system. Kook served as the first chief Ashkenazi rabbi (until his death in 1935), alongside a chief Sephardi rabbi.[50]

Kook was initially concerned that earthly politics would corrode Judaism, but he eventually drew on Jewish sources to establish a redemptive theology supporting the Jewish state.[51] He came to view the defiantly secular Zionist leaders as (unwitting) agents of a larger cosmic process of redemption. "[T]he resettlement of the Land of Israel, even by blasphemous atheists, is a step on the road to salvation," the political scientist Shlomo Avineri writes of Kook's thinking. For Kook, the secular, civic state was never an end but a means for the "godless Zionists," whom he also called "our adversaries," to fulfill Jewish destiny. Devout Jews, therefore, were obliged to seek to bring them back to the fold of believers.[52]

Civil law and institutions represented a compromise on the road to redemption, but Kook hoped that the rabbinate would ultimately lead all institutions and spheres of life in the national entity.[53]

Both Haredi and religious Zionist groups in the pre-state decades would insist that any future state adopt Jewish law. Thus, when representatives of Agudath Israel testified to the Woodhead Commission in 1938 (the group that was charged with making technical plans to implement the recommendation of the Peel Commission of the previous year—that the region should be partitioned into Jewish and Arab states), they were already worried that the Mandate authorities and the League of Nations would impose a secular constitution on a future Jewish state, which would override Jewish religious law. The commission reported that Agudah representatives "regard the State and Church as indivisible," and demanded that a future state would guarantee autonomy of religious schools and that it would grant religious courts authority over marriage, divorce, and burial.[54]

Scholars have since observed that the religious communities were not necessarily opposed to a constitution during the pre-state years, but, as the Woodhead Commission reported: "What they desire is that the constitution shall be so drafted as to ensure, not only that the law of the Torah shall prevail, but also that *it shall never not prevail.... In matters which they consider vital to the Jewish religion, the will of the majority, if it does not coincide with the views of the Orthodox, shall not prevail*"[55] [emphasis mine].

Agudah leaders drafted a constitution in which failure to keep Torah discipline would be a violation of the law.[56] Their Council of Torah Sages resolved that "a Jewish state that refuses to recognize the Torah as its constitution denies the source of Israel, negates the correct character of the nation ... [and] cannot be called the state of the Jews."[57] The religious Zionist party Mizrahi was slightly less stringent but maintained the same basic approach to religion and state.

Thus for the Haredi or religious Zionist leadership, a constitution was to be primarily theologically-driven or informed—even the moderate versions examined below.[58] The secular state was instrumental; they hoped that the entire future state would adopt Orthodox Jewish laws in full.

The most accommodationist religious Zionist figure, who understood the need to harmonize Torah law with emerging democratic norms, was Isaac Herzog, the second chief rabbi from 1936 and, from 1948, the first Ashkenazi chief rabbi of independent Israel. Herzog was deeply attuned to global processes of liberation and state-building. He had served as a rabbi in Ireland since 1916, and he became chief rabbi when the country won independence in 1922. He was personally close with Eamon de Valera (the Irish statesman who later oversaw the drafting of Ireland's 1937 constitution).[59]

Herzog sought to meld democratic principles into Jewish law. He began working on an eighteen-point constitution in the late 1930s, an effort that stalled and then revived in 1947, when statehood was imminent. Herzog had an elaborate grasp of the institutions of governance, such as elections, courts, and civil and criminal codes. He was prepared to modify halakhah—Jewish law—to hammer out the deepest possible integration of religion and democratic legal systems, but the Torah was to hold the ultimate authority. His approach would become the dominant element of religious Zionism after independence.[60]

The triangle of tensions between non-Zionist ultra-Orthodox streams, the religious Zionist attempts to mold the state in a theocratic image, and the secular basis of statehood remain living challenges to democracy in Israel today; they are not residual. In some areas, the tensions have become conflicts for democracy in Israel that have deepened over time, as the following chapters will show.

From Ideology to Institutions

The socialist, nationalist, and religious Zionism streams generated ideological competition within the early Zionist movement; by the 1920s, under the British Mandate, statehood was becoming conceivable. Ideology was now manifested in Zionist institution-building, creating the skeletal structures for a future state. These institutions grew at an extraordinary pace over the Mandate years through 1948, and Ben-Gurion and his party, Mapai, would come to dominate nearly all of them. The vigorous growth in the Yishuv was largely enabled by the financial and institutional partnership with the World Zionist Organization (WZO), the body that was raising funds from world Jewry, and from increasingly enthusiastic American Jews. The land-acquisition arm of the WZO, the Jewish National Fund, helped Yishuv leaders purchase and settle land, which prohibited Arabs from leasing, and later working in, its holdings.[61]

Ben-Gurion believed that only Jewish economic power would earn statehood —this was his vision for the Histadrut.[62] Early Zionist institutions therefore espoused what Dowty calls "socialist separatism," and the most iconic example was the kibbutz, an all-Jewish, mostly-Ashkenazi socialist agrarian project.[63] Ben-Gurion insisted that the Histadrut would accept only Jewish members, and he got his way; Arabs were allowed to join only in the 1950s.[64] The Jewish Agency was founded in 1929 to advance immigration to pre-state Palestine and to serve as the Yishuv's representation to foreign governments.

The Histadrut held elections, but their quality was compromised. Under Ben-Gurion's leadership, there were few institutional constraints on its executive body. The Histadrut gained control over the Haganah—a relationship with armed forces that endured in the postindependence years between the labor organization and the army. Ben-Gurion banned the Palestine Communist Party from the Histadrut in 1924; he not only opposed communism but resented the party's Jewish–Arab cooperation, particularly its pro-Soviet, anti-Zionist position at that time. By 1930, the Histadrut was the "single largest banker, employer, insurance agent, manufacturing engine, and provider of housing and social services."[65] For this reason, as new waves of immigrants arrived in the 1930s desperate for jobs and material support, participation was hardly voluntary but a matter of dependency.

In its commitment to higher wages, respectable housing, and social services, at least for Jews, Ben-Gurion's vision was progressive. However, from the mid-1920s, his party, Ahdut Ha'avodah, had energetically constructed no less than a full party "mechanism"—*manganon*, in the language of Jonathan Shapira—to anchor its control over the organization from bottom to top. As Shapira writes:

> Like the Communist Party in the Soviet Union, they organized party cells in all Histadrut institutions. They established these cells in the workplace and in the workers' councils, in the welfare and health institutions, and in its factories and financial institutions. All of the cells were connected to the center of the party from which they received orders, and in this way their party held influence over these bodies and directed their activities.[66]

The party ensured loyalty through financial remuneration to activists, choice positions, or benefits from financial institutions and the social welfare organizations. Its cells reciprocated not only by voting for the party in Histadrut elections and for constituent institutions but also by recruiting others to vote for the party; thus in 1927, Ahdut Ha'avodah won its first outright victory at the Histadrut's convention.[67] The reward mechanism also generated a class of party bureaucrats, mostly established immigrants from a European (Ashkenazi) background, which sharply contradicted the idealized egalitarian ethos of the Labor Zionist movement. With generous salaries, this new class established demand for larger apartments, restaurants, household and domestic help, and travel abroad. These new lifestyles were a sharp contrast to the spartan socialist ethos, and eventually contributed to a Mizrahi underclass as Middle Eastern Jews arrived, while leaving out Arabs entirely. The party-loyalist arrangements were unwritten and completely opaque. The institutional character of the Labor Zionist movement by this time was broadly "counterproductive ... for the prospects of liberal democracy."[68]

In 1930, the two main labor movements unified to form Mapai under Ben-Gurion's leadership, which now easily dominated the Histadrut. Mapai won the 1933 Zionist Congress election, and took over the Political Department of the Jewish Agency. Mapai won its power through formal democratic procedures, but as the scholar Joel Perlmann writes, "they manipulated those procedures as much as they could."[69]

When Revisionists also accused the Jewish Agency of being undemocratic, apparently due to the influence of foreign money, including funds raised from non-Zionist Jews from abroad, Ben-Gurion responded: "We have a principle more dear to us than democracy, and it is the building of Palestine by Jews."[70]

Ben-Gurion was appointed chairman of the Jewish Agency Executive in 1935. Thus, by the mid-1930s, Ben-Gurion and Mapai effectively controlled the sprawling agencies of power in the Yishuv: Mapai, the Jewish Agency, and the Histadrut.[71]

Nevertheless, Ben-Gurion never held unchecked power. He relied on all layers of the institutional structures, and the multiparty competition held back authoritarian tendencies.[72] But he also favored the highly concentrated mode of leadership and fostered institutions that ran secretive, patronage-based sources of power. Over time, he stated his commitment to democracy and equality more prominently, but these aspirations were invariably subject to his own tendency to compromise, or contradict those values in governance.

Chapter 3: Democracy and International Legitimacy

By the 1940s, the international community was increasingly expecting the future Zionist state to advance equality, at least in terms of economy and living standards, but also in regard to cultural autonomy and the political rights of the Arab population alongside the Jews.[73] The Zionist leadership was well aware that democracy was a rising global force, though over the prewar decades, democracy is often cited mainly through the lens of majority rule and elections, or foreign alliances, rather than as a specific constitutional order or value system.

For example, recalling the years of World War I, Chaim Weizmann wrote in 1941: "I believed our destiny lay with the Western democracies."[74] Weizmann also wrote in 1918 to Lord Balfour—the British foreign secretary who authored the Balfour Declaration, recognizing a Jewish national home—that "the democratic principle, which reckons with the relative numerical strength and brutal numbers, operates against us, for there are five Arabs to one Jew."[75] Zionist leaders lobbied hard against a short-lived idea that the US would administer the region after World War I, worried that the Americans would establish a constitutional republic and Jews would be overwhelmingly outnumbered.[76]

The Balfour Declaration of 1917 was therefore the greatest triumph for Zionism so far, since it recognized the national rights of Jews to a homeland—but no national rights for other groups, although Jews represented barely 10 percent of the population. The declaration did call to avoid "prejudice" against the non-Jewish communities of Palestine, but even Ben-Gurion acknowledged that the move ran counter to democratic principles.[77]

Ben-Gurion was also a shrewd observer of Cold War politics, and at points in the 1930s, he seemed to consider, or even gravitate toward, the Soviet sphere of influence—instrumentally. But overall, as fascism spread and World War II loomed, Yishuv leaders sought to convince global leaders that a new Jewish state would be an upright member of democratic society.

A Changed World

In the aftermath of World War II, two historic processes would profoundly change the global political landscape. The Cold War pitted the democratic against the communist world, with each side racing to expand its pool of allies and spheres of influence. At the same time, the war drove a radical new vision for a world ordered by supranational laws devised to contain conflict and promote global peace; these would become known as the liberal, rules-based international order. The late 1940s saw intense activity to consolidate ideas about the conduct of war, human rights, and international law that had been evolving in various forms since the late nineteenth century, and to bind them into international commitments. The values of peacefully settling international disputes, as well as notions of self-determination, human rights, civil liberties, and even social rights, became paramount.

No assessment of Israel's history and democratic developments can work without understanding that Israel was born alongside this system, figuratively speaking. Israel's final sprint to statehood reflected both the international concepts in the process of codification and exploited its ambiguities. In some ways, Israel owed its legitimacy to global penance and hope for redemption in a new world. At the same time, the founding of the new state entailed some of the darker aspects of the old, prewar world.

The emerging global order explicitly favored democracy. The UN Founding Charter of 1945 does not mention the word "democracy," but it invokes "we the people" and portrays states as equal international citizens. Chapter 1, "Purposes and Principles of the United Nations Charter," outlines the principles of equality and human rights, universal freedom, and nondiscrimination; the charter is also a legally binding treaty.[78] No international body could prescribe a type of regime that would interfere in sovereign affairs, but these documents established the principles expected of members of the international community as Israel was founded.

The Universal Declaration of Human Rights (UDHR) followed three years later, in December 1948, asserting the basic aspects of democracy and human rights: regular elections of a government by the people, equality before the law, right of habeas corpus, and freedom of opinion, expression, religion, assembly, and association.[79]

Israel declared independence in May 1948, before the UDHR was adopted. But leaders of the Yishuv were well aware of the ideas under construction. Some of the towering figures of international law, including Hersch Lauterpacht and Jacob Robinson, who influenced the Universal Declaration and other emerging international human rights efforts, were lifelong Zionists advising the Yishuv leadership.[80] The two years that it took to draft the UDHR overlapped almost precisely with the UN deliberations over the fate of Palestine and, from 1948, Israel.

International Paths to Independence

By the 1940s, the Zionist leadership was using the language of democracy in international forums. The Biltmore Program of 1942, reflecting Ben-Gurion's and Weizmann's deepening relationship with American Jews, called for "Palestine [to] be established as a Jewish Commonwealth integrated in the structure of the new democratic world."[81]

But the international authorities were increasingly concerned about the fate of democracy in the region. In 1946, British foreign secretary Ernest Bevin's Anglo-American Committee of Inquiry reported that the "Palestinian Jews" (referring to Jews in Mandate Palestine) had always prided themselves on "free democracy" but noticed the "corroding effects" of fanaticism, propaganda, a feverish conspiratorial mind-set, and widespread support for terrorist groups among the Zionists. The authors even worried about "totalitarian tendencies to which a nationalist society is always liable."[82]

Ben-Gurion still weighed Israel's Western- or Eastern-bloc orientation. The Biltmore Program implies that the choice was made, but he retained a measure of neutrality. At the same time, the Zionist leadership had been wooing the Soviets, an unlikely courtship, given anti-Zionism and anti-Semitism under Stalin, as well as the Palestine Communist Party's anti-Zionist position, noted earlier.

But in 1943, the Soviets seemed to shift. Stalin apparently became intent on breaking what he saw as a British "stranglehold" on the Middle East.[83] The Soviet deputy foreign minister visited Palestine, touring Jewish settlements in the hills outside Jerusalem, with Ben-Gurion and Golda Meir, among others.[84] In 1945, Ben-Gurion shocked the Histadrut with a sudden statement welcoming communists back to the Histadrut, apparently hoping to impress the Soviet delegation at an upcoming conference in London.[85]

In February 1947, Bevin announced that Great Britain was turning Palestine over to the UN General Assembly. The US still presumed that Stalin would oppose the Zionist aims. Instead, Andrei Gromyko, the Soviet representative to the UN, made a surprising statement in May, recognizing the claims of both the Jews and Arabs in Palestine and supporting a federated state for both. If not, he conveyed, the Soviet Union would support partition.[86] Bevin thought that the Soviet Union hoped to pour "indoctrinated" Jews into the region and turn it into a communist state.[87]

The Soviet Union was also quietly helping the Zionist leadership in the way it needed most desperately—facilitating Jewish immigration to Palestine, via Poland and the West.[88]

By contrast, following World War II but prior to Israeli independence, the US was still somewhat divided over the issue. President Truman broadly supported the Jewish cause, but the State Department was wary, and some of its staff outright opposed an independent Jewish state, concerned that it would fall under the Soviet sphere of influence.[89] Yishuv leaders hedged their reliance on the US at that stage, and it was only in 1949, after Israeli independence, that Ben-Gurion stated: "In the ideological debate, Israel is democratic and anti-communist."[90]

The Road to Partition Runs through Democracy

In 1947, the Yishuv stood at the threshold of its half-century quest for Jewish statehood. Tension and violence between Arabs and Jews rose; Bevin worried about civil war. For these reasons, in just the previous year, the Anglo-American Committee had recommended continuing the Mandate.[91]

The committee heard from a series of Arab representatives arguing that the Palestinian Arabs deserved an independent state like the other Arab countries of the region. These representatives from Palestine and other Arab countries protested bitterly against expanding Jewish immigration until Jews held a majority before independence, which would thwart Arab self-determination in Palestine. The various Arab delegations reminded the committee that they were not responsible for the terrible persecution of the Jews of Europe.[92]

The committee report on the Zionist attitude toward Arabs, meanwhile, held marked echoes of certain themes heard in the present:

> Too often the Jew is content to refer to the indirect benefits accruing to the Arabs from his comings and to leave the matter there. Passionately loving every foot of Eretz Israel, he finds it almost impossible to look at the issue from the Arab point of view, and to realize the depth of feeling aroused by his "invasion" of Palestine. He compares his own achievements with the slow improvements made by the Arab village, always to the disadvantage of the latter, and forgets the enormous financial, educational and technical advantages bestowed upon him by world Zionism. When challenged on his relations with the Arabs, he is too often content to point out the superficial friendliness of everyday life in town and village... . [I]n so doing, he sometimes ignores the deep political antagonism which inspires the whole Arab community; or ... explain[s] it away by stating that it is the "result of self-seeking propaganda by the rich effendi class."[93]

Nevertheless, the committee found that the Jews of Palestine were surely fit to manage a democratic government at a future time. The committee recommended allowing 100,000 more Jewish immigrants, ending land-sale restrictions, and disarming all groups. But violence was rising: Jewish militias killed Lord Moyne, the British resident minister of the Middle East, in 1944 in Cairo. In 1946, they bombed Jerusalem's King David Hotel (where the British Mandatory authorities had their headquarters), killing nearly a hundred people; they blew up bridges and kidnapped British soldiers. These attacks were the work of the Revisionist militias but also involved the Haganah—the force controlled by the Yishuv leadership.[94]

The UN took over the problem in February 1947, establishing the UN Special Committee on Palestine (UNSCOP) to study the region and propose the best political solutions.

The man who initiated UNSCOP, Ralph Bunche, was a rising academic and diplomatic star. Bunche was a Black American, deeply committed to decolonization and self-determination and to advancing democracy through US foreign policy. He had played a key role in drafting the UN Founding Charter, which he saw as a means to advance peace and democracy; he also believed that the US had to commit to values of equality and freedom from oppression globally, specifically in Asia and Africa.[95]

Bunche was named as special assistant to UNSCOP and leader of its secretariat.[96] Abba Eban, then the Jewish Agency liaison to UNSCOP and later Israel's first permanent representative to the UN (and future foreign minister), recalled concern that Bunche would favor Arab self-determination:

> Some of us were rather apprehensive: Would not [Bunche's] background lead him to a greater sympathy with the third world? ... The Arabs seemed to represent that third world more than we did, and how would he absorb the whole point of a Jewish nation which was trying to establish itself in the country where we were not yet the majority—in other words, the normal laws of self-determination did not seem to apply.[97]

The British government also indicated that democracy ought to factor into its foreign policy. Richard Crossman, a Labour legislator who had served on the Anglo-American Committee, criticized British hesitancy in its policy for Palestine, saying that the approach did not reflect "humanity and democracy."[98]

In 1947, the Palestinian Arabs were represented by the Arab Higher Committee (AHC), established following the Arab Revolt that began in 1936; Haj Amin al-Husseini, grand mufti of Jerusalem, represented the AHC. This leadership saw the Balfour Declaration as the original sin for the neglecting of Arab national rights in Palestine. Its demands had not changed over time: an end to Jewish immigration, an end to land sales to Jews, and political independence.[99]

The AHC was furious that a decade after the Arab Revolt, the 1946 Anglo-American Committee report recommended only a large new wave of Jewish immigration and an extension of the Mandate. The AHC thought that "the solution lay in the Charter of the United Nations, in accordance with which the Arabs of Palestine, who constituted the majority, were entitled to a free and independent State."[100]

The AHC therefore declined to participate in the subsequent UN-led processes seeking a solution ahead of the UN decisions, conveying its decision to the first UN secretary general, Trygve Lie, on June 13, 1947: "Palestine Arabs natural rights are self-evident and cannot continue to be subject to investigation but deserve to be recognized on the basis of principles of United Nations charter ends."[101]

In other words, Palestinian Arabs felt that for three decades they had been excluded from the global convergence around ideals of self-determination. Emil Sandström, the Swedish judge leading UNSCOP, was unable to persuade them to participate.[102] But other Arab UN member states provided statements appealing to democratic values: "The Governments of the Arab States, looking toward the democratic principles on which the United Nations was founded as the best defence and surest guarantee of that right, demand the full application of those principles in Palestine" and an "independent Arab Government based on democratic principles."[103] They even directly addressed specific Jewish fears: "Thanks to the victory of the democracies, there is no longer any hotbed of anti-Semitism anywhere in the world."[104]

The Zionist leadership hardly believed these appeals, but it didn't matter: the Zionist movement would never have accepted living as a minority in an Arab state, no matter how democratic. After seeing all their demands dismissed, the Arab states and AHC rejected the partition plan.

The Zionist Case for a State

The Zionist leadership was eager to prove to UNSCOP the widespread commitment to Jewish statehood by the various Jewish communities. When UNSCOP toured Palestine in 1947, the Zionist community provided institutional representatives of religious and community organizations, including Chaim Weizmann and David Ben-Gurion; other representatives of the Jewish Agency; the Histadrut; the National Committee (the de facto Yishuv executive power); the Palestine Communist Union; and even the binational party Ihud, founded by Judah Magnes, which mainstream Zionists detested. Each claimed to speak in the name of the whole Jewish people, while proposing fundamentally different visions.[105] Their testimonies display conscious attention to questions of democracy and awareness of how important it was for the international audience.

Agudath Israel again insisted that "divine Torah alone forms the eternal constitution of the Jewish people.... . Whatever is formative in Palestine and within the Jewish people can be of lasting value and can have a right of existence only inasmuch as it is connected with and flowing from, the Almighty's Torah."[106]

Weizmann argued that the Jewish settlement in Palestine had contributed extensively to improving the economy, agriculture, and infrastructure and that these improvements had benefited the Arab population as well. Ben-Gurion used the word "democratic" generously, repeatedly advocating a free and democratic state. At times, he asserted that democracy meant the equality of all citizens, without elaborating.

Ben-Gurion was well aware of Arab national aspirations; back in 1937, he had told the Histadrut that "the Arab inhabitants of Palestine should enjoy all civic and political rights, not only as individuals, but as a *national* group, just like the Jews."[107] But now, Ben-Gurion accused the Arabs of supporting a deceptive democracy in which Arabs would restrict Jewish settlement. Ben-Gurion still focused mainly on releasing all restrictions on Jewish immigration—for him, the Jewish majority was the primary meaning of a Jewish state.

It was the Palestine Communist Union representatives and Ihud, the binational party, who advocated most eloquently for democracy. They presented ideas about the structure, substance, and procedures of democratic governance. They called for total equality, not in general terms as did Ben-Gurion, but "full equality of civic, national and political rights," including religious rights.[108] These representatives insisted on a single binational state in a federal arrangement, or possibly confederal, and insisted that this was the only path to a democratic state. The committee reasonably asked why, if the communists were so sure that Jews and Arabs could cooperate, the party itself represented only Jews, having split from the Arab communist faction.[109]

International Decision: Two Democratic States

UNSCOP was not thoroughly convinced of any one proposal. Ralph Bunche drafted a majority and a minority opinion—the first for partition between a Jewish and an Arab state, and the second for a single federated state. In either case, the new state or states were to be democratic:

> In view of the fact that independence is to be granted in Palestine on the recommendation and under the auspices of the United Nations, it is a proper and an important concern of the United Nations that the constitution or other fundamental law as well as the political structure of the new State or States shall be basically democratic, i.e., representative, in character, and that this shall be a prior condition to the grant of independence.[110]

Democracy was not a thin concept but spelled out in detail, in the recommendations of the committee's report to the General Assembly:

In this regard, the constitution or other fundamental law of the new State or States shall include specific guarantees respecting

A. Human rights and fundamental freedoms, including freedom of worship and conscience, speech, press and assemblage, the rights of organized labor, freedom of movement, freedom from arbitrary searches and seizures, and rights of personal property; and

B. Full protection for the rights and interests of minorities, including the protection of the linguistic, religious and ethnic rights of the peoples and respect for their cultures, and full equality of all citizens with regard to political, civil and religious matters.[111]

The General Assembly accepted the majority recommendation for partition. UN General Assembly Resolution 181 reiterated the requirement for democratic regimes:

> The Constituent Assembly of each State shall draft a democratic constitution for its State and choose a provisional government... . The constitutions of the States shall ... include inter alia provisions for:

> (a) Establishing in each State a legislative body elected by universal suffrage and by secret ballot on the basis of proportional representation, and an executive body responsible to the legislature.

The constitutions were to include provisions for civil rights and freedoms inherent to liberal democracies: "Guaranteeing to all persons equal and non-discriminatory rights in civil, political, economic and religious matters and the enjoyment of human rights and fundamental freedoms, including freedom of religion, language, speech and publication, education, assembly and association."[112]

If the Zionist leadership was concerned by the strong and detailed requirements for a democratic constitution guaranteeing full civil rights and equality to all, it had more immediate problems. The borders that UNSCOP had proposed for the Jewish state were deeply troubling, generating major discord and controversy. More than 40 percent of the population in the proposed Jewish state would be Arabs.[113] Jewish immigration was insufficient to guarantee a Jewish majority for the future. Nevertheless, the Zionist leadership chose to embrace statehood immediately, in sharp contrast with the Arab representatives—a contrast that would define history. Yet the Zionist leadership was never satisfied with the UNSCOP boundaries, and may already have hoped to undermine them.[114]

The General Assembly passed Resolution 181 on November 29, 1947. Zionists rejoiced, and Zionist leadership quickly set about appointing leading Yishuv figures to begin drafting the constitution, discussed in Section III. In fact, efforts to write a draft began even before UNSCOP had submitted its report; outside figures such as Jacob Robinson, the Jewish American jurist (originally Lithuanian, born in Czarist Russia), helped as well. Will Maslow, general counsel to the American Jewish Congress and a tireless fighter for Jews but also for the African American civil rights movement, also provided feedback on the drafts.[115]

These constitutional efforts would all come to naught.

Conclusion

The evolution of the Zionist movement over a few decades, from scattered thinkers to a formidable set of institutions and a savvy international presence, reflected a blend of ideology, strategy, and urgent, evolving needs. Zionism was born in an age when democracy was often viewed in broad strokes of majority rule, equality, and elections, while the great ideologies—nationalism, self-determination, socialism, and, ultimately, a Jewish-majority state—were the true engines of the movement. Democracy emerged as a global currency as the Zionist movement found itself on the cusp of statehood.

The Yishuv leaders established democratic procedures of parliamentary electoral processes, for institutions built by Jews and for Jews. These institutions were highly centralized and tightly controlled by nontransparent, consolidated, mostly unchecked, and often patronage-based party rule. Religious Zionists either resisted the state itself, or the idea of authority derived from people rather than God. When the international community advanced elaborate versions of democratic governance as a condition for statehood, the Yishuv leadership could plausibly agree to comply. But the roots of democratic thinking were shallow and compromised among the dominant Zionist leadership. Democracy in a robust sense was compromised, secondary, and subordinate to the overriding aim of a *demographically* Jewish state.

Section III
Independence and the Least Democratic Decades, 1948–66

To declare independence, or to wait? In 1947, just fifty years after Herzl's audacious declaration predicting the establishment of a Jewish state, it was almost a reality. The Yishuv leadership was torn over the timing and worried about dividing the land according to the borders of the Partition Plan.[1] Nevertheless, the leadership finally decided to declare statehood when the British Mandate was scheduled to end, at midnight on May 14, 1948. By that time, about one month remained to write a declaration of independence.[2]

The declaration would be a seminal statement articulating the historical justification for the new state and the vision for the country—a message both to the world and to the country itself. Various figures within the Zionist leadership in Jerusalem and Tel Aviv began working on drafts, only partly aware of one another.[3] Apparently unknown to them, in New York, the law scholar Hersch Lauterpacht was also writing a draft. Moshe Shertok (later Sharett)—head of the political department of the Jewish Agency—carried this draft to the acting (and future) justice minister in Tel Aviv, Felix Rosenblueth (later Pinchas Rosen) just days before the end of the Mandate.

Lauterpacht was a renowned pioneer of international law. Born to a Polish- and Yiddish-speaking family in Galicia, he studied law in Lemberg and Vienna, and eventually settled in the United Kingdom, where he rose to prominence for his scholarship on international law. Lauterpacht advised the Nuremberg trials, and in 1945 published *An International Bill of the Rights of Man*, advocating for the international legal structures to enforce such rights.[4]

Lauterpacht's involvement in drafting a declaration captures the dilemma of Israel itself, caught between two poles: universalist values, on the one hand; and the particularist justifications for the Jewish state, on the other. His work on the draft was sensitive, even secret, due to his prominent work shaping universalist ideas of the new international system.[5] Yet he was also passed over for representing the United Kingdom to the commission drafting the Universal Declaration of Human Rights in 1947 and 1948, due to his Jewish identity and Zionist involvement.[6]

Lauterpacht described the future country as a "republic" that would commit itself to the UN Charter, accept the jurisdiction of the young International Court of Justice, and commit itself to "any international treaty or Bill of Rights adopted in pursuance thereof." Historian James Loeffler writes: "Lauterpacht promised

https://doi.org/10.1515/9783110796582-004

that in exchange for sovereignty, the Jewish state would become a model of how all states should approach the new ideals of human rights."[7]

The Yishuv leadership in Palestine had different priorities. When Lauterpacht's draft was presented at a meeting of the National Administration just days before the Mandate ended, Ben-Gurion interrupted the discussion, and appointed a small drafting committee, which drew on the local drafts instead—Lauterpacht's was mostly forgotten.

The committee weighed each word: the phrase "sovereign and independent state" was dropped to avoid conveying a political break with the larger Zionist movement and world Jewry.[8] Future Supreme Court justice Zvi Berenson had drafted text defining the state as "Jewish, free, independent, and democratic," but in Shertok's late-stage draft, the word "democracy" was intentionally dropped.[9] Ben-Gurion purposely avoided any mention of borders, in contrast to Lauterpacht's draft proclaiming the state "within the frontiers approved by the General Assembly"; Rosenblueth also thought that the declaration must mention "international." But Ben-Gurion told Rosenblueth: "Everything is possible. If we decide now not to discuss borders, then we won't discuss them."[10]

Israel's final Declaration of Independence is largely devoted to the Jewish history of ancient exile, persecution, and yearning to return. It lays the groundwork for liberal and democratic values, guaranteeing freedom and justice; "complete equality of social and political rights of all its citizens"; and freedom of religion and conscience, language, education, and culture. In accordance with the UN resolution, the declaration promised that an elected Constituent Assembly would pass a constitution no later than October 1, 1948, and stated the country's commitment to the UN Charter.[11]

Israel's Declaration of Independence symbolizes the ambiguity and contradictions of the new country. The document gave moral weight to robust democratic principles but does not name democracy, and it lacks legal authority. Israel was unable to meet the Declaration of Independence's 1948 deadline to approve a constitution. In 1950, the Knesset broke the promise to adopt a constitution altogether, adopting a poorly defined, incrementalist approach instead, to be discussed in Chapter 4. The declaration remains the only complete national vision for democracy and equality of all citizens; it has played a role in Israeli law over time, but its authority has remained partial and debatable over the years.

Chapter 4: Stillborn Constitution

The declaration committed the new country to electing a Constituent Assembly, and then writing and ratifying a constitution, in the ambitious timeline of four and a half months after the May 14 declaration (independence formally began on May 15). But after the UN adopted the Partition Plan in November 1947, inter-communal violence escalated severely, followed by full-scale war with Arab countries after the declaration. Israel's first election was postponed to January 1949. The war went on until armistice agreements were signed in the first half of 1949. During this time, approximately 750,000 Palestinian Arabs left, fled, or were expelled, and became refugees. The events drastically changed Israel's demographic balance; by the end of the war, about 85 percent of the new state's population was Jewish.[12]

When elections were finally held for the Constituent Assembly, turnout was an enthusiastic 86.9 percent, giving that body a robust popular mandate for its role to produce and ratify a constitution.[13] But the task soon foundered.

Although prominent Zionist actors had been thinking about a constitution at least from the 1930s, the content varied widely, from advanced liberal democratic systems to theocratic, halakhah-driven principles. As UNSCOP got under way in 1947, Yitzhak Ben-Zvi, president of the National Council (the executive arm of the Yishuv), announced that Zerach Warhaftig would prepare a draft constitution. Warhaftig was a religious Zionist (and, later, a Talmud scholar) and headed the law division of the Yishuv's National Council; he worked eagerly, focusing mainly on the design of state institutions.[14]

After the adoption of the Partition Plan, the Jewish Agency took over from the National Council, and gave the task of drafting the constitution to the secretary of its political department, Leo Kohn. Kohn was an Orthodox Jew, born in Frankfurt. His PhD in law focused on constitutions, especially the 1922 constitution of Free Ireland, and he had a role in drafting the 1937 constitution of Ireland.[15] In 1944, Kohn had written in the *Palestine Post* (later, the *Jerusalem Post*) that non-Jews would have full equality in a future state and would live under identical laws as Jews, to be enacted by a democratically elected government. They would enjoy religious and cultural autonomy, with constitutional guarantees for freedom of worship and protection for their property and lands. At the time, the *New York Times* noted that Kohn had the full backing of the Jewish Agency, still chaired by Ben-Gurion.[16]

From late 1947, Kohn developed his drafts methodically, in several stages, soliciting input from constitutional experts around the world and rounds of feedback from local leadership, including religious leaders. He drew inspiration from the constitutions of France, the US, the Weimar Republic, China, and Ireland.[17] His draft became the basis for Israel's Constitutional Committee under the new Provisional State Council established with independence, prior to the election for the Constituent Assembly.

Kohn's draft established Israel as a "sovereign, independent, democratic republic."[18] It included equality before the law for all citizens and, critically, defined citizenship to include all people living as subjects of the Mandate on the eve of independence. Human dignity and life were to be a cornerstone of the state's values. The draft laid out basic rights, abolished the death penalty, established habeas corpus, and protected civil rights such as free speech, assembly, and association, unless they were being used to subvert human rights or democracy. Kohn's constitution would establish a national health-care system and the right to unionize and strike—both issues would be important arenas for political struggles of the early decades.[19]

At the urging of Jewish religious leaders, Kohn incorporated elements of Israel's Jewish identity. The drafts would therefore include text stating that Israel was a national home for the Jews, immigration would be open to all Jews, Hebrew was the official language, and the law would draw on Jewish sources. The draft broadly envisioned separation of religion and state but also left personal (family) law to religious courts. (Twenty-five years later, practically on his deathbed, Ben-Gurion would admit that he regretted maintaining a version of the Ottoman millet system, which refers family law to religious courts.)[20]

Kohn also defined the judiciary in detail, granting the Supreme Court the power to review legislation of the Knesset, to ensure that no laws would violate constitutional principles. His draft allowed the Knesset to amend the constitution itself with a two-thirds majority, or eighty members of the 120-seat legislature.[21]

After independence, there was a certain urgency to the task, given the international commitments that Israel had made; justice minister Rosenblueth also assumed that Israel would need a constitution in order to join the UN, as Israel prepared its application. Warhaftig became head of the Constitution Committee of the postindependence Provisional State Council, and endorsed Kohn's draft; the committee then worked assiduously, debating Kohn's draft and others. Warhaftig later stated that the committee held twenty-five meetings and agreed on 60 percent of the items.[22] But despite Warhaftig's own earlier drafting efforts, he increasingly opposed what later scholars called the "ideological" content, addressing issues of identity of the state, citizenship, and the bill of rights, while Warhaftig solicited further input from rabbinical figures and advocated a greater grounding in Jewish tradition. The constitutional debate became a tug-of-war between religious figures insisting on greater Jewish content, while secular political forces insisted that there was already too much. Warhaftig would have preferred a "lean" constitution limited to institutional design, but when it became clear that an actual constitution would go further, he turned against a formal document altogether.[23]

In February 1949, the Provisional State Council disbanded, passing its legislative authority to the newly convened elected Constituent Assembly. Two days after convening, the Constituent Assembly passed its first act, transforming itself into a regular legislature, called the Knesset.[24] The move was controversial, since the body had been elected primarily to write a constitution, not as a permanent legislature. The new Knesset retained the Constitution, Law and Justice Committee, but the debate increasingly turned to whether the country should adopt one at all.[25]

By that time, Ben-Gurion had expressed firm opposition to adopting a formal constitution. His most immediate problem was the wall of rejection of the Jewish religious parties to the content of a liberal constitution. In the lead-up to the Partition Plan, Ben-Gurion had taken a step that would prove fateful for the long-term character of Israeli society. He was concerned that Agudath Israel was still staunchly against a modern Jewish state and would testify against it to UNSCOP. Intent on winning their support, and hoping that they would appear under the rubric of the Jewish Agency in a show of unity, he wrote a letter via the Jewish Agency, offering far-reaching incentives to the ultra-Orthodox parties. The four critical promises would become the bedrock for religion–state relations following independence. First, in the new state, Saturday would be the day of rest. Second, all public establishments would preserve kosher rules. Third, family law would fall under religious authorities, as it had during Ottoman times. Fourth, religious education would retain its autonomy.[26] These four elements form what Israelis to this day call the status quo. Ben-Gurion later provided an exemption for yeshiva scholars from the war that followed independence and from the mandatory draft, generating one of the deepest intra-Jewish rifts of Israeli life.

Despite Ben-Gurion's later misgivings about retaining religious authority over family law, his efforts to co-opt the religious leadership succeeded—at least, enough. The leadership of Agudath Israel testified to UNSCOP and did not openly reject statehood, the ultra-Orthodox parties joined the national institutions and the governing coalition after independence, and they clung to the initial agreement.[27]

Six months after independence, Tom Segev observes, Ben-Gurion also admitted that he had made a mistake by promising a constitution by a specific date in the Declaration of Independence.[28] By that time, Ben-Gurion knew a constitution could endanger their coalition support, or precisely the opposite: he may have been worried that a constitution would entrench the religious demands. But the dependence on the Orthodox parties was only one of the reasons that he came to oppose a constitution.[29]

Publicly, Ben-Gurion had also argued that a constitution could not represent the masses of Jewish immigrants who had not yet arrived and that future generations in general should not be limited by a higher law of the present.[30] But historian Shira Robinson argues that officials were also reluctant to define rights, or guarantee suffrage or equality to the Arab population.[31] The military regime governing Arabs in Israel for the first two decades, discussed in Chapter 8, would certainly have been constrained by a bill of rights and guarantees of equality. Even if the concern about future Jewish immigrants was true, it meant that the lack of a constitution prioritized the interests of noncitizens—potential immigrants and generations of the future—over the rights of Arabs in the country, in the present.

Finally, Ben-Gurion came to oppose the very principles of limiting the power of the state and the legislature, or hindering the rule of the majority. He gave poetic speeches about the undemocratic nature of a constitution that elevated some laws above others, and particularly worried about entrenching the system in a law that would be hard to overturn.[32]

Ben-Gurion's opposition to a constitution based on principles of governance also reflected his desire to avoid constraints on his own power. Ben-Gurion was viscerally opposed to the Revisionist opposition, Jabotinsky's party, now led by Menachem Begin, and to the Communist Party as well, with its (revived) Jewish–Arab partnership and anti-Zionist history. "If democracy in Israel is to develop, it must be armed with defensive mechanisms and safety barriers to prevent any minority, non-Jewish or Jewish, domestic or Soviet-launched, from usurping government," he said.[33] Institutionalized minority protections were not his concern. After Jews were a majority in Israel, Ben-Gurion expressed considerable commitment to democracy in the sense of majority rule.[34]

In a speech to the constitutional committee in July 1949, as it was still deliberating, Ben-Gurion elaborated further: "The American constitution has turned into a conservative, reactionary institution that stands against the will of the people."[35] He was referring primarily to judicial review of legislation, which he considered absurd, rejecting the idea that any law had higher status than another. He opposed constraining, for any reason, the right of the legislature to make any law. With overtones of a twenty-first-century populist, Ben-Gurion continued: "I think that I am capable of understanding things as well as the best judge in the world... . The most knowledgeable person in the world knows not just the law but also has common sense."[36]

As Israeli political scientist Gideon Doron states, "The old collectivist leader was more comfortable ruling without the boundaries of the law."[37]

It was unclear as to whether there would be international consequences for not having a formal constitution. In one view, Ben-Gurion may have accepted the Partition Plan and included a constitution in the Declaration of Independence, largely to satisfy the United States. But the US quickly provided de facto recognition, and relations quickly solidified anyway.[38] Meanwhile, concerns that the UN would require a constitution in accordance with Resolution 181 dissipated. In fact, the UN did reject Israel's application for membership in December 1948, primarily because of the war, concerns over the status of Jerusalem, and the growing Palestinian refugee problem. But the UN finally approved Israel's next application by a two-thirds majority vote on May 11, 1949.[39]

In 1950, the Knesset held its final discussion on the matter of a constitution, before voting on how to proceed. Yizhar Harari, a member of the Progressive Party, had provided one of several proposals: instead of a formal written constitution, the Knesset would incrementally pass a series of "basic laws" to define the government institutions and citizens' rights, which would add up to a constitution over time.

Like the constitutional debates over the previous two years, the discussion was heated. The smaller parties mounted spirited substantive arguments in favor of a constitution, all clearly worried that Ben-Gurion's Mapai held too much political power. Among the most forceful supporters of a constitution was Begin of Herut:[40] "There is one thing you wish to prevent[:] ... the existence of a law of freedom, of justice, that will take precedence over all other laws and that you will not be able to nullify one fine morning by a mechanical majority."[41] Begin also took a dig at the Knesset for transforming itself into a regular legislature, which he considered an undemocratic violation of the voters' will.

To the left of Mapai, the socialist Mapam representative Yisrael Bar-Yehuda argued that a constitution was urgently needed, both to help achieve "coexistence" with the Arab minority after the war and to unify the far-flung Jewish immigrant communities. "Basic rules should be formulated, which will obligate everyone," he insisted.[42] Another Mapam representative, Nahum Nir, warned that a "patchwork" of basic laws would be easily undermined. In the meantime, under the ordinances adopted from the Mandate system, the government was simply too powerful; it could even dissolve the Knesset. "I beg of you not to think that I suspect anyone," Nir reassured the committee, "but this is the juridical situation, though I am certain that the government would never take advantage of the possibility." Herut member Yohanan Bader blurted in response, "Don't trust it."[43]

Finally, Bar-Yehuda of Mapam argued that opposing a constitution was "a constant legislative irresponsibility, with all depending on the moment, the [person], or the circumstance."[44]

But in June 1950, the Knesset passed Harari's proposal, and Israel adopted an incremental process of passing "Basic Laws" instead of a constitution. These brought their own complications. The Harari decision does not define the Basic Laws in detail, and the constitutional authority of these Basic Laws is subject to debate.[45] It took ten years after independence for the Knesset to pass the first Basic Law defining the Knesset itself, in 1958.

Most of the Basic Laws passed before 1992 defined governing institutions and procedures, such as the Knesset, the army, the presidency, economic competencies of the state, and other institutions. But the Knesset also passed significant legislation expressing Jewish national interests, such as the Law of Return of 1950 (not a Basic Law but regular legislation—discussed in Chapter 8); the Basic Law: Israel Lands (1960), one of the laws intended to perpetuate Jewish ownership of Israeli land; and the Basic Law: Jerusalem, the Capital of Israel (1980), effectively formalizing Israel's annexation of the eastern part of the city.

Laws providing the basic rights of citizens would not be passed until more than four decades after independence (discussed at length in Chapter 13). The missing bill of rights is a gaping hole in the democratic foundations of Israel's early decades; even at the present time, the legislation providing such rights is both partial and highly disputed.

The Provisional Government had carried over British Mandate laws until regular legislation could replace it; this included Mandate-era Defence (Emergency) Regulations that allowed forceful measures against people perceived as a threat. The Provisional Government made rapid changes, such as abolishing all Jewish immigration restrictions. Due to the war of 1948, the country also declared a state of emergency, which is in force to the present; among other powers, this allows the government to temporarily override regular legislation.[46]

The (Non-)Constitutional Consequences

The accumulation of Basic Laws and Supreme Court rulings in Israel is often viewed as holding the legal and moral weight of a constitution, even if not formalized in a single written document.[47] Even if this is true, Israel definitely has a constitutional deficit. Opponents of judicial activism, such as Daniel Friedmann, a conservative law scholar and minister of justice in the late 2000s, believed that the Harari compromise "excelled at confusing the main argument" over whether Israel has supreme law.[48] But Court rulings and scholarship have established constitutional law in Israel and use the term "constitutional" as a matter of course, which appears throughout this book as well.

But as noted, the supremacy of the Basic Laws is debatable. These laws can be passed by a plurality of legislators present in the Knesset, rather than a majority of all lawmakers (61 out of 120)—Israelis call this a "regular majority" to indicate the same process of passing a normal law. By default, these laws can be overturned by the same plurality—a majority of legislators who show up to vote that day, unless the specific law or clause is explicitly protected ("entrenched") by requiring a special majority to amend it.

The lack of a formal constitution is not the exclusive source of Israel's democratic deficits, nor would it be a panacea: "Constitutions alone do not create democracies," in the words of the political scientist Matt Qvortrup.[49] But the constitutional paralysis at the start of statehood is among the most prominent manifestations of underlying disagreements about Israel's identity and how it intends to govern. The void leaves room for irreconcilable values and permits policy and lawmaking without the guidance of fundamental values, while allowing certain constituencies to maintain skeptical and selective attitudes toward the authority of the law. The lack of a formal constitution has pushed the Israeli Supreme Court into a highly controversial role defining certain democratic values, as will be seen. Constitutional law deepened in Israel over time, but the skeptical constituencies also grew in both numbers and influence, and new ones joined. These processes are shown in the following chapters.

Religious Exemption and Coercion: Origins of the "Status Quo"

Every Israeli knows at least two words in Latin: status quo. As the status quo agreement between Ben-Gurion and the Orthodox religious Jewish leadership crystallized, the majority of Israeli citizens, who do not live strict Orthodox religious lives, nevertheless fell under religious rules for specific aspects of personal and public life.[50] Once again, these included the requirement for kosher food in all public institutions, commercial closure on the Sabbath (including of public transportation), educational autonomy for ultra-Orthodox Jews (exempting them from secular curriculum), and granting the religious authorities control over marriage and divorce (these authorities being the chief rabbinate for Jews, and Muslim and Christian religious authorities for their respective communities).[51] Soon the mandatory draft became another profoundly divisive aspect of the status quo arrangement.

The chief rabbinate eventually came to be dominated by ultra-Orthodox leaders, although the ultra-Orthodox Jewish community is a small minority in Israel.[52] Ben-Gurion's arrangement therefore gave vast power to a minority to impose its will on a majority in society, since non-devout citizens of any religion are subject to religious authorities over family law. As such, there cannot be equality in family law, since each religious group may have different rules, conservative religious systems broadly favor men over women, and secular people do not enjoy freedom from religion.[53]

The status quo arrangement did not retain its informal character, but became anchored in law or government policy for each of the core areas, including, for example, the 1953 Law of Rabbinic Courts, which formalized the exclusive control of rabbinic courts over marriage and divorce, preventing civil marriage or intermarriage between people of different faiths from being officially performed in Israel.[54] Warhaftig, who was then the deputy minister of religious affairs, admitted that the law was a form of religious coercion but argued that it was justified for the sake of Jewish unity—a recurring theme over the years.[55]

The status quo not only gave the Orthodox Jewish leadership disproportionate power but also created multiple forms of self-exclusion from critical social institutions.

Autonomy in the education system meant that the ultra-Orthodox (also called Haredim, or "God-fearing") could neglect to teach core curriculum in favor of religious education, a situation that endures to the present. The aim of ultra-Orthodox leadership was to prepare boys for a life of studying in religious seminaries, rather than learning core skills needed for employment or social integration; this insularity is one of the fundamental distinctions between the Haredim and the Jewish religious Zionist (non-Haredi Orthodox) communities. Educational autonomy also avoided teaching children about civic principles regarding the meaning of state and society, perpetuating the self-imposed isolationist life of these ultra-Orthodox communities.

Army service represented the second major form of exemption for ultra-Orthodox Jews from Israel's social institutions. During the War of Independence, Ben-Gurion had granted an exemption from fighting for approximately 400 full-time yeshiva students; after the war, rabbinic leaders and a political representative of Agudath Israel asked to defer the draft, and Ben-Gurion agreed. Ben-Gurion appeared to view this level of religious observance as a disappearing relic and the exemption as a worthwhile sacrifice to maintain coalition cooperation.[56] The trends were quite the opposite of what Ben-Gurion expected. Israel's 1949 law allowed the defense minister to defer drafts.[57] From the 1970s, the number of deferrals for yeshiva students increased dramatically, reaching 50,000 by 2011.[58]

Because of the disproportionate power over politics and certain aspects of life, along with exemptions from major social activities, with an institutionalized basis for ongoing social isolation, the Haredim could easily view themselves as existing outside the bounds of regular life and beyond the realm of civic, secular laws.

Not only the Haredi leaders took this position. Historian Alexander Kaye observed that many religious Zionist leaders resented the state for supplanting rabbinic authority and even rejected civil courts, although the Sephardi chief rabbi took an accommodationist position.[59]

Religious Zionist rabbis often concluded that the civil courts of the Jewish state were in fact illegitimate "Gentile courts," and prohibited their followers from using them. It is an astonishing fact that, from the 1950s until the present, rabbinic leaders of the religious Zionist community have commonly publicly prohibited Jewish use of Israel's civil courts.[60]

Finally, the status quo arrangement set a tone for coalition politics: the participation of religious parties or their ability to topple governments became the ultimate leverage for religious figures and communities to win concessions. In September 1952, the religious parties unsuccessfully fought against legislation that required religious women to perform national service, prompting Agudath Israel to leave the government in protest.[61] In December of that year, the remaining religious parties also left in protest over disagreements regarding religious education, and the government collapsed.[62]

The practice of achieving religious concessions by threatening coalition stability (or actually pulling the government down) became routine in Israel and represents a pronounced feature of Israeli politics, as well as a frequent trigger for early elections. Since modern Israel's founding, the demand for deeper influence of religion on the Israeli state, or resisting attempts to weaken religious power, has not only challenged civic sources of law but also the stability of governance.

The Judiciary: Independent but Cautious

The judicial branch was established as an independent branch almost immediately following statehood, creating a firm institutional basis for democratic governance. The Supreme Court was inaugurated in Jerusalem in 1948, and its powers carried over from the Mandate era, as both a final court of appeals and a court to review government action, as the High Court of Justice. In 1953, the Judges Law became a critical basis for judicial independence, removing the judicial selection process from the political branches of government, and entrusting selection to a committee including jurists, bar members and elected politicians. The procedure created a de facto limit on party influence on the judiciary. In 1957, a law was issued defining the courts. Thirty-six years after independence Israel passed the Basic Law defining the judiciary.[63]

Religious Zionist leaders viewed the establishment of the Supreme Court as a grave injustice, "the ultimate symbol of the state's abandonment of halakha," according to Kaye. The Ashkenazi chief rabbi Isaac Herzog wrote that it should have been a day of mourning or even a fast day, being "'the climax of the abolition of the Holy Torah from Israel."[64]

The tension was not one-sided. Isaac Olshan, one of the original justices and the second chief justice, was a staunch secularist who believed that "Zionism would liberate the Jew of religious bondage." When taking his oath, Olshan boycotted the Bible; both the Ashkenazi and Sephardi chief rabbis boycotted the Supreme Court's inauguration ceremony altogether.[65]

"From time immemorial, the court has been the fortress of the citizen," wrote Hebrew University law professor Shimon Shetreet in 1989.[66] But without a constitution, the Court's support for citizens had its own limits. Almost immediately, citizens seeking constitutional protections drew on the Declaration of Independence; the Court was not easily convinced. In 1948, two property disputes made this claim, both involving Jewish Israelis whose apartments in Tel Aviv the state had taken in order to house state bureaucrats, based on the Mandate-era Defence (Emergency) Regulations. The government had seized one of them, on Chen Boulevard, for the use of the new attorney general, Yaakov-Shimshon Shapira. In a separate case, Tzvi Ziv owned an apartment on Balfour Street, and the state issued orders to seize the property to house a bureaucrat from the Interior Ministry. Petitioners argued that the state had contravened the spirit of the Declaration of Independence. In this and another case regarding the use of administrative detention, the justices ruled that the Declaration of Independence was intended to establish the state and to win international recognition but did not confer constitutional rights.[67]

Citizens were thus poorly protected against the state, but political figures enjoyed a measure of de facto legal impunity. "In the phase following the establishment of the state, the possibility of investigating a minister and putting him on trial for criminal [charges] was practically unimaginable," writes Friedmann, the law scholar. Moshe Dayan famously looted antiquities with total impunity, writes Friedmann, but "during the time of boundless adulation towards him, the authorities were helpless."[68]

Nevertheless, in the early years, the Court occasionally ruled against the executive branch, sometimes sparking backlash from politicians.[69] Despite the ambiguities and the chaotic start of statehood, the Court played an active role in establishing democratic principles—filling in some of the legal and constitutional lacunae.

In the heated twenty-first-century debate, many have argued that the Court was playing a passive role in its earliest years, supporting the government. But Itzhak Zamir, who served as attorney general and later as a Supreme Court justice (discussed in Section IV), emphasizes the Court's key role in establishing values of equality, civil rights, and limitations on state power, even in its earliest years.[70]

Chapter 5: Institutions: One Man, One Party

Israel's earliest decades saw the greatest concentration of powers in the country's postindependence history. One man, David Ben-Gurion, dominated the ruling Mapai Party, and Mapai, in turn, dominated the most powerful institutions ruling Israeli life, including the government, the Histadrut, and the Jewish Agency. Since Israel's government is made up of a Knesset majority, the government also largely controlled the legislature.

It seems counterintuitive to view Israel as a country of consolidated power, given its notoriously fragmented party system. Even in 1949, twenty-one parties competed in the elections for the Constituent Assembly, and twelve parties crossed the electoral threshold.[71] No single party won a majority, and never would. All governments have been coalitions.

But Israeli society was unusually dominated by parties in general. They controlled "schools, theatres, sport clubs, youth movements, consumers' and producers' cooperatives, suburban developments, urban housing projects, health insurance schemes, and convalescent homes," as Israeli law professor Benjamin Akzin wrote in 1955.[72] Parties dominated the Histadrut labor federation and health-care services, making most people dependent on specific parties for jobs and basic services. These establishments injected party ideology into everyday life. Mapai resisted efforts to nationalize health care, preferring a captive audience.[73]

Since parties select their own leaders, and a party leader serves as prime minister, there is no term limit. The president holds a ceremonial position. For a limited time from the mid-1990s through 2001, Israel introduced direct elections for prime minister, but reverted to the original system after less than a decade. There are no structural constraints on the power of a government, led by a ruling party, other than de facto judicial review, and elections.[74]

Moreover, in the early decades, parties were controlled from the top. Candidates for the Knesset were selected by central committees, through an internal, nontransparent bargaining process, immortalized in Israeli collective memory by the image of closed doors and smoke-filled rooms. Top party leaders could place candidates in a higher or lower spot on the party list, determining that person's chance of entering the Knesset. As a result, legislators sought to please their senior party figures through loyal voting behavior in the Knesset. And as legal scholar Eyal Benvenisti noted, since Israeli coalitions are established by a majority of Knesset seats, "every government from 1948 until 1992 [when primaries were adopted by the two large ruling parties] enjoyed a subservient Knesset, and there were no real checks and balances in place between the legislature and the executive."[75]

Parties were not always sufficiently tolerant of debate. "Without going to the extreme of denying the validity of democratic procedures," wrote Akzin, "most parties in Israel, because of their dogmatic attitude toward politics, find it rather difficult to practice that tolerance of opposition without which the free discussion of issues and their amicable solution by the ballot lack the proper atmosphere."[76]

Party patronage was central to employment in the civil service. For the first decade of statehood, the "party key" was used to distribute government and civil service jobs, reflecting the proportion of each party in the Knesset. A decade after independence, in 1959, Israel would adopt a merit-based system for civil appointments.[77] But the law allowed numerous exceptions and was slow to take effect; party appointments ebbed, but in the mid-1970s, one study found that there was "one resolution which exists in law and another in fact," and another observer described "the omnipotent control of party mechanisms by Bolshevik means."[78] (Despite significant transitions of power since the early decades, Israel still has more political appointments than most developed countries.)[79]

In reality, one party mattered most: Mapai. How did a single party gain so much power, given that Israel held competitive elections with full suffrage from its very first years? The answer lies in the pre-state institutions that carried over, like the parties themselves, and effectively led the country alongside the elected leadership.

Histadrut and the Jewish Agency: Para-Governmental Governance in Israel

By the time of statehood, the Histadrut labor federation had become a leviathan. Still open only to Jews, the Histadrut came to handle housing, education, pensions, and vacations. ("Wellness facilities" were a common concept at the time, where workers could take time off for leisure activities—but only if they belonged to the Histadrut.) The Histadrut founded a theater and sports activities, and it conveyed information through its newspaper, *Davar.*

Although some of the Histradut's pre-state social functions had been taken over by the state—mainly education and national insurance—the labor federation still controlled numerous industries. It had established the workers' bank, Hapoalim; the health-care fund (*kupat holim*—lit., "sick fund"), called Clalit; the construction company Solel Boneh; and other industries. The Histradut also owned and managed factories, construction operations, and shipping companies; and it ran building contracts, agriculture, and other production sectors.

Jobs were distributed according to party membership: Mapai members secured the most, and the best, jobs. The Histadrut was, in effect, the gatekeeper to getting by in Israel: its Hevrat Ovdim—Workers' Corporation—owned major industries and therefore was the country's largest employer, and the right party members were destined to have the best opportunities. Yet the Histadrut was the country's largest trade union—in other words, it simultaneously represented both the employers and the employees.[80]

The Histadrut's health-care fund became the greatest symbol of the party and of Histadrut's combined control over society—and the lack of boundaries between Histadrut and Mapai. The newly independent state had no nationalized health-care option. Clalit was the country's biggest health-care provider, and one had to join the Histadrut to receive it; in 1948, about half the Jewish population was insured, most of those, about 46.5 percent of the Jewish population, by Clalit. Mapai was omnipresent within the Histadrut and dominated the management of health services. By 1968, about 75 percent of the population was insured by the Histadrut's health fund—the massive rise due largely to an agreement with the Jewish Agency to funnel new immigrants into the Histadrut's health fund and pay their fees for several months, on the condition that they join the Histadrut, which helped funnel votes to Mapai.[81]

Moreover, by the 1950s Ben-Gurion had personally opposed the establishment of national health care, though he had expressed support in the past, because it would have taken the critical service away from the Histadrut.

The Histadrut supported an ethos of equality, and the government advanced a policy of full employment as a higher priority than productivity.[82] The Histadrut policies of equal pay within specific sectors and universal employment made income distribution "the most egalitarian in the free world," according to Bernard Avishai, and economic growth was robust. Immigration drove an injection of money, enabling the state and the Histadrut to undertake major construction projects. From the mid-1950s, Mapai invested in industrialization and encouraged exports, and German reparation money boosted the economy. Industrial production, employment, consumption rates—and the private sector—all grew significantly.[83]

In fact, the system had major achievements in developing the economy and society—at least the Jewish economy, in the face of daunting pressures. In the first few years of statehood, the country absorbed nearly 700,000 immigrants, with vast differences of language, education levels, health challenges, and cultural disparities, including during the war of 1948–49.[84] Conditions were rough for immigrants; many were sent to quarantine camps to contain disease; many (up to 60 percent of the poorer Middle Eastern immigrants, twice the rate of European immigrants) were placed in transit camps with squalid conditions.[85] To cope with shortages of food, Mapai established an austerity and rationing policy through 1952.

But the state- and Histadrut-dominated economy and social policies also laid the foundations for some of Israel's deepest class and social cleavages, which had begun prior to statehood. Arabs were allowed to join the Histadrut only from 1953, and as full members only in 1959, a decade after the establishment of the state.[86] Arabs who were not members of organized labor earned wages far below either organized or non-organized Jewish citizens.[87] Mapai of the 1950s was already becoming a party of the middle class—which, up to then, was still associated with the General Zionists Party. By the late 1950s, economic policy under Mapai's leadership was already nurturing the private sector, productivity, and export-based growth, while the party retained the symbols, or "festive dimension," of socialism.[88]

The Histadrut generally channeled Jewish immigrants from the Middle East and North Africa into blue-collar, working-class jobs; although the government was now responsible for education, high schools also sent students to technical and vocational training or to preparation for higher education, with Mizrahi students largely marked for working-class training.[89] These policies affected the poorest, including some Holocaust survivors and Eastern European Jews, but ultimately helped form an ethnic, Mizrahi-based underclass, to the point that the political scientist and longtime Israeli left-wing politician Dov Khenin described it as a "strategy of ... constructing a separate caste of cheap Jewish workers."[90] The established "old-timer" European Jewish communities now represented a middle class, generating an economic and cultural schism that did not dissipate but would affect social and political dynamics for years to come. Workers, especially blue-collar and lower-level employees, felt themselves to be at the mercy of the institution and therefore the party—forced into its bureaucracy, blackmailed for services and jobs, or ostracized if they didn't conform.[91]

One of the other most powerful quasi-government institutions was the Jewish Agency. Mapai maintained its position as the dominant party in the organization's leadership. The Jewish Agency had primary responsibility for mobilizing immigration to Israel from Diaspora Jewish communities. In 1959, sociologist Amitai Etzioni observed that the parties had "cognate" parties abroad. Since new Jewish immigrants quickly gained voting rights once in Israel and the Jewish Agency was responsible for immigration, it, too, functioned as a supplier of future voters for Mapai.[92]

Even the Israeli Defense Forces (IDF), the new state army, was interwoven with party politics. During the War of Independence, the *Altalena* affair became the great symbolic showdown between the new country's political rivals. The *Altalena* was a ship bringing arms and fighters bound for the Irgun militia under Menachem Begin's command, while Ben-Gurion struggled to consolidate all armed forces under the IDF. When Begin refused to completely integrate his forces into the IDF, Ben-Gurion ultimately ordered the new state's forces to attack the ship off the shore of Tel Aviv, and nearly twenty people died.[93]

The incident holds an outsize place in Israel's national mythology, but from a political perspective, it is possible to see the events as an inevitable effort of any state to establish its monopoly on the use of force, with the tragic special circumstances of internecine bloodshed. From a democratic standpoint, however, the politicized nature of the IDF was a bigger problem, though less visible than the collective memory of the *Altalena* burning on the beach. The new state maintained the de facto overlap between the ruling political party and the IDF. Mapai promoted officers according to party affiliation and invited senior military figures to political meetings. This lack of separation between politics and the army formed the roots of the Israeli political-military elite. Even today, the circulation of personnel between the military and politics is prominent in Israeli life, but the specific party orientation of the military elite was one of the "most salient anti-democratic features" of the early decades of statehood.[94]

Mapai's dominance of some Israeli institutions started decades before Israel achieved statehood. Etzioni observed in 1959 that Mapai had held unrivaled power for twenty-eight years, though Israel had only been independent for eleven years.[95]

The statist and party-driven centralization of power cast a shadow over elections. The electoral institution was Israel's most solid and visible democratic practice. Numerous parties competed, vigorous debates were held in the media and on the streets, suffrage was universal, and turnout was high.

But the integrity of electoral choice was eroded by the party patronage, citizens' dependence on institutions dominated by a single party, and the access to jobs and even health care, based on party affiliation. The situation was particularly coercive for Arabs under Israeli rule, a phenomenon that is examined in depth in Chapter 8.

Mapai never won a majority in elections, which mitigated its power somewhat. But it maintained a "hard core" of roughly 30 percent of the voters whose loyalties flowed from its institutional dominance, and the party usually won about a third or more of votes in the elections of the 1950s, far ahead of the runners-up. Under the general conditions characterizing Israeli society and economy in the 1950s, Etzioni wrote, it was unlikely that even 10 percent of Mapai voters would shift."[96]

Scholars debate whether, deep in his heart, Ben-Gurion was a true democrat— or a "semi-authoritarian."[97] The complicated man may have been both, but the society that he created ensured what was effectively one-party rule for nearly three decades, despite the appearance of a vibrant multiparty system.

Chapter 6: Partial Rights, Limited Freedoms

Mapai's institutional dominance not only helped it win elections; the party was also able to significantly constrain society, with few formal anchors for civil liberties. Citizens lived with significant limitations on aspects such as labor representation, travel, and access to information, within a largely conformist, party-oriented media environment during this era.

Organized Labor

Workers regularly staged strikes, but laws protecting this right were enacted only in 1957.[98] In the first years of statehood, the Histadrut retained its monopoly over workers' actions while simultaneously representing their employers (since it owned so many companies in the economy). People who felt that the Histadrut did not adequately represent their interests discovered just how powerful the organization could be and how indistinguishable it was from the ruling party and arms of the state.

In mid-1951, workers of Shoham, a shipping firm founded by the Histadrut and the Jewish Agency, demanded better working conditions. The employees' labor union representatives were dominated by Mapai; they were unelected and overlapped with the management of Shoham. The seamen decided to elect their own independent representatives, and called a strike.[99] Their ship, *Negba*, sailed from Marseille, while independent representatives reached an initial agreement with management; but when the ship reached Haifa, the police met them at the port and hauled them off by force, and the men were promptly drafted for IDF service. The state and the army had been mobilized to effectively abduct the workers and suppress the strike.

The dispute escalated. The Histadrut found replacement workers for more than 200 seamen from the *Negba*, but then the entire fleet of more than 800 seamen went on strike. Ships docking at Haifa piled up at the port, workers refused to unload them, and ships abroad refused to sail. People demonstrated in solidarity, as the issue moved from labor demands to a political standoff: Ben-Gurion, Mapai, and the Histadrut came to view the strike as practically mutiny. Mired in Cold War dynamics, the Histadrut portrayed the seamen as communists and even traitors, while Mapam, the socialist party to the left of Mapai, embraced the strikers.[100] Ultimately, Mapai could not tolerate the workers' democratic election of their representatives, or it could not tolerate political competition (or both).[101]

Pinhas Lavon, then minister of agriculture, stated: "Not every strike is sacred; the workers have no right to declare a strike independently without the agreement

... of the Histadrut... . [T]o protect the 'state in the making' ... the freedom to strike is a matter of national responsibility."[102]

In December, the police violently raided the boats in Haifa, in what became known as "Black Friday," and crushed the strike. The Histadrut negotiated the original demands, demonstrating and consolidating its power. The state used similar tactics against locomotive drivers who were also on strike at that time and seeking independent union representation. The transportation minister proposed using emergency powers to force them back to work; once again, the government and Ben-Gurion stepped in and used the army, both to operate trains to distribute cargo and to draft the striking workers.[103]

Restrictions on Movement

The new state placed constraints on people's freedom of movement, including leaving the country. Ben-Gurion, apparently concerned about Jewish emigration and foreign currency shortages, insisted that the ongoing state of emergency justified restrictions on travel. From the start of statehood until 1961, Israelis had to apply for an exit permit for each trip, for which they could be denied.[104] In 1950, "Mrs. D" applied for a two-month trip abroad and was rejected more than once; government lawyers wrote of their concern that she might extend her trip while abroad: "We may suspect that the applicant is sick with the infamous Jewish illness known as 'Travelitis.'"[105] A Supreme Court decision in 1953 had recognized the "natural right" of citizens to leave the country that should be fundamental in "every democratic country," in the Court's wording—even prior to US courts recognizing this right in 1955. But Israel routinely rejected applicants on various grounds, often citing security.[106]

The practice was not unique. Both the US and the UK restricted exit and passport rights (beyond criminals), mostly during the Cold War, in order to restrict citizens suspected of communist political affiliations abroad. But Israel's policy went beyond specific groups; the aim was to curtail foreign travel in general.[107]

While the state incrementally liberalized policies to attain exit permits in the 1950s, it simultaneously imposed heavy taxes on exiting and on ticket purchases. "Thus travel was made more difficult, while presenting the appearance of a relatively liberal policy."[108] The government canceled the requirement for exit permits in 1961, but continued to require them for reserve soldiers for years afterward.

The exit tax far outlasted the permit requirements, and continued in various forms and changing rates until canceled for good only in 1993. In the 1980s, the government considered levying the tax based on emergency regulations (the attorney general rejected the idea).[109] In 1989, J. Michael and Susan B. Jaffe, residents of Zichron Yaakov, pleaded to legislators: "The most fundamental right in a free society is the right to leave that society, without molestation or penalty," but "to the detriment of all who live in Israel, we are denied this right," due to the prohibitive tax.[110]

The Press and Expression

Freedom of expression represented a particularly complex issue. While the media operated freely and critically—for Jews—newspapers were subject to both top-down restrictions and bottom-up, voluntary self-censorship. No primary Israeli legislation guaranteed free press or information. Most newspapers in this period were party organs—each party had its own newspaper, as did the controlling institutions of society, such as the Histadrut.[111]

Dissenting opinions encountered resistance. The magazine *Ha'olam Hazeh* ("This World") is a legendary example. The paper had an oppositional, often sensationalist, tone. Its editors paid little mind to the ethos of *mamlakhtiyut*, which was moving from a pre-state cause of unifying the Jewish people to an ethos of support for the state institutions (or even etatism). *Ha'olam Hazeh* investigated corruption, criticized government policy, and exposed patterns of discrimination and marginalization of various communities.

Other media outlets viewed *Ha'olam Hazeh* as a rogue actor. The charismatic editor was a defiant and prolific German immigrant named Uri Avnery, who had joined Etzel, the Revisionist pre-state militia, as a teen before fighting in the War of Independence. After the war, he started a column at *Haaretz* but left a year later, claiming that he had been pressured to suppress articles about mass expropriation of Arab-owned land.[112] In 1950, he bought *Ha'olam Hazeh*, along with Shalom Cohen, establishing investigative and iconoclastic journalism that did not always win friends.

In 1953, the two newspaper editors were beaten outside their offices by men with sticks. The thugs ran off after a group of paratrooper passersby rushed to help. Cohen sustained a head injury, while Avnery suffered injuries to his hand, including broken fingers.[113] The attackers were never found, and the incident was reported only in newspapers affiliated with opposition political parties: Menachem Begin's *Herut* and the newspaper of the Communist Party, *Kol Ha'am* ("Voice of the People").[114]

Two years later, a bomb exploded at the offices of *Ha'olam Hazeh*. This time, the Israeli Federation of Journalists denounced the violence in a statement in the newspaper *Haaretz*. The statement carefully distanced itself from endorsing *Ha'olam Hazeh*, which did not belong to the federation.[115] *Maariv*, one of the country's leading daily papers, hinted at a false flag attack: "[W]hat drives the logic of this strange terrorist organization? It makes sure that *Ha'olam Hazeh*, its editors and its struggles over the freedom of the press will gain the greatest publicity possible... Is there a better way to attract public attention than by an explosion?"[116]

Ha'olam Hazeh clearly had enemies in high places. David Ben-Gurion hated *Ha'olam Hazeh* so much, according to Avnery, that he did not speak its name, calling it only "a certain weekly."[117] Ben-Gurion may have been involved in commissioning a polemical play in 1958 from Israel's national theater, Habima, called *Throw Them to the Dogs*, in which a character is called to break the bones of a sinister journalist similar to Avnery. The play prompted accusations of physical incitement against the media. Ben-Gurion even asked the state intelligence agency, later known as the Shin Bet, or Shabak (whose existence was still a secret then), to establish a competing publication to counter the accusations and criticism of the government in *Ha'olam Hazeh*.[118]

Israel employed military censorship to review all material related to security affairs prior to publication. Such censorship still exists today. But the media also employed self-censorship. Prior to independence, Hebrew newspaper editors set up a committee that coordinated their responses to the Mandate authorities seeking to delegitimize the Zionist movement. After independence, the editors declared that the committee would transition "from a wartime council opposing foreign rule, to a joint council ... working with the Hebrew government and helping it get established." This became the legendary "editors' committee," which aimed to "establish joint positions" on major issues, by working closely with the authorities to decide what to publish. In the limited media environment of the 1950s, with no television and only state-controlled radio broadcasts, such control could be nearly hermetic.[119]

The single electronic broadcasting service, radio, was run by the government until 1965, when the Israeli Broadcast Authority (IBA) was created as a public, non-governmental authority—a "reluctant" surrender of power.[120] Ben-Gurion resisted introducing television throughout the 1950s, worried about the intellectual decline of the "people of the book, [lest they] become people of the screen."[121] The government was concerned that Israel's Arabic-speaking Jewish immigrants would embrace what it considered the low culture of broadcasts from neighboring Arab countries.

Legend holds that Ben-Gurion began to relent after realizing the educational potential of television; in 1962, Charles de Gaulle explained that television had been valuable for transmitting his messages directly to citizens regarding Algeria. "Why doesn't Israel have television?" he reportedly asked Ben Gurion. "You are so much more photogenic than me."[122] In 1966, the government began experimenting with educational television. Officials were becoming increasingly concerned with anti-Israel propaganda from Arab television stations. The 1967 war accelerated the urgency, and the government approved national television shortly afterward—with an emphasis on Arabic-language programming.[123] The aim of advancing Israel's national image and countering Arab broadcasts was hardly hidden: survey researchers in 1968 asked the Jewish public: "What do you think will be the impact of television broadcasts to be established, on the attitude of Arabs in the territories towards the state of Israel?" Fifty-six percent thought that the impact would be positive.[124] Israeli news was provided by a single public channel for approximately the next two decades.

Israeli legislation did not establish freedom of expression (and still has not), while a Mandate-era press ordinance gave the government the power to limit the press, which it soon used. In the early 1950s, Ben-Gurion continued to loathe the Communist Party. The government made various efforts to harass the party and to shutter its newspaper, *Kol Ha'am*. First, Ben-Gurion, as prime minister and defense minister, took the paper to court for defamation, following an aggressively critical editorial, and the government demanded to shut the paper down; the court found the editors guilty and sentenced them to a fine but declined the request for a shutdown.[125] In January 1953, Ben-Gurion suspended distribution of the paper in the IDF temporarily; two weeks later, the minister of the interior (under pressure from Ben-Gurion) suspended publication for ten days. The paper appealed to the Supreme Court, which backed the government. Then in March, *Kol Ha'am* and the Arabic communist paper, *Al-Ittihad*, ran another provocative, and probably false, story playing into Cold War fears. The minister suspended *Kol Ha'am* again, and then *Al-Ittihad*.[126]

Kol Ha'am petitioned the Supreme Court again, but this time, the justices departed from the decision earlier that same year, and issued a landmark ruling. Now they argued that "freedom of expression is closely bound up with the democratic process." Although the ruling noted some limitations on freedom of expression, it also provided an eloquent lesson in democracy that, they explained, was "the regime of 'the will of the people,'" in which "the commanders have been chosen to represent the people. The people have the right to judge and criticize them, or to remove and replace them in elections."[127]

The case became a watershed for establishing freedom of the press in Israel. It was also a touchstone case of the Court confronting government action, while acting to establish democratic values and civil liberties not explicitly provided by laws.[128] The case also represented victory for the newspaper of a Jewish-Arab political party, however disliked. A nationalist Arab newspaper met a different fate, to be examined in Chapter 8.

Finally, during these early decades of statehood, the ruling party only barely tolerated political opposition. The secret intelligence agency, operating in the shadows in the 1950s, unconstrained by laws, was used for political surveillance. Ben-Gurion and Mapai had the agency spying on Mapam on the left and Herut on the right. Menachem Begin claimed that his apartment had been bugged; in 1953, Shabak agents were caught breaking into Mapam offices to change the batteries on listening devices.[129] The government employed the agency to aid the police in constraining political or economic demonstrations, in addition to its would-be role as propagandists to counter *Ha'olam Hazeh*.[130]

Chapter 7: Political Violence

The 1950s were also a time of significant political violence, indicating ongoing struggles to shape society through force, rather than through civic institutions. The War of Independence of course represented a full-scale military conflict, that included violence against civilians; but this chapter analyzes political violence when the country was no longer at war.

Prior to statehood, political violence was common in the struggle against British colonial rule by Jews and Arabs, as well as between the two communities. Palestinian Arabs killed Jews in the riots of 1929, and, from 1936 to 1939, the Arab revolt against the British sowed further violence. Jewish–Arab violence escalated throughout the 1940s, especially following the Partition Plan, when both Jews and Arabs committed massacres against civilians; as preceding chapters have described, Jewish militias carried out attacks against other civilians, from the assassination of Lord Moyne to the King David bombing.

In the pre-state years, there was political violence among Jews as well. Chaim Arlosoroff, the charismatic head of the political department of the Jewish Agency, was assassinated in 1933. The main suspects were Revisionists who might have resented Arlosoroff's interest in binationalism and his conciliatory approach toward Arab leadership, or his negotiations with the new Nazi regime for the emigration of German Jews. Three men were arrested and one was convicted, but the verdict was overturned, sparking various theories, while the killing remains unsolved.[131]

In September 1948, members of Lehi, a Revisionist-affiliated militia, murdered the UN-appointed Swedish mediator Count Folke Bernadotte in a shocking, mafia-style shooting, apparently opposed to Bernadotte's cease-fire plans that would oblige Israel to cede territory conquered during the war and allow Palestinian refugees to come back.[132] The assassins also killed a French colonel seated next to Bernadotte; the colonel had replaced deputy mediator Ralph Bunche, who was supposed to have been there but hadn't yet reached Jerusalem.[133] Bunche took over for Bernadotte and brokered the final armistice agreements.

Political violence continued in the first few years of independence. On January 7, 1952, Menachem Begin led a protest against Ben-Gurion's plan to accept reparations from Germany, which developed into a riot at the Knesset. With 10,000 demonstrators gathered at Zion Square in Jerusalem, Begin exhorted that "we are all prepared to sacrifice our souls" to prevent the deal. "Today I give you the order," Begin said. "This time, we will have no mercy for you either, and it will be a war to the death." The crowd surged toward the Knesset (still located in the center of the city), clashing with police, who used tear gas and batons. Smoke poured into the building, and wounded police were carried inside for treatment—Ben-Gurion's wife, Paula, was a nurse and helped treat them.[134]

Extremist splinters of Lehi gave rise to new underground groups, including "Kingdom of Israel" and the ultra-Orthodox "Alliance of the Zealots." Kingdom of Israel sought to combat European anti-Semitism and conquer more biblical lands in order to establish a Hebrew empire. Instead, it shot at the Jordanian legion positions in Jerusalem, attacked nonkosher butcher shops, and plotted to attack the Knesset over debates in 1951 regarding women serving in the army. Kingdom of Israel was foiled by Israel's secret security agency. A Lehi operative infiltrated the Ministry of Foreign Affairs in 1951 with a bomb (he was arrested just in time), in protest over the negotiations with Germany.[135] In the early 1950s, Kingdom of Israel tried to bomb the Czechoslovakian diplomatic mission, torched the car of a Soviet diplomat, and set fire to nonkosher butcher shops.[136] In February 1953, it bombed the Soviet Embassy with seventy pounds of explosives, wounding several, including a house cleaner and the ambassador's wife, and sparking a major diplomatic rupture: the Soviet Union cut ties with Israel for several months.[137] Members of the group were finally arrested and charged under the Defence (Emergency) Regulations held over from the Mandate authority, by a military prosecutor at the Tzriffin army base who renamed the group "the Tzriffin underground."

Menachem Begin quickly decried the violation of the Kingdom of Israel militants' rights, since they were tried in military proceedings. Constitutional protections would have prohibited the practice, but the civil rights argument may have been lost on the defendants, anyway, whose overall aims were "the establishment of an Orthodox regime, based on the principle of God's justice, [and] a dictatorial regime with no democracy."[138]

The military court sentenced the Tzriffin leader, Yakov Haruti, to ten years in prison. The defense minister approved lighter sentences for the others. However, all sentences were commuted within two years.[139] The suspects were portrayed as patriots, as some had fought in the War of Independence. Following public protests, the Defence (Emergency) Regulations were never used against Jews again for terror activities.[140] The incident was therefore an important legal turning point, on the one hand, for advancing the rights to due process. On the other hand, the end result displayed leniency for terror activities, at least for Jews.

Kingdom of Israel was apparently undeterred. In 1954 and 1955, members plotted to attack American and British senior envoys, bomb the Soviet embassy (again), and attack Israeli prime minister Moshe Sharett.[141] Assassins linked to the Tzriffin group killed Rudolph Kastner in 1957, following the highly emotional trial over Kastner's role in negotiating with Nazis during the war. Investigation of that killing led to an important development: following *Ha'olam Hazeh*'s accusations that Shabak was involved in a conspiracy to kill Kastner, Ben-Gurion finally openly admitted to the existence of the organization, a first step toward transparency and oversight. Three assassins were caught, tried, and sentenced to life—but were released six years after the killing.[142]

In 1957, someone threw a grenade into the Knesset, aimed at the government cabinet. The attack sent Golda Meir, David Ben-Gurion, and others to the hospital. As the explosion hit, someone cried "Arab, Arab!"—but the attacker turned out to be a Jew. The case was never fully solved, but some suspected that the attacker was angry about Israel's withdrawal from Sinai and the Gaza Strip following the Sinai campaign of 1956.[143]

Two years later, riots erupted in the Wadi Salib neighborhood of Haifa. This was not right-wing Revisionist or religious violence, or a nationalist protest against Israeli policy. Wadi Salib had become a slum, where Mizrahi Jewish immigrants from North Africa moved in after it was depopulated of Arab residents. Demonstrations over rumors of a police killing turned into riots and vandalism, which spread to towns around the country over the course of a month. The rioters were clearly enraged at the state and its ruling institutions: among the first targets were Mapai and Histadrut local offices.[144] It turned out that some of the activists had been trying to establish a party representing North African immigrants that would join Mapai, which had treated them instead as "vote contractors," feeding their anger. The uprisings were quelled; the leader of this effort was arrested during a demonstration in July 1959, and sentenced to two years in jail.[145]

Political violence was not an everyday occurrence, but there was more of it than at any other period, at least in Israel's sovereign territory. The "ideological crimes were part of the struggle for power in the country," wrote Tom Segev, reflecting challenges to authority through violence rather than institutions.[146] But the consequences of these incidents were also telling: it was not unusual for Jewish perpetrators to face light consequences, or to have their sentences commuted or overturned. Lehi leader Yitzhak Shamir, who oversaw Bernadotte's assassination, became a prominent politician and eventually prime minister. By contrast, actions that crossed the interests of the ruling party met a heavy-handed response.

Chapter 8: Military Regime, the Non-Democracy Within

For all that was missing or wrong with democratic governance of Jews in Israel, little compares to the situation of Palestinians Arabs who remained after the war.[147] This group enjoyed nothing like freedom and nearly nothing by way of genuine representative government. Arabs could not even be called "citizens" at the earliest stages, for reasons to be explained. The regime governing Arabs in Israel creates such a dramatic problem for characterizing democracy that literature of the early years most often trivialized or dismissed it, and formal democracy indexes did not yet exist.

But the military regime governing Arabs was not separate or alien. It rested on the foundations of law and the governing institutions of Israeli life. The same decision makers created this system and sustained it. Unlike the occupation that began in 1967, the undemocratic regime was imposed on Israel's own people—people who would eventually become citizens—in the same sovereign territory.

The premise of this chapter is that the military regime governing much of the Arab population is not marginal to the story of democracy in Israel—not in the early years, or even in the decades after it ended. It is essential.

The Start of the Military Government

After the UN General Assembly approved the Partition Plan in November 1947, violence between Jews and Arabs escalated. Even before independence, the Haganah and the Irgun, Israel's pre-state fighting forces, took control of Haifa and later Jaffa, the latter outside its boundaries as designated in the Partition Plan. After independence, Israel conquered Ramle and Lydda—perpetrating expulsions and a notorious massacre—and then the Galilee and the remaining parts of the Negev, similarly expelling many residents.[148] By the end of the war, Israel had gained about 40 percent more territory.[149]

During the fighting, the Provisional State Council placed those regions and their Arab towns and villages under temporary military rule. It was not yet clear whether Israel would ultimately be compelled to relinquish the territories, as Count Bernadotte advocated. But as armistice agreements were signed in 1949 with Egypt, Lebanon, Jordan, and, finally, Syria, Israel retained the areas beyond the Partition Plan, its new boundaries demarcated by the 1949 armistice lines.

In October 1948, the ad hoc military administration was replaced with a military government, which defined zones of control in 1949.[150] The new regime operated under six of the Defence (Emergency) Regulations (DER) established by the

British in 1945. The DER included 162 draconian laws that had been used to suppress the Yishuv's Jewish militants, earning widespread hatred.[151] Israel's government also adopted emergency regulations to transfer lands now emptied of Arab residents to the state.

By the war's end, approximately 160,000 Arabs remained in Israel's new boundaries, or about 15 percent of the country's population.[152] Approximately 85–90 percent of them now lived under the military regime.[153] Many were internally displaced and scattered within the state, due to the fighting. More than 400 villages had been depopulated or destroyed, ensuring that there would be no physical or social infrastructure for mass return.[154]

The remainder of Palestinian society had been torn into fragments. Approximately 750,000 Palestinian Arabs fled the country or were expelled by Israeli forces, and during the war, the Israeli cabinet determined that the refugees would not be allowed back during the hostilities.[155] Despite pressure from both Bernadotte and the Americans, the Israeli line hardened into a complete ban on return after the war.[156] Refugees were dispersed throughout the Middle East and other countries, or had joined Palestinian communities in the West Bank or Gaza, under Jordanian and Egyptian control, respectively. Those who fled lost their land, property, social structure, and way of life. Those who remained were subject to rapidly accumulating laws that would expropriate their land and property as they looked on, under military guard. These are the events that Palestinians would come to call collectively "the Nakba" ("the catastrophe").

This book does not not re-litigate the Nakba, which has generated an extensive body of historical research. However, two critical points are important to note from a democratic perspective: first, this chapter shows how the state avoided formally designating Palestinians as Israeli citizens in the first years of statehood. Second, among the main reasons Israel so rigidly resisted Palestinian return was precisely to preserve its democratic status, in the limited sense of maintaining a Jewish voting majority.

The Missing Legal Basis for Citizenship

Approximately half of the 750,000 refugees were displaced after Israel declared independence.[157] The Declaration of Independence had promised "complete equality … to all its citizens irrespective of religion, race or sex" and called on "Arab inhabitants of the State of Israel to preserve peace and participate in the upbuilding of the State on the basis of full and equal citizenship and due representation." Did Israel thus expel its own citizens and prevent their return? Was it expropriating property, land, and livelihood from its citizens? And how did it justify ruling its own citizens through a military regime that lasted long past the war?

In fact, the declaration obscured a legal lacuna: Palestinian Arabs in Israel following independence were not technically citizens; legally, no one was a citizen.[158] While the Mandate Palestinian Citizenship Order-in-Council was not formally canceled, the state had superseded the Mandate, and Israel would not pass any citizenship law until July 14, 1952—four years after independence.[159]

The situation was inconvenient in general. When senior ministers debated how to define its people on *laissez-passer* documents, Ben-Gurion proposed "Israeli citizenship," but the director general of the justice ministry informed him that experts agreed that no Israeli citizenship existed. Ben-Gurion retorted: "I'm not interested in what experts say! There are no experts in this matter." Ben-Gurion got his way, and went on to reject eighteen different drafts of a citizenship bill.[160]

Ben-Gurion worried that citizenship for Arabs would stymie the aim of a Jewish majority and restrict his policy options. In 1947, just ahead of the UN vote on the Partition Plan, he told Jewish Agency colleagues that citizenship would make it impossible to deport the Arabs of the future state: "It is better to expel [them] than to imprison them."[161] After 1948, Arab residents of a few small villages were, in fact, transferred to Jordan, Gaza, or other parts of Israel.[162] Ben-Gurion was also concerned that citizenship would allow Palestinian refugees abroad to claim residency and return. In April 1949, he told his party: "We have no need of a law of citizenship [because civil rights for Arabs] undermine our moral right to this country." And in May, he argued that, in a stable country, "the question of citizenship is a simple one. But here you are asking to make decisions about matters that we are not interested in finalizing."[163]

While the country was, in fact, still at its chaotic beginnings and the tail end of the war, Ben-Gurion's statement nevertheless indicates Israel's general reticence to define rights, or establish laws for equality and inclusion of Arabs. "He sought to keep Palestinians in a liminal position between law and lawlessness, governed by a state of temporariness," states Lana Tatour.[164]

In 1950, Israel passed the Law of Return, the flagship legislation allowing all Jews to immigrate to Israel (while avoiding the word "citizen").[165] Mass Jewish immigration remained the main hope for solidifying a permanent Jewish majority, which the Zionist leadership viewed as an existential need.

The Law of Return inherently prefers one group over all others for immigration policy, and "return" became a national metaphor rather than a literal concept. The law applied to people who may never have been to the country at all, as well as to their direct ancestors. Privileging one group for immigration purposes is not, in itself, unusual for democracies, except that people who were actually from the region—refugees, not immigrants—were not allowed to come back. Further, the law favoring Jewish immigration later became one of the bases for citizenship, when Israel finally adopted the Citizenship Law in 1952. The first two articles of that 1952 law stipulated that Jews everywhere are eligible for citizenship through the Law of Return. The remaining categories cover groups not eligible under the Law of Return but who are entitled to citizenship by residency and birth or a naturalization process; these groups were subject to additional requirements. Thus, the 1952 law created two different grounds for citizenship, privileging hypothetical immigrants, who may never have visited the country, over people born and raised there.[166]

Critics estimated that up to 90 percent of Arabs in Israel could theoretically have been excluded from citizenship under the new legislation.[167] In practice, about 40 percent received citizenship at that time, and another 40 percent incrementally, over decades, as if they were immigrants.[168] Opponents petitioned to change the law and eventually won concessions regarding the birth and residency requirements, starting in 1968. A third amendment in 1980 allowed tens of thousands of Arabs—native to the country or who had managed to return following 1948—to finally achieve citizenship. Many of these individuals had spent many years stateless.[169]

Jacob Robinson, a legal adviser to Israel's UN delegation, praised the Citizenship Law as one of the world's most liberal and generous, regarding rights for aliens and noncitizen residents, while briefly acknowledging the law's inherent inequality between Jews and Arabs.[170] One scholar wrote in 1953 that the new law was a laudable compromise between providing "special status" to Jews and an "ardent desire to enact a nationality law so fair and liberal ... [that Israel would] serve as a forepost of democracy in the Middle East."[171]

Military Rule: Movement, Law, Suppression, and Surveillance

The heart of the military regime was restriction over physical movement, which had consequences for a wide range of social and economic activity. The DER laws regulated whether a person could enter or leave the area of residence.[172] Arabs needed an army permit to reach a medical clinic or visit family, and there was a nightly curfew on Arab villages.[173] In fact, Shira Robinson writes, "virtually every aspect of daily life required a military pass ... [t]o open or maintain a shop, to harvest one's land or graze one's animals on it, to find work in a nearby quarry or town or in the fields and orchards expropriated from refugees ... to fish or bathe in the sea."[174]

Arabs had to apply for permits at offices that were distant and scarce, with limited opening hours, for permits printed only in Hebrew with extremely specific terms of movement. Permits were approved or denied under "security considerations," with no obligation to provide reasons.[175]

The army could banish internally displaced people from their former residences or prohibit them from leaving their homes. Arabs could be required to appear at any police station at any given time and could be arrested and held in administrative detention, with no access to cause or counsel.[176] The military used arrest quotas and incentives to exceed them, sometimes stopping buses so that the security forces could check for permit violations.[177]

It was nearly impossible to be in full compliance. All infractions were tried in military courts, where Robinson notes that up to 95 percent of military tribunal hearings were for administrative offenses. Proceedings were held in Hebrew, and for fifteen years, until 1963, there was no appeal for military court judgments.[178]

During the war, the army had seized a vast amount of property and land from the Arab residents under the emergency rules, and movement restrictions kept owners from returning to claim the lands, while deterring refugees from returning. Movable property was confiscated or looted, sometimes while the military commanders ordered residents to leave their homes for identification lineups that could include physical abuse.[179] In 1950, Israel passed the Absentee Properties Law, which designated that for people who were absent—for example, if they were displaced by the war, including within the country—their properties could revert to a state custodian.[180] The 1953 Land Acquisition Law followed, which further legalized the state's expropriations of privately owned land even if the owners were not "absent." On the basis of these laws, the state transferred some 2.3 million *dunams* (over half a million acres) of Arab-owned land to state authorities.[181]

Military Justice and Permanent Injustice

Enforcing the regulations entailed the construction of an extensive military legal system, overlaid with the civilian laws, as seen above, to facilitate property expropriation. As noted, Arab citizens could not appeal military court rulings. Theoretically, they could petition civil courts, but few had the means to do so. Most often, if such a petition reached the Supreme Court, it was rejected; at best, the Court "sharply criticized" the DER, but mostly upheld the regulations.[182]

Other legal figures had been openly critical of the regulations when they were implemented in 1945 by the British colonial rulers. At that time, Yaakov-Shimshon Shapira, later the first attorney general (and later, minister of justice) called them "without precedent in a civilized country... . Only one kind of system resembles these conditions—that of a country under occupation... . [The regulations] mean the destruction of the rule of law in this country."[183] Once Israel was independent, there was less protest, but at least one district court judge refused to rule based on the laws.[184]

The system rested on ambiguity of status and authority. The lack of clear citizenship rights and fragmentation of Arab society would have been invisible to Jews because of the near-complete separation of the Jewish and Arab populations. But it shaped everyday life for Arabs in Israel. The situation created a gulf of perceptions and experiences between Jews and Arabs about Israel's legal and political culture.

One watershed incident captures the dissonance, yielding completely opposing memories and perspectives on the same events in Israeli history.

On October 29, 1956, Israel began its Sinai campaign, in response to infiltration and attacks. (A stunned Moshe Sharett, former foreign minister, wrote in his diary: "We were in an initiated war! We were the aggressors!")[185] That day, the IDF began the nightly curfew earlier than usual in a number of Arab villages in Israel near the West Bank. Agricultural laborers who were unaware of the time change returned from the fields after the curfew had begun. In some villages, the border police allowed their return, but in Kfar Qassem, at the eastern edge of the country, police opened fire instead. The shooting went on in waves, killing forty-nine civilians, including a pregnant woman. A child of seven was shot and bled to death overnight and was the fiftieth victim; the child's grandfather died of a heart attack shortly afterward and is counted as the fifty-first.[186] To date, it is Israel's biggest state-perpetrated killing of its own citizens since independence.

The events were reluctantly exposed, and the border police unit was court-martialed. Several members were convicted and sentenced to seven, twelve, and fifteen years in prison, and the unit's commander received seventeen years. The defense argued that the unit had followed orders, but Justice Benjamin Halevy's verdict swept aside the claim, which was eerily reminiscent of the Nazi arguments in Nuremberg. In a judgment that became legendary well beyond legal circles, Halevy ruled that every soldier is not only allowed but obliged to disobey a "manifestly illegal order," one that is so heinous that its illegality "should fly like a black flag above the order given."[187]

But it would have been difficult to identify a black flag in a gray zone. As one analysis has it, "the structure of authority and the scope of operational freedom given to local commanders were unclear. The Border Police, in particular, were located in a twilight zone of authority between police and army."[188] There is evidence that the entire order and massacre were part of a secret plan to cause mass dislocation or the flight of Arab citizens.[189] These military and political conditions formed the context of the curfew policy, the orders, and the killing itself.[190]

The memory of Kfar Qassem would split into diverging paths. For Israeli Jews, the famous obligation to refuse a manifestly illegal order is the end and the moral of the story. They recall the massacre as a terrible anomaly, followed by sober self-reckoning in pursuit of justice, even in the face of war.

Arab citizens experienced the events as continuity—another manifestation of arbitrary rule and state violence against them, albeit the most extreme up to that point, since the end of the war. Arabs recall what happened after the events: new curfews forcing residents to remain in their homes until the victims were buried; and prohibiting entrance into or exit from the town. The government initially sought to keep the full information out of the media. The sentences of the perpetrators were eventually commuted; like the Tzriffin underground leaders, none served their full term. Two years later, the highest-ranking officer, Issachar Shadmi, was charged for the killing of half the victims. Ben-Gurion told Shadmi to choose the judges; the military prosecutor clarified that he didn't truly hold Shadmi responsible for the deaths but only for violations relating to ordering the curfew. The court acquitted Shadmi of most charges, and famously fined him ten *prutot* (a tiny amount) for the technical charge. A bevy of high-level military figures attended the reading of the verdict in a show of public support, including Yitzhak Rabin, Ariel Sharon, and Rehavam Ze'evi, all of whom would become defining military and political leaders in the coming years.[191]

Many decades later, nearing death at the age of ninety-six, Shadmi asserted that the trial itself had been largely for appearances. It was intended, he believed, to divert attention from the responsibility of the highest political levels—Ben-Gurion and Chief of Staff Moshe Dayan—while portraying due process to the international community.[192]

For the citizens of Kfar Qassem and future generations, the events came to represent state violence and exclusion and a shadowy plan to drive them out. The authorities sought to suppress annual commemorations, and the army shut down a ten-year anniversary event in 1966, declaring the town a closed military zone.[193] Arab citizens recall ersatz justice, disappearing jail sentences, and the ten-*prutot* fine.

Suppression of Political Expression, Organization, and Leadership

Despite living under a military regime, Arabs in Israel were allowed one major democratic concession: the right to vote. Universal suffrage was the foundation of Israel's claim to be a democracy; women's suffrage from the start of statehood (and in the pre-state Yishuv era) put Israel ahead of even many democratic regimes.[194] Yet Arab voting rights were not a given. After statehood, the fraught debate about Arab participation ultimately favored the franchise—but this decision was largely to show the international community a commitment to liberal democratic principles and to establish Israel's sovereignty over newly captured territory.[195]

Electoral participation for Arabs lacked any of the civil liberties associated with a "free and fair" process. The military regime imposed sweeping restrictions on freedom of expression, freedom of association, and freedom of the press. Under the emergency regulations, publishing a newspaper required a license, subject to the military's discretion; the interior minister had the authority to shut it down. Organizing for practically any purpose involving national identity, political demands, or material demands was generally prevented and independent Arab organization was suppressed; the historian Yair Bauml noted six attempts at political organization that were stifled from 1958 to 1968.[196]

The Mapai leadership established local "satellite" lists of candidates, cultivating local elites, to ensure fragmentation and prevent unified, independent Arab political organization. Arabs were blackmailed through bureaucracy to campaign for the ruling party. Methods included denying civil identification cards, which could lead to expulsion.[197] The government tolerated Arab participation in the Israeli Communist Party, where the majority of the leadership was Jewish, but the Arab political movement al-Ard ("the Land") met a different fate.

Established in 1959, al-Ard demanded the right of return, full equality, cessation of military rule, and an end to discriminatory laws and policies. It demanded that the state return confiscated land, while seeking educational and economic improvement for the Arab community. The movement's leaders saw these as the terms of full citizenship; its open anti-Zionist position had set it apart even from the Communist Party by this time.[198]

The minister of the interior rejected al-Ard's application for a press license. Activists found a technical loophole and began printing its journal, using a different name and editor for each issue, in order to avoid the designation of a regular publication. In 1960, after thirteen issues had been published, authorities shut down the paper, arrested activists, and convicted six of them for publishing without a license and for incitement. Al-Ard appealed and reached the Supreme Court, which reduced the sentences for incitement but did not intervene in the original decision to deny a license.[199]

Several more cat-and-mouse rounds of legal struggle to register the movement and receive a press license followed. In 1964, the defense minister finally shut the group down entirely and arrested top leaders. One memo, cited by the historian Leena Dallasheh, advocated making generous use of emergency regulations to "decontaminat[e] the disease."[200]

But in 1965, some of the same figures who had been involved in al-Ard established a political party called the Socialist List. The Central Election Committee banned the party from competing, on the grounds that certain candidates had been members of an illegal organization, banned for seeking to harm the state. In a landmark judgment known as "Yardur," the Supreme Court rejected the appeal, with two of the three justices arguing that a "defensive democracy" must undertake even grave constraints on electoral rights to protect itself from internal threats. Justice Haim Cohen wrote a dissenting opinion: he found insufficient evidence of a threat to the system or to the existence of the state. Without legislation explicitly prohibiting a group with perceived subversive opinions from competing, Cohen thought that the ban contradicted Israel's proud "constitutional regime."[201] The only independent Arab party during the time of the military government was thereby banned. Instead, Arab parties were established as loyal satellites attached to the ruling Mapai.

These frameworks convey that Arabs had representative political organization, as long as they received official sanction. They had no actual political independence.

Nearly twenty years later, the Supreme Court came to the opposite conclusion, allowing the candidacy of the Jewish radical leader Meir Kahane, arguing that there was no law available to ban him. This is discussed in Section IV.

Surveillance, Informers, Psychological Control

One of the least visible elements of the regime left an enduring, collective psychological imprint even decades later: surveillance. Informers were essential to the regime. The military government coerced, bought, bribed, and blackmailed informers by dangling vital resources that citizens needed to survive, such as movement permits, jobs, and privileges. Israel's nascent (and still-secret) security organization, Shabak—not a military authority—similarly employed material or political incentives to local leaders, as well.

Shabak kept oversight of school councils in order to vet principals, supervised all teachers and principals in the Arab school system, and sometimes directly intervened in their appointments and curriculum. Shulamit Aloni writes that schools were prohibited from teaching Arabic poetry and Arab history—including Saladin's victories in the twelfth-century crusades—for fear that they might instill a sense of pride or rebellion.[202]

These policies involved a patchwork of civilian and military bodies, including the Central Security Committee, chaired by Ben-Gurion's adviser for Arab affairs, the Israeli police, and Shabak, as well as the military government commander.

They developed surveillance files on the grassroots leadership, schools, teachers, parliamentarians, and an unspecified number of regular citizens.[203] The psychological impact of the informant-surveillance-collaboration regime included self-censorship, passive acceptance for many, and reflexive distrust of authorities—effects that linger even today.

Once again, the interweaving of civil and military bodies was critical; this method appears later as a key aspect of the occupation governing the Palestinian territories after 1967.

Security Justifications, Political Results

The core justification for the military regime was security. The early years saw a stream of refugees trying to return despite Israel's ban, and within a few years, *fedayeen* (militants), seeking to commit attacks, appeared. Many assumed that the Palestinian Arab population remaining in Israel might seek retribution as well. Other government officials viewed them as mostly shocked and scared.[204]

Historian Tom Segev concludes that most posed no security threat and identified three primary aims of military rule. The first aim was to prevent refugees from returning, by expropriating their property (returnees who were caught were routinely expelled again). The second aim was to keep people dislocated internally—which broke down social structure, left more land for expropriation, and kept the Jewish and Arab populations separated. The third aim, Segev argues, was political control, which meant both suppressing organic political leadership among Arabs and creating a captive, dependent base for vote harvesting: "The Arab voters were secured through the military government," said one of Ben-Gurion's advisers. Joshua Palmon, the government's adviser for Arab affairs, told Segev in the 1980s that the regime helped "maintain a democratic regime within the Jewish population alone," while supporting Ben-Gurion's rule.[205] The founding chief of Shabak, Isser Harel, wrote that he tried to persuade Ben-Gurion during the late 1950s to dismantle the "anachronistic" regime, explaining that even if Ben-Gurion did not personally exploit the system, others in the party did.[206] Local *mukhtars* or other community figures who helped ensure compliance and marshal votes for Mapai in local and national elections were rewarded with permits and jobs, which the people desperately needed.[207] That gave the community leaders enormous power, reinforcing their ability and incentive to supply votes.

Political figures, especially in opposition parties, were skeptical of the military regime almost from the start. Mapam and the Communist Party opposed the policy from the left, but even Mapai-affiliated figures were skeptical. In 1951, Pinhas Lavon, then leader of the Histadrut, secretly recommended dissolving the regime, and later argued that implementing military rule "must impair something ... in the soul of Jewish youth."[208]

Political opposition grew after the Kfar Qassem massacre, whether for moral concerns, or, in one view, because even this event failed to spark an Arab exodus.[209] In the late 1950s, Mapam proposed legislation to abolish the system, together with Herut and the Liberal Party; they submitted six different bills from 1959 to 1963.[210]

But Ben-Gurion was devoted to the policy. At one point, he threatened to resign if the regime was abolished. He desperately engineered votes to defeat the bills, and even strong-armed the Arab representatives of Mapai's Arab satellite parties to vote against bills to end the regime.[211]

When Levi Eshkol became prime minister in 1963, he announced that he would dismantle the regime, but it would take, in practice, another three years to do so. In December 1966, Eshkol announced the end of military rule, and most cite this date as the end of the regime.

Little changed on the ground. The DER laws that had been implemented under military rule were simply transferred from military apparatus to civilian bodies. Moshe Dayan said in 1966: "According to this change, the military mechanism ... will be converted and replaced by a police mechanism, which will take charge of fulfilling the very same law."[212]

The permit regime continued to govern physical movements, even tightening during 1967, and fell out of use only after the war. Implementation of the DER measures used against Arab citizens finally ceased in 1968.[213] Yet the surveillance regime and the network of informers went on supplying the police and Shabak— civilian agencies—with precise details about Arab life, in schools, political parties, student unions, religious committees, and clubs. Local authorities reported on anti-Israel or pro-Arab statements by teachers and others. Individuals who applied for licenses, loans, or permits requiring interaction with a state agency such as the Histadrut or government entity could be placed under surveillance.[214]

The Kfar Qassem massacre looms large in Israeli and Palestinian collective memories; but its long shadow can be misleading. In addition to diverging recollections of the events among Arabs and Jews, Kfar Qassem highlights a specific moment in history.

But from a political perspective, it was the sustained system, more than an incident, that shaped state–society relations. For about twenty years, most Arabs in Israel learned that under democracy, they lived at the margins of the citizen body, in a gray zone of the law, governed by a patchwork of civilian and military authorities under arbitrary, nontransparent rule. Compliance itself overshadowed daily life and ensured physical, political, and economic segregation, under a chimera of justice and coercive political participation. Yet Jewish citizens executing the policy—from political leaders to bureaucrats, military court clerks to foot soldiers—learned that these practices were commensurate, justified, and integral to Israel's version of democracy in the founding years.

Early Decades: Conclusion

The earliest decades were marked by a severe democratic deficit. The multiparty parliamentary system and widespread political participation, on the surface, belied the reality of highly centralized control of state or quasi-governmental institutions, lack of sufficient protection of civil rights, and minimal intervention of the judiciary—all before considering the military regime over the majority of Arabs. "In states where one group controls so many of the nodes of power in the state —the army, the police, the professional guilds, industry, government bureaucracy, welfare and health organizations, universities—there's no dialogue and no democracy," states Jonathan Shapira, who concluded that even formalistic democracy was only partial at this time. He cautiously concludes that "the question arises how much a political regime like this is even democratic."[215]

Nevertheless, the country did establish institutional mechanisms for change, particularly through elections and an independent judiciary. The universal suffrage, a culture of electoral participation, and a cadre of political and legal figures who advocated constitutional democracy represented potential.

But the military government over Arabs could not be reconciled with democracy. To preserve that system, the state delayed a citizenship law and neglected a bill of rights, with consequences for both Jews and Arabs. Religious parties stymied the adoption of a constitution, leading to an unstable, blackmail-based coalition culture of governance that has persisted over the decades (and spread beyond religious parties).

The state built partial and compromised foundations for democracy in these decades, while certain legs were simply missing. The source of these problems never dissipated.

Section IV
Diverging Paths: Occupation, and Democratic Progress, 1967 – 77; 1977 – 92

An old joke about Levi Eshkol, Israel's prime minister during the Six-Day War, holds that he was "half coffee, half tea," and his tergiversating policy regarding the fate of the Occupied Territories is a good example.[1] But the quip is also a fair observation of Israel's democratic trends in the next decade.

The year 1967 is widely viewed as a turning point that reshaped Israel's political destiny and possibly its political regime. But the image of a rupture doesn't reflect the long view regarding Israel's pre-state territorial aspirations, nor does it reflect the long view of its politics. Prior to statehood, Ben-Gurion kept the Partition boundaries out of the Declaration of Independence; Shimon Peres later related that "Ben-Gurion hoped all along that our right to the entire Land of Israel would be preserved somehow."[2] The Revisionists dreamed of both sides of the Jordan River. From 1948 to 1967, the country existed within the 1949 armistice lines. But for the fifty-six years since 1967, Israel has clung to all areas west of the Jordan River with varying degrees and mechanisms of control. The smaller Israel with a larger Jewish majority turned out to be the nineteen-year historical anomaly, although Jews remain a firm majority of citizens.

Israel also displayed a certain continuity in enacting military and civilian regimes simultaneously throughout its history. The military occupation established in 1967 borrowed heavily from Israel's military government over Arab citizens, whose colonial-era Defence (Emergency) Regulations (DER) laws remained in force when the occupation began. From 1967, a new military regime ruled civilians, despite the fundamental difference that the new occupation governed non-sovereign territory. But the regime flowed from the same state that was governing Israeli citizens. The occupation only deepened the fissures in democracy: it generated confrontations with international law and bled into Israeli politics and society. Israeli settlements added a whole dimension of structural inequality and undemocratic practice.

Yet the decades after the 1967 war saw certain democratizing tendencies inside Israel (a geographic distinction from the Occupied Territories that was still relevant at that time). Weaker social groups became more assertive. The public mounted civic protests, which fueled organized demands for good governance and won some victories. The judiciary increasingly held the government to account, and these forces contributed to Israel's first transition of power. The occupation even contributed to accelerated awareness of human and civil rights, social activism, and political opposition.

https://doi.org/10.1515/9783110796582-005

The country's two personalities appeared to be pulling in two directions at once. This section first addresses the occupation in its first decade (1967– 77), and then returns to 1967 to consider other Israeli social and political developments during that time. The next phase begins with the transfer of power in 1977 through 1992, including greater liberalization but also deadweights on democratic progress.

Chapter 9: Occupation

During six days of war in June 1967, Israel captured swaths of territories that tripled its size and brought approximately 1 million Palestinians under its control.[3] Israel conquered the West Bank and East Jerusalem from Jordan, which had annexed those areas in 1950, though most of the international community did not recognize Jordan's sovereignty. Israel captured the Golan Heights from Syria; it also captured the Sinai Peninsula and the Gaza Strip, which had been under Egyptian control. The new territories were placed under military rule.[4]

Did Israel view the possession of the territories as permanent? The answer depends on who was responding to the question. In contrast to his earlier yearnings, Ben-Gurion argued very quickly after the war that Israel should withdraw from all territories except the Golan and Jerusalem; he was no longer prime minister but a regular legislator, and his influence was waning.[5] In September 1967, Foreign Minister Abba Eban assured the US Ambassador to the UN that Israel would return the West Bank to Jordan under the right terms.[6] But a survey among Israeli Jews in 1969 showed that 90 percent supported returning none of the territories, or just a small portion.[7] Eshkol's government was divided, and Eshkol himself decided not to decide, in a common reading.[8] It is also possible that Eshkol recognized, consciously or instinctively, that nondecision was a useful way to obscure incremental changes on the ground.[9]

The occupation opposed democratic practice in some of the same ways as the military government had with Arab citizens. But the new occupation outlasted the military government by decades and included substantively worse violations of rights and representation. Nearly six decades later, the occupation has become deeply entrenched, with multiple dimensions and manifestations visible and invisible, too elaborate to include in full here. It hardly bears repeating that the occupation itself is not a democratic regime. The aim here is selective, not exhaustive: to describe the regime at its start and to consider three main implications for democracy.

First, unlike the old military regime over Arab citizens, ruling over areas beyond Israel's recognized sovereign territory generated confrontations with international law and challenged Israel's image as part of the democratic world, which generated disagreements between Israel's own political and legal authorities. Second, the settlement project established a new system of legal, physical, infrastructure, and resource-based inequality, along with renewed political violence. Finally, the occupation generated confrontations between another group of *citizens* and Israeli legal authorities.

The analysis here shows that the occupation is not truly separate from Israel's government or society. The remainder of this book does not treat the occupation separately but incorporates its policies into the overall analysis.

International Tension

In contrast to the territories that Israel captured in the 1948 War of Independence, and then retained under the internationally brokered armistice agreements, Israel did not annex the territories of 1967 wholesale. Eshkol did consider annexing Gaza; but annexing all the land would have raised a troubling question of voting rights for more than 1 million non-Jews, which was certainly counter to the leadership's aims. Still, Eshkol hinted that he did not want to give up the West Bank, either.[10] Israel did immediately extend the municipal boundaries of Jerusalem to include the eastern part of the city and additional areas reaching into the West Bank; by late June 1967, these were placed under Israel's "law, jurisdiction and administration," a move often viewed as a form of annexation. (This expansion was formalized in a 1980 law, just ahead of a similar law effectively annexing the Golan Heights, discussed in Chapter 11.)[11] International law also established rules for the treatment of civilians under military occupation and barred actions leading to permanent possession.[12]

Compliance with international law is not a specific indicator of democracy, per se. (Needless to say, some democracies have committed profound violations of international law.) Nevertheless, there is a general connection: democratic countries took the lead in building the postwar international institutions and international law, and Israel aligned itself with these countries following independence.[13] Israel's behavior vis-à-vis international law reflects on its commitment to the postwar order that aspired to support democracy. No less important, if not more important, Israel was building its strongest alliances with democratic countries, especially the US, partly predicated on the notions of shared values and of both having a democratic society.

In addition to challenging international law regarding territorial conquest, the new military control over civilians quickly raised questions about international humanitarian law. From an early stage following the war, Israeli officials developed favorable interpretations of these laws that supported its overall aim of maintaining control, even if the international community rejected the approach. Meir Shamgar was key to establishing these interpretations. (His name was still Sternberg when he was appointed as Israel's military advocate general in 1961.) During the 1967 war, Shamgar provided legal advice for the military, as more and more land fell under its control.

Shamgar immigrated to Israel in 1939 from Poland, and was active in the pre-state Revisionist militia groups Etzel and Lehi. In 1944, British authorities arrested and deported him, along with other militia members, to detention camps in Africa.[14] Menachem Begin's Herut supporters, mindful of Mapai's broad influence among IDF leadership, welcomed his appointment as military advocate general.[15]

In 1963, Shamgar developed a legal plan in the event that Israel was to take over the West Bank. The plan copy-pasted from the British DER, the same general source of the military government over Arabs, to build a new system for the West Bank.[16]

When the war ended, Shamgar began developing the argument that because the West Bank, East Jerusalem, and Gaza were not sovereign territories prior to the war, the land was not "occupied" and the territory was instead "disputed."[17] Therefore, in his view, the Geneva Conventions regarding the laws of occupation were not binding but should be applied to civilians in a distinction between land and people that invited selective and ambiguous interpretations.[18]

Shamgar advised the government to apply the 1907 Hague Regulations, which, like the Geneva Conventions, stipulated that the laws prior to the military occupation should be retained. In this case, prior laws included a thicket of ordinances based on Ottoman, British, Jordanian, and Egyptian legal systems.[19] Following the war, the commander could pick and choose from these systems or even from specific articles within the laws. Neve Gordon, a human rights scholar, argues that the complex patchwork legal system and bureaucracy were meant to obfuscate the permanence of the policy, while demonstrating a rule- and law-based approach that belied the near-total arbitrary nature of life under occupation.[20]

About six months after the Six-Day War ended, a different Israeli legal authority warned against imminent violations of international humanitarian law. This issue involved the nascent steps toward civilian settlements on occupied land. In September 1967, Foreign Minister Abba Eban asked his ministry's legal adviser for a legal opinion on the matter.

The adviser, Theodor Meron, issued his opinion to Eban in a top-secret document on September 14, excavated only decades later by historian Gershom Gorenberg. Meron noted that the request for an opinion regarding "the limitations and permissions according to international law for occupying states, when considering land use," was somewhat vague.[21] But the director of the prime minister's office, Aviad (Adi) Yafeh, clarified that the main questions were the legality of civilian settlements in the West Bank and in "the Heights," as well as the resettlement of Palestinian refugees from Gaza in the West Bank. Meron did not provide creative interpretations of international law, and he observed that the international community did not accept the argument that the territory was disputed rather than occupied.[22] His opinion was blunt: Article 49 of the Fourth Geneva Convention, which Israel had ratified, "categorically" prohibited civilian settlements in occupied areas. This violation was likely to spark diplomatic pressure, even from Israel's allies. Therefore, any such settlements should be established only as temporary military installations.

Meron also noted that even a military settlement would be obliged to respect land-ownership rights of the protected population (Palestinians) under international law. The memo was delivered to the prime minister's office on September 18; just days later, Eshkol approved the settlement in Kfar Etzion in the West Bank—to be labeled a military base.[23] The memo was "either forgotten or ignored," writes Gorenberg, and civilian settlements soon sprouted up in each of the occupied areas.[24]

The government thereby demonstrated its willingness to sidestep both international law and Israel's own legal authorities in its occupation-related policies.

Military Regime: Similar Mechanisms, Different Aims

Many of the basic contours of military rule were familiar from the regime within Israel. Within months, the army had conducted a census of the new populations under occupation and required registration for identity cards, creating the basis for a permit regime.[25] Once again, permits regulated where Palestinians could live and where they could go. The system extended to areas of life that had no clear link to Israel's security needs, restricting economic and agricultural activity: Palestinians required a permit to hold foreign currency, export goods, hold jobs in the public sector, and grow specific crops.[26] Military orders regulated the use of parks, exchange rates, and "duties on tobacco and alcoholic beverages, postal laws, and the transportation of agricultural products," and they regulated the production of information and knowledge by restricting publications. Applicants could be subject to interviews by Shabak, a vehicle for recruitment as collaborators.[27] These kinds of restrictions on daily life, which were not connected to security, violated international humanitarian law and naturally undermined any degree of freedom.

Permits could be rejected or approved but also revoked without explanations. Applicants could be sent to different offices, receive conflicting responses, or have their applications ignored.[28]

What is known as administrative detention—detention without due process, including on a preventive basis—was used freely with no requirement to show evidence of involvement in crime or terrorism. The regime also employed unrestrained interrogation methods, home demolitions, and deportations.

Military orders defined most forms of opposition as insurgency, including meetings, flags and national symbols, and singing or listening to nationalist songs. Security forces sought to suppress political expression, organizing, and protest.[29] By 1984, 1,300 books were prohibited from entering the territory, when restrictions were loosened and the number was *reduced* to 300.[30]

The regime quickly cultivated collaborators and informers, using permits, vital services, protection, assistance, and travel permission as incentives. Informers could make money from other Palestinians by representing their needs to the Israeli authorities.[31] Shabak, Israel's internal security service, was among the most powerful forces on the ground and, at the time, operated outside the bounds of any law; Gordon refers to the agency as a "legal specter" that became "king of the land," by unwritten agreements with other government agencies.[32]

While establishing a military regime that made no or few pretenses to democracy, the government also quickly began blurring the distinction between Israel and the captured territories, while at the same time avoiding the appearance of annexation.

Thus, in contrast to policies regarding Arabs in Israel in the early decades, which had sought to contain and separate them from Jewish areas, in the first years after 1967, Moshe Dayan envisioned economic (not social) integration of Palestinians with Israel and supported broad permission to move between the West Bank, Jordan, and Israel. He believed that an "invisible occupation" could be inobtrusive, while improving material conditions for Palestinians by employing them in low-skilled labor, including in major new infrastructure projects in the new territories.[33] The Israeli economy had fallen into recession the previous year, following the government's austerity policy of late 1965; the consequences of the occupation helped lift Israel out of the recession but generated long-term economic dependence of Palestinians on Israel. Occupation policies restricted and rapidly damaged Palestinian industry, finance, and local labor markets, making them increasingly dependent on Israel for low-paid jobs.[34] One Palestinian economist referred to the era from 1967 to 1993 as "imposed integration"; between 1968 and 1974, the portion of Palestinians employed in Israel rose from 6 to 32 percent.[35] In light of the far more restrictive movement regime following 1993, the ease of physical movement during the first years might have seemed preferable; but ultimately, the policy helped entrench Israel's control.[36]

While conveying that only the military authorities governed the area, civil institutions were almost immediately mobilized to manage the region and its population, as well. Military and civilian authorities, and even laws, thus worked side by side, complementing each other, or simply intertwined. As the IDF occupied the West Bank, on June 7, 1967, the IDF commander issued two proclamations establishing military rule, declaring himself the authority for legislation and governance, as well as administrative functions. The second proclamation declared that prior laws of that region would remain in force, as per the Hague Regulations and customary international law.[37] On July 4, the Knesset, a civilian body, enacted an emergency regulation law regarding Judea and Samaria (the biblical term for the West Bank), establishing that Israeli citizens in those areas would be viewed as residents of Israel for the purpose of Israeli criminal law. The Knesset eventually attached a cluster of seventeen additional Israeli statutes that also apply to Israeli citizens in the territories under that same emergency law. Importantly, these laws were applied to people but not to the territory itself, which could imply annexation; the application of Israeli law was augmented by other mechanisms of establishing civilian-like law for Israelis, through the military commander, described in greater detail below.[38] Israel has argued that the Defence (Emergency) Regulations from 1945, from the colonial Mandate regime, were among the laws that remained in force in the West Bank and Gaza.[39]

From the early days of the occupation, the state decided, via the attorney general and military advocate general (Meir Shamgar), that if Palestinians challenged IDF policies in Israeli courts, the state would not challenge the jurisdiction of the Supreme Court (in its role as the High Court of Justice).[40] Palestinians petitioned within weeks of the occupation, and the Court decided that it had the jurisdiction to rule in non-sovereign territory. The decision was reinforced by an important 1971 ruling in the Christian Society petition against the IDF; the state did not challenge the Court's jurisdiction, and the Court ruled in favor of the state. Shamgar indicated that Israel genuinely preferred that Palestinians have legal recourse. But extraterritorial jurisdiction also supports efforts to project the legitimacy of occupation, while some argue that it is effectively a form of "judicial annexation."[41]

The Court did, in fact, provide legal recourse for Palestinian claims against the state. Yet its decisions, over time, repeatedly backed the Israeli state's policies and only rarely ruled against individual state or army actions, and never against policies. This situation creates a fine balance of tolerance and arguably helps sustain the long-term policy of occupation.[42]

While the Supreme Court reviewed Israeli actions, other Israeli civilian bodies actually administered Israel's policies in the territories. Shlomo Gazit, IDF's first coordinator for government affairs in the territories (now known as COGAT) wrote that civilian ministries and institutions were involved from the "first stages":

> As per international law, formal responsibility for activities in the territories was in the hands of the military commander ... and the civilian government actors had no status in this area. Nonetheless, beyond the formal responsibility, each Israeli government ministry took responsibility for its area of activity in the territories, exactly as they worked within Israeli territory.[43]

Gazit makes this point more than once about the first decades of occupation: "Even if the territories being held were outside Israel's territorial jurisdiction, in fact from the first days, a policy was adopted recognizing the de facto responsibility of Israeli institutions and authorities in the full range of activities in these territories."[44]

These institutions included lower courts, the comptroller, internal supervisors within each ministry, a "Ministerial Committee for the Affairs of the Administered Territories," and two inter-ministerial committees.[45] Therefore, all three branches of government, and both civilian and military institutions, had a role in the occupation. Shamgar himself would soon move from the military legal system, where he helped shape Israel's laws of occupation, to become attorney general, representing the state in court; he later joined the Supreme Court and eventually became chief justice, highlighting the circulation of personnel in Israel between the military, legal, and political institutions of the country.

The war and occupation were also integral to economic developments leading up to, and following, 1967. In late 1965 and early 1966, the new government adopted an austerity policy, sparking recession. Although the economy had grown impressively from the late 1950s, it had been buoyed by the massive immigration and influx of external unilateral "gift" funds—mainly German reparation payments, which together fueled large-scale construction, industry, and growth. When these waned, Israel's trade deficit grew and previously robust growth fell.[46] The impact of the austerity policy was twofold: unemployment and poverty soared (eventually leading the government to prioritize and formalize the welfare system); and Mapai (now the "Alignment") moved more firmly toward a market orientation.[47]

The 1967 war ended the recession, injecting the country with a newfound self-confidence, and it changed the regional balance of power. The occupation and ensuing policies also meant an infusion of cheap labor for Israel and a new market for Israeli products.[48] The occupation laid the groundwork for Israeli investment in what would become one of the most essential pillars of growth: military industries. Arms production became an Israeli export boon from the late 1970s, and eventually contributed to the emergence of Israel's high-tech industry; by association, the occupation has had a towering long-term impact on Israel's political economy.[49] But the occupation also generated major economic pressures, as the defense budget soared. These dynamics will be examined in future chapters.

Settlements: Government, Land, Violence

Settlement efforts began within months after the war, ushering in the most iconic, and eventually the most permanent, institutionalized inequality under Israeli rule. The various governments of Israel mostly tolerated, backed, or actively promoted settlements. The project is predicated on privileged legal status for the settlers and a tight military regime over Palestinians; the settlements also depend on vastly unequal use of land and resources and contributed to the resurgence of political violence over the decades.

At first, the Labor government projected ambiguity toward settlements, but soon supported the efforts—first tacitly, and then explicitly. Yigal Allon, a minister of the Labor Alignment, published his plan for splitting the West Bank and settling the Jordan Valley, the eastern portion of the West Bank.[50] Religious settlers returned to the Etzion bloc south of Jerusalem, where Jews had lived prior to 1948, when they were defeated by Arab forces. In the spring of 1968, a messianic religious group held the famous Passover seder in Hebron, farther south, leading to the establishment of Kiryat Arba. This group led the religious settlement effort, establishing the Gush Emunim movement ("Bloc of the Faithful") in 1974. Settlements were also built in the Golan Heights, Gaza, Sinai, and East Jerusalem. Each of these regions took a different political trajectory; today, West Bank settlements represent the oldest, and most formalized, undemocratic framework of governance, with populations in the same land living under different, unequal laws.[51]

Theoretically, all residents of the Occupied Territories—Palestinians and Israeli Jews—fell under the military regime, following the proclamations of the military commander in 1967. But after Israel had passed the "Emergency Regulations—Judea and Samaria (1967)," mentioned earlier, its citizens in the Occupied Territories fell under large sections of Israeli law. The law establishing this mechanism was temporary, but the Knesset has extended it every five years.[52] The Knesset has amended numerous other laws to extend them to its citizens residing in the occupied areas, such as its own electoral law so that settlers can vote outside sovereign territory.[53] The result has been described as a "turtle" approach, in which the home country laws follow the citizen beyond territorial boundaries, or a "pipeline."[54] Palestinians remained governed by military authorities, tried in military courts, drawing on the selective layers of preexisting Ottoman, Jordanian, or Egyptian (depending on the territory), Mandate laws, and IDF orders.

A second legal mechanism was employed to help "remove [settlers], in practice, from the jurisdiction of military law," so that they could live mostly like other Israeli civilians: the military commanders issued orders that applied or mirrored regular Israeli law.[55] These orders could be tailored to apply only to the settlements; they branched out into a whole system in themselves, with local courts for the settlements and military regulations that tunneled in a new cluster of Israeli laws governing civil affairs, such as welfare, education, health, trade, and labor law.[56] Decades later, the Supreme Court also recognized settlements as legal enclaves, ruling that Israelis who were there should live as much as possible like Israelis in sovereign territory: "[T]here is no real difference between the law applying in Israel and the one that should apply in these enclaves."[57]

The effect was that Israel blurred the lines between sovereign and occupied territory for Israelis living beyond Israel's sovereign areas. Almost immediately, the government changed the terminology of the land, using the biblical names (Judea and Samaria) in formal documents; it quickly removed the Green Line from official maps and, within a few years, from textbooks.[58] Civilian and military institutions also worked elaborately together to enable life in settlements.

Yet while fusing the areas, Israel constructed elaborate systems separating governance and life for the Jewish and Palestinian populations in the Occupied Territories. One group enjoyed the civil rights and protections of democratic rule (with accompanying services and infrastructure favoring this group), while the Palestinians remained under an authoritarian military regime that curtailed basic human and civil rights, deprived the population of its property and resources, and governed through a patchwork of impenetrable layers of law.

Land use became an essential battleground for the settlement project. One of the first measures was to limit Palestinian participation in decisions regarding how to use their own land. In 1971, the army issued Military Order 418, which amended the old Jordanian planning laws, and abolished local and district planning committees where Palestinians had representation.[59] The consequences of this esoteric bureaucratic change were enormous: it removed Palestinian influence over how and where their communities could grow, for residential or public purposes. Instead, the Higher Planning Committee took over, eventually falling under the Civil Administration (established in 1981 under the authority of the IDF). In the 1970s, the military authorities approved most Palestinian applications for residential construction; but in later years, approvals would fall to a bare minimum.[60] Anything not approved was technically illegal and subject to destruction. In recent years, playgrounds and even water tanks have been bulldozed, becoming iconic images of the occupation.

Political violence soon escalated. The Palestine Liberation Organization (PLO) was formed by Palestinian nationalist factions in 1964, prior to the war, but stepped up terror attacks after 1967, mostly abroad.[61] In the West Bank and Gaza, Palestinians mostly carried out demonstrations and strikes, often leading to clashes with the army. They also threw stones and committed vandalism and individual attacks while expressing support for the PLO.

There was a lull in political violence in Israel after the 1950s, but violence against Palestinians by the militant elements of Jewish settlers increased over time. Settlers reflexively defended their actions as a response to Palestinian violence, but Gazit recalls that many attacks were unprovoked.[62]

Law enforcement and justice were applied through different systems to the two populations. Palestinian violence was met with military force, and suspects were subject to Shabak investigations and military courts. Settlers, for their part, became accustomed to operating in a legal gray zone. Gazit states bluntly: "The legal situation of many of the settlers wasn't clear." On the one hand, they were subject to the authority of civilian police. But according to the military law, the civilian police itself was subordinate to the military government. These ambiguities were "ideal conditions for the settlers," recalled Gazit, which allowed them to take "punitive steps towards the local Arab population, with no particular concern that the authorities would seek to impose law and order on them."[63]

Israeli Citizens Confront Israeli Courts

In the first years after 1967, the settlement movement theoretically fought state policy, as the government appeared to constrain civilian settlement efforts. In practice, Gush Emunim enjoyed support from key political leaders in the first decade, including Defense Minister Shimon Peres of Labor (Alignment). Government support accelerated significantly after Likud won power in 1977.[64] When settlers were unable to win permission for a specific spot that they had chosen to establish a settlement (called Elon Moreh) in 1974, some tried "wildcat" action and even confronted the army.[65] Prime Minister Yitzhak Rabin resisted, but they found support from then-opposition right-wing politicians, including Geula Cohen and Ariel Sharon. When soldiers were sent to remove settlers, Sharon exhorted them to disobey an "immoral order." This kind of support, writes Gorenberg (specifically about Shimon Peres a few years later), "concisely articulat[ed] the ethic of illegalism, which valued patriotic purpose over the rule of law."[66]

The Supreme Court (in its role as the High Court of Justice, hearing cases against the state) upheld the state's arguments in certain key cases; for example, in 1978, petitioners fought against a civilian settlement called Beit El, built on private Palestinian land. But the Court ruled in early 1979 that in the case of security threats, there was "no better medicine" than preemptive measures.[67] The justices agreed with the state that the security needs for this settlement meant that the army had met the conditions justifying infringement on Palestinian property rights. However, in that case, the state had tried to convince the Court that the Palestinian petitioner lacked standing to sue for his property and that the Court should not rule. The Court rejected both arguments, finding the issue justiciable—at least as an individual claim rather than a challenge to the policy itself, which the Court would later rule was not justiciable (discussed in Chapter 15).[68]

After clashing with the army and meeting mixed reactions from politicians, the settlement movement had its first serious confrontation with the Supreme Court, in 1979. Settlers had been trying to establish Elon Moreh in a location near Nablus; but the government, despite the right-wing leadership of the time, was involved in sensitive peace negotiations with Egypt and was wary of endangering the process.[69] The IDF found a new location on private land that it seized for the settlement; Palestinian owners challenged the move. This time, the Court was not convinced by the security needs justifying the settlement on private land—reaching this conclusion largely because the settlers themselves had initiated the settlement, not the army, and had declared their religious, biblical justifications to the court. The Court ruled that the land should be vacated and returned to its owner.[70]

The ruling was a bombshell; the settler activists responded desperately. Some considered simply defying the Court order.[71] Ariel Sharon stated that the Court should not be dealing with settlements and should be "relieved of the burden of having to make political decisions."[72] The National Religious Party sought emergency laws that would enable the settlers to bypass a Court judgment.[73] Gush Emunim produced a series of proposals, from barring the Court from ruling on petitions against West Bank settlements, to outright annexation.[74] "If democracy begins to stand in the way of building a Jewish state, then give up on democracy," one supporter reportedly said.[75]

Over the years, the *Elon Moreh* judgment has been often cited as an example of how the Court restrains settlements. But the truth is nearly the opposite: the decision was a shock to both the settlers and the government; it became a galvanizing moment that sparked vast expansion of settlements by other means. Itzhak Zamir, attorney general, reassured a worried Prime Minister Menachem Begin that the ruling did not seriously threaten existing or planned future settlements, since the justices did not rule against settlement on "government land," or even on private land, if there were sufficient security needs.[76] Lawyers for Palestinians in the *Elon Moreh* case were initially giddy, but soon faced a series of losses.[77] The most important consequence of the *Elon Moreh* judgment was that the state seized the mechanism of declaring vast portions of the West Bank to be "state lands"—lands that Zamir had called "government lands." This mechanism is examined in Chapter 11, as it accelerated over the 1980s. The formal term is "public land"—under the Hague Regulations, land to be used for the benefit of the local population. It was state lawyers who adopted the term "state land" instead, and the land is hardly used for the benefit of the local Palestinian population, even as the Court came to recognize settlers in that category. The largest portion of Israeli settlements today are built on these lands.[78]

The demarcation of settlements built on "state land" ultimately contributed to the distinction between settlements that *Israel* considers legal, or "unauthorized" settlements or outposts. But under international law, an occupying power cannot transfer its civilian population into occupied territory, and *all* Israeli civilian settlements in the West Bank are considered illegal. Moreover, settlement construction on private land would eventually resume over the years.[79]

The messianic-territorial elements of the settler community never quite forgave the Court for *Elon Moreh*, which prompted the settler movement to mount its first significant arguments about the need to limit or circumvent the Court's authority, with hints of support from hawkish secular politicians. Over time, this movement would become another community, in addition to the ultra-Orthodox, that treated the law and Israeli courts with skepticism or even hostility.

Summary: Occupation and Democracy

For some, the occupation's threat to democracy was obvious. Yeshayahu Leibowitz, Israel's iconoclastic prophet-scientist-philosopher and an Orthodox Jew, warned in 1968 that "the corruption characteristic of every colonial regime would also prevail in the state of Israel." By 1976, he had freely referred to a "colonial regime"; in 1981, he stated: "There can be no democratic system in such a state, no human rights."[80]

The predominant view within religious Zionist Jews was that the territorial conquest represented the will of God. Given that Israel had yielded to religious parties in political bargaining from the start, indulging divinely inspired messianic communities on settlement policies was not a great leap. Moreover, there was some common cause between the settlers and secular, security-oriented territorial expansionist leaders, including within Labor. In terms of democratic concerns, Israel was accustomed to governing Arab citizens even in sovereign territory under martial rule for two decades; justifying military rule over noncitizens would not have been a great conceptual leap.

For these reasons, the common analytic separation between Israel's political culture and the occupation is artificial. The laws, agencies, and institutions implementing the two regimes are inextricable; civil and military laws and enforcing bodies coexist in complex, complementary layers in the occupied areas, flowing from—and, in turn, influencing—Israel itself.

For longevity, the occupation beat out the military government over Arab citizens by decades. The regime was clearly undemocratic for Palestinians. It also deepened the rupture with democratic practice in Israel, generated confrontations with international law, and drew in civil and military institutions alike. The policy led Israel to construct a new, formal system of inequality between settlers and Palestinians, at a time when the world had seen a wave of democratization and decolonization following World War II. The new reality fueled political violence between Israelis and Palestinians, alongside hostility and challenges to state authority and the Supreme Court by Israelis themselves.

The occupation also generated opposition from certain communities in Israel, almost from the start. Some of these communities threw a spotlight on human rights and contributed to growing movements of civic activism, examined in the following chapters. But just as the state of Israel moved into the territories, the occupation seeped into Israel, eventually dominating politics, ideology, and, in some ways, society itself.

Chapter 10: Democratic Progress

Even as Israel laid the foundations for the occupation, it simultaneously experienced democratic progress following 1967, which accelerated in the 1980s. This chapter considers the same decade as the last, 1967–77, in order to chronicle the country's incremental democratic turn.

After 1967, the military regime governing Arab citizens finally ended. The social mobilization of Israel's marginalized Mizrahi underclass marked the emergence of antiestablishment civic opposition that accelerated with the 1973 Yom Kippur War and culminated in Israel's first transfer of political power. And the judicial branch became more bold and independent, as legal action forced greater government accountability, hastened the transition of power, and boosted awareness of the need for a stronger constitutional order. The new right-wing government gave way to political parity between the two major parties and a mixed, complicated democratic legacy through 1992—the subject of the next chapter.

Arab Citizens Unchained

The year 1969 marked the first time when Arabs voted in national elections, no longer under military rule.[81] Equality would be an ongoing struggle, and the social-psychological impact of living in fear of authorities would linger for decades. The Arab satellite parties attached to the Alignment (led by the Labor Party, the former Mapai) were still prominent, and the authorities still sought to suppress certain forms of independent Arab organizing, as will be shown. Arabs were technically free but had, as yet, little reason to trust in the democratic process, and voter turnout fell slightly, from around 80 percent under the earlier regime, to around 75 percent in the 1970s. Participation declined to 68 percent in 1981—high, by most democratic standards, but reflective of the changing circumstances.[82]

The portion of Arabs who voted for satellite parties quickly declined from 40 percent in 1969 to just 13 percent in 1981. By the following elections in 1984, the satellite parties were gone.[83]

One of the few independent Arab frameworks was Arab-led Rakah, which splintered from the Communist Party in 1965. In the decade after the military government, parties began to reflect more pluralistic ideological debates, such as nationalist versus accommodationist themes, the position of the Arab minority in Israel, attitudes for or against a future Palestinian state, and the extent to which Arabs in Israel identified with Palestinians under occupation.[84]

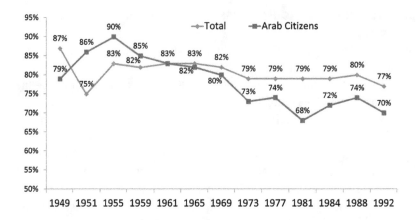

Figure 1: Voter Turnout in Israeli Elections. Graph created by author. Data sources: Arab turnout data: Schafferman, "Participation, Abstention and Boycott"; total turnout data: Israel Central Election Committee.[85]

Arab civil activism grew in the 1970s, and then hit a deadly wall. The practice of land and property expropriation implemented almost immediately after independence, described in Chapter 8, continued unabated under military rule. By 1973, a UN commission estimated that 4 million *dunams* of privately owned land had been seized for Jewish settlement.[86] Buildings, homes, shops, and agricultural lands had all been expropriated, and the loss of land became a particular focus of public anger.

In early 1976, the Rabin government published a plan for yet a new wave of land seizures in the Galilee, an area heavily populated by Israel's Arab citizens, which Israel sought to "Judaize" by encouraging the development of Jewish towns in the region.[87] The Communist Party leadership urged community strikes and demonstrations against the plan, possibly inspired by Palestinian unrest in the West Bank and Gaza in the 1970s. Israeli authorities worked to sever the identities of Arabs in Israel and Palestinians under occupation, but Arab leaders resisted the sense of imposed identity and were influenced by events in the territories, more than in the first decades.[88]

The community now planned large-scale marches and strikes. What became known as Land Day turned violent; the government placed curfews on some of the towns and sent in the army to enforce the curfews. Clashes ensued. By the end of the night, six citizens had been killed. "The violence was by far the worst to erupt among the normally quiescent 450,000-member Israeli Arab community since the foundation of the state," reported the *New York Times*.[89] Land Day became the next iconic and deadly rupture between the Arab population and the government following the Kfar Qassem massacre in 1956 and the first such incident after the end of martial law. The anniversary of Land Day is marked annually, both in commemoration for the victims of 1976 and in continued protest against the policy itself. Once again, the authorities showed few compunctions about using lethal force against Arab citizens.

The government sought to suppress critics of the land expropriation policies, even among Jews. In 1978, the Film and Play Censorship Board rejected an application by the socialist group Matzpen to screen a documentary film titled *The Struggle for the Land of Palestine in Israel.* The Supreme Court upheld the decision to block the film, based on fear of incitement of the "minority against the state and its citizens" and possible violence.[90]

Nevertheless, Arab political activists, academics, merchants, and students continued organizing in the 1970s, especially in the Nazareth area but also spreading around the country.[91] Activists established the National Council of Arab High School Students, a committee of Arab university students, professional guilds, and political coalitions. In 1977, a new political list emerged around the kernel of the old Communist Party of Jews and Arabs, called the Democratic Front for Peace and Equality.[92] The Hebrew acronym was Hadash, meaning "new," and it soon became the dominant political force among Arab citizens.

After the end of military rule, Arab participation in elections began to increase once again in the 1980s. In the 1990s, turnout reached over 70 percent, close to Jewish rates—until another cataclysmic rupture in the 2000s.[93]

People in the Streets: Civil Society

Israel's most marginalized Jewish citizens had also reached a breaking point. As in 1959, Mizrahi immigrants and the second generation were seething in neighborhoods that had become urban slums. After decades of cultural condescension, social marginalization, and economic deprivation, they once again took to the streets. Inspired by the Black American community, the demonstrators took the name Black Panthers. Its leaders said that there was no political platform or organizational structure at first, only large demonstrations of 10,000–15,000 protesters fighting discrimination in living conditions, housing, wages, and education. They were furious about their poor long-term housing conditions, while empty high-quality units awaited a wave of Russian Jews in the 1970s. Activists also occupied schools to demand better education resources and education policy reforms in Mizrahi communities, and longer school hours.[94]

In 1973, the Black Panthers ran as a political party in Histadrut elections, winning 1.7 percent of the vote.[95] The movement then set its sights on the Knesset elections.

But the war that October devastated the country. The elections were postponed to December, and the Labor Party knew that the country was infuriated by its failure to head off the Yom Kippur surprise attack. In its desperation, the party distributed a platform to active-duty soldiers, promising a package of enviable benefits, including a return to prewar jobs, priority for soldiers to receive public service jobs or receive assistance from the Labor Services, funds for completing high school, preferential housing, state support for higher education, and professional training.[96] Legislation for these benefits passed on December 25, six days before the election, prompting a member of Gahal—the combined list of Begin's Herut with the Liberal Party, which would soon become Likud—to fume that the party was politicizing the army for elections.[97] Perhaps ironically, the platform was called the "soldiers' bill of rights," though the country had no bill of rights for anyone else.

Labor managed to win the elections, and the Panthers won 18,000 votes, missing the minimum threshold by a few hundred votes. Shalom Cohen, one of its leaders, lamented that the war had robbed public attention from the socioeconomic issues of the movement's base—presaging a complaint of left-wing parties decades later.

But the electoral victory could not save Labor, and Mizrahim were not the only citizens erupting in protest. The government's failures over the war opened a floodgate. Broad swaths of the public saw widespread political incompetence and inertia from a party that had governed far too long.[98] Under heavy pressure, Prime Minister Golda Meir agreed to the formation of a special commission of inquiry. The Agranat Commission concluded that the top military and intelligence brass had fallen for a *conceptzia*—a fixed notion that neither Egypt nor Syria would dare start a war after being routed in 1967. But Golda Meir and Defense Minister Moshe Dayan were, famously, found not responsible for this failure.[99]

The commission's findings made many angrier still. A returning soldier named Moti Ashkenazi began a one-man demonstration and hunger strike, and his effort burgeoned into mass demonstrations. As many as 10,000 people signed a petition, between 4,000 to 5,000 protesters gathered for demonstrations in February 1974, which continued through April, including at the prime minister's residence. Many were first-time activists and from higher socioeconomic classes, indicating fury from deep within the established and elite communities of Israel. [100] Golda Meir finally resigned, but protesters' demands went further: they wanted big political change. The bottom-up protests would converge, in the following years, with criticism of the ruling party from another branch of government: an increasingly assertive judiciary.

Judicial Evolution

Several developments led by the judicial branch demonstrated greater willingness to constrain the other branches of government around this time. One of these was a landmark 1969 Supreme Court ruling that struck down primary legislation for the first time—an event made more important, given common perceptions that the Court invented judicial review of legislation only in the 1990s (discussed in Sections V and VI).

In 1969, Mapai was deep in debt. So was its longtime left-wing rival party, Mapam. The parties decided to merge ahead of that year's elections, and then backed a law introducing public campaign financing. The law budgeted public funds for existing parties, based on their size in the outgoing Knesset.[101]

The campaign financing law passed its first, sleepy reading in late January 1969, with just 24 out of 120 members in favor; apparently, 94 didn't even show up.[102] In the final reading on February 19, the coalition—an enlarged government formed during the 1967 war—easily passed the law, with only one legislator opposed. Tensions were already brewing with Egypt, which entered the War of Attrition in March through 1970; and the previous day, the Popular Front for the Liberation of Palestine (PFLP) attacked an El Al flight in Zurich, prompting a dramatic shootout on the ground—the third such attack on Israeli flights in recent months.[103]

Uri Avnery, the erstwhile editor of *Ha'olam Hazeh*, had left the newspaper in 1965 to run for office. He and the magazine had taken a bold stance against the occupation during the 1967 war, arguing for peace and recognition of Palestinian statehood—a position almost unheard of at the time. Avnery entered the Knesset as a one-person faction; he was the lawmaker who opposed the campaign financing law in its final reading.[104] Avnery argued that the law favored the large ruling parties and suppressed new parties. He advocated retroactive financing instead, in order to reimburse parties based on the number of seats that each won, including new parties if they entered the Knesset.[105]

Aharon Bergman, a lawyer then serving as director of the Maritime Bank of Israel, found the law scandalous. He opposed public funding for campaigns (in fact, public funding was not common in the Western democratic world until the 1950s, when numerous countries introduced it to reduce dependency on nefarious private funding sources).[106] Bergman took an unusual step: he petitioned the Supreme Court against Knesset legislation.

Bergman argued that the law violated the Basic Law of the Knesset from 1958 in both procedure and spirit. The Basic Law held that the elections for legislature must be conducted in an equal manner. This clause was also entrenched, requiring a majority of Knesset members (sixty-one votes) to make amendments.[107] Bergman argued that the law implied equal rights not only to vote but to *be elected* and that unequal funding undermined the equality for new or small parties. Since it violated an entrenched clause, he also claimed that the new law was invalid because just twenty-four members supported it in the first round—a plurality but not a majority.[108]

The defendants—the Ministry of Finance and the State Comptroller—didn't bother to challenge Bergman's standing or the justiciability of the case, believing that the entire argument was too weak to warrant the effort. Bergman was so certain that he would lose that he did not even show up to hear the ruling.[109]

The justices did reject several of his arguments but surprised everyone by upholding Bergman's most critical argument: the campaign finance legislation *did* violate the principle of equality of elections stipulated by Israel's Basic Law, and, as such, it violated the law's requirement for majority support. The justices suggested just how the lawmakers could amend the legislation, which the Knesset promptly did, in ways that still favored large parties but provided a funding mechanism for new and smaller parties, too, depending on their results.[110] Nevertheless, the Court had struck down primary legislation for the first time.[111]

The justices hardly conveyed a revolution, but certain legal observers treated the case as an understated earthquake because the Court had reviewed legislation. In a report for the Israeli Ministry of Justice, American law scholar Melville Nimmer gave the decisions the greatest metaphorical weight possible in Israel: "[I]n years to come [the Bergman ruling] may prove to have a greater impact in shaping the destiny of the State than anything that occurred at Suez during the same period."[112]

The Bergman ruling is rarely viewed as Israel's *Marbury v. Madison* (the 1803 ruling that established the precedent of judicial review in the US). This is likely because, in Israel, the Court carefully limited its intervention, facilitating changes to help pass the law rather than asserting the authority to review legislation in principle, as the Court did after the Knesset passed Basic Laws establishing human rights in the 1990s (discussed in the following chapters).[113] But Bergman's petition established the precedent for judicial review of legislation. Over the next decade, it was the attorney general who took an increasingly central role in holding the government, as well as the ruling party, accountable.

Corruption Spoiled the Party

After Golda Meir resigned in 1974, the Labor Party replaced her with Yitzhak Rabin. He brought the credibility of a military hero but was not blamed for the failures of the war, having spent most of the previous five years in Washington as Israel's ambassador to the United States. Rabin took office in June 1974.

In late 1976, Rabin faced a coalition crisis. A ceremony for the arrival of American F-15 fighter jets was scheduled for a Friday afternoon, but the delivery ran late. When the ceremony was over, the secular Rabin drove home after Sabbath had begun, a violation of Jewish law. The ultra-Orthodox Agudath Israel, then in opposition, was furious and initiated a vote of no confidence; the National Religious Party (NRP), a coalition partner, abstained instead of supporting the government. Rabin was so angry that he ejected NRP from the coalition, which left him with a minority of seats; he then resigned.[114]

"Only 20 percent of Israeli Jews are strictly observant," reported *Time* in 1977, "but the religious parties ... are a potent factor in the nation's politics."[115] Yet the problem from a democratic perspective was not only the numerical minority but the fact that government stability itself depended on theological, rather than civic, considerations. Fresh elections were planned for May, and Rabin remained as head of a caretaker government.

But by that time, Labor was already reeling from a different blow, related neither to policy debacles nor instability but to corruption.

The Histadrut still retained enormous control over Israeli society and still controlled the country's largest health provider, Clalit; the director and treasurer of Clalit's health services was Asher Yadlin, a political operator who had held top spots within the Histadrut for years. His cousin Aharon Yadlin was a respected Mapai figure who served as education minister under Rabin's government, and Aharon's son Amos eventually led IDF intelligence services, and almost entered politics briefly himself in the 2010s.[116]

In 1976, Asher Yadlin was tapped to lead the Bank of Israel, but reports of corruption had been circulating for several years involving Yadlin and his friend and Histadrut figure, Avraham Ofer. *Ha'olam Hazeh* published an exposé in early 1973 about rotten real-estate deals between Yadlin and Ofer involving the health fund's properties, from which Yadlin was accused of lining his pockets. After Yadlin's appointment, a fairly new attorney general began investigating: Aharon Barak.[117]

The affair was immediately compared to Watergate. At one point, Yadlin clogged his sewage pipes trying to flush incriminating papers down his toilet, which his plumber revealed.[118] Yadlin was arrested in late 1976, and broke down after Ofer, by then housing minister, committed suicide after falling under suspicion, as well.

Yadlin then admitted to taking the money but insisted that it was for the party, not for personal gain. (It probably did not help Labor's image to be seen as sucking funds from its own medical system for political purposes.)[119] Yadlin reached a plea bargain in early 1977 and served a jail sentence. But his initial response to the affair, captured by his ghostwriter Zeev Galili, revealed the prevailing political culture: "The man didn't understand what was happening to him. He could find no fault in anything he had done, and put all the blame on the Prime Minister, Yitzhak Rabin, who didn't know how to bang on the table and stop the investigations, as all prior prime ministers had done each time an investigation was opened into some corruption case."[120]

Aharon Barak was pressured to close the case, but said: "There is no justification for closing this file. If the evidence ... is true—there is apparently a basis for criminal indictment. We must continue the investigation ... in order to reveal the truth."[121]

Seven years after the Supreme Court had first challenged the legislature in 1969, the attorney general was now directly challenging Labor (then known as the Alignment, an amalgam of several parties). Yadlin's sensational case was just one of a series of corruption revelations that, at the time, was affiliated with the ruling party. But even these were soon overshadowed.

In March 1977, two months before the election, Yitzhak Rabin visited Washington. The Israeli journalist Dan Margalit was trailing Rabin in Florida and New York when his wife called from Washington with a rumor that she had heard at an event hosted by Israel's military attaché. According to the rumor, Rabin's wife, Leah, was holding a US-dollar account in Washington, which was illegal at the time, beyond a very limited sum. The couple was allowed to keep an account when Rabin was serving as ambassador to the US and they lived in Washington, but his term had ended four years earlier.[122]

Margalit admired Rabin, whom he viewed as a modest and honest war hero. He hoped that the rumor might not be true and, by his own admission, even offered to bury the story if Rabin's press secretary would simply deny it. The denial didn't arrive. Margalit learned that the account was located at a branch of the National Bank in Dupont Circle; he visited the bank and asked the teller to deposit a fifty-dollar check into Leah Rabin's account. The teller complied and asked him for the account number, which he didn't have; but she found it and wrote the number on the check. Margalit watched, memorized the number, and then published his article in *Haaretz*. By one account, *Ha'olam Hazeh* had the story earlier but refrained from publishing it for fear of bringing down the government—indicating, if true, that even the good-governance fighters had political considerations.[123]

The ensuing scandal was the final trigger for Rabin's downfall and Labor (Alignment) itself. Leah Rabin first said that the couple had simply forgotten to close the account, which held about $2,000. In fact, there were two accounts with tens of thousands of dollars between them.[124]

Finance Minister Yehoshua Rabinowitz, a Labor man, sought to address the issue the old way. He proposed to the attorney general that Rabin pay a fine, and the indiscretion could be quietly closed.

But Barak refused, and warned that the fine wouldn't stand up in court. "You can rest assured, Aharon," Rabinowitz responded, "there will be no High Court [petition] because no one had the standing to submit a petition."[125] Barak was incensed. "They gave you the wrong advice," he retorted. "It's true that only an interested party can petition, but I know one... . [I]f you pay the fine, I will submit a petition against you."

Rabinowitz relented. Barak then visited Rabin and explained that he could not close the file, describing his approach as "rule of law, and law for the rulers." Rabin said that he would resign if the charge moved ahead, and Barak recalled that he heard about Rabin's resignation on his car radio.[126]

Political Opposition Gains Force

Aharon Barak was appointed to the Supreme Court the following year, in 1978. One of his chief legacies was to expand standing before the court, to no small controversy. Debates about the practice continue to the present.

Between the Bergman verdict, the high-profile corruption cases, and Rabin's bank accounts, the third branch of government was becoming a watchdog on government power. Cases such as the corruption files benefited from an increasingly independent, less party-loyal, media exposing corruption. Daniel Friedmann, an advocate of judicial restraint in the 2000s, wrote that "the judiciary toppled Rabin's first government."[127] But one could also describe this as a phase when an independent investigative media helped expose government corruption, leading to suspected politicians being held accountable by the law; and a phase when the media and the judiciary advanced transparency and accountability, helping to check the abuse of political power.

The scandals undercut another core populist theme of the twenty-first century —that judicial activism in Israel was a form of revenge by the Ashkenazi liberal elite (the historical Left) on the elected right-wing leadership. In fact, Aharon Barak's prosecution of government corruption was the final blow that triggered Labor's downfall.

Labor should have known that it was in trouble. In 1969, the Alignment won fifty-six seats, or 46 percent of the vote, which looked like its best result ever.[128] But the Alignment formed after the 1965 elections, combining the historical

Mapai with two other parties (Mapam and Rafi, a splinter party founded by Ben-Gurion, along with Moshe Dayan). Thus, going into the 1969 elections, Labor held sixty-three seats combined; the election result of fifty-six seats was actually a seven-seat decline.

Moreover, in Histadrut elections just a month before the 1969 Knesset elections, Mapai lost 15 percent, while three right-wing parties increased their vote share over time and eventually combined to form the largest party in Israel at the time of this writing: the Likud.[129] All this was compounded by the upheaval of the Yom Kippur War, which destroyed the already-fraying faith in the political leadership. The Black Panthers had been unable to enter the Knesset in the 1973 election, with their socialist-left outlook, but right-wing Likud was becoming the protest party for the Mizrahi working class and urban poor.

Thus, ethnic (Jewish) and class-based anger was compounded by anger at the government for incompetence, complacence, *and* corruption. Investigative media and assertive legal figures held the government accountable; together, they created an almost perfect storm. The final factor was a new political party known as Dash (the Hebrew abbreviation for "Democratic Movement for Change"), which challenged the old Mapai-led hegemony from deep within the political, intellectual, and military elite. Like so many Israeli parties, this one was an amalgam of two factions: the Democratic Movement and Shinui ("Change"). The Democratic Movement was led by Yigael Yadin, the famed archaeologist and military hero. Shinui emerged from the protests against the government following the Yom Kippur War, led by reservists, who recruited a group of academics, including law scholars Amnon Rubinstein and Daniel Friedmann, mentioned earlier, along with the sociologist Jonathan Shapira, business figures, and others.[130] They sought to channel the public demands for better governance in the mid-1970s into political action.

In contrast to Labor's statist-socialist ideals, Dash represented a liberal, free-market economic ideology, while focusing heavily on democratic governance and individual and civil rights. Shinui had nominally stated its support for negotiations with Arabs and possible land concessions but did not take a sharp position on the Palestinians; Dash similarly established a perfunctory position but stated that it would focus on domestic issues—specifically, electoral reform.[131]

At the time, the idea that a former chief of staff with impeccable military credentials, untainted by corruption, would form a new party that could transcend, and perhaps break, the major political divide was an exciting innovation (to be repeated numerous times over the decades). Dash set about recruiting key figures from the major parties on both sides.

Ahead of the 1977 elections, Dash did something unprecedented in Israeli party politics: the leadership decided to begin its political reform agenda by establishing a democratic process *within* the party. Up until then, the central committee and party leaders (the "smoke-filled rooms") selected candidates, and regular party members had no say. After early elections were called in December 1976, Dash held the first primary in Israel, allowing regular party members to vote (and compete) for the list of candidates.

The decision sparked a wave of excitement. Citizens rushed the party's barely operational offices to sign up. The party was logistically overwhelmed but managed to register mass numbers, growing from 8,000 to about 33,000 in less than two months.[132] Rubinstein recalls that citizens were desperate to volunteer in the registration process, while others ran around to party branches to boost their profile, hoping to win high spots on the list.[133]

But democratization had its limits. As a Jewish Zionist movement, Shinui preferred to avoid Arab registration. At one point, the party negotiated with Druze leaders to set a quota of Druze who would be allowed to register—in the hundreds.[134]

One activist for Dash was Issachar Shadmi, the officer who was tried for the Kfar Qassem massacre twenty years earlier and who had been severely injured in a helicopter crash during the 1973 war. By 1977, he was a fervent supporter of Dash and played a key role in wooing prominent politicians away from Labor, contributing to Dash's success.[135]

On election day, Dash acted as a wrecking ball for the Alignment. The party won nearly 12 percent of the vote and fifteen parliamentary seats, almost entirely at the expense of Labor, whose share declined by nineteen seats.[136] Likud won the 1977 election, but Dash ensured that Labor lost. Yet after all the excitement, Dash's fortunes would soon fade. The party's factions broke up within one cycle, foreshadowing the fate of later high-volume celebrity-centrist parties headed by former generals. Shinui ran alone in 1981, winning two seats and receding as an electoral force until the late 1990s. However, Amnon Rubinstein remained in the Knesset and made some of the most significant contributions to democratizing trends in governance over time, despite minimal parliamentary strength.

From 1973, Labor also faced a new kind of challenge from the left. Shulamit Aloni was an upstart politician, ahead of her time. Born in Tel Aviv in 1927 to parents who had immigrated from Poland, Aloni (then Adler) lived in a working-class neighborhood of Tel Aviv. She served in the War of Independence, and then worked as a teacher while completing a law degree.[137] Aloni also hosted a radio show in which she encouraged citizens to learn and demand rights from government authorities. In 1958, she published what has been called Israel's first civics textbook, *Citizen and His State: Foundations of Civic Theory.* The book exudes a sense of pride in the institutional foundations and values of democracy in Israel.[138] The book also conveys a full awareness of democratic ideals and norms in the earliest years.

Aloni joined the Labor-led Alignment in the mid-1960s, but her focus on civil rights and individual freedoms was not an easy fit for Labor's collectivist ethos. Golda Meir considered human and civil rights to be "'bourgeois legal egoism,'" wrote Aloni.[139]

By the early 1970s, Aloni felt that the Alignment was marginalizing her political program to advance civil rights and that it had pushed her into a low place on the list of candidates. She broke away and established her own party, the Movement for Civil Rights (also called Ratz). The party advocated equality, separation of religion and state, civil marriage, reducing class inequality, improvements for slum neighborhoods, women's advancement, and opposition to gender discrimination by religious authorities. Aloni supported a constitution and an end to religious coercion; like Dash, she was deeply critical of the Alignment's closed-door selection committee process, and she supported personal primaries.[140] In contrast to Dash's splashy first result and later decline, her party won three seats in 1973 and one in 1977, slowly gaining seats in elections through the 1980s. Ratz helped carve a new space in the Israeli political culture for the liberal Left, in contrast to the socialist Left—reflecting changing notions in Israel about the very meaning of the concepts of left and right (discussed in future chapters.)

It was a right-wing party that finally reshaped Israeli politics. The Herut opposition, led by Menachem Begin, took second place in elections throughout the 1960s —still well behind the Alignment, but gaining. Herut and other allies advocated free-market economics and liberalization, the traditional opposition to Labor Zionism and the more socialist parties, at a time when ideology was defined more prominently by social and economic values; in 1965, Herut and the Liberals created Gahal together. Territorial dreams seemed remote until 1967; but after the war, territorial ambitions ignited once again. In 1973, Gahal incorporated more factions and ran under a new name, Likud.[141] This time, it won thirty-nine seats.

Labor's long rule, with its complacency and sense of impunity, had demolished its credibility among large segments of Israeli society. For many, the party's image would never recover. But the change was not born only of anger. It also reflected a growing confidence and willingness among both mainstream and marginalized citizens, legal authorities, military, and political insiders to challenge the hegemony.

For Jewish Israelis, at least, the Six-Day War seemed to boost confidence on an existential level (despite the downfall of 1973). Self-sacrifice, economic austerity, the trials of mass immigrant absorption, and perhaps immediate memories of the Holocaust were fading by the late 1960s. Israel was turning toward a messier, but more democratic, polyarchy of power, even as the democratizing trends hit the roadblocks of its least democratic elements.

Chapter 11: Transitions of Power

Ahead of the 1977 elections, Begin and Likud appealed directly to Mizrahi Jews, seeking to capitalize on their decades-long alienation under Mapai. Tom Segev found that, even in 1949, Mapai leaders were worried that these voters (specifically, Moroccans) were leaning toward Herut in the very first election of 1949, due to their resentment of Mapai.[142]

In the early 1970s, the Black Panthers offered a left-wing, class-based struggle for social justice, but Begin's appeal was stronger. He issued a broadside attack on the upper crust of Israel's ruling class and lashed out at the "heg'mony" (Israelis tended to drop the second syllable). "They try to turn the citizens into a frightened herd, to do the bidding of the Ma'arach"—the Alignment—he told an audience in the working-class neighborhood of Yad Eliyahu, the backside of Tel Aviv.[143] Likud's campaign material exhorted voters: "You see what everyone sees: bureaucracy, corruption, depravity... . You search for who is to blame—and you find the Ma'arach."[144]

Herut, the main hub of Likud, was still deeply nationalist and had only recently drifted from its commitment to Israeli sovereignty over *both* banks of the Jordan River.[145] In 1973, the Likud platform accused the Alignment of seeking to redivide the "western" land of Israel (in other words, west of the Jordan River), and spent several pages addressing the right of the Jewish people to the land, advocating sovereignty in the "liberated areas," rejecting withdrawal and emphasizing settlements, plans for Palestinian refugees, foreign relations (including assistance from the United States to "avoid pressure"), and the urgency of security and further Jewish immigration, before presenting its plans for a full constitution, followed by a social and economic program.[146]

In 1977, Likud's campaign material showed a marked emphasis on domestic socioeconomic themes. The platform of its student group opened with three short bullet points, declaring that Likud would not give away Judea and Samaria and that Israel would be the only sovereign west of the Jordan River, while striving for peace with Arab states. The platform then launched into detailed plans for tax breaks, social support, a minimum wage, and investments in education, culture, sports, and municipal improvement in impoverished neighborhoods; it presented a full draft constitution. The document guaranteed democracy and equality, with a heavy emphasis on fortifying the courts and the judiciary.[147]

After three decades under Mapai (now the Labor-led Alignment), many of its voters had been nurtured on disdain for Begin and his movement. Ben-Gurion hated Herut as much as he hated the Communist Party, and banned both of them from his coalitions. He had called Begin "a classically Hitlerist type," echoing his "Vladimir Hitler" sentiment for Jabotinsky.[148] And those were the instances when he referred to Begin at all; sometimes, Ben-Gurion just called him "the person sitting next to Mr. Bader" in the Knesset.[149]

The fading political and cultural elite seemed unwilling to see what was coming. The only public-opinion expert who predicted the 1977 results ahead of the vote was terrified to publish her findings, with all other polls indicating the usual Labor victory. But that pollster, Mina Tzemah, was vindicated on election night—and she was lucky that her boss had insisted on publishing her poll in a small financial newspaper.[150] When the results came in, Likud won forty-three seats, while Labor crashed to thirty-two, marking Labor's first-ever loss. The anchor of the state news channel (the only Israeli news), Chaim Yavin, called the vote result a *mahapach.* The word literally means "upheaval" but is often translated as "the earthquake," in order to convey the colossal political event. Yavin also likened the outcome to Yom Kippur, the Jewish Day of Atonement, without clarifying whether he meant for the party or for the country.[151]

As the country was witnessing its first transition of power nearly thirty years after independence, the Labor leadership, along with Israel's social elite, lamented the demise of democracy. Following the elections, prominent authors filled newspaper columns with accusations of fascism, fanaticism, irrational extremism, and militant rule committed to destroying rights and freedoms.[152] Ahead of the 1981 election, Shimon Peres, leading the Alignment, warned: "There is a real danger to the future of Israel's democracy. There is a real danger to the future of Israel," accusing Begin and his supporters of fomenting election violence and populism.[153] There had, in fact, been campaign skirmishes. Peres compared these to the tactics of Iran's Ayatollah Ruhollah Khomeini.[154]

In June 1981, a *Jerusalem Post* editorial stated that a segment of the population —referring to Begin's supporters—"takes a dim view of the country's system of democracy, and would be happy to see it scrapped and replaced with an authoritarian 'strong-man' regime," while members of the Central Election Committee referred to some of the voters as illiterate, "hot-tempered," and too ignorant to understand the true nature of the candidate they supported.[155]

Begin led the country for six years, and, like that of Jabotinsky, his impact on democracy was complex, while his legacy has become selective and politicized. Begin's government broke down state centralization; he oversaw policies intended to liberalize the economy but confronted major economic crises and runaway inflation in the early 1980s, caused partly by the residual economic damage of the Yom Kippur War.[156]

The power of the Histadrut had declined somewhat since the pre-state and earliest years, and the government was the biggest employer by the late 1970s. But the institution still held enormous power, controlling about 25 percent of the economy; about 80 percent of the country's workforce were Histadrut members.[157] Though the government and the Histadrut were still somewhat mutually independent, the loss of a near-symbiotic relationship with the state was part of a long Histadrut decline. The Histadrut became weaker as independent unions gained power; and its decline ultimately culminated in the 1990s—ironically (or logically, as will be discussed), under a Labor government.[158]

Begin's government also brokered a historic peace agreement and started a war leading to yet another occupation, while establishing policies that vastly facilitated settlement expansion.

Beyond top-down change, the spontaneous street presence of public demonstrations gave way to new organizations and movements seeking to institutionalize the spontaneous public engagement, in order to influence the government and policies.

Something's Happening Here: Turning Points in Civil Society

The 1970s were a decade of growth for third-sector welfare groups, which stepped in to help provide social services for children and the elderly, as well as education and religious services. These organizations worked closely with the government.[159] But the 1980s also saw the growth of interest groups and opposition citizen groups —the heart of civil society. As Tocqueville noticed in the nineteenth century, associations among citizens provide a crucial counterweight to government power while elevating citizens above pure individualist concerns.

These interest groups had political agendas and sought social change, challenging the government and advocating for women's equality, religious freedom, environmentalism, improvement of poor neighborhoods, and other causes.[160] Beyond specific policy change, Israelis increasingly focused on the underlying need for human and civil rights protections. In the early 1970s, the large Black Panther demonstrations sometimes ended in clashes with police. Other demonstrations could be tiny, yet the police still used heavy-handed tactics, according to the jurist David Kretzmer. "If they saw five people with placards, they would say, 'You don't have a license,'" and then disperse and arrest demonstrators, even if the law did not require a license, he recalled.[161] Kretzmer and his other activist friends notified the police that they would send observers to the demonstrations; they hoped that the police would restrain themselves if they knew that people who knew the rules were watching.

Kretzmer, a lawyer, immigrated from South Africa in 1963, swearing that he would never visit again under the apartheid regime. A colleague in Israel, Daniel Amit, had studied at the University of California–Berkeley and was impressed by the student activism of 1968. The two agreed that true political action was impossible if the authorities did not respect full civic freedoms, including the right to assembly (demonstrations) and freedom of expression.[162] In 1972, together with colleagues and modeling themselves on the American Civil Liberties Union, they formed the Association for Civil Rights in Israel (ACRI).

The ethos of collectivism and socialist conformism was beginning a slow decline. Shulamit Aloni had called her party the "Movement for Civil Rights," although, in politics, it was mostly the right-wing Herut or the Liberal Party that had advocated for individual and minority rights in politics in the first decades. Aloni's party became the kernel of the liberal political camp that opposed occupation. These groups and related civil society organizations (discussed below) later came to be seen, fairly or unfairly, as "left-wing" in Israeli terms, as notions of ideology began a long shift away from previous connotations of socialism versus liberal or free-market orientations.[163] In the 1960s, Yitzhak Hans Klinghoffer was a lawmaker from the Liberal Party (then part of Begin's Gahal). He was a law scholar from Vienna and a war refugee who had fled to Brazil, before arriving in Israel to become a professor of constitutional law at the Hebrew University. During his three terms in the Knesset, he worked doggedly to advance a full bill of rights (discussed in Chapter 13). When he left the Knesset, Klinghoffer served as president of ACRI from 1976 to 1982.

Arab citizens began to organize more openly after military rule ended, establishing dozens of civil society groups by the 1980s (the number would eventually reach thousands).[164] Arab political activity continued: in 1980, activists planned a "Congress of Arabs in Israel," envisioned as a nationally representative body for Arab citizens. The draft charter named the Land Protection Committee and the National Committee of Local Councils as representatives within Israel and stated that the PLO was the national representative of Palestinians outside the state.[165] For Jewish Israelis, the PLO of the era was synonymous with terror; the PLO would not declare its renunciation of violence in favor of diplomacy until 1988. Employing the old colonial-era Defence (Emergency) Regulations, the Israeli government banned the Congress, which became known as "the forbidden convention."[166]

Peace and Opposition to Occupation

Opposition to the occupation took shape through civic organizations as well. In 1978, 348 IDF reserve officers sent a letter to Begin, expressing their longing for peace and the end of the rule over "millions of Arabs." As "citizen-soldiers," they felt that such rule damaged the Jewish and democratic character of the state. Their letter led to the formation of Peace Now, which opposed settlements and occupation and supported peace agreements with Israel's neighbors.[167]

The letter did not arrive in a vacuum. In November 1977, Anwar Sadat made his historic trip to Jerusalem, which stunned Israelis and established a basis for negotiations. Begin wanted an agreement with Egypt but resisted Sadat's demand—shared by US president Jimmy Carter—to link peace with Egypt to Palestinian self-determination. The Israeli officers hoped to boost the opportunity for peace. In 1978, Menachem Begin and Anwar Sadat did reach the landmark agreement at Camp David; and the following year, they signed a full peace treaty, in which Israel agreed to return the Sinai Peninsula to Egypt and remove its settlements there, in exchange for full normalization of relations with Cairo. Regarding the Palestinians, Begin did, in fact, make striking proposals during the negotiations: autonomy and an end to military rule over Palestinians—even allowing Palestinians to apply for full Israeli citizenship.[168] He resisted a Palestinian state but, when pressed, acknowledged that both Arabs and Jews claimed sovereignty in the West Bank and that, in the future, the question of sovereignty might be revisited.[169] Begin described the proposals in terms of "fairness" and Israel's desire to avoid becoming like Rhodesia, where a white minority government was losing control to an African-nationalist insurgency demanding majority rule.[170] The return of Sinai seemed like a dramatic reversal for Likud, which had broadly opposed territorial withdrawal and passionately supported settlements. Likud's 1973 platform even asserted the freedom of "all citizens" to settle in "all parts of the land of Israel."[171]

But its platform in both 1973 and 1977 also recommitted Likud to the detailed constitutional vision of Israel as a liberal and democratic society, with "freedom of conscience and expression and the equality of all before the law, with no differentiation of race, origin, sex, nationality, religion, ethnicity or outlook" (including a decisive role for the Supreme Court in reviewing legislation, in the role of a constitutional court). These elements were consistent with Jabotinsky's historical commitment to democracy, alongside Jewish nationalism and the settlement drive in the Occupied Territories. Begin's tentative proposals and characterization of the Palestinian situation seemed to acknowledge that indefinite, ongoing military occupation inevitably contradicted democratic values; yet Likud's commitment to settlement and Jewish control only deepened over time.

The final Camp David agreement reduced the Palestinian issue to basic principles for future autonomy, which would wait years for further progress, and did not include the citizenship option.[172] The agreement with Egypt, by contrast, was cataclysmic. Israel demonstrated that it could withdraw from territory in return for security guarantees; and that the Israeli government—under a right-wing leadership, no less—was able to dismantle Jewish settlements in the Sinai desert, despite visceral resistance from the settlers.

The Begin government also went to war. Israel invaded Lebanon in 1982 for the immediate purpose of destroying the PLO infrastructure there. Defense Minister Ariel Sharon hoped to rout the PLO from Lebanon entirely and engineer a friendly Lebanese government.[173] Even after the IDF partly withdrew in 1985, the ongoing presence in the "security zone" of southern Lebanon was a new, protracted occupation of a sovereign country. The war generated deep controversy within Israel, at an early stage.

Yishai Menuhin was a combat soldier who had served in the late 1970s; from his first encounter with the occupation in Gaza as an officer, he opposed the regime.[174] After his service, he became active in Peace Now as a student, and then found a more radical group that began discussing the refusal to serve in the occupation, following growing Palestinian resistance and IDF crackdowns. When the Lebanon war began, the group's support for refusal carried over. Menuhin was called up to serve in Lebanon as his first tour of reserve duty; while there, he decided that he would not serve in Lebanon again. When he received a second reserve call up for Lebanon, Menuhin refused, and went to military prison instead. The activists issued a petition against serving in the war, and became an organization called Yesh Gvul, whose name meant "there is a limit" (*gvul* also means "border").

The call to refuse IDF service never generated widespread support. But when Lebanese Phalanges militias committed a massacre of Palestinian civilians in the Sabra and Shatilla refugee camps under IDF cover, the Israeli public took to the streets again in protest. Peace Now had been demonstrating over the summer of 1982 against the war (which had begun in June). After the massacre in September, approximately 350,000 people showed up to demonstrate, in what was described at the time as Israel's largest demonstration in history (often called "the demonstration of 400,000").[175] The protesters demanded that the government establish an investigating commission, and the public pressure had some success. The Kahan investigation commission found the minister of defense, Ariel Sharon, and other officials indirectly responsible for the massacre, and recommended that they be removed from office. International media lauded Israel's democratic character for its willingness to investigate the massacre.[176]

Peace Now was angered that the government did not immediately act on the commission's recommendations, and staged a demonstration in Jerusalem. A right-winger threw a grenade into the marching crowd, killing the peace activist Emil Grunzweig, in another internal, internecine incident of political violence. Nevertheless, the occupation of the "security zone" in southern Lebanon dragged on for eighteen years. Ariel Sharon did resign as defense minister, but soon moved to other ministries; nearly two decades later, he became prime minister.

Palestinians in the West Bank and Gaza had protested in waves during the 1970s, foreshadowing the major Palestinian grassroots uprising in 1987, the Intifada. The Intifada sparked tougher Israeli crackdowns, which, in turn, accelerated small but passionate groups opposed to the occupation within Israel. In 1988, Lotte Salzberger, a German-Dutch war refugee with a PhD in social work, established HaMoked: Center for the Defense of the Individual, which provided legal representation to Palestinians facing occupation-related human rights violations. Salzberger's story was remarkable: she was born into an ultra-Orthodox family in Germany, which had fled to Amsterdam before the war. There, the family was arrested and sent to the Ravensbrück concentration camp, and later moved to Theresienstadt. Upon arriving, Salzberger was personally interrogated by Adolf Eichmann, who promised that if she revealed what she knew about death camps, "Then you will go through the chimney"—as Salzberger testified at the 1961 trial in Jerusalem, while Eichmann listened.[177] In later years, she devoted herself to Palestinian human rights; her tombstone notes that she died on the International Day of Human Rights (December 10, 1994).[178]

In 1989, B'Tselem was established as the dedicated flagship organization documenting and exposing Israeli violations of Palestinian human rights. In 1990, Menuhin was among those who formed the Public Committee Against Torture in Israel, in order to oppose interrogation practices involving torture.

Israel's emerging newer types of right-wing groups also successfully leveraged civil society. Gush Emunim was a form of nongovernmental civic activism as well, with considerable impact. As seen earlier, the messianic settler group (and other settlers) at times enjoyed tacit or open government support but also vigorously confronted the government when faced with any limitations on their settlement aims.

In a sense, the civilian settler movement depended on democratic norms that allowed it to take brazen actions to influence the policy and future of the state. Yet settlers' political freedoms were put into the service of a fundamentally undemocratic project that entrenched occupation and military rule and undermined Palestinian self-determination. Gush Emunim was driven by "religious, messianic, and anti-democratic arguments ... [with] no compunctions about breaking the law. Its confrontations with the army and with law enforcement agencies ... became a matter of routine," states sociologist Uri Ben-Eliezer.[179] Thus, the movement leveraged the democratic concept of civic action but not in order to advance democratic values.

Lurching toward Liberalization

Alongside the turbulence of the Lebanon war, the increasingly influential settler movement, and the growing civil society engagement, Israel experienced major economic turmoil in the 1980s. In the 1984 and 1988 elections, the two large parties were almost evenly matched and unable to form coalitions on their own; under pressure to address the economic crisis of the early 1980s, Labor and Likud established a unity coalition in 1984 and again in 1988. The two parties increasingly converged around a broad liberal orientation, specifically in terms of economic policies. This phase had the dual effect of laying the groundwork for the significant liberalizing changes of the 1990s (the subject of Section V) but also cleared the ideological stage for nationalist divisions regarding the future of the land, which would come to define the country.

The roots of the economic crisis of the 1980s went back to 1970s and deeper structural causes; the more proximal factors included (but were not limited to) heavy military spending, major state subsidies for exporting industries, and state financing of the emerging military industry sector, as well as the welfare state—what the political economist Arie Krampf calls, simply, overextension.[180] As in the past, the state financed these needs partly through foreign aid and loans, leading to expanding foreign debt. Since the late 1970s, Begin's finance minister, Simha Erlich, had tried to implement a rapid series of plans to liberalize the economy—too fast and too shocking to the system—and his first efforts failed. But he devalued the currency and liberalized foreign exchange.[181] And other changes during this time significantly weakened the Histadrut. For example, in 1979, when the Histadrut resisted wage restrictions, the government ended a long-standing practice of allowing the institution to use pension funds to invest in its companies and of providing low-interest (subsidized) credit. These changes eroded its industries and prompted privatizations in the year to come.[182] In 1983, a bank share crisis led the government to buy out bank stocks, effectively nationalizing the banks, including the Histadrut's Bank Hapoalim (before selling them off again to private investors in the years to follow)—further weakening the Histadrut's power.

Inflation was spiraling out of control, reaching dizzying rates (over 500 percent in the fourth quarter of 1984 and an annual average of 466 percent), while government debt was approaching 150 percent of GDP.[183] Israeli economists called on the government (the unity coalition) to reduce the state budget drastically, and another important actor urged the same: US secretary of state George Shultz. Since 1967, the US had become a major source of military and financial aid, in order to balance Soviet power, thereby gaining leverage. Now, the US had an interest in stabilizing the Middle East and encouraged "scaling down" Israel's military power.[184]

In 1985, the Israeli government's Stabilization Plan seemed stuck between external interest groups and internal disagreement within the government, until pressure from the increasingly independent Bank of Israel finally forced the government to implement it.[185] But the plan became a turning point toward liberalization of Israel's economy, with far-reaching consequences for its politics as well. At the political level, the two major parties now openly converged around liberal, market-based economic policy. In practice, Mapai had established a robust market-oriented system over the years, while Begin's Likud supported key aspects of social welfare; the parties were not as polarized as often thought. By the 1980s, Shimon Peres of Labor was increasingly interested in economic cooperation in the Middle East as a basis for peace, an early indication of the connection between economic and political liberalization and support for peace. But Krampf argues compellingly that a liberal economic orientation is not inherently tied to peace-related aims and can similarly serve nationalist ideology and interests. In other words, both parties could embrace a liberal economic agenda in the service of their political-national ideology, and each side did so in the decades to come.

The Stabilization Plan of 1985 accelerated the transformation of the Israeli economy. The government stabilized inflation and reduced public expenditure, including defense spending. The plan also helped reorient Israel's economy toward a more internationalist positioning; in the early to mid-1990s, foreign direct investment rose dramatically, imports and exports grew, and foreign companies bought more shares in Israeli firms.[186]

The institutional power of the Histadrut was now rapidly decaying. The near-demise and reconstitution of Koor Industries represented one of the biggest such changes. Koor was the massive manufacturing conglomerate held by the Histadrut's Workers' Corporation. Even after the stabilization plan, Koor had 130 subsidiaries and employed more than 30,000 people. It earned one description as a "symbol of Israeli-style statism, an arteriosclerotic, union-owned behemoth."[187] In the 1980s, the Workers' Corporation significantly reduced its holding shares in Koor; in the late 1980s and early 1990s, a determined executive sold off the many money-losing enterprises and slashed payroll, debts, and also jobs, laying off fully 40 percent of employees. Koor was "radically and brutally transformed," and was ultimately sold to private investors.[188] It is impossible to overstate the importance of these changes for the Israeli economy and society. The economy went into recession, and unemployment rose, though the jolt was limited and replaced by fairly steady growth after 1989.[189]

Due to the economic crisis, the social impact of the changing economic environment, and the turbulence of the war, the public was increasingly troubled by the political situation. Though the unity coalitions did ultimately stabilize the economy, they had been formed mainly because of electoral deadlock, in the context of the economic crisis. Israel looked briefly like a two-party system, but, in fact, small parties continued to draw votes, which is why neither large party had a clear victory. Religious parties gained more bargaining power, which some Israelis began to view as blackmail; and the Palestinian uprising, discussed in the next sections, was dragging down the mood by the late 1980s. Sociologist Ben-Eliezer claimed that "the public expressed its disgust at the functionaries, at the parties' leaders, and at the extortionist virtuosity demonstrated by the small parties," leading to cynicism and declining idealism by the 1988 elections.[190]

In mid-1987, against this background, four law professors from Tel Aviv University, some with ties to Shinui and Dash, established a new effort to advance a constitution as well as electoral reform.[191] The academics proposed another draft constitution, with a bill of rights, alongside far-reaching electoral reform measures. In Israeli public discourse of the time, the focus on good governance and constitutional democracy without prominent statements about the occupation seemed to rise above traditional right- or left-wing politics, as a mainstream, middle-ground antidote to the perceived failings of the large parties. Right-wing prime minister Yitzhak Shamir and Israel's president, Chaim Herzog, originally from Labor, both conveyed support for their aims.[192] Yet the political crisis only deepened in the late 1980s, driving fresh civil protests in the early 1990s (discussed in Chapter 12).

Democratic Deadweights: Occupation, Militarism, and Ideology

The transition of power, growing activism of civil society, and a deepening focus on civil rights represented incremental but important democratic steps. From its start in the early 1970s, the "Freedom in the World" index by Freedom House consistently ranked Israel as a free country overall; the only other Middle Eastern country in that category was Lebanon, for three years in the mid-1970s. In 1977, Israel's score for civil rights improved slightly, moving from the "partly free" to "free" (apparently partly because of the transition of power). The occupation was then a decade old, but Freedom House had categorically separated the issue: "Freedom House's rating of Israel is based on its judgment of the situation in Israel proper and not that in the occupied territories."[193] The dismal freedom ratings of the Palestinian territories were included as a separate and distinct category.

Yet the occupation was increasingly intertwined with Israeli life, society, and government. By the mid-1980s, more than 46,000 Israeli settlers lived in the West Bank and Gaza, and over 96,000 lived in East Jerusalem (see the table below).[194] The 1979 *Elon Moreh* judgment prompted a race to declare swaths of the West Bank as "state land," which the Court did not address in its judgment.

Table 1: Population of Israeli Jews and Palestinians in West Bank, East Jerusalem and Gaza, 1967 and 1985.

Area	1967		1985	
	Palestinians	**Israeli Jews**	**Palestinians**	**Israeli Jews**
West Bank	598,637[195]	0/unknown	813,000[196]	44,200[197]
East Jerusalem	65,857[198]	0/unknown	126,900[199]	96,500[200]
Gaza	356,261	0/unknown	526,000[201]	2000[202]
Total	1,020,755		1,465,900	142,700

The mechanism of establishing state lands itself displays the intricate partnership of Israeli civilian state authorities and military bodies. In 1967, an IDF military order halted the registration of West Bank lands to the Jordanian authorities, including by private owners; only about one-third of West Bank lands had been registered by then.[203] As observed, Israel adopted the Hague Regulations of 1907—specifically, the regulation to maintain existing laws and another regulation permitting the occupier to manage government lands of the occupied area. Another military order, from July 1967, designated a military-appointed "custodian for government property" to possess property registered to the Jordanian government. Then, to figure out if more lands could be registered as government property under existing laws, the authorities drew on a nineteenth-century Ottoman law defining land ownership. The term "public lands" eventually gave way to "state lands," with its clear political connotation, referring to the only state in the region.[204]

In the years after the *Elon Moreh* case, the effort to identify such land accelerated: the Custodian and, separately, the Civil Administration (the latter established in 1981, both under IDF authority) now conducted a "double investigation" to identify more land, aided by the State Attorney's office, a civilian body.[205] If land was eligible, the Custodian would inform local *mukhtars*, who could inform anyone who might want to appeal the decision; the burden of proof was on parties claiming rights, and the standards of proof were almost unattainable.[206] For areas ultimately designated as "state land," another military order created a special registry to transfer usage rights to bodies such as the Ministry of Housing or the World Zionist Organization, to be administered under the Israel Lands Authority—the same (civilian) body that manages most land in sovereign Israel.[207] About 40 percent of the West Bank is currently designated as "state land," and approximately 0.25 percent of those areas went to Palestinian development. Nearly all state lands have been used for settlements or other purposes, such as military zones. By 1985, about 90 percent of settlements were built on state lands—though the portion has declined significantly over time as building continued on privately-owned land in practice.[208]

Other similarly complex patchwork legal and bureaucratic systems are used to expropriate land in the West Bank for "public needs," and a separate mechanism is used for such expropriations in East Jerusalem—including privately owned land —and another mechanism for "abandoned property."[209]

In 1984, the tunneling-in of Israel's criminal law and other statutes to its citizens in the territories was amended to apply to anyone eligible for Israeli citizenship under the Law of Return. Thus, even noncitizens fell under those areas of Israeli law in the settlements, if they were Jewish, while Palestinians remained under military rule.[210]

In 1978, the Knesset amended its tax laws to apply to "areas" specified as Judea and Samaria, Gaza, Sinai, and the Golan.[211] In the 1980s, Israel extended laws involving taxes, national insurance, military bureaucracy, and the population registry to apply to Israeli citizens in the Occupied Territories. Legislators had no illusions about the political implications: in a parliamentary debate about extending certain real-estate taxes in 1984, Chaim Ramon of the Alignment referred to both annexation and apartheid: "You claim that this is being done in order to collect more taxes. I don't buy it. There is an intention here to annex the West Bank without granting rights to the residents... . You cannot create a regime that has more than a hint of apartheid."[212]

In 1988, the Knesset voted for a law defining preferential regions and "development towns" that would apply to local authorities and Israeli citizens, including in "the areas" (without Sinai, by then), the first extension of Israeli law to actual territory, rather than people.[213]

But in addition to extending regular Israeli civilian laws on an extraterritorial, personal basis, another mode of law for settlers utilized the military commander, who issued military orders very much like regular Israeli law, mainly for defining local government, applied to settlements. Indeed, the Supreme Court has ruled in this context that the settlements are enclaves; in one case, a justice ruled that "their lives [i.e., Jews in Israeli settlements] should be as close as possible to that of other Israeli nationals."[214] These mechanisms cast doubt on the idea that Israel applies laws in a way that distinguishes between people and territory.[215]

These civilian and military mechanisms complemented each other, deepening Israel control over land, helping to expand settlements, and facilitating life for settlers, while ensuring that Palestinians lived subordinate lives under separate and unequal laws, which they had no hand in creating and which were implemented by military authorities. The bureaucratic mechanisms of the occupation can seem impenetrable and are practically invisible to observers. But this bureaucracy enables the project, and it was established by mainstream parties in Israel's executive and legislative branch, not by radical settlers. The embroidery of military and civilian authority was stitched tightly together almost from the start. This not to assume that the processes were either deterministic, nor are they entirely irreversible—Israel completely reversed and dismantled its settlements in Sinai and Gaza. But the geographic boundaries between sovereign Israel and the Occupied Territories have been blurred by settlement spread, while the state and occupation can hardly be separated. Where does one end and the other begin?

Violence between Palestinians and Israelis escalated in the 1980s. Israeli and Palestinian perpetrators were, of course, tried in different courts. But there was also a difference in the responses to violence, based on the identity of the victims: when Palestinians attacked settlers, the latter demanded more settlements, and the Likud government increasingly met their demands. When Israelis attacked Palestinians, justice was delayed and partial.

During the first decade of the occupation, Palestinians protested mainly through civil activities, demonstrations, and stone-throwing, though there were also more violent attacks. In January 1980, Palestinians killed a yeshiva student in the city of Hebron; in response, Gush Emunim settlers began squatting in buildings in the historic Jewish quarter, determined to reestablish the pre-1948 Jewish community there. In May, Fatah-affiliated Palestinians conducted the most lethal attack since 1967, killing six Jews at Beit Hadassah, a historic building. Now, Begin acquiesced to demands for Jewish settlement inside Hebron, which became one of the most bitter and violent flash points of the occupation in the years to come.[216]

In June 1980, Israeli settlers targeted three Palestinian mayors—of Ramallah, Nablus, and al-Bireh—in bomb attacks. Begin condemned the violence and called for an investigation but warned that the authorities must follow due process. Shabak knew whom it was looking for, but no one was apprehended for another four years; for Jews, Shabak was "not allowed to use administrative detention, not allowed to arrest and isolate suspects for fourteen days … and they could not use administrative punishment such as home demolition," relates Gazit; in other words, Shabak could use the old Defence (Emergency) Regulations for Palestinians, but Jews were investigated according to regular Israeli criminal law.[217]

More attacks occurred in 1983: Jewish Israelis committed a shooting attack at an Islamic college in Hebron that killed three; a bus bombing killed six Palestinians; and there was a shooting spree in a school and grenades in mosques and churches, injuring clergy members. Attackers even laid explosives at the al-Aqsa compound, apparently intended to attack both mosques.[218]

In 1984, the authorities foiled a plan to blow up five Palestinian buses during rush hour. Twenty-five suspects were arrested and charged for the plot and other attacks, twelve were released, and thirteen were convicted; two received a life sentence. Once again, domestic and international media generally praised Israel's willingness to police itself. But when the affair died down and attackers began their sentences, some Israelis organized a movement advocating for their pardon. The activists struck a deal: the convicts wrote to the president expressing regret, and all of them were pardoned well before the end of their terms.[219]

The occupation continued to violate international law, beyond the constant growth of settlements. In 1980, Menachem Begin's government pushed through a new Basic Law: Jerusalem, the Capital of Israel. Unified Jerusalem was now viewed as sovereign Israeli territory, under Israel's "law, jurisdiction and administration," as per the language of the 1967 legislation. Palestinians of East Jerusalem therefore represented another population under Israeli control with murky citizenship status. They were considered permanent residents after 1967; they could apply for citizenship, but many refused to recognize the authority of the state, and applications could also be rejected. Most Palestinian East Jerusalemites today hold residency status rather than citizenship. They cannot compete or vote in national elections; though they have the right to vote in municipal elections, most do not do so. Most importantly, authorities can revoke their residency status entirely and also that of their families, which can act as a form of forcible, bureaucratic transfer out of the region.[220]

The following year, in 1981, a new regular law applied using the same "law, jurisdiction and administration" language to annex the Golan Heights. Here the government took the opposite approach and sought to force approximately 13,000 Syrian Druze residents of the Golan to accept citizenship, in order to legitimize Israeli sovereignty. Members of this tiny religious sect traditionally avoid political activism, but now they were indignant. The Golan Druze organized a surprisingly effective civil boycott. The Israeli army closed the area and tried to distribute blue identification cards by force, but eventually backed down. To this day, most of the Golan Druze remain permanent residents.[221]

Security threats flowing from the occupation generated further clashes within Israel's own political institutions. One such incident demonstrated that the ongoing conflict generated specific crimes, as well as clashes between the highest political levels and the law itself.

On April 12, 1984, four armed Palestinians hijacked bus number 300 from Tel Aviv to Ashkelon and drove toward the Egyptian border. They intended to hold the passengers ransom, demanding the release of Palestinian security prisoners. But Israeli security forces overtook the hijackers en route, leading to a standoff; finally, late at night, the IDF commando unit Sayeret Matkal stormed the bus. Troops killed two of the hijackers and captured the remaining two.

The army then interrogated the two Palestinians, and handed them over to Shabak agents. In the predawn hours, Shabak agents led them away, holding them tightly, while photographers from various newspapers snapped images of the men, dazed but alive. Furious agents tried to stop the photographers, but the photos survived. By morning, the two captured terrorists were dead.

The details of how the security agents beat them to death emerged in slow-burn fashion. Local photographer Alex Levac had a photo of the agents leading one of the hijackers away, taken for *Hadashot* newspaper, which was blocked by the military censor but leaked to international media.[222] Anat Saragusti, another photographer, also managed to take a photo of the hijacker still alive, and wrote an article for *Ha'olam Hazeh*, which the military censor heavily redacted. The newspaper ran Saragusti's photo on its cover, and published her article with large white blots over the censored portions.[223] An investigating commission was established, and, based on testimonies of security personnel involved, suspicion fell on Itzik Mordechai, commander of the IDF's commando unit. Over the course of two years, he was charged with manslaughter and court-martialed, but eventually acquitted.[224]

Eighteen months after the hijacking, in October 1985, three senior Shabak officials accused the agency's chief, Avraham Shalom, of approving the killings and orchestrating a frame-up, including planting a Shabak member on the investigating committee in order to incriminate Mordechai, the IDF commander. The officials managed to speak with the prime minister, Shimon Peres (Yitzhak Shamir had been in office during the original incident; Peres replaced him after the 1984 elections). Shabak chief Shalom had already warned Peres that the agents were conspiring to topple him. The three agents told Peres about a cover-up and sham investigation with faked testimonies; they were certain that he would be scandalized, but Peres believed Shalom. He sacked the top agent, and the others were pressured to leave Shabak.[225]

The agents persisted, telling the deputy state attorney what had happened, and then telling the attorney general, Itzhak Zamir, who had been on the job for seven years and had announced that he would leave when a replacement was found. In the meantime, he resolved to investigate.[226] Peres mounted a wall of opposition and recruited support from former prime ministers Shamir and Rabin. Zamir began to realize that the Shabak chief might have approved both the killing and a cover-up. Shalom, for his part, would lie to police, claiming that the prime minister, Shamir, ordered the killing.[227] Peres insisted that Zamir drop the case. Finally, Zamir offered to resign if Shalom, the Shabak chief, would resign, too. Peres refused; Zamir insisted on a police investigation, and in June 1986 the cabinet found his replacement; Zamir said that he was "relieved," but it looked as though he had been forced out.[228]

The showdown roiled the country. The dean of Tel Aviv University's Law School, Uriel Reichman, called it "a constitutional drama. Never before was the attorney general isolated, fighting the government."[229] The *Washington Post* argued that a complete investigation was needed to ensure a "viable democracy." In 2016, Zamir recalled his greatest fear: that if the deception was not investigated, the affair would establish a norm, creating a "secret police, in the style of countries we don't want to be compared to."[230] By contrast, an intelligence figure said: "When you fight terror, there are many situations that cannot fit under the laws of democracy... . You must break the normal rules of democracy."[231] A poll reportedly showed that over 70 percent of Israelis agreed with Peres.

Weeks later, Shalom resigned. But in return, President Herzog pardoned him and numerous other Shabak officials before they were even indicted.[232] The preemptive pardon was so controversial that a dozen private petitioners appealed to the High Court of Justice, which upheld the pardons; Meir Shamgar wrote the majority opinion, and Aharon Barak wrote the dissenting position.[233] Later, the legal scholar Leon Shelef would argue that, while certain preemptive pardons can be justified, in the bus number 300 affair, it mainly helped suppress the truth by burying the issue.[234]

In 1987, following another major Shabak scandal involving the use of torture to extract a confession—and another cover-up—the government established a special commission, headed by retired chief justice Moshe Landau, to investigate Shabak's interrogation practices and their veracity in court. The commission found that the security agency routinely used force to extract information. But it was more disturbed to find out that security agencies regularly used conspiracy, cover-ups, and what the journalist Ronen Bergman called "a strict policy ... of institutionalized lying to the outside world."[235] Moreover, the commission found that outside figures knew and "were complicit by their silence," including "civil and the military prosecutors, the courts and the political levels."[236]

The security apparatus, it turned out, was yet another group in Israeli society accustomed to behaving outside and above the law. Both military and civil courts had believed "countless" false testimonies by Shabak officials, incriminating hundreds or thousands of defendants, who the agents said had freely given their confessions.[237]

Landau's 1987 report concluded that "moderate physical pressure" could be used in security interrogations. This generated an outcry among liberal critics, who read the conclusions as a license for torture. The interpretation devastated Landau, who had cited international conventions against torture and proposed limited "special methods" to prevent imminent attacks; notably, he purposefully sought to end the reality of Shabak operating in a "twilight area" of the law.[238] The government adopted the report's recommendations just before the Intifada began; in fact, three years later, a study found that the use of torture was widespread for investigating Palestinians. Formal limitations on torture in interrogations would wait until 1999, when the Supreme Court ruled against it—even then, leaving loopholes. The Court, for its part, regularly ruled in favor of the state on petitions against the use of torture for investigations, changing its position only after the Court ruling of 1999.[239] There was no law defining Shabak until 2002.

Bad Crop of Jewish Supremacy

Finally, among the forces counteracting democratic progress, Israel in the 1980s saw one of the most undemocratic ideological movements in its history leap from the social fringes to the political mainstream arena. Subsequent generations are still grappling with whether Kahanism was an aberration or an outgrowth.

Meir Kahane hailed from Brooklyn; he was a rabbi and a thug with a rap sheet. In the late 1960s, he founded the Jewish Defense League, which stockpiled and trafficked in explosives, was tracked closely by the FBI, and faced numerous indictments in the United States.[240] In the 1990s, both Israel and the US would designate his successor organizations as terrorist groups.

Kahane moved to Israel in 1971. His ideology evolved from Jewish militarism to include outright Jewish supremacy. He was arrested more than sixty times and detained in jail, and Israel labeled his organization a terrorist group. Nevertheless, Kahane began running for the Knesset, starting in 1973.[241] His racism against Arabs was fanatical: "There is no coexistence with cancer, and Arabs are a metastasizing cancer!" he thundered at crowds.[242] In each cycle through 1981, his Kach Party won thousands of votes but fell short of the minimum 1 percent threshold for entering the Knesset.[243]

In 1984, Kahane tried again. The party's campaign posters railed against the disloyalty of Arabs to Israel's national identity and flag.[244] His program and later proposals included anti-miscegenation laws between Jews and non-Jews, including prison sentences for prostitution between Jews and non-Jews and direct expulsion of Arabs from the territories.[245]

In 1984, Israel's Central Election Committee (CEC) tried to ban him from competing:

> This list advocates racist and anti-democratic principles that contradict the Declaration of Independence of the State of Israel, openly supports acts of terror, seeks to fan hatred and hostility among different parts of the population in Israel, a formula for harming the feelings and religious values of some of the citizens of the state, and its goals negate the foundation of democratic governance in Israel.[246]

Kach challenged the ban in court, together with a left-wing party that had also been banned (on different grounds). The Supreme Court reversed the CEC. The justices emphasized their "revulsion" at Kahane's ideas, but they lacked the legal basis to reject his candidacy. They recalled that the Court had upheld the ban on the Arab "Socialist List" in 1965 because some members had been involved with an earlier organization deemed illegal; this was not (yet) the case with Kach. Kahane was allowed to run; he won nearly 26,000 votes and entered the Knesset in 1984 with a single seat.[247]

Surveys began to show a wave of support for Kahane's ideas among young people. In August 1985, the *Washington Post* reported "a drift by the country's burgeoning adolescent population toward radical right-wing ideologies."[248] Mina Tzemah, the pollster who had predicted Likud's first victory, conducted a survey of the Jewish population, offering several options for "Arabs in the Occupied Territories." Nearly half (44 percent) responded that Arabs could remain in the region without full citizenship rights or the right to vote. Another 15 percent chose deportation— in total, nearly 60 percent of Jews chose something akin to apartheid or worse.[249]

These trends were greeted with shock. In July 1985, Chaim Ramon of the Labor Party told the Knesset:

> Last Friday's papers were full of the phenomenon of Kahanism in schools. This is terrifying. This should give no peace to people from any side of the political spectrum. Anyone who thinks that the threat of Kahane is a threat only to Arabs ... [or] only to the left or the center parties, is mistaken. Kahane threatens the entire democratic structure of the state of Israel with no exceptions... . [Right-wing parties] will never succeed in competing with Kahane– he will always be more radical, more anti-democratic, than Likud members or Tehiya members.[250]

Ramon was speaking during discussions ahead of a vote to amend Israel's electoral law, following Kahane's electoral success. The proposed amendment would modify Article 7 of Israel's "Basic Law: the Knesset," to prevent parties that "incite to racism" from competing in elections. The law would give the Supreme Court a legal basis to uphold a ban on such a party.

But the new law (amendment), known as 7 A, raised worries about democracy in its own right. Did it conflict with the essential right to equal competition in democratic elections? The Knesset debates were stormy. Who was to interpret the draft language citing a "reasonable basis for suspicion" that a party might violate the new terms? Ramon himself thought that the wording was "Orwellian," too easily weaponized. The minister of justice shot back that one need not look to George Orwell for amorphous formulations in Israeli law.[251]

As a legislator, Kahane also got his turn to speak. He insisted that he represented only a natural continuation of Israel's own founding ideology: Zionism. On July

31, 1985, in a final debate on the amendment, Kahane, who had studied law, gave an eviscerating speech: "Jews, know that if this [law passes], we will have to ban all Zionist lists. We will have to ban Zionism … because in fact Zionism is in its essence anti-democratic… . The state that was established is confused and schizophrenic, and has entrenched its schizophrenia and its confusion in the Declaration of Independence."[252]

Kahane argued that the Declaration of Independence focused primarily on Israel as a Jewish state, "but democracy says precisely the opposite. In a democracy there are only people, human beings, and it doesn't care if they are Jewish or goy. And as such, there's a contradiction. There is a conflict, there is a war between these concepts."[253]

The Knesset passed clause 7A of the Basic Law. The final version seemed to concede Kahane's point. What if a ban against racist parties was used against Zionism itself, particularly the right-wing parties? The amendment was adjusted to open with a clause that parties could be disqualified for negating Israel as the "state of the Jewish people" and, after that, for undermining the democratic character of the state. The third clause names incitement to racism as a basis for disqualification.

The law was applied to only one whole party—banning Kahane's list ahead of the 1988 elections and two Kach successor lists in 1992. He was assassinated in 1990 in New York by an Egyptian American who was later found to have ties to al-Qaeda —still a little-known extremist organization that had been founded two years earlier.

The 7A amendment sparked a process of legally codifying Israel as a state belonging to the Jewish subset of its population. In 1992, the term "Jewish and democratic" was included in a Basic Law (discussed in later chapters), and in 2002, the Knesset amended section 7A, merging the first two clauses to ban parties that negate "the Jewish and democratic character of the state." That amendment also added a new ban on parties that support armed struggle against Israel.

Defining Israel as a Jewish state in Israeli Basic Law can be considered a statement of identity that appears in many democratic constitutions. One example is Spain's 1978 constitution, which refers to "the Spanish Nation, desiring to establish justice, liberty and security." Another is Germany's "Basic Law," which functions as its constitution and states that "Germans … have achieved the unity and freedom of Germany in free self-determination. This Basic Law thus applies to the entire German people."[254]

Opponents argue that the current version of clause 7A of Israel's electoral law violates the sacrosanct right to compete in elections for anyone who would challenge the identity of Israel as a Jewish state, or who believes that the law elevates Jews above other citizens by privileging the Jewish identity. Debating the 2002 amendment, the Arab parliamentarian Taleb al-Sana argued that the "Jewish and democratic state" wording "guts the concept of [democracy] of any substance."[255]

The 1985 law is routinely used by parties attempting to ban Arab and extreme right-wing parties or candidates. Since Israel's Central Elections Committee (unlike most other democracies) is largely made up of party representatives, its decisions are challenged, and the Supreme Court is the final arbiter—usually overruling challenges to lists (while occasionally supporting a ban on individual candidates).[256] In practice, the right wing often accuses the Court of taking sides and expressing a political view when it upholds Arab parties.

Conclusion

The post-1967 decades were a time of social transition and initial democratizing trends: a transition of power, buoyant party competition, and realignment of ideologies, not just parties. Likud actually presided over many of these changes, such as legitimizing liberal values in Israeli society, eroding the party dominance and centralization of state institutions, and advancing a peace treaty with Egypt. With some irony, the occupation and the Lebanon war contributed to burgeoning political opposition from civil society actors. It is also significant that Israel acceded to some of the critical international treaties at this time. The International Convention on the Elimination of All Forms of Racial Discrimination (CERD) and the International Covenant on Civil and Political Rights (CCPR) were originally signed in the 1960s, under Mapai-led governments. But Israel bound itself legally to the treaties when it ratified them in 1979 and 1991, respectively—under Likud governments.

Yet these stirrings of greater democratic practice emerged alongside deepening undemocratic policies. The occupation may have seemed like an external appendage in the early years, but it was becoming entrenched physically and legally. In a contest between security and democracy, there was no contest for most Israelis. Israel's religious, messianic, and racial supremacist Meir Kahane saw no contest between democracy and Judaism. In a way, democracy seemed present but subordinate to numerous higher priorities.

But viewed in a more favorable light, the 1967–92 period also saw trends pulling for and against democracy, almost evenly matched. One direction was bound to give out, and in the next era, it looked as though Israel might be choosing the democratic path.

Section V
The Liberal Potential: 1992–2009

Israel of the 1990s felt very different from Israel of the 1970s. A robust liberal ethos was completing the process of replacing the statist, or semi-socialist ideals of earlier decades (romanticized as they had been). After the brief recession of the late 1980s, the economy was transforming; GDP in the mid-1990s was seven times higher than in 1975, per-capita income rose and was ranked twenty-first in the world, and, by 1997, the IMF had placed Israel in the category of developed countries, alongside fast-growing Asian countries.[1]

The economic environment was matched by changing cultural norms. Israel was moving away from both the austere spirit of the early decades and the economic instability of the 1980s, and the decades of state and quasi-state institutional domination of society were fading. Expectations of individual rights and freedoms rose, while citizens experienced a newfound consumer culture and a more global outlook.

At the same time, from 1987, Israel was coping with a Palestinian uprising, which carried social, political, and international costs. This section argues that it was no coincidence that the country took its first serious steps toward a political solution with the Palestinians at this time.

With the political leadership largely converging around a free-market, liberal orientation, the axis of ideology itself was changing. Polling over the years has found that political labels such as left and right in Israel are moderately, even inconclusively, related to the economic outlook of those polled, such as whether they have a socialist or capitalist orientation.[2] But from the mid-1980s, the issue of the Occupied Territories became the "overriding dimension" of the party system and the defining factor of left and right labels: "[T]he left became the 'peace camp' and the right the 'national or nationalistic camp,'" state Asher Arian and Michal Shamir, veteran scholars of public opinion in Israel. As early as 1967, the two scholars also observed the increasing connection between high religious observance among Jews and nationalist attitudes.[3] The axis of the nationalist, territorial-expansion camp versus the "peace" camp supporting land conditions now came to eclipse, or encompass, the other major divisions in society.[4]

In the 1990s, the liberal universal side appeared to be driving the country's destiny, and not only in Israel. The Cold War ended, and tantalizing "end of history" notions reverberated around the world, if briefly and naively. Democratization rose sharply in Eastern Europe, but not only there; according to the V-Dem Institute's 2018 global democracy analysis, even the stubbornly authoritarian Middle East and North Africa saw modest gains from 1992 to 2012.[5]

https://doi.org/10.1515/9783110796582-006

From 1967, the occupation and control over Palestinians ran broadly counter to global trends of decolonization and the emerging international order. Now, it looked as though Israel's liberalizing trend was proceeding in tandem with historical currents: democracy was experiencing a "big bang" of accelerated growth, from 45 percent of the world's countries in 1990, to 61 percent in 2005, according to the political theorist Larry Diamond.[6] But in this phase too, Israel's liberalizing and democratic gains ran into underlying obstacles, eventually reaching a limit and causing a backlash.

The year 1992 is critical for understanding democracy in Israel. That year, the Knesset passed two Basic Laws that signaled a transformation of its political culture, while reflecting the accelerated changes in society. The elections that year represented a turning point, the massive influx of Soviet immigrants from 1990 had a significant impact, and the economy, as mentioned, was both recovering and completing its transformation. The starting point of 1992 requires a return to the late 1980s and early 1990s for context.

Chapter 12: Political Standoff and Democratization

The specific political context for the critical democratic developments of the 1990s had its roots in the late 1980s. Like the economic crisis that had led to economic liberalization in the mid-1980s, a political crisis in the latter half of that decade triggered the important changes to come. In 1986, Yitzhak Shamir returned as prime minister, replacing Shimon Peres in a rotation agreement. After the 1988 elections, Labor and Likud were nearly tied once again, and they established another unity government; but this time, Shamir became prime minister—with no rotation deal. By 1990, Peres had begun secretly wooing the ultra-Orthodox parties to form a new coalition that he would lead.

Peres thought that Shamir was reneging on a coalition agreement to prioritize Israeli-Palestinian peace, which Peres conveyed as the reason for the ensuing government crisis. Peres had completed his transformation from a settlement-supporting Labor hawk to an advocate of peace.[7] He became a firm believer in the "internationalist neoliberal vision," part of which was regional Middle East cooperation. Peres was apparently inspired by European integration; he believed that peace would facilitate a common market, while the economic interdependence would play a reciprocal role and help advance peace.[8]

And peace did appear increasingly urgent. In December 1987, an Israeli army truck collision killed four Palestinians in Gaza and ignited the mass Palestinian grassroots uprising known as the Intifada—later, it would become the "First Intifada." While the PLO claimed to represent Palestinians from its base in Tunis, Palestinians throughout the territories now organized rapidly, somewhat unexpectedly, through local networks. They held strikes and demonstrations and clashed with the Israeli army, which, in turn, cracked down, and violence escalated.

The US made new efforts for a peace process. In 1988, toward the end of Ronald Reagan's presidency, Secretary of State George Shultz proposed a peace process calling for Israeli withdrawal and negotiations in accordance with UN Security Council resolutions and fulfillment of the "legitimate rights of the Palestinian people."[9] Shultz urged a multilateral peace forum, including direct Palestinian participation under a Jordanian delegation and a rapid timeline of eighteen months to reach a transitional arrangement, and subsequently, a permanent status agreement. Shamir, a land of Israel maximalist and former militant who had overseen the assassination of Count Bernadotte in 1948, defiantly rejected the initiative, while also managing "to play a sophisticated political game—not to say 'no' and not to say 'yes.'"[10] After George H. W. Bush took office, he was quickly dismayed when Shamir reneged on what the president saw as a commitment, in one of their first interactions, to cut back on settlements.[11]

The fall of the Soviet Union changed the Middle East, just as it changed the world. American dominance in the region grew, as the erstwhile patron of some of the Arab states declined. After the US fought the first Gulf War in early 1991, Washington had additional leverage, and Bush's administration doubled down on peace efforts (discussed in Chapter 15).

Peres's insistence that the peace process move forward therefore had a genuine context. But in popular memory, it was pure ambition that led Peres in early 1990 to engineer the fall of the unity government. He believed that the ultra-Orthodox parties supported his gambit, after he had offered tens of millions of shekels for their autonomous education system; he now set a government crisis in motion. The coalition agreement with Likud would have required early elections, but Peres persuaded Israel's president (Chaim Herzog) to tap him to form a coalition instead.[12] Though Peres and Labor figures linked his move to the peace process, critics grumbled about his sheer ambition. Longtime Labor rival Yitzhak Rabin referred to the maneuver as the "stinking trick," and the name stuck.[13]

Peres's plans unraveled when the ultra-Orthodox parties broke the whispered deals, setting off political chaos. Now both Peres and Shamir launched a frenzy of horse-trading, seat-jockeying, party-jumping, and budget-related incentives to the religious parties. Once again, angry citizens turned out to protest; they demanded electoral reform, pitched tents on the Knesset gardens, recruited mayors, and some held hunger strikes.[14] Signs read, "We want statesmen, not wheelers and dealers" and "Stop the blackmail." A huge demonstration in Tel Aviv produced the slogan that would symbolize the era: "Crooks, we're fed up" (*mushchatim, nim'astem*).[15]

In mid-1990, Shamir formed the next government, after all: a narrow, right-wing coalition that governed through 1992. Many saw the crisis as a low point for democratic governance, and in response, the events prompted a series of small but important political reforms, along with civil society activism.[16] One demonstrator went on to establish the Movement for Quality Government, an anticorruption and good-governance group that still exists today.[17]

The Knesset passed laws to deter party-hopping and political bribery for coalition-building. Chief Justice Meir Shamgar upheld a Court petition against Shimon Peres, demanding that parties publish their erstwhile secretive coalition agreements. Shamgar's opinion advised the Knesset to pass legislation regarding these agreements, and it did; the law now requires parties to publish coalition agreements ahead of swearing in a new government.[18] Labor, seeking to prove its credentials regarding better governance, transparency, and a break from its past image, held its first primary election in 1992, which Rabin won. Likud did the same in 1993, choosing a different Israeli diplomat who had also served in the United States, Benjamin Netanyahu, as its first popularly elected leader. These processes boosted transparency and participation, seeking to revive public trust.[19]

Also ahead of the 1992 elections, the Knesset passed a dramatic electoral reform. After years of debate over how to stabilize Israel's fractious system, the legislature adopted direct elections for prime minister, in addition to a separate vote for the party list, like the system for municipal and mayoral elections established in the late 1970s. The new reform was first implemented in 1996 and canceled before the 2003 elections. As such, while seen as dramatic at the time, it did not leave a significant mark on Israel's overall governance and political life.[20]

But it was against this background of crisis that Israel, at the tail end of the Shamir government in 1992, made the most important change to its constitutional culture since the Harari decision of 1950, by passing two new Basic Laws. The story of these laws is essential for understanding both the democratizing developments of the 1990s and the attacks on Israeli democracy in years to come.

Chapter 13: Piecemeal Bill of Rights

At the beginning of 1992, Israel had nine Basic Laws, most (though not all) defining the procedures and institutions of government. There was (and is) still no law establishing the general equality of all citizens and no general bill of rights.

Many had tried to advance a bill of rights over the years. Among the prominent efforts was an elaborate proposal by Yitzhak Hans Klinghoffer, then a legislator for the Liberal Party, in 1964. His bill of rights included eighty-five items, expansive civil rights, and generous protections for social welfare and economic rights; Mapai was among the strongest opponents. Mapai's justice minister, Dov Yosef, delivered a lengthy refutation in the Knesset, with marked echoes of Ben-Gurion's arguments in 1949: a constitution with higher status constrained Knesset legislation, gave the courts the power to overturn laws, and enshrined amorphous rights that could be misused. He noted critically that the US Supreme Court established its own authority to review the legislature, and warned of an unrestrained court: "Who will stand guard over the guardians?"[21] Uriel Lynn, a former lawmaker also originally from the Liberal party, believed that Mapai assumed that it would remain in power indefinitely, and still rejected constraints on its power.[22] The vote failed in its first reading.

Benjamin Halevy made the next significant attempt. The former justice had presided over the 1956 Kfar Qassem military tribunal, served on both the Kastner and the Eichmann trials, and had become a Supreme Court justice, before becoming a lawmaker with Gahal, forerunner to Likud, in 1969.[23]

In the 1970s, Halevy proposed a scaled-back bill of rights with various compromises intended to overcome political obstacles.[24] This draft included equality of all citizens (while stipulating that the new law would not affect the 1950 Law of Return), as well as the right to defend life, body, soul, dignity, and property; due process; privacy; and freedom of movement, occupation, expression and creativity, assembly, and religion. Halevy's draft did not call for a special majority to amend the bill of rights but explicitly included judicial review, stating that future laws contradicting the Basic Law could be canceled.[25] Halevy's biggest concession was that the bill of rights would not prejudice prior legislation. This was intended to win over the religious parties by protecting the "status quo" arrangement, but they remained mostly opposed. The chair of the constitutional committee was again Zerach Warhaftig, of the National Religious Party (religious Zionists), and he particularly opposed judicial review.[26] Once again, the bill was "buried" in the committee stage.

In the early 1980s, Amnon Rubinstein of the liberal Shinui Party (seen as centrist in Israeli terms) tried again. He was a tireless advocate for a constitution and studied both the content and the politics of earlier efforts. Rubinstein tried to frame his bill as a continuation of the Likud legacy, but to no avail. Likud was governing the country for the first time and did not wish to antagonize the religious parties. His bill passed a first reading but also stopped at the committee stage.[27]

How the Legislation Finally Passed

Uriel Lynn entered the Knesset in 1984, representing the Liberal faction of the Likud. He was a lawyer and a strong advocate for a bill of rights. Lynn's 2017 book *Birth of a Revolution* chronicles the story of the 1992 Basic Laws in detail and provides much of the information in this chapter. In the book, Lynn made a valuable observation: by the 1980s, resistance to a bill of rights was not so much about basic human rights, which he believed the political leadership largely accepted after years of legislative debates and Supreme Court rulings. The problem, Lynn believed, was granting those rights higher status than regular laws, by making them harder to overturn (usually by requiring a special majority, as with a constitution—called "entrenchment").[28] In other words, Israel seemed prepared to adopt democratic norms, while retaining the right to circumvent those norms in practice when it wished to. In sum, the problem was commitment.

In 1988, Dan Meridor became justice minister under Shamir's unity government between Labor and Likud and other parties. He was a lawyer and scion of a Herut-affiliated, intellectual Jerusalemite family. On taking office, Meridor announced his commitment to passing the bill of rights, which he saw as the essential missing piece of Israel's constitutional system.[29]

Meridor hoped to capitalize on the broad political partnership of the unity government, and quickly assembled a committee to provide a new draft. Once again, the bill included equality before the law, as well as the main human rights and civil liberties of earlier drafts. His bill also protected existing legislation but tried to mitigate this concession to religious laws by stipulating that existing laws should be interpreted "in the spirit of this Basic Law."[30]

Meridor's bill required two-thirds, or eighty members, of the Knesset, in order to amend the law. The Supreme Court was to act as a constitutional court, and anyone could challenge a law that was thought to violate the constitutional principles.[31] Meridor had the bill of rights published in the newspapers for public debate, and Shamir claimed to support the effort.[32] But the religious parties in the coalition opposed this effort.

Amnon Rubinstein, concerned that another failure was looming, proposed, from the opposition, a private bill that was identical to Meridor's. Meridor decided to support Rubinstein's bill, which passed a first vote, generating momentum. The bill was under extensive discussion in committees, with Ministry of Justice officials and professional consultations. But in March 1990, the government collapsed.

Following Shimon Peres's "stinking trick" maneuver and the ensuing political standoff, Shamir and Peres were both desperate to woo the ultra-Orthodox parties; each hoped to gain sufficient support to form the next coalition. The ultra-Orthodox parties now felt that the forces converging in favor of a bill of rights were coming together, so their resistance grew; they now made the issue into a bargaining factor. Peres offered to freeze the legislation to win their support. Shamir promised that the rights legislation could advance only with the consent of the Haredi leadership—just a slight difference.[33]

Shamir won the political battle, and the tiny opening under his agreement became meaningful. Meridor was justice minister again, and liberal-leaning figures from Likud to Shulamit Aloni's Ratz—the coalition and the opposition—forced the crack open a bit more. But the opening was still too small for a whole bill of rights to fit through, so Rubinstein, in opposition, made a new proposal: just as Harari had proposed breaking down the constitution into incremental chapters, now he and Uriel Lynn, chair of the constitutional committee, developed four separate bills. These were Human Dignity and Liberty, Freedom of Occupation ("occupation" referring to employment or vocation), Freedom of Association, and Freedom of Expression. With support from the justice minister, these bills passed preliminary readings, and negotiations began.[34]

The Ashkenazi Haredi parties still fought against any constitutional law that could challenge the status quo arrangements for the four original issues: Sabbath restrictions, rabbinic authority over family law, educational autonomy for religious schools, and kosher food in public institutions, as well as the exemption from army service for yeshiva students, which had ballooned since the start of statehood.

The new bills were also committed to preserving existing legislation, a painful compromise for liberal figures. But National Religious Party (NRP) leader Yitzhak Levy, representing religious Zionist Israelis (who are mostly modern Orthodox Jews), signaled some openness, at least, to the Basic Law of Human Dignity and Liberty—an important breakthrough. Levy asked that the law be amended so that it could not hold *future* religious legislation to human rights requirements (mainly concerning religious laws), but Lynn drew the line at this demand.[35]

The religious parties also rigidly opposed the item at the heart of most democratic constitutions: equality. They were terrified of losing both Jewish and ultra-Orthodox privileges in Israel, worried about judicial review of the Law of Return and threats to their exemption from the IDF draft, and particularly feared the growing recognition of non-Haredi streams of Judaism. Rubinstein recalls that the attitude of religious parties was "over my dead body."[36] The equality clause that had appeared in all historical drafts for an Israeli bill of rights was dropped.

Lawmakers were left to hope that "human dignity" would be interpreted as conferring equality.[37] The ultra-Orthodox Agudath Israel also rejected entrenchment.

Finally, Levy raised the bill's reference to Israel as a "democratic state," worried that the Jewish character of Israel was not sufficiently represented. Levy asked Rubenstein: "Would it bother you if we say 'democratic and Jewish'?"[38] The first article in the bill for "Human Dignity and Liberty" was amended to read: "The goal of this Basic Law is to protect the dignity of individuals and their freedom, in order to anchor in the Basic Laws the values of the state of Israel as a Jewish and democratic state."[39]

Meridor initially opposed specifying "Jewish state" in stand-alone human rights legislation, concerned that it could convey to minority groups that they were not truly included. He consulted with Chief Justice Shamgar, who proposed adding that the rights in this law would be interpreted in the spirit of the Declaration of Independence, which would have provided the basis for both Jewish identity and equality, indirectly.[40] Yet even this solution is ambiguous: Does it signify a hidden anchor for a powerful Jewish-centric national identity, or a commitment to equality that might evade the religious opposition? Both concepts exist in the declaration. Liberal communities assume that the declaration is an anchor for democratic values; by contrast, Yitzhak Levy claimed that it was his idea to refer to the declaration, in order to protect the Law of Return under the Jewish-identity basis of the founding document.[41] For the moment, the point was moot and the declaration was left out.

The remaining pressure points were judicial review and entrenchment. Instead of the two-thirds requirement of Meridor's original bill, Rubinstein and Lynn reduced this to sixty-one, a bare majority of lawmakers, as another concession.

But Shamir's coalition also teetered, once again because right-wing partners were angry about the initial steps toward a peace process. Elections were called for June 1992, prompting advocates of the Basic Laws to accelerate their efforts. In early March, the Knesset passed the Freedom of Occupation law, with a requirement of sixty-one legislators to amend it. Rubinstein told *Haaretz* that, for the first time in its history, Israel had placed human rights above regular law and had allowed the Court to review regulations based on those rights.[42] Two weeks later, the Knesset held a final vote on the Basic Law: Human Dignity and Liberty. The Haredi parties made a last-ditch effort to have Shamir strike the bill from the agenda, but the vote went ahead.[43]

In the voting, the entrenchment clause failed by a single vote. To this day, Israel's only constitutional-level legislation for broad human rights can be overturned easily, not just by a majority of legislators but by even a small plurality.[44]

In practice, the laws have developed a normative stature, and there have so far been no serious efforts to overturn them.

Explicit judicial review was dropped from final versions. But the Human Dignity and Liberty law allowed "limitations" of rights under specific conditions. The Knesset protocols leave no doubt: legislators understood that the article beginning: "The rights in this Basic Law cannot be harmed" meant that citizens could challenge future laws that they believed threatened their rights. Religious parties, in particular, anticipated challenges to future religious legislation that citizens might deem coercive.[45] The article went on to define when a new law *could* legitimately limit those rights, under specific, defined conditions. The most explicit statement came from Likud member Michael Eitan, who opposed constraints on the legislature: "From this day forward, all laws that the Knesset legislates can be struck down on the grounds of violating the Basic Law, and whoever thinks [that they should be struck down] will go to the High Court of Justice or to the court whose role it will be to strike down laws that we have passed."[46]

Rubinstein later explained that he had always hoped to include judicial rule explicitly in a future Basic Law of Legislation, after passing the original four bills; but none of these efforts advanced.[47]

Thirty-two legislators voted in favor of Human Dignity and Liberty, and twenty-one were opposed; one abstained.[48] Lax attendance is a standard feature of the Knesset, but later opponents of the laws would argue that lawmakers did not realize how important the Basic Laws were. Defenders explain that Labor members were assured that the laws had sufficient support to pass and preferred to be on the campaign trail of the first Labor primary election. Others argue that low attendance signifies *consensus*, while controversial legislation brings legislators out in force.

What is clear is the broad, cross-party support for the Basic Laws: Human Dignity and Liberty won support from figures from both the coalition and the opposition: eleven Likud lawmakers, seven from Labor, five from Ratz, three from Mapam (the latter two parties would soon merge to form the left-wing Meretz), three from Hadash, two from Shinui, and one from NRP—Yitzhak Levy. Despite future accusations that the entire constitutional shift was a left-wing project, the legislation was approved under a right-wing governing coalition, and Yitzhak Shamir was one of the country's most right-wing leaders. Weeks after the laws passed in 1992, Meridor called them a "constitutional revolution."[49]

Judicial Activism, Criticism, and Amendments

Judicial review was neither formalized nor resolved. But based on the new legislation, in November 1995, the Supreme Court ruled on *United Mizrahi Bank v. Migdal Cooperative Village*, a case in which the plaintiff argued that a new amendment to an earlier law violated the rights of the 1992 Basic Law on Human Dignity and Liberty. Aharon Barak had become chief justice just over two months earlier; Meir Shamgar was still on the Court but preparing to retire. They concurred that the Basic Laws established the authority for the Court to strike down legislation (though they refrained from doing so in *United Mizrahi Bank*).

The *United Mizrahi Bank* case is widely seen as the turning point for judicial review of legislation, as well as the heart of later right-wing accusations that the Court, and Barak in particular, unilaterally established judicial review.

But judicial activism was broader than the review of legislation. Since the 1980s, as we have seen, the Supreme Court has widened the right of standing to accept petitions from individuals not directly affected by the issue at hand, in order to argue matters of public interest.[50] More cases were considered justiciable, and more government actions also fell under review. Critics and supporters alike would characterize Aharon Barak's doctrine as "everything is justiciable." But some believe that Shamgar, chief justice in the 1980s, was just as responsible for the activist Court as Barak.[51]

The relationship between religion and state was the perennial flash point for these changes. In 1986, Yehuda Ressler, a lawyer and major in the IDF reserves, petitioned the Israeli Supreme Court against the exemption of yeshiva students from Israel's draft. It was his third such petition and the fourth in total. This time, the Court's decision (two years later) in *Ressler v. Minister of Defense* granted the plaintiff standing (even while rejecting his claim). Former Supreme Court justice Shoshana Netanyahu said that the decision "mark[ed] a leap in liberalizing the standing of a petitioner without a [personal] interest," although she noted that, by that time, the Court was already moving toward "liberalization," in the sense of relaxing requirements for a petitioner to have standing. The ruling also expanded justiciability.[52]

The Court's willingness to rule on the deeply fraught question of religion and state drew accusations that it would be seen as intervening in political matters to favor a liberal agenda. In the *Ressler* decision, Aharon Barak wrote: "I am less afraid of judicial occupation with political matters leading to politicization of adjudication than I am of the court's reluctance to deal with political matters leading to the violation of the rule of law and shattering the public faith in law."[53]

In other words, the activist direction was already becoming clear. The trend toward accepting judicial review of legislation was clearly emerging, well before the *United Mizrahi Bank* decision. In October 1993, the government denied a permit to a food import company wishing to import nonkosher meat; the company challenged the state's decision as a violation of the new Basic Law: Freedom of Occupation. The court agreed, angering the religious parties, which began to argue that the Basic Laws had deceptively introduced judicial review, which would soon be applied to legislation as well.[54]

Shas now led an effort to amend the Freedom of Occupation law to permit exceptions; in other words, if the Court finds that a law violated the principle, the proposed amendment would allow the Knesset to override such a ruling. Reportedly, Barak himself helped devise the compromise, by which the Knesset could pass a law violating freedom of occupation, with a majority of legislators and for a limited four-year period.[55]

In March 1994, the Knesset voted on the amendments, and the discussion yielded even more explicit statements about the meaning of judicial review. David (Dedi) Zucker of Meretz, who now chaired the Constitution, Law and Justice Committee, told the plenary that the laws clearly granted the Court authority to strike down legislation. Religious legislators acknowledged—and bemoaned— that the Court had the power to interpret the Basic Laws. Lawmakers approved several amendments that replaced the Freedom of Occupation law with large majorities, ranging from seventy-seven to eighty votes. In response, Dan Meridor, now a regular Likud legislator, told the Knesset:

> Today we are taking a very important step in the constitutional overhaul that Israel began two years ago.... This time, not with a small majority but with a large majority of nearly two-thirds, the Knesset has authorized the Supreme Court to strike down laws of the Knesset.... [I]f not for [Shas's initiative and the prime minister's agreement,] we would continue to hear claims that through some accident in 1992, laws were passed in a clandestine way that suppressed the rights of the Knesset.... This time with a large majority the Knesset has limited itself and bestowed on the Supreme Court the authority to strike down laws that contradict the basic principles of our system.[56]

But Meridor also urged the government and the Knesset to advance the remaining Basic Laws to complete the piecemeal human rights legislation—warning that otherwise, the current Basic Laws would generate more Court activism "instead of the Knesset making laws. It's not proper and it's a pity."[57]

The amendments that replaced the Freedom of Occupation law included a terse amendment to the Basic Law of Human Dignity and Liberty. The change stipulated that the law would be interpreted "in the spirit of the principles of the Declaration of Independence." In the first reading on this package of amendments, eighty-two voted in favor and sixty-seven in the final reading, with five supporting votes beyond the coalition and only nine opposed.[58]

These discussions were held more than a year and a half *before* the *United Mizrahi Bank* ruling.

Moreover, even after the ruling of 1995, the Court did not actually strike down legislation for another two years, doing so only in 1997.[59] There was no longer any doubt that the Court viewed the Basic Laws as conferring judicial review of legislation. For five years, from 1992 to 1997, the Knesset could have amended the Human Dignity and Liberty law without even an absolute majority, but it never did.

Another common retroactive accusation is that the lawmakers of 1992 never intended for the laws to confer judicial review. Uriel Lynn, as well as Amnon Rubinstein, argues that the laws indeed conferred judicial review. In Rubinstein's analysis, support for judicial review was connected to the lawmakers' awareness of global democratic currents. In the years leading up to the legislation of the Basic Laws, Rubinstein observed that members of the Knesset were participating as observers in various European institutions, "where they learned from watching how judicial review of legislation was advancing and spreading around the democratic world." The portion of democracies that provided explicit authority for (or de facto acceptance of) judicial review of legislation around the world rose sharply in the previous decades, he notes, and "this is an important process that members of Knesset could not ignore.... . Many of them would not want to isolate Israel from the democratic world and continue being seen as an impaired state in terms of human rights in the European community."[60]

Outside the court, certain liberal and conservative legal scholars have argued that the Court *should* exercise more restraint on issues considered sensitive, divisive, or political. Such scholars include Menachem Mautner and Ruth Gavison on the liberal side; and Daniel Friedmann and others on the conservative side. But the question of *whether* the Court has the authority of judicial review of legislation should be put to rest. The Court has reviewed administrative decisions of the executive branch from the early years of statehood. Aharon Barak formally asserted the authority to review primary legislation, in light of legislation passed legitimately by the Knesset and then reaffirmed with a large majority and more explicit acknowledgment of the implications. Accusations that he invented it ex nihilo contradict the historical record. To be sure, as with many other aspects of Israeli political life, the reluctance to establish explicit and committed principles openly in the law is one of the main reasons the Court and legal authorities have taken on the role of protecting rights, contributing to bitter rifts over the legitimacy of either side's position. Any true democracy should make its basic democratic values and constitutional order clear and transparent to all.

Chapter 14: Social Liberalization

The Israeli election campaign of 1992 saw ideology moving rapidly away from the competing domestic-social-economic outlooks that had been more prominent in earlier decades. By the early 1990s, the two large parties were not terribly far apart in their economic worldview: Labor was moving toward a liberal, free-market economic approach that was once Likud's domain, and its younger guard was eager to challenge the lingering power of the old Mapai institutions. Although the economy had become significantly more liberal, less statist, and more privatized since the mid-1980s, the major parties still supported the basic welfare state that put Israel in the camp of social democracies, rather than American-style capitalism. Globalization represented new opportunities, as well. Ahead of the 1992 elections, the political scientist Daniel Elazar wrote:

> There [was] very little difference between the two major parties or any of the others these days on economic matters. They are all in favor of the principle of a free market, but none of them want Cousin Mordechai to be unemployed... . The only difference between a Labor-led government and a Likud-led one is that more money will go to Kupat Holim ... and less money to settlements.[61]

As we have seen, by the late 1980s, Peres and Labor opposed settlement expansion, while Shamir's governments raced ahead. Shamir dragged his feet on peace, but the Madrid Conference in 1991 and tension with the US over settlements (discussed below) kept the issue high on the agenda. By contrast, Shimon Peres had begun to legitimize contacts with the PLO, and in the 1992 campaign, Rabin promised to seek a peace agreement with the Palestinians (for autonomy) in six to nine months.[62] Labor linked peace to domestic social priorities, promising to prioritize investment in the economy and other social services, rather than investing in settlements.

Momentum appeared to favor dovish parties. The historical Mapam and Shulamit Aloni's Ratz joined forces with the liberal-centrist Shinui, Rubinstein's party, calling their new formation Meretz. This party represented the most elaborate argument linking occupation with the inevitable erosion of liberal democratic values. Its 1992 platform stated: "The state must establish full equality for all its residents and citizens... . [It] must be a state of progressive law, a full member of the family of enlightened, democratic, thriving countries... . We must choose between protracted war with the Arab world and economic and social burden, and peace, welfare, and [economic] achievement." Controlling a population through military occupation, the party asserted, is incompatible with democracy:

> The longer the occupation over the territories lasts, the greater the threat to the democratic character of the state of Israel... . The rule of law in Israel is increasingly challenged by re-

peated and severe damage to human rights in the territories, and due to the creation of two distinct systems of law—one for Jews and one for Arabs... . Until there is a peace agreement, Israel must run its governance in the West Bank and Gaza by adhering to the laws of the state, the rules of natural justice and international law.[63]

The party advocated including the PLO in negotiations, supported "autonomy in the territories" pending a final agreement that would respect Palestinian self-determination, and opposed settlements even in the Golan Heights, anticipating eventual peace negotiations with Syria.[64] In Israeli terms of the 1990s to the present, Meretz is classified as firmly left—the furthest left of the Zionist parties.

Hadash, mentioned in earlier chapters, was the Jewish-Arab amalgamated list whose name is the Hebrew abbreviation for "the Democratic Front for Peace and Equality." The party devoted its platform largely to peace and, like Labor, linked the occupation with economic hardship. "They're having a ball in the [West] Bank— while you don't have a job," stated one poster.[65] The party took the more radical step of advocating "two states—Israel and Palestine," rather than autonomy.

Another party running for the third time was to become important: Shas was founded in 1984 as a religious party representing Mizrahi Jews. The name Shas is an acronym, which in Hebrew stands for "Sephardi Guardians" (of the Torah), and became a counterpart to the Ashkenazi ultra-Orthodox parties. Shas's spiritual leader was Rabbi Ovadia Yosef, who served as chief Mizrahi rabbi for a decade and established a theological approach tolerating land concessions, such as the Sinai withdrawal, that stood in marked contrast to the positions of both the Ashkenazi chief rabbi and the Ashkenazi Haredi parties.[66] The rising political star of Shas was a young charismatic figure named Aryeh Deri. Shas's voter base included ultra-Orthodox but also less religiously strict "traditionalists," as well as Orthodox but non-Haredi Jews. Its voters shared a Middle Eastern heritage and, for many, a sense of being treated as subordinates in Israeli social, economic, political, and even religious institutions. Shas was not a left-wing party but played a key role in the next government.

On election day, the parties now considered left-wing (in terms of the fate of the territories) had a strong showing, never again to be repeated (to date). Labor won, with 44 seats to Likud's 32, almost precisely reversing Likud's 1977 results and breaking the near-parity of the two parties for much of the 1980s. Meretz won 12 seats, giving the two left-liberal Zionist political parties a combined 56 seats in the 120-seat legislature. Rabin, like most Israeli leaders, added a religious party to his coalition—Shas. Rabin also took a bold step by making an agreement with Hadash: the left-wing Jewish-Arab party would support Rabin's government by blocking any no-confidence votes "from the outside," without formally joining the coalition, in return for a commitment by Rabin to advance a peace process and a series of policies to improve the situation of Arab citizens in Israel.[67]

Changing Institutions

Labor's comeback in 1992 was partly due to efforts by its younger guard to shed its lingering, burdensome historical image. Holding primaries was a step toward participation and transparency; now the party had a young generation of leaders that was prepared to challenge even the historical sources of its own power: the Histadrut.

In the 1980s, as we have seen, the Histadrut underwent its sharpest decline. The government had nationalized its Bank Hapoalim even before the Stabilization Plan, and the bank was eventually privatized. The Histadrut and the Workers' Corporation had privatized most of their companies during that time, including the dramatic restructuring and downsizing of Koor Industries (discussed in Chapter 11). In the 1980s, about 80 percent of Israeli workers were still unionized; by the end of the 1990s, only 41 percent were—a decline seen in many democratic countries— but striking, considering the outsize historical power of the organization in Israeli life.[68]

The system linking health care to unions, associated with political parties, had dragged on for decades, dating back to the earliest years of statehood, when Ben-Gurion fought nationalized health insurance so as not to threaten the status of the Histadrut. As mentioned in earlier chapters, the organization's health-care plan required people to join the Histadrut, making union-based health care a critical source of "patronage, dependency, and political persuasion ... which brought [Mapai] considerable electoral support" in the early decades.[69] Like Histadrut's other assets, its health-care provider, Clalit, was facing a crisis; the organization accused the Shamir government of failing to transfer government subsidies, and service had become abysmal. But up to 70 percent of Israelis belonged to Clalit, and there was widespread public fury at this provider due to its declining quality of service.[70] Ahead of the 1992 elections, both of the major parties promised to advance a national health-insurance law.[71]

Rabin appointed Chaim Ramon as health minister after the elections. Ramon was a key figure of Labor's younger, rising generation and made it his mission to sever Labor from the Histadrut for good. He decided that passing a national health-care law would be his signature policy. When his efforts were stonewalled by the Histadrut, which undermined Labor's backing, Ramon angrily called the organization a "beached whale," resigned as minister, broke from Labor, and ran for the leadership of Histadrut himself in early 1994. His new party for the Histadrut election included figures from both Meretz and Shas; when he won, his victory indicated the broad, cross-sector popularity of his mission.[72] The name-calling closed a certain circle among the competing political forces: for Ze'ev Jabotinsky, back in the early 1930s, the Histadrut was an "obese sarcoma" and a "malignant tumor."[73]

The Knesset finally passed the National Health Insurance Law, a watershed event in the history of health care in Israel; it went into effect in 1995.[74] The new system made health care compulsory and provided a single government budget for four competitive nonprofit providers, with funds allocated per member. Since the passage of the law, these providers have covered all basic health care specified in the law. Private health care is available, but the quality of basic public health-care plans improved dramatically with the adoption of the new system.[75] The change led to near-universal coverage and contributed to other positive indicators, including high life expectancy and low infant mortality.[76] Despite the usual inadequacies of public health care, including insufficient state funding, the change freed citizens of one of the last lingering mechanisms of political interference into essential services. Vastly improved health care for all marked another democratizing development.

Changing Values and Laws

The general orientation of the country now yielded what felt like an accelerated push to change the social climate toward a more liberal state, with civic universal values. The changes were manifested in policy and legislation in the critical fields of religion and state, gender equality and LGBTQ rights, a changed media environment, and access to information. Developments in these areas happened roughly over the same period of time and are outlined thematically below.

Religion and State

Challenges to the religion and state "status quo" accelerated during the late 1980s and 1990s. Secular communities attempted to weaken the hold of religious forces over society, which they viewed as coercive, and other elements of the status quo. These challenges continued through the 1990s, long after the Labor government expired; they encouraged secular communities to challenge the religious influence over the state and reignited religious anger from the start.

From the late 1980s, ultra-Orthodox communities in Jerusalem sought to close a main traffic thoroughfare called Bar-Ilan Street on Saturdays, in accordance with Jewish prohibitions on driving during Sabbath. Secular activists sought to keep the road open, but the minister of transportation ordered it closed, and a standoff ensued. Citizens and some opposition politicians petitioned the Supreme Court, which issued an injunction to keep it open.[77] Ironically, the minister of transportation was Yitzhak Levy, the religious politician who had supported the Basic Laws that underscored both the secular petitioners' claims and parts of the judgment.[78] In response, a prominent ultra-Orthodox newspaper editorial referred to Chief Justice Barak, who authored the decision, as "a 'dangerous enemy' of both Judaism and democracy."[79]

The issue of ultra-Orthodox IDF exemptions was also coming to a head. By 1998, approximately 30,000 yeshiva students held exemptions, and the numbers were rapidly rising.[80] The *Ressler* ruling of 1988 had opened a door. In 1998, Yehuda Ressler and others, including Amnon Rubinstein, argued new petitions against the exemption. In an expanded panel of eleven judges, two of them religious, the Court found that the number of exemptions had grown so significantly that the situation had fundamentally changed from the early years.[81] Citing the principle of equality, the Court ruled against the longtime policy of near-automatic exemptions by executive power, and ordered the Knesset to come up with primary legislation on the matter within one year.[82] The ruling was a dramatic reversal that made international headlines and set the stage for a new collision.

Finally, the Court touched the rabbinic monopoly over family law. The ramifications of religious authority over marriage and divorce had become a festering source of anger among nonreligious Israelis (or religious people who did not share the ultra-Orthodox rabbinate's interpretations). Marriage or divorce—activities that touch most people in society—meant subjecting oneself to religious authorities and rituals (for all faiths). Many Israelis chose to fly abroad for secular weddings that could be recognized later in Israel. Anyone wishing to marry a non-Jew, or whose Judaism was questioned by the rabbinate, could not do so officially in Israel; all marriage and divorce proceedings under religious courts could undermine gender equality, with ramifications for custody and property as well. In Judaism, a recalcitrant spouse can refuse to grant a divorce, for example, which severely limits the freedom of the other partner to remarry. "[I]n view of the patriarchal nature of the system, it is usually women who will be the victims of such pressure," writes law scholar Frances Raday.[83]

In 1994, the Supreme Court compelled the Rabbinical Court to ensure equal division of property in a divorce settlement, in order to comply with gender equality provisions guaranteed by Israeli law.[84] The religious authorities reacted with "violent opposition" and did not implement the ruling.[85] But the court's activism was pointing out the inherent contradiction between religious dominance over private life, threats to freedom of and from religion, and principles of equality. A mature and active feminist movement was becoming more vocal in Israel, just as gender and sexual norms were also changing in the country.

Gender Rights and LGBTQ Progress

Gender equality advanced in the late 1980s as well, under right-wing and center-left governments alike. The infrastructure for gender equality was established early: the Labor Zionist movement established its women's "worker's council" in the 1920s; the country established universal suffrage, and though Israeli law does not guarantee equality of all citizens, Israel had already adopted a gender equality law in 1951. Still, the first phase of the country's history saw a certain de facto regression regarding women in politics and social equality. In the 1970s, Shulamit Aloni, together with activists such as Marcia Freedman, made women's rights and gender equality integral to the human rights agenda of Aloni's political party. In the 1970s and 1980s, gender studies led to an increase in feminist scholarship.[86] The 1980s saw new organizational efforts: the Israel Women's Network was born in 1984 and became a major civil society organization, advocating social change and feeding into legislative debates.[87]

A salvo of laws for gender equality advanced from the late 1980s: the Equal Retirement Age Law (1987) and an Employment (Equal Opportunity) Law (1988). Rape statutes were amended to strengthen the victims' legal position, and in 1991, the Knesset passed the Prevention of Violence in the Family Law.[88] A new law for equal pay for male and female employees followed in 1996, replacing an old law from 1964. In 1998, Israel passed its first law against sexual harassment in the workplace, including in education, health, and the military.[89] In addition to legislation, the government during this time established infrastructure to support gender equality: in 1992, the Knesset established a parliamentary committee for the advancement of women and gender equality; and in 1998, the National Authority for the Advancement of Women was established, now under the Ministry of Social Equality.[90]

In 1993, Uzi Even, a Tel Aviv University chemistry professor, claimed that the IDF had shut him out of his longtime sensitive military research and stripped his officer's rank because he was gay. The Knesset held its first hearing on homosexual people serving in the military.[91] An El Al employee, Yonatan Danilovich, sued the national airline in 1988 for spousal benefits for his male partner; in 1994, the Supreme Court ruled in his favor on appeals. Uzi Even then went to labor court for *his* partner's benefits, and won.[92] Both cases were argued by the Association for Civil Rights in Israel—the civil society infrastructure established in the previous era, which was now bearing new fruit.

The legitimization of LGBTQ sexuality burst into the cultural sphere in the 1990s. The gay activist power couple Eytan Fox and Gal Uchovsky created the hit prime-time television drama *Florentine*, about twentysomethings in a bohemian neighborhood of Tel Aviv, featuring a gay main character.[93] In his 2002 film, *Yossi and Jagger*, Fox tackled the big taboo by portraying a clandestine male couple in the army. An all-woman rock band, The Witches, put unofficial lesbian chic onto the cultural map (with the necessary clues in their lyrics). And in 1998, twenty-nine-year-old transgender woman Dana International won the campy Eurovision song contest that Israelis adore (partly for the simple fact of being included in the European club at all). Her triumphant victory earned an invitation to the Knesset, where she enthused to reporters that Israel was "free and democratic, believes in and respects individual freedom, creative freedom and democracy," while ultra-Orthodox lawmakers fumed.[94] Her winning song, "Diva," name-checked a pantheon of female goddesses, symbolically asserting her own place among them. The lyrics of "Diva" had nothing to do with Israel but revealed a great deal about the country at that moment.

The changes in gender equality and LGBTQ progress reflected efforts to legislate equality in general. Though Israel still did not adopt laws establishing the general equality of all citizens, equality was established in specific fields. In 2000 the Knesset passed a law to prohibit discrimination in public services or by private service providers. After several years of lobbying in the 2000s, largely by women's organizations, in 2006 the Knesset amended its 1988 law to create an Equal Employment Opportunity Commission, formed in 2008, which has since received more than 10,000 citizen requests, naming fifteen categories of discrimination.[95] In 2000, the Knesset revised its archaic 1953 law defining the aim of public education; now education was to "instill the principles of the Declaration of [Independence] and the values of Israel as a Jewish and democratic state, and to develop respect for human rights, basic freedoms, democratic values ... to strive for peace and tolerance... ." Public schools were to teach about the Arab population, and to "recognize the equal rights of all citizens of Israel."[96]

Media and Information

Information was an essential cause and accelerator of the trends toward cultural liberalization; by the 1990s, there was simply a great deal more of it.

The establishment of Israeli television in the late 1960s had been an information leap, but it was also a guardian of social conformism that was ensured by a single, state-owned channel and news source.[97] The nightly news broadcast was a shared civil ritual that, by the 1990s, was becoming a relic.

In the 1980s, foreign cable packages were threatening the state television's monopoly on Israeli viewers' attention. The government allowed local cable providers to compete from 1992, and by the end of that year, 40 percent of households had subscribed; two years later, two-thirds of households had a cable package.[98] International news stations were now available, often supplying open secrets about Israeli news that were stifled by the military censor. No less important, during the same years, Israeli television diversified. In 1990, the Likud government led the establishment of the Second Authority for Radio and Television, and commercial broadcasts began in 1993. Private Israeli franchises now competed to provide both news and other original Israeli content.

The end of the state's television monopoly was a breakthrough for Israeli consumers, but it also contributed to the ongoing decline of a shared social realm and deepened individualism. The trend was sweeping the world, but given Israel's restrictive and conformist starting point, the social shift felt palpable.

Israelis increasingly demanded to know secrets of the state. In 1988, the edgy Tel Aviv newspaper *Ha'ir* wrote a story about the Mossad chief. The military censor requested changes to the story three times before it was published, until the editor and the author finally took the censor to court. Aharon Barak ruled in the newspaper's favor, finding that the Mandate-era colonial rules needed to be reinterpreted to suit a democratic society. While affirming that security is a national priority, Barak's opinion asserted that "free expression and public debate contribute to state security."[99]

Buoyed by these successes, a group of civil society organizations now formed a coalition to agitate for a full-fledged freedom of information legislation. From the first draft in 1993, it took four years of legislative wrangling. But in 1998, the Knesset passed the Freedom of Information law, under Benjamin Netanyahu's first right-wing government, with a unanimous vote. Israel thus joined a major wave of similar legislation in other countries as part of the global democratization. However, implementation and true access were often uneven—in 2001, observers found that Israel still maintained a "culture of secrecy in all branches and levels of government," relative to other democracies.[100] But the new basis for accessing information was a boon to civil society, media, and academia alike.

Chapter 15: Horizon for Peace

The fact that Israel undertook its first serious steps to establish a peace process with the Palestinians at this time raises important, if not entirely answerable, questions. Did the liberalizing trends in society raise an implicit awareness that Israel could not continue its most undemocratic policy and continue moving in the globalizing and liberal democratic direction that it seemed enthusiastic to pursue? Addressing the perennial debate over democracies and peace, Fareed Zakaria noted in 1997 that "when divining the cause behind this correlation [between democracies and peace], one thing becomes clear: the democratic peace is actually the liberal peace."[101]

Did the economic horizons of liberalization at home—and globalization, in general—signal to Israelis that peace was a necessary condition to fulfill the potential, reflecting the connection that Peres had drawn from the mid-1980s? Israel's business community certainly thought so. As with other institutions, from the judiciary to the Bank of Israel, state involvement in the private sector declined significantly during that time; by the 1990s, business leaders were taking more initiative to express their political views and interests. "The public campaign of the Israeli business community on behalf of peacemaking was unprecedented," write Gershon Shafir and Yoav Peled.[102]

These factors may have complemented growing discontent with the economic costs of ongoing conflict, as the left-wing parties had argued in the 1992 campaign. To be sure, Israel's defense budget as a portion of GDP had declined from a peak of 30 percent in 1975, to just over 15 percent by the early 1990s. But this was far higher than other Western countries (throughout the 1990s, the US defense budget was below 5 percent of GDP).[103]

Repressive policies toward Palestinians fueled undemocratic measures at home for Israelis. Dana International may have won the Eurovision, but artists who expressed anguish about the political situation could run into the limits of official tolerance. Two examples include pop singer Nurit Galron's "After Us, the Deluge," whose lyrics conjured tableau-like images of violence in the territories; and beloved singer Chava Alberstein's haunting rendition of the traditional "Chad Gadya," sung on Passover, the Jewish holiday of liberation, which was repurposed as a metaphor for the strong devouring the weak. Both songs were censored by the Israel Broadcast Authority in 1989. The attorney general reversed the decision; but another song, "Shooting and Crying," was removed from IDF radio by the station's IDF commander.[104] One popular song released in 1995 (that was not banned) mourned that normalcy itself was unattainable at home. The narrator longed "to live in New Zealand," where one hears cannons only on the queen's birthday:

Sometimes I think to myself,
Maybe I should live on a verdant isle
In a faraway ocean
And grow up in a tranquil town
Without wars and special taxes
For guns and tanks.[105]

The lyrics of "To Live in New Zealand," were cowritten by Yosef Lapid, known as Tommy, a charismatic journalist and cultural figure. He inherited Amnon Rubinstein's Shinui party later in the 1990s and went into politics; his son, Yair Lapid, served as prime minister in 2022.

Peace Process Under Way

Of greater concern to policymakers and perhaps to the public, the occupation generated a rare bout of public friction with the United States. Under George H. W. Bush, Secretary of State James Baker had pushed a grudging Yitzhak Shamir toward a peace process in 1991. Against this background, the Bush administration took an unusually tough position against settlements, delaying guarantees that Israel badly needed in order to borrow huge sums of money, so that it could absorb hundreds of thousands of immigrants arriving from the collapsing Soviet Union. Shamir finally agreed to a breakthrough multilateral summit in Madrid in October, with Palestinian participation (under the Jordanian delegation). The Madrid Conference did not yield an agreement, though it did establish parameters for a future process. The Bush administration continued to insist that Israel freeze settlement expansion and avoid settling its immigrants across the Green Line, including in East Jerusalem. Tensions with Shamir and the administration ran high and apparently worried the public, contributing to Likud's defeat in 1992. After Rabin took office in July 1992, he quickly negotiated a settlement slowdown, and Bush supported the loan guarantees.[106]

The Palestinian cause was gaining some global sympathy; the image of women and children confronting tanks with stones was different from the 1970s image of PLO plane hijackers. With far more news options, Israelis were well aware of how they were being seen in the world. Rabin's government moved more decisively in favor of negotiations.

Rabin allowed his old rival Shimon Peres to oversee a secret back channel in Oslo that eventually led to the "Declaration of Principles" (DOP), signed in 1993 on the White House lawn. The immediate politics around the Oslo process led to at least one important democratizing step within Israeli politics: a breakthrough role for Arab political parties in the government.

Like so many Israeli governments, Rabin's coalition quickly encountered a crisis over religion and state tensions, when his ultra-Orthodox coalition partner Aryeh Deri of Shas demanded that he fire the secular, liberal Shulamit Aloni from her role as education minister.[107] That crisis passed, but a bigger one was brewing: Deri had been under investigation since 1992 for several counts of corruption, including influence-peddling and bribery for personal enrichment (prosecutors' charges included using the money for lavish properties and vacations). But he was also accused of siphoning off large funds from state budgets into religious institutions. In August 1993, the draft indictment was ready—just weeks before the Oslo agreement was announced.[108] Rabin and Deri had already agreed that once the indictment was served in court, Deri would resign. But the Movement for Quality Government petitioned the Supreme Court to demand that Deri be fired forthwith. In a landmark ruling, the Supreme Court agreed, finding that it was "extremely unreasonable" for Deri (and Shas deputy minister Raphael Pinchasi) to serve while facing serious corruption charges. The "Deri-Pinchasi" ruling, along with the "reasonability" criterion, became a prominent source of tension in the public debate over judicial review of government action in later years.[109]

With Deri gone, Shas eventually left the government just as Rabin needed support for the peace process. When the Knesset held a vote on the Oslo process in September 1993, Rabin depended on the supporting votes of the Arab parties from "outside" the coalition to reach sixty-one members in favor, in a vote that he had turned into a motion of confidence in the government. Fifty legislators voted against.[110] In fact, Shas did not join the opposition but abstained—evidence that the religious Jewish parties in Israel have not always been committed to blocking a peace process.

That first vote on the first stage of the Israeli-Palestinian peace process became the first time that independent Arab parties had played an executive-level decision-making role—and not on a marginal issue: their vote helped enable Israel's first-ever breakthrough toward peace.[111] The backlash was swift: the right wing was furious. Even before the vote, the new leader of Likud, Benjamin Netanyahu, argued that a "Jewish majority" must block the Oslo agreement. The notion of a "Jewish majority," conveying that Jewish lawmakers count more than non-Jews, has become routine and accepted in Israeli political discourse, at least among Jews.[112] Netanyahu continued to harangue the government for failing to win a Jewish majority ahead of the vote on the next major stage of the Oslo process, in October 1995, for the agreement known as "Oslo II."

Opposing Peace with Violence

Opponents of Oslo viewed the peace process that involved redeploying the Israeli army, restraining settlements, and establishing Palestinian autonomy as an existential danger, or as a violation of God's will for Jewish sovereignty over all the land. Macabre forces were rising against the process; just ahead of the October vote, right-wingers rallied against it, filled with violent threats against Rabin. Fully fifty-nine legislators opposed the agreement, including Shas this time. Yet once again, the vote passed, with sixty-one seats. All 120 lawmakers were present.[113]

Opposition to Oslo had already burst the constraints of civil protest. In 1994, Baruch Goldstein, a settler from Kiryat Arba, killed dozens of Palestinians in a mass shooting attack as they prayed in the Ibrahim Mosque (at the site known to Jews as the Tomb of the Patriarchs) in Hebron. After the vote, in November 1995, Rabin told hundreds of thousands of peace demonstrators at a rally in Tel Aviv that "violence was undermining the foundation of Israeli democracy." It was one of the last things he would ever say. As Rabin descended from the stage, Yigal Amir—a man prepared to sacrifice his life for permanent Jewish control over all the land and people—shot Rabin in the back. The prime minister died within hours.[114]

Failed Peace, Aborted Democracy

Many believe that Amir killed not only Rabin but peace itself. In fact, the Oslo process was already on a troubled path. Some Palestinian factions also opposed the effort (reflecting internal Palestinian political competition), and perpetrated a series of suicide bombings against Israeli civilians, many within the Green Line. It is quite possible that right-wing opposition would have defeated Rabin, had he lived, in the next elections scheduled for 1996, and ended the process.

Moreover, there is no certainty that the Oslo process would ultimately have brought peace, thereby making Israel—and the Palestinians—more democratic. The initial declaration in 1993 never explicitly mentioned the aim of a Palestinian state (Israel officially negotiated over full Palestinian statehood only in 2000). Oslo slowed the settlement boom under the previous Likud governments, but they still grew; when Rabin took office, there were about 112,000 Jewish settlers just in the West Bank and about 150,000 by 1996.[115] Immigrants from the former Soviet Union did, in fact, settle over the Green Line, in the 1990s. Just days after the first announcement of the process in August 1993, the Supreme Court rejected an ambitious petition initiated by Peace Now, challenging the legality of the entire settlement project, based on several arguments. The court determined that the issue was nonjusticiable, a political matter in the hands of the executive. The Court's opinion contrasted sharply with the Court's growing activism in other areas, observes leading human rights lawyer Michael Sfard.[116] On settlements, the court became "nonintervention[ist]."[117] Whether building on "state land" (originally "public land," as noted), or even private lands, Israel kept racing ahead to build.

The role of the Supreme Court is an apt metaphor for the processes of the 1990s regarding democratization and liberalizing trends. The Court played a key role in advancing these trends, regarding challenging government action and legislation, confronting corruption, advancing equality, and supporting incremental steps toward separating religion and state. But the Court's willingness to confront the state and to advance equality or liberal values hit a wall when ruling on occupation policies.

The peace process itself encouraged some democratic developments, such as the participation of Arab parties in national decision-making and the potential for one day ending the overall policy. Yet opposition—legitimate at the political level—supported an undemocratic policy. It also ultimately resorted to the worst kind of violence: terrorism and political assassination.

Opponents of Oslo also began embracing the term "democracy" to justify violence or incitement, foreshadowing later trends of exploiting the term to support undemocratic policies. Following the assassination, a settler from Kiryat Arba insisted that Rabin was the dictator; another settler told a reporter that celebrations for the killing were a matter of free speech in a democracy. In 1996, the assassin, Yigal Amir, wrote that the government and the media had brainwashed people and that the public was afraid to openly support him, which meant, he claimed, that "it's not a democracy any more."[118] These statements recall the response in a Haredi newspaper to the Court ruling to open the Jerusalem street to traffic on the Sabbath: "Democracy has ended. The rule of the people has ended."[119]

The Palestinian side of the equation is also a central question: Did the Oslo process advance democracy? It gave Palestinians a horizon for self-determination and established institutions intended for them to govern themselves. The agreements led to the first—broadly free and fair—national Palestinian elections in the Occupied Territories, in 1996. Turnout was nearly 76 percent and almost 87 percent in Gaza.[120]

Palestinian critics of the Oslo Accords, such as the prominent academic Edward Said, immediately warned that the accords were not conducive to building a democratic society. Yasser Arafat's leadership quickly moved in the opposite direction, with a cohort of self-anointed governing figures who lacked financial or decision-making accountability and who displayed authoritarian behavior in the name of the national cause.[121] And the Palestinian areas ultimately remained under occupation, despite some limited areas of local authority.

Palestinians quickly viewed the Palestinian Authority (PA) as authoritarian and corrupt, not committed to civic freedoms, and intolerant of political opposition. Freedom House's 1995–96 report noted that PA laws allowed it to suspend newspaper outlets, and it regularly detained journalists or pressured them to drop stories critical of the PA, while the judiciary was not independent and ran kangaroo courts with security personnel as justices to try suspected Islamic radicals. The PA also used arbitrary arrest, detention, and torture of suspects. PA governance therefore recalled the practices of the occupation; the Israeli army and Shabak continued to use similar tactics. Freedom House described the Palestinians as "military and PLO administered," under the heading of Israel.[122]

Young Palestinians were especially despairing. "The more disillusioned the students are with the PA about issues like corruption, mismanagement, and lack of democratization, the more opposed to the peace process they become," wrote Khalil Shikaki in 1998; Shikaki tracked public attitudes among Palestinians through systematic survey research.[123] Palestinian national elections were held only once more, in 2006.

Israel also seemed to view democracy among Palestinians as undesirable for Israel's purposes. Rabin had sought to placate opposition against Oslo by insisting that Arafat would fight terrorism effectively, "without Bagatz [the High Court], without B'Tselem, without Mothers Against Silence," he said, possibly several times, in a quote that became famous.[124]

Many recall the statement as evidence that Rabin resented these bodies within Israel. But he was talking about Palestinians, conveying a demarcation that was self-evident to most Israelis: Israel is a democracy, with all the inconveniences. Palestine should be what Israel needs it to be. The quote—or, more often, exploitations of the quote to justify attacks on these groups in Rabin's name—would later feed the extreme populist narrative in Israel that the Supreme Court and critical civil society groups were an obstacle to fighting terrorism, or that they even supported it.

The peace process appeared linked, at least circumstantially and logically, to the liberalizing and globalizing trends of the 1990s. What seems clearer is that as the process failed, the worst violations of democracy returned, and ultimately became worse.

Chapter 16: Seeds of Backlash

Benjamin Netanyahu won the 1996 elections after Rabin's death, beating Shimon Peres, ushering Likud back into power. Netanyahu slowed the Oslo Accords but didn't abandon them entirely; three years later, Israelis elected a leader who promised not only to revive the peace process with the Palestinians but to finally withdraw the IDF from the "security zone" in southern Lebanon, where Israel had maintained its occupation since 1982. Ehud Barak and the Labor Party also campaigned on addressing Israel's soaring economic gaps, poverty and unemployment, and problems in health care and education; and rejecting what had already become Netanyahu's signature alliance with the ultra-Orthodox parties. As in 1992, Israelis appeared to make a firm decision in favor of Barak's liberal and peace-oriented promises, when he won in a landslide in May 1999 (Israel still held direct elections for prime minister at that time). Meretz won ten seats, indicating that its general support for liberal and progressive social values, minority and LGBTQ rights, separation of religion and state, and commitment to peace with the Palestinians had a core constituency. On election night, Barak's supporters flooded the renamed Rabin Square in Tel Aviv; he announced the "dawn of a new day" and built a colossal coalition of seventy-five seats and seven different parties.[125]

But the victory for the parties now viewed as left-wing was deceptive, or limited. Meretz lost power relative to 1992. Despite Barak's heady victory in the direct ballot, the Labor Party fared poorly, losing eleven seats despite combining with other factions.

Ahead of the 1999 elections, the ultra-Orthodox backlash against the courts and the liberalizing trends was boiling over. Haredi communities were increasingly antagonistic toward the Supreme Court rulings, challenging their power and erosion of the "status quo" arrangements. The broad status quo framework remained in force, of course, as it remains in the present, and the Court did not always rule against the religious authorities. In one 1997 ruling in an appeal against rabbinic courts by a woman unable to attain a divorce, justices acknowledged: "The situation of a Hebrew slave was preferable to that of a wife under Jewish law, since even a slave would be released in the seventh year." She still lost.[126]

After the watershed ruling challenging the IDF service in December 1998, the court heard petitions related to non-Orthodox Jewish conversions abroad in 1999; early that year, the Court also ruled against the ultra-Orthodox on a municipal matter in Jerusalem. The ultra-Orthodox community, seemingly at a breaking point, staged its biggest demonstration in memory—an estimated 250,000 people—specifically to oppose the Supreme Court. Their leaders denounced the Court as "anti-Semitic." Rabbi Ovadia Yosef, the Shas spiritual leader, "described the justices as 'wicked, stubborn and rebellious,' 'empty-headed and reckless' and 'the cause of all the world's torments.'" His son called Supreme Court president Barak "the enemy of the Jews," a reference to Haman, the ancient and archetypal enemy of the Jews.[127]

All those events preceded the verdict against Aryeh Deri. About a month after the Haredi demonstration and two months before the May 1999 elections, the Jerusalem district court finally ruled in the long-running corruption case. Deri was found guilty. By this time, he had achieved towering status; the ruling made him a martyr and touched off a tidal wave of support. At a stadium-size event, a beatific-looking Deri sat alongside the movement's rabbinic leaders, while a singer wailed the now-iconic: "He's innocent, Aryeh Deri, he's innocent." Footage of the event became one of the party's television campaign ads; the spot also showed ultra-Orthodox women weeping and swaying in prayer and teenage girls buttoned to the neck, singing, "Aryeh Deri will never fall!" The wizened Rabbi Kadouri declares that "they brought liars as witnesses and investigated them poorly and they convicted Deri, and therefore this touches the entire Sephardi public."[128]

On election day, Shas won its highest showing ever: seventeen seats. The result stunned the country and showed the power of an emerging accusation that the judiciary had sought to destroy Deri, with the subtext of Ashkenazi elites seeking to suppress Mizrahim. This group, too, joined the earlier communities that viewed the law as instrumental, at best, and as an enemy, at worst.

Ehud Barak included Shas in his sprawling, cross-ideological coalition, which shocked his voters, but the government was short-lived. Once again, controversies over religion and state cracked its cohesion. Instead of Rabin's F-15 fighter jets, the first crisis involved a heavy electrical turbine that needed to be transported slowly on Sabbath, rather than suffocating traffic during the week. Shas threatened to bolt the coalition rather than violate the Sabbath; that crisis passed, but the coalition could not withstand the renewal of the peace process.[129]

Ehud Barak first sought to hold negotiations with Syria, but the effort failed. Next, he turned to the Palestinians: in July 2000, Barak and Palestinian leader Yasser Arafat opened direct negotiations, hosted by US president Bill Clinton at Camp David. Barak arrived prepared to negotiate the details of a comprehensive, final status agreement in which the Palestinians would have statehood—in other words, a two-state partition.

But as the broad outline of compromises began to take shape ahead of the negotiations, Shas and other parties could not tolerate the anticipated concessions. The coalition collapsed inauspiciously just before the Camp David talks. Even Barak's foreign minister, David Levy—whose faction had run within Barak's "One Israel" list—did not attend.[130] The negotiations reached the most advanced final status draft agreement so far. But after fourteen grueling days, the talks collapsed, leaving analysts to battle out the blame for decades to come. That September, Ariel Sharon, leader of Likud and the political opposition, strode across the Temple Mount in Jerusalem. The provocative move sparked clashes that became the second Palestinian uprising, also called the al-Aqsa Intifada.

Almost immediately, the events triggered another incident of the state using lethal force against its own citizens—once again, against its Palestinian Arab citizens. In October, days after the Intifada began, Arab citizens demonstrated throughout towns of northern Israel. Over the course of a week, and in a number of towns, police opened fire, killing thirteen—the worst attack on Arab citizens since Land Day in 1976, and twice as deadly.[131]

It was a devastating rupture for the Arab community. When Israel held special elections in February 2001 for prime minister, the Arab community called for a full boycott. Only 18 percent of Arabs turned out to vote, the lowest level in any national election before or since.[132] Ariel Sharon beat Barak by a wide margin and became prime minister; Arab turnout rates rose in the next parliamentary elections but would never again match the rate of Jewish turnout. A government commission investigated the October 2000 killings of Arab citizens, and criticized police actions. But unlike even the compromised effort at justice following the Kfar Qassem massacre of 1956, in 2008, the attorney general announced that no one would be indicted.

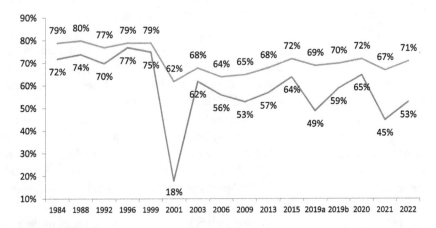

Figure 2: Arab and General Voter Turnout in Israeli Elections, 1984 – 2022. Graphic by author. Data source: Total Israeli turnout and Arab votes: Arik Rudnitzky, "Arab Votes in the 2022 Election," Israel Democracy Institute, November 9, 2022, https://en.idi.org.il/articles/46271; from 2001, see Staff and Wire Reports, "Sharon Claims Victory in Israeli Election," CNN, February 6, 2001.

The Second Intifada sparked a far more violent phase. A new wave of Palestinian suicide bombings targeted Israelis, often civilians. In 2002, the IDF reoccupied major Palestinian towns for a period. In 2002, the government began building a massive concrete wall to create a physical barrier in parts of the West Bank and Jerusalem. The wall jutted into the West Bank, well beyond the Green Line, cut through villages, severed Jerusalem neighborhoods from the West Bank, and cut off Palestinian farmers from their lands. The wall soon became one of the most ubiquitous new symbols of the Israel occupation.

In 2004, the International Court of Justice (ICJ) issued an advisory opinion, finding that the wall violated Palestinian rights while effectively annexing occupied territory. Days before the imminent ICJ ruling, the Israeli Supreme Court ruled on a group of petitions against the wall by human rights activists. Aharon Barak's judgment found that specific, limited segments of the wall caused undue harm to Palestinian life and had to be rerouted. Did the ruling prove the Court's independence and the country's commitment to law and justice, even in the face of dire security needs? Or was the Supreme Court ruling a useful tool, as critics charge, for confronting international pressure by proving that Israel could prosecute itself? Still others believe that the Supreme Court simply betrayed Israelis: upon learning the verdict, an IDF figure angrily told the media that the Court handed a victory to the PA and "made a mockery of all victims of terrorism."[133] The ruling did not affect the overall policy of the wall, which remains in place today.

In 2005, Ariel Sharon implemented a highly controversial plan of unilaterally dismantling all settlements in Gaza. The policy is most often remembered as a turning point in the conflict, but it also raised difficult questions about democratic practice in the settlers' eyes, since the policy meant displacing them against their will. The consequences for Israeli democracy turned out to be very far-reaching.

Likud, deeply conflicted over Sharon's plan, held a referendum among party members; nearly 60 percent rejected the pullout. Sharon went ahead, firing two ministers who would have opposed the plan so that it could pass a vote in the government. The Knesset voted in favor of two different laws for the plan, in October 2004 and early 2005; the first law for the general plan passed with a strong majority of sixty-seven votes.[134] The political process can be described as legal, democratic, and procedurally correct, but roughshod—Sharon perhaps lived up to his "bulldozer" nickname.

Large portions of right-wing Israeli society mobilized against the disengagement. Some opponents called on soldiers to refuse orders to remove settlers who refused to leave. Twelve different petitions were submitted to the Supreme Court against the plan. Ten out of eleven justices on an expanded panel rejected all twelve petitions.[135]

But the government implemented the withdrawal; the country watched as IDF soldiers dragged anguished people out of their homes. The religious Zionist community was shattered; some even felt profoundly betrayed. From their perspective, argues Yair Sheleg, an expert on Israel's religious Zionist community, this group had tolerated the Supreme Court ruling, tolerated the weakening of Jewish religion over the public sphere, and served enthusiastically in the IDF—the most important distinction from the ultra-Orthodox. Religious Zionists thought that they had a fair bargain: as model citizens, they believed that secular state leadership would support settling in "all parts of the land."[136] Given the forward motion of settlements under all governments, with variations only in the pace of growth or geographic locations in the West Bank, the assumption was well-founded.

Over the following decades, the post-disengagement, right-wing activist, pro-settler movement turned its attention beyond hilltops.[137] Now, they hoped to settle deep within "hearts of Israeli society," in a popular expression; this included leveraging the arenas of civil society, academia and higher education, the media, the judiciary, and Likud itself.

Ariel Sharon broke from Likud and established a new party; but he fell into a coma before the next elections, in 2006. Sharon's successor, Ehud Olmert, tried to revive the peace process with Palestinian leader Mahmoud Abbas (known as Abu Mazen) in the late 2000s, but conditions could hardly have been worse. The Second Intifada and the disengagement had soured many Israelis. In the second Palestinian elections for national leadership in 2006, a plurality of voters, angered by a decade of corrupt, authoritarian Fatah-led PA leadership and an ineffective peace process, supported Hamas. Fatah nonetheless formed the next government; in response, Hamas took over Gaza in a violent coup. Israel quickly placed Gaza under a near-hermetic siege starting in 2007; with some adjustments, the closure policy remains as of 2023. Since 2007, Palestinian leadership has been divided between the theocratic Hamas regime in Gaza and the PA regime under Fatah, which Palestinians view as deeply corrupt. Both areas remain under some mechanism of Israeli control.

The negotiations of 2007–08 failed, though the proposals for a two-state solution by this time were detailed and advanced. But Olmert fell under corruption investigations, too. Benjamin Netanyahu, now leader of the opposition, called for him to resign, famously saying that he was "up to his neck" in the investigations and might make policy decisions for personal reasons.[138] Although a prime minister can remain in office unless convicted, Olmert resigned in September 2008, before being indicted; he was eventually convicted and served sixteen months in prison—representing the bittersweet privilege of democratic accountability.

Netanyahu, it is worth noting, had served as finance minister from 2003 to 2005.[139] In that role, he seized on the economic liberalization under way from the 1980s, under both Likud and Labor governments, slashing taxes and the public sector, further privatizing national companies, and, in particular, deepening cuts to child allowances that had benefited large families over the years. (For a time, these cuts to child allowances cost him politically with the essential ultra-Orthodox allies.)[140] But Netanyahu was simultaneously digging into his fervent nationalism, which drew a contrast with Sharon's perceived pragmatism and also characterized his future leadership. There was little sign that Netanyahu believed that continued robust economic growth or liberalization depended on a peace process, nor was the absence of an eventual peace agreement an obstacle to his economic vision. In later years, Netanyahu made the opposite case, indicating at points that "economic peace" could replace peace itself and, finally, that there was no need for peace with the Palestinians in order to forge new global allies and expand Israel's economic horizon. The latter view was the basis of the Abraham Accords (discussed in Chapter 20).

As a new election campaign got under way in late 2008, war broke out between Israel and Hamas in Gaza. Under Kadima's new leader, Tzipi Livni, the party that Sharon had established won first place in the 2009 elections, with one more seat than Netanyahu's Likud. But only Netanyahu was able to form a coalition, and he returned to the leadership.[141]

Conclusion

The late 1980s were a prelude to what became a decade of accelerated democratization, when the country seemed to orient itself decisively in a more democratic direction. The Basic Laws of 1992, though piecemeal and vulnerable to challenges over their authority, charted a course. In contrast to the decades when the democratizing or liberalizing steps were small and the expansion of occupation was large, the opposite dynamic happened in the 1990s. As the country seemed to embrace liberalizing trends, it embarked upon a process with the Palestinians, despite Israel's continued unwillingness to name a final endpoint in the early stages, and the actual detrimental outcome of the Oslo process for both Israelis and Palestinians. Israel began the peace process because of a combination of growing pressure from the US, the fall of the Soviet Union, and the Palestinian uprising.

But the decision to embark upon such a process cannot be isolated from the context of a dramatically changed society in the 1990s, relative to Israel's earlier decades. Many Israelis argued that the accelerated leaning toward liberal democracy and a globally-oriented economy, alongside an increasingly individualist, bourgeois culture, depended on ending the violent conflict, a local and international albatross. Ending the occupation would not have solved Israel's democratic problems, which had begun long before—but embarking on the path would have pointed the way.

This is not the place to reopen the blame game regarding who missed an opportunity for peace at the negotiating table; the deeper social and political forces undermining peace were no less potent than specific decisions, while Israel holds vastly more power. When the peace process collapsed (mostly by 2000 – 01), the democratizing developments of the 1990s did not vanish, but the vehicle hit potholes and the engine stalled. Renewed conflict inflamed sentiments and fed the rise of Israel's new right wing: a populist, nationalist, illiberal movement rose from the late 2000s and flourished in the next decades.

Olmert made one more important decision while in office: he appointed law scholar Daniel Friedmann to serve as justice minister, beginning in 2007. Friedmann, a respected academic, had begun to express critical, even hostile, opinions about the Court, surprising some of his colleagues.[142]

Friedmann broadly opposed the trend of judicial activism and developed plans to curb its components. He believed that the Court had become "the author of the constitution," which was unacceptable.[143] Friedmann's plans included reducing the number of justices on the judicial appointment committee and proposals for allowing the Knesset to "override" a Supreme Court ruling striking down legislation, among other changes. He also opposed giving more power to rabbinic courts, which he saw as detrimental to women.[144] Friedmann's main reforms did not pass, other than capping the terms of the chief justice. But Friedmann legitimized the notion of a "counterrevolution," against what some felt had become an orthodoxy in support of judicial activism. Perhaps unwittingly, he gave prestigious professional weight to the groups in Israel that resented the law itself when it was not on their side—the ultra-Orthodox, the more extreme ends of the settler community, security and intelligence agencies (at times), and Shas supporters who felt that the law had been used to persecute their leader. The ingredients of Israel's own illiberal populist backlash were coming together.

Section VI
Backlash: 2009–present

When did the global illiberal backlash against democracy begin? From the vantage point of 2023 and following a decade that produced Donald Trump and Brexit; antidemocratic leaders in Brazil, India, the Philippines, Hungary, and Poland; and Russia's war on Ukraine, it is easy to forget that the initial illiberal wave began earlier.

In 1997, democracy theorist Larry Diamond predicted that liberal democracy would cease to expand and could regress if the institutional norms of liberal democracy were not consciously deepened and consolidated.[1] That same year, Fareed Zakaria observed a trend of leaders and processes undermining constitutional liberal protections, often by exploiting the democratic system: "Illiberal democracies gain legitimacy, and thus strength, from the fact that they are reasonably democratic."[2]

Diamond showed that the number of countries categorized generally as democracies began to decline in 2006; the number of *liberal* democracies—which had risen significantly since 1975—peaked and also began a slight decline.[3]

Viktor Orbán returned as prime minister of Hungary in 2010. In 2012, Vladimir Putin returned as president of Russia, as an unrestrained autocrat (which eventually gave way to a violent dictatorship). Western European countries saw a first generation of populist hardliners in the 2000s: Jean-Marie Le Pen's National Front surprised France in the 2002 presidential election by reaching the second round on a nationalist, anti-immigration, Holocaust-denying agenda, while Pim Fortuyn in the Netherlands embraced a xenophobic and anti-Muslim platform; he was assassinated in 2002. Both gave rise to a second generation of populists: Marine Le Pen also reached a second round of presidential elections in France in 2022, performing far better than her father; while in the Netherlands, Geert Wilders continued the ultranationalist, anti-immigration, anti-Muslim themes that Fortuyn had unleashed; his party gained significant ground in the 2010s.[4]

The initial illiberal trends of the late 1990s and 2000s were the global backdrop to Benjamin Netanyahu's return as prime minister in 2009. But Israel's populist, illiberal right-wing movements are not exclusively about Netanyahu. Despite his towering presence in Israeli politics—on or off for nearly three decades, as of this writing—neither Israel's illiberal backlash nor its long-term vulnerabilities can be reduced to one man.

https://doi.org/10.1515/9783110796582-007

Chapter 17: Twenty-First-Century Populism in Israel

To be sure, Netanyahu presided over, cultivated, and unleashed some of the most undemocratic forces in Israel's history, reaching new and dangerous heights as this book is being completed. These include political attacks on the judiciary, alongside both policies and rhetorical pressure targeting civil society, minorities, media, cultural figures, and left-wing critics of the government or Israeli policy. Throughout his leadership, Netanyahu displayed a sharp grasp of emerging international trends and adapted them to support his aims; his personal role is examined in Chapter 18.

But, as this book has documented, there were numerous historical antecedents to undemocratic practices in Israel. And Netanyahu was not the first to identify the electoral potential of targeting internal enemies, haranguing the country's Arab Palestinian minority, and advocating illiberal, strongman rule.

The New Populist Leader

Avigdor (originally known as Yvette) Lieberman, a pugnacious immigrant from Moldova (then part of the USSR), arrived in Israel in the 1970s. A right-wing student activist, he moved to a West Bank settlement and became active in Likud politics.[5] When Netanyahu took office for the first time, in 1996, he appointed Lieberman director general of the prime minister's office.

Israel had just absorbed a massive wave of immigration from the former Soviet Union. In 1990, Israel's population was about 4.8 million; by 1996, 700,000 immigrants had arrived from post-Soviet states. Eventually, more than 1 million immigrants would arrive from that region, making a powerful demographic, political, and economic impact on Israel.[6] Political camps quickly began vying for their vote, initially uncertain as to whether these immigrants would be sympathetic to left-wing ideas, out of familiarity—as the left wing hoped—or to the right-wing, in reaction. The answer, for a time, was both: in the 1990s, this group swung between the major political camps.

Ultimately, the former Soviet immigrants gravitated significantly to the political right.[7] The former Soviet dissident Natan Sharansky established a right-leaning party in the 1990s, hoping to win their support, which joined Netanyahu's first government (1996–99).

In 1999, Avigdor Lieberman, who had become a trusted Netanyahu adviser, broke with Likud and started a party called Yisrael Beiteinu—Israel Is Our Home. The party was considered more militant and hawkish than Likud on the Israeli-Palestinian conflict, though it was staunchly secular, like its constituents.

Lieberman seemed to have a natural populist streak. He excelled in outrageous statements, famously threatening to bomb Egypt's Aswan Dam and stating that Arab lawmakers who had met with Hamas figures should be treated like Nazi collaborators who had been tried at Nuremberg and executed.[8] From four seats in 1999, the party's vote rose during the 2000s; days before the 2009 election, *Haaretz* revealed that Lieberman had briefly been a member of Meir Kahane's Kach. Lieberman responded with hyperbole and deflection, the kind of remarks made famous by politicians like Donald Trump a few years later: "Our opponents [have generated] an incredible number of lies and fictional defamation never before seen in politics and media."[9] That year, Lieberman also had a new campaign asset: Netanyahu's former American campaign adviser, Arthur Finkelstein, known for attack-dog negative campaigning for right-wing American politicians that often included race-baiting. Lieberman's 2009 campaign launched an open broadside against Israel's Arab citizens that seemed shocking at the time. His slogan was "No Loyalty, No Citizenship." The party's ads targeted specific Arab political figures in Israel, and the closing slogan was "Only Lieberman Understands Arabic."[10]

In 2009, twenty-five years after Meir Kahane's anti-Arab diatribes, Lieberman soared to fifteen seats, nearly four times more than his first run in 1999, and his best result before or since. Likud recovered from its dismal result in 2006 (when Kadima sapped its strength), and won twenty-seven seats. However, Likud should have done better. Earlier in the campaign, polls showed Likud winning more than three times as many seats as Lieberman. But Yisrael Beiteinu directly siphoned off potential Likud voters, winning a substantial portion of nonimmigrant, right-wing Israelis for the first time. The Eighteenth Knesset now had sixty-five seats going to right-wing and Jewish religious parties. Likud could not have missed the fact that its polls showed serious defections to Lieberman, with his populism and Arab-baiting and surprise success.[11]

From 2009, anti-Arab political rhetoric became routine, and not only during elections. Likud figures, and later Netanyahu himself, expressed increasing hostility against these citizens in the coming years. Why did it work? What social sentiment had Lieberman, and then Netanyahu—perhaps in competition with Lieberman—tapped?

Arabs, Palestinians, and Jews

The previous decade of the 2000s, with the Second Intifada and the Gaza disengagement, was not only a murky time for democratic progress. It was also a "lost decade" in terms of Arab–Jewish relations and relations between Arab citizens and the state, according to sociologist Sammy Smooha.[12] Although Arab political and social empowerment had grown, so had the socioeconomic gaps, largely because of increased privatization and rollbacks of the welfare state (one of Netanyahu's signature policies as finance minister). But the critical sources of tension were political: the Intifada and the killing of Arab citizens in October 2000; the second Lebanon war, in 2006; and the first Gaza war, in 2008–09. Some Arab citizens demonstrated against the wars, in solidarity with Palestinians under occupation.[13] The proportion of Arabs in Israel who recognized a Palestinian component in their identity rose in survey research during the 2000s, hovering around 60 percent from 2006 through 2009, while the proportion who identified with their Israeli citizenship declined.[14]

Lieberman zeroed in on the solidarity with Palestinians. In 2004, he introduced his version of a two-state solution.[15] Instead of making "adjustments" to the Green Line (as most of the official two-state negotiations had proposed), Lieberman wanted to radically redraw borders by ethnicity and transfer large Arab towns to a future state of Palestine, making the residents into Palestinian citizens. The plan, in effect, would strip their Israeli citizenship—building up his theme that they were not loyal citizens.[16]

The charge was fake. For all the solidarity and contiguous identity of Arab citizens with Palestinians under occupation, the Arab community in Israel has never mounted a serious secessionist movement.[17] In the late 2000s, after Lieberman raised the political transfer plan, surveys found that a firm majority, 66 percent and 58 percent of Arab citizens in 2009 and 2010, respectively, rejected the idea.[18] Some argue that the findings demonstrate a democratic achievement, since the state has fostered Arab loyalty to Israeli citizenship. However, when the same survey probed the reasons that respondents preferred Israeli to future Palestinian citizenship, few selected the response that Israel was more democratic than a future Palestinian state. Their main reason, by a wide margin, was the expectation of a better quality of life.[19] Yet the Arab citizens' preference to remain part of Israel is notable, since numerous ethno-national minorities in the post-Soviet arena had fought wars of secession, while others had sought to secede through democratic means as well.[20]

Over the decades, the main demand of Arab citizens in Israel has invariably been for full equality as citizens in politics and in economic and professional life. They hold ongoing demands for equitable social services, since the state has historically neglected or underfunded health, education, infrastructure, and planning in Arab localities. Over time, more Arabs have sought opportunities to live in "Jewish" areas, where they face barriers of discrimination and a culture of separation, and the historical pillar of Zionism, Jewish-only cooperative villages such as kibbutzim, and other types of semi-cooperative Jewish villages. There are mixed cities in Israel, but fewer than 10 percent of Arab citizens live in those areas.[21]

For Jews, the more controversial demands include collective, national rights within Israel, or anti-Zionist attitudes that would either strip the state of its Jewish identity or remove the policies and symbols that privilege Jews. For most Jews, the greatest threat from Arab citizens—which many even see as a betrayal—is the demand for "a state of all its citizens." Many Palestinian Arab citizens of Israel view this as natural—the foundation of any democracy; for most Jews (in Israel and abroad), the phrase "a state of all its citizens" is reflexively understood as the destruction of Israel.

Toward the late 2000s, Arab community leaders began to formally articulate the community's vision. The violence of that decade had sparked a sense of urgency; in addition, Jewish civil society leaders had renewed efforts to advance a constitution, and Palestinian community leaders in Israel felt that their efforts ignored the needs of Arab citizens, while entrenching the already-dominant Jewish and Zionist identity of the state.[22]

Arab communities in Israel had, by this time, established various civil society representative bodies. These groups began a series of consultations that eventually produced several documents outlining their political aspirations in Israel, known collectively as the "future vision" documents. These differed in certain aspects but generally called for a fundamental change in the structure that privileges Jewish citizens. Political scientist Amal Jamal characterized one of the proposals as a "transformation of the State of Israel from a state that defines itself as Jewish and democratic to a state that belongs to all its ethno-national groups."[23] For Israeli Jews, the documents represented sabotage, even a "declaration of war."[24] One organization that was involved was Mada al-Carmel, an Arab policy and social-science think tank that published its "Haifa Declaration" in 2007, after five years of study. This was one of the more liberal documents, urging dialogue with the Jewish community to advance "justice and equality for all citizens." Nevertheless, the effort prompted an assault on the organization's foreign funding sources by NGO Monitor, a right-wing group established in 2001 and devoted to sabotaging NGOs that it deemed insufficiently loyal to the state. Mada al-Carmel lost a major grant from the Canadian government and was forced to shut down its survey research unit.[25]

Lieberman's vocal anti-Arab orientation gathered momentum after the 2009 elections and drew in other politicians, particularly from Likud—whose members were developing a more hostile, extreme, and populist rhetoric. The Eighteenth Knesset put the rhetoric into action, with a new kind of legislative agenda, explored throughout this section. But Netanyahu was leading the country; he managed to constrain Lieberman's rise and was poised to remake both the Likud and right-wing politics in Israel.

King Bibi

Netanyahu is among the most complex political figures in Israel, with a range of political skills. By the time he returned to power in 2009, he was a master at the game of politics, practically inviting comparisons to a chess player. He strategized his moves vis-à-vis other politicians, parties, coalition dynamics, and even international actors, keeping competitors close or far, depending on his calculations. One of his repeated and successful tactics was to cultivate extreme right-wing forces if they supported his leadership, and then present himself as either beholden to their demands, or as the only one capable of restraining them.

In another role, Netanyahu was becoming a full-blown populist in his political style. This persona was already evident in the 1990s. Even then, he relished orchestrating crowds to chant "Bi-bi! Bi-bi!" or "Bibi, King of Israel," but there were also more thematic chants. In 1999, days before the May elections, Netanyahu led his thrilled audience in chorus for the now-iconic "They! Are! Afraid!" He was referring to the media, which he viewed as part of an embittered, vanquished old Left that was determined to bring him down.[26] The slogan tapped into older collective wounds among the historically marginalized Mizrahi underclass and the nationalist right-wing Herut—two core Likud constituencies that still resented the old Mapai/Labor elites. These elites, Netanyahu conveyed with the slogan, knew that they were losing and were afraid to let the true *people* take power.

Netanyahu's 1990s populism also touched on Jewish identity. In 1997, Netanyahu was caught on a hot mic whispering to Yitzhak Kaduri, a nonagenarian kabbalist rabbi who was influential among Shas voters, saying that "the Left forgot what it is to be Jews." Netanyahu's whispers, pitting the left-wing against Jewishness, created a mini-scandal at the time, sounding haughty and cynical. But the remark planted the darker political implication that left-wing politics was a betrayal of Jewish identity and of the state itself. When Kaduri died in 2006, an obituary noted that the 1997 incident had been "embarrassing for Israel's secular right."[27] By the 2010s, Netanyahu and Likud had changed; accusations against the Left were no longer an embarrassing mistake but a rallying cry.

Netanyahu's combined skills as a pragmatist, a political mastermind, and a populist served him well. He staved off early elections in 2012 with a surprise coalition remake. *Time* magazine named him "King Bibi" in a cover story; the name stuck, and his political stature became unrivaled.[28] Given Netanyahu's near-continuous rule from 2009 to the present, except for an eighteen-month hiatus, his influence can appear towering. But just as he harnessed, rather than pioneered, Israel's liberalizing economic directions, so Netanyahu leveraged, exploited, and adapted Israel's oldest democratic vulnerabilities, rather than inventing them.

Chapter 18: The New Illiberal Ideology

In his second term, beginning in 2009, Netanyahu gave free rein to the newly emergent illiberal forces, appearing confident that he could reel them in when it suited him.

Netanyahu's coalition of 2009 included Lieberman's party, along with religious parties and even Labor; but it was Yisrael Beiteinu and Likud that set about putting "No Loyalty, No Citizenship" into action during the term of the Eighteenth Knesset (2009–13). The two parties sponsored bills, sometimes cosponsoring them, that were designed to threaten and intimidate Arabs in Israel and entrench institutional discrimination. Likud figures began to sound more like Lieberman in tone and program.

Legislating against Equality and Civil Liberties

New laws affected housing discrimination and freedom of speech. The Admissions Committee Law of 2011 provided a legal basis for de facto discrimination, conveyed in the language of democracy and fairness. According to the law, small Jewish cooperative communities were prohibited from discriminating against applicants for residency based on "race, religion, sex, nationality, disability, personal (family) status, age, parental status, sexual orientation, country of origin, outlook or political-party affiliation." But their admissions committees could reject applicants who threatened "the social-cultural fabric of the community," or if "the candidate is not suited to the life of the community."[29] To understand the law means going back once again to 2000, the year of a breakthrough Supreme Court ruling, *Ka'adan v. Israel Land Administration*. In 1995, the Arab Ka'adan family had applied to the local committee to live in a small all-Jewish community nestled among large Arab towns adjacent to the northern West Bank, along the Green Line. The community had been established by the Jewish Agency and was intended for Jews; its rules for admission never named Jews or Arabs but required residents to have performed army service; by mutual agreement, Arabs have historically been exempt.[30] The Ka'adan family was rejected, and they sued. In 2000, the Court ruled in their favor, emphasizing once again that equality is a core value in Israel. Aharon Barak was the lead author of the decision, which touched off a visceral right-wing backlash, defending decades of privileges for Jews in planning and housing. The head of the Jewish Agency at the time insisted that Jewish communities near the Green Line were essential to entrench Israeli sovereignty.[31] The decision particularly angered a lawyer, Simcha Rothman, who later wrote: "There's nothing like the Ka'adan decision … to demonstrate how the judicial branch has invaded the issues at the heart of Zionist values."[32]

The Admissions Committee Law of 2011 gave legal protection to discrimination and looked like the right-wing's defense against the fear that Jews, the rightful owners of the country, in this view, were losing their status. Did most Jews feel this way?

Analyzing democratic decline in the 2020s, political scientist Mads Qvortrup found that people who feel "let down and humiliated" can develop a sense of inferiority and may gravitate toward a strong figure. Summarizing Alexander Hamilton, Qvortrup notes that such demagogues employ a "mask of zeal for the rights of the people" who are feeling aggrieved and usurped. Qvortrup, like many observers of democratic decline, observes that the aggrievement is exacerbated by economic deprivation.[33]

By the 2010s in Israel, economic conditions could certainly have augmented nationalist tensions. The great liberalization of markets and the growth of preceding decades fed large-scale economic gaps, rising costs, and only limited wage increases among most workers, compared with robust increases for a small group of high-production industries. Socioeconomic gaps increased from the 1990s until, in 2013, Israel had the second-highest level of income inequality among countries of the Organisation for Economic Co-operation and Development (OECD); in 2014, Israel had the second-highest level of poverty in the OECD.[34] The losers of this growing inequality, not surprisingly, were those who had historically found themselves at the lower end of the Israeli economic and social structure. Among Jews, this largely meant Mizrahi Jews and the ultra-Orthodox—both groups that vote mostly for right-wing or religious parties. Meanwhile, during the 1990s and 2000s, as seen in earlier chapters, the country took steps to rectify historical social inequalities, including for Arabs, partly through the courts. The Labor Party, responsible for the historical class stratification in the earliest decades, now remade its identity around peace with the Palestinians and seized on the cause of social liberalization and equality within Israel, as did Meretz. Once again, the Jewish cultural and economic have-nots felt that those parties, or "the Left" in general, were passing them over, adding a key ingredient to the coming backlash.

The emerging populist right-wing politicians now challenged the liberalizing direction, which was increasingly associated with the Left. In their telling, the liberal Left, with its universal values, was robbing the country of its Jewish identity, and the Court was helping, by weakening the status quo power of religion in public life, or by weakening the privileges of Jewish Israelis.

The right-wing parties justified rough-edged laws to defend the people's identity, dismissing the fact that illiberal consequences could affect *all* citizens. The Admissions Committee Law, for example, could be employed to block ultra-Orthodox or Mizrahi applicants, as well, from living in traditionally Ashkenazi cooperative communities. But the right-wing parties were directing their fire at Arab citizens; the public debate centered entirely on the Jewish–Arab fault line.

Civil rights groups, including ACRI and the Arab minority rights group Adalah, petitioned the Supreme Court against the Admissions Committee Law, but in 2014, the Court upheld the law by a narrow margin.[35] The right wing did not seem to notice when the Court ruled in its favor.

These efforts established a "thousand cuts" approach, or what could be viewed as small infringements when seen on their own but that add up to a more serious threat to democracy. In Qvortrup's examples, the cuts begin with proto-dictators attacking the media and the courts; Israel was more subtle and Netanyahu was more savvy than that.[36] During this phase, it was mostly lawmakers from various parties in his government proposing the changes—he positioned himself as above it all.

Instead of attacking the press, two laws touched a category of political speech that were unlikely to gain any sympathy from most Jewish Israelis: expressions of solidarity with Palestinians. The Nakba law was possibly the first Israeli law (excluding military law) to explicitly target specific political expression. Submitted by a member of Lieberman's party, the original bill proposed a criminal statute and a prison sentence for commemorating the Nakba; the final version stipulated that a public institution commemorating the Nakba on Israeli Independence Day could lose its public funding.[37] Thus, the final law was less draconian than the first; once again, civil rights groups lost a Supreme Court appeal.[38]

Another law was intended to suppress the growing popularity of political boycott. The bill arose in the wake of Israeli cultural figures refusing to perform in West Bank settlements, along with growing Palestinian efforts to advance international boycott activity.[39] Once again, the original version of the boycott law was severe, including criminal sanctions for those who called for a boycott, while the final law retained only the civil statute: a citizen could sue someone for supporting a boycott, and the plaintiff was not required to prove personal damages.[40] The law had an immediate chilling effect on left-wing media outlets reporting on boycotts, lest coverage be interpreted as advocacy. Again, civil rights groups petitioned the Supreme Court, and an expanded panel of judges struck down the provision regarding compensation without proof of damage but upheld the rest of the law.[41]

Another bill sponsored by Yisrael Beiteinu would ban the use of loudspeakers for the Muslim call to prayer. Even some Likud figures, including Dan Meridor, Michael Eitan, Benny Begin (Menachem Begin's son), and Limor Livnat, found the "muezzin" bill too explicitly anti-Arab.[42] All of them would leave the party within a few years.

The muezzin bill never passed, but the intensive debate around all these bills could go on for years, through future Knesset terms. The bills could legitimize their own aims through public discussion, which became a showcase for deeply illiberal arguments, full of political grandstanding and vilifying the Arab community at large. Other bills debated implementing some form of a loyalty oath to Israel as a Jewish and democratic state, originally intended to target Arabs.[43] Actions followed rhetoric: in 2014, a Jewish-Arab bilingual school, run by a coexistence organization called Hand-in-Hand, was torched in an arson attack; the assailants sprayed the walls with graffiti: "Kahane was right"; "death to Arabs"; and "no coexistence with cancer."[44] In 2003, the Knesset amended the Citizenship Law to create formidable bureaucratic obstacles for Palestinians who were married to Israeli citizens from living in Israel. The original amendment was designed to prevent the rare terror attack by Palestinians who could access Israel by virtue of a spouse; but the Intifada was long over. The law had effectively become a family separation law; yet the Knesset repeatedly extended it in the 2010s.[45]

The vilification of civil society groups, particularly those critical of the state, began at this time, too (discussed in Chapter 19). In the early 2010s, the Knesset also began debating the Nation-State Bill, which would codify and privilege Israel's identity as a Jewish state. The law is also discussed in Chapter 19.

Jewish identity itself was a resurgent theme in an increasingly religion-oriented government. In 2011, the Knesset Committee for the Advancement of Women, led by a Likud member, invited the extreme anti-miscegenation group Lehava, known a few years later for harassing mixed Jewish-Arab couples and staging demonstrations at mixed weddings while shouting "Death to Arabs!" and "Mohammed is dead!"[46] Lehava's regular attorney was Itamar Ben-Gvir, an extremist settler activist and a follower of the teachings of Meir Kahane. The group considered itself "anti-assimilation," and the discussion focused on saving young women from Muslim partners, while Lehava's representative argued that this was not a racist position.[47]

Democracy advocates were deeply alarmed by the wave of legislation. "There is no precedent for the wave of anti-democratic legislation," wrote analysts from the Israel Democracy Institute (IDI) in a 2015 report about the Eighteenth Knesset (2009–13). "The number of bills is unprecedented ... adding to a widespread assault on the foundations of democracy."[48]

Political Pressure on the Supreme Court

Following Daniel Friedmann's brief term as justice minister in 2007–09, the Eighteenth Knesset developed a concerted political effort to erode the authority of the

Supreme Court. Legislators were clearly concerned that the Court would continue to rule on the illiberal legislation, and eventually constrain their efforts. Another likely immediate source of anger was the Court's involvement, once again, with the ultra-Orthodox yeshiva students who avoided army draft. After the 1998 decision ordering the Knesset to legislate on the issue, the Knesset had finally passed a law in 2002 designed to encourage incremental participation, known as the Tal law. The law had been challenged in the Court, and in a 2006 decision, the Court deferred ruling on the constitutionality of the law, finding that more time was needed.[49] Finally, in 2012, the Court decided that the law had not sufficiently increased the Haredi draft rate and that it entrenched inequality in Israel. The justices struck down the Tal law—deepening the near-total break with the ultra-Orthodox and earning bitter accusations against judicial activism from the right wing in general.[50]

Aharon Barak retired from the Court in 2006. After declaring the authority to review Knesset legislation in 1995, the Court did so only occasionally. Still, the Knesset chafed at the Court interfering on issues that were portrayed as socially "sensitive"—the ultra-Orthodox draft—but that also risked coalition turmoil from the ultra-Orthodox parties. Governing parties were likely just as worried, if not more so, about losing their coalitions as about the constitutional principles.

Sometimes the Knesset preferred to avoid clarifying its policies. In another ruling from 2012, the Court found that tax codes created nontransparent criteria for tax breaks that were provided in practice to Jewish towns, discriminating against Arab, Druze, and Bedouin localities (as per the language of the Court's ruling). In their decision, the justices recounted that the proceedings had taken seven years and included numerous hearings, while the Court entreated the government to create clear criteria, in order to head off judicial intervention. The justices wrote that legislators over the years had repeatedly promised, apologized, and delayed but never did clarify the criteria for the benefits. In 2010, the Speaker of the Knesset personally wrote to the finance minister—both from the ruling Likud—to take action before the Court was forced to rule, "[which] I believe that you and I both vigorously oppose."[51] The government did not act, the justices ruled against the existing tax code, and, once again, they told the Knesset to create clear criteria. Attacks mounted against the Court.

The government and the Knesset were increasingly prone to neglecting to implement Court rulings. The Association for Civil Rights in Israel (ACRI) had observed the worrying trend already in 2009, meaning that it had begun before Netanyahu came back to office. When the government sought to re-legislate an amendment that the Court had struck down, in a unanimous ruling of an expanded nine-member panel, ACRI stated: "This is an unbelievable phenomenon." The report cited a number of Court rulings that the state simply "ignored," prompting

Dorit Beinisch, chief justice at the time, to state that "the Court's judgments are not in the realm of recommendation." The examples mainly involved Arabs, Palestinians, foreign workers, and the security barrier.[52]

The Supreme Court also issued rulings that protected the rights of security suspects, rejecting extending their detention without arraignment, which angered security hardliners. Starting in 2013, the Court made several decisions that particularly incensed Israel's right wing—among them, decisions that protected certain rights of migrants seeking asylum in Israel. In the preceding years, a wave of migrants from Sudan and Eritrea, as well as Ethiopia, had reached Israel, after fleeing violent conflict in their respective countries. Many traversed the Sinai desert and fell victim to traffickers—smugglers who employed extortion and violence against them. The influx of non-Jewish migrants inflamed the debate over Jewish identity, converging with growing anti-migrant currents fueling populist politics in other Western countries. "Infiltrators" became a new flash point of Israel's illiberal backlash.

When the Court struck down legislation in 2013 allowing the government to imprison asylum seekers for up to three years, right-wing figures revived new calls for an override law specifically to address the issue of asylum seekers.[53]

Under the previous government, Daniel Friedmann had established the outlines of a program to constrain the Supreme Court and legitimized the idea of a "judicial counterrevolution." But there was little evidence that his proposals were intended to support specific policies. Now the Knesset began to move his ideas forward, apparently convinced that the Court was holding back their policy agenda.

Likud legislators submitted a bill to limit standing, i. e., who would be allowed to petition the Supreme Court. The bill would also require disclosure of foreign funding sources by civil and human rights groups that challenged occupation policies in court.[54] Funding information for NGOs was already a matter of public record; hence "disclosure" was mainly intended to mark these groups as foreign subversives. Another bill would have prevented the Court from ruling on security matters altogether.[55]

According to IDI researchers, the aim of the bills was "to tarnish the authority of the Supreme Court and to politicize justice." They warned that the politicized attacks would damage public trust in the Court.[56]

The signature proposal was a new bill allowing the Knesset to override a Supreme Court ruling, striking down legislation deemed unconstitutional. Again, the bill did not advance beyond the early stages. But politicians now regularly conveyed the urgency of reining in a runaway court that was destroying the will of the people. Years later, in 2021, Labor Party leader Merav Michaeli said that Netanyahu's governments had a "drill": they advanced "laws they knew were unconstitutional, knowing they would end up facing petitions in the Court, where the laws would be reviewed, and then they would attack the Supreme Court."[57]

The new dynamic regarding the Supreme Court differed fundamentally from the earlier types of tension over the authority of the law, seen in earlier chapters. In the 2010s, the parties in power sought to limit the judicial branch through legislation, while mounting a sustained public campaign portraying the Court as a subversive actor in Israeli society: arrogant, dangerous, interventionist, forcing liberal secular values on the population, undermining Jewish identity, and all-powerful. These themes set the course for the antiliberal backlash against democracy in Israel.

Netanyahu portrayed himself as a restraining force on his right-wing political partners—and, in certain ways, he was. He knew how to convey gravitas for the independent judiciary. At certain points in the 2010s, Netanyahu stalled the efforts to pass an "override" law and maintained a good relationship with retired justice Aharon Barak.

Chapter 19: Israeli-Palestinian Conflict and the Attack on Civil Society

The year 2009 was marked not only by Netanyahu's return and illiberal governance. That year also saw a new nadir for the Israeli–Palestinian conflict, leading to even greater deterioration of the peace prospects in the next decade. Occupation policies continued to violate Palestinian human rights and settlements grew steadily, until about 400,000 Israelis were living in the West Bank by 2016 and more than 200,000 in East Jerusalem.[58] As in the past, some Israelis opposed the occupation and advocated peace or the defense of Palestinian human rights; more organizations emerged, even as public attitudes among Jewish Israelis toward Palestinians and the conflict grew toxic. Then in the 2010s, the leading political forces governing Israel, alongside right-wing media and influential figures, unleashed a new attack on what Israelis now saw as far-left NGOs, or possible internal enemies.

As anti-occupation activists realized that the occupation was increasingly permanent, new organizations formed to address specific topics: Yesh Din was founded in 2005 to provide legal assistance to Palestinians and document patterns of human rights violations. Gisha was founded the same year, focused on Palestinian freedom of movement (mainly in Gaza), also through documentation and legal advocacy. These groups joined older NGOs focused on planning and land use under occupation: Bimkom, established in 1999; Physicians for Human Rights, established in the 1980s but also active in occupation-related issues; B'Tselem and HaMoked, mentioned in earlier chapters; and others.[59]

At the end of 2008, Israel and Hamas fought their first war, stretching into 2009, alongside the political campaign. Israel called the military assault on Gaza "Operation Cast Lead."[60]

The background to the war was Hamas's takeover of Gaza in 2007. In response, Israel imposed near-hermetic restrictions on all movement of people and goods into and out of Gaza. The closure slashed personal freedoms and economic livelihood, isolated Gaza in general, and largely cut its people off from Palestinians in the West Bank and Jerusalem. Israel argued that these were security measures, while critics charged that the aim was political: to pressure the population and thereby topple Hamas through arbitrary restrictions such as limits on food imports unrelated to security.[61] Gaza was buckling under the pressure; by 2009, truckloads of imports had plummeted by 80 percent, unemployment had shot up to 44 percent, and the export restrictions had shut down 96 percent of local industry.[62] Hamas had been firing rockets from Gaza into civilian areas in Israel's southern region for years; the group accelerated its attacks following the closure, leading up to the war.

Operation Cast Lead involved an air campaign and a ground invasion that wreaked massive destruction in Gaza's densely packed civilian areas. B'Tselem documented more than 1,300 Palestinians killed, approximately 800 of whom were not involved in the fighting. Palestinian sources reported nearly 1,000 Palestinian civilians killed. Israel's air campaign leveled neighborhoods, including public and private property and civilian infrastructure.[63] Israel suffered fourteen deaths, eleven of them soldiers.[64]

The war was a profound shock: Palestinians experienced vast destruction and high casualties in Gaza's already-miserable conditions. Israelis suffered few actual casualties but cowered under rockets fired at civilians in the south. The lopsided power dynamics sparked international outrage; after the fighting, the UN Human Rights Council established a fact-finding commission led by the Jewish South African justice Richard Goldstone.[65] The Israeli government branded the commission rigged and biased and the Human Rights Council as anti-Semitic, and it declined to cooperate with the investigation.[66] Israeli human rights groups, however, had worked extensively during the war to document evidence and events. Independently, a number of these groups supported the investigation and submitted material to advance its research.[67]

The Goldstone report published later in 2009 investigated crimes on both sides. One of its findings—that Israel targeted civilians—ignited fury in Israel. The government responded that the report contained "vicious" assertions, "bending both facts and law," while giving credence to "anti-Israel allegation[s]."[68] Netanyahu's government went into public-relations "overdrive" to discredit the findings.[69] Right-wing activists—and many mainstream Israelis—were enraged by the cooperation of Israeli NGOs, which they saw as no less than crossing lines to help Israel's enemies. The idea that the UN was singling out Israel became axiomatic, and the organizations were on the side of Israel's existential enemies, in this view.

The Israeli–Palestinian conflict became the platform for a major, sustained attack on Israel's civil society organizations that advocated the least popular positions in Israeli society. Today, NGO Monitor, the organization targeting left-wing groups and funding sources, articulates the position on its website:

> NGOs such as B'Tselem, Adalah, and Breaking the Silence receive massive amounts of funding from foreign governments, claiming to promote a human rights agenda in Israel. In reality, these groups focus on delegitimizing and demonizing Israel before international audiences, seeking to generate external pressure outside of Israel's democratic framework.[70]

The text contains the core accusation that soon became ubiquitous in Israeli life: "human rights" was a cover for anti-Israel activity; foreigners were funding these subversive activities. Right-wing activists portrayed these funders as the enemy; they particularly targeted the New Israel Fund, which raised money mostly from liberal American Jewish donors for a range of progressive causes, including the human rights groups that supported the Goldstone commission.[71] In 2010, a right-wing NGO called Im Tirzu ran a public campaign against the president of the New Israel Fund in Israel, with ads stating: "Fact! Without the New Israel Fund, there could be no Goldstone Report, and Israel would not be facing international accusations of war crimes."[72]

Im Tirzu and related groups targeted NGOs and academics who encouraged the growing call to boycott Israel or advocated radical positions such as trying senior IDF or political figures in international courts for war crimes. Right-wing groups published lists of left-wing lecturers, arguing that anti-Israel forces were exploiting academic freedom to traduce Israel.[73] In Israeli discourse, terms such as "academic freedom" and even "freedom of speech" came to stand for the accusation of cynical exploitation of those concepts by left-wingers, in order to undermine Israel.[74]

An offshoot right-wing group planted moles in the human rights groups or left-wing anti-occupation groups, seeking to elicit anti-Israel statements or portray activists as criminals. Prominent human rights groups kept their office addresses out of the public eye and hired security firms. When left-wing activists labeled Im Tirzu "fascist" in a public forum, the organization sued for libel, and lost.[75]

Im Tirzu and similar organizations worked closely with the ruling right-wing parties. In 2011, these groups wrote a secret report providing elaborate mappings of the funding sources of left-wing NGOs; the Knesset then approved an initiative by Lieberman's Yisrael Beiteinu to investigate numerous anti-occupation groups. A shouting match erupted in the Knesset over the vote, as right-wing and left-wing legislators traded accusations of defaming the IDF and McCarthyism (respectively).[76] The idea stalled, Likud lawmakers were split, and Netanyahu himself opposed it.

The term "human rights" was increasingly used to imply anti-Israel activity. In 2011, the Knesset began debating a bill to tax the relevant human rights civil society groups at a rate of 45 percent for donations from "foreign government entities." The original bill specified that the law applied to organizations that were opposed to Israel as a Jewish and democratic state; supported putting Israeli figures on trial for war crimes in international or foreign courts; supported refusing IDF service or supported boycott. Likud and Yisrael Beiteinu sponsors stated: "These organizations, which sometimes call themselves 'human rights organizations,' receive funding from states and sources that are anonymous, whose aim is to harm ... public political discourse in Israel."[77]

In 2016, the Knesset finally passed an amendment targeting left-wing NGOs, under another Netanyahu-led, right-wing coalition. Again, the initial draconian bill had been diluted; but the law was still tailored to the funding structure of anti-occupation human rights groups, requiring these organizations to label all their materials to indicate that they receive foreign entity funds.[78] It hardly mattered that such information was already public, and the vast majority of such funds came from friendly, democratic allies, such as foundations affiliated with the EU and governments of the US, the UK, Canada, Germany, and countries of Scandinavia.

The law allowed private donors to remain anonymous; a new array of far-right groups had sprung up in the 2000s and received much of their funding from sources listed in public records as simply "private donor." Michal Rozin of Meretz called the new NGO funding disclosure law a "targeted killing" of left-wing groups. "The law will not expose the fat donations enjoyed by organizations such as Elad [a group working to expand settlements in Palestinian neighborhoods in East Jerusalem] or Im Tirzu, or those of the Prime Minister." Isaac Herzog, then leader of the opposition and the Labor Party and future president of the state (descended from the first chief Ashkenazi rabbi and the son of the sixth president), said that the NGO law symbolized the "seeds of fascism."[79]

After years of battering the concept of human rights, surveys showed declining support among the public. In a 2011 poll, 65 percent of the Jews surveyed gave favorable marks to "human rights," but by 2016, that portion had dropped 20 points, to just 45 percent, later hovering around the 50 percent mark. Just 19 percent of all Israelis (including both Jews and Arabs) expressed favorable opinions toward Israeli organizations dedicated to protecting Palestinian human rights, as seen in the graph in figure 3.[80]

Legislation continued to put pressure on left-wing political activities through civil society: in 2017, a new law restricted funding and certain voter turnout efforts by civil society groups, developed in response to civil society activism on the center-left.[81] Another law permitted authorities to deny entry to foreigners who had expressed support for boycott efforts. After a two-year court battle, the representative of Human Rights Watch in Israel and Palestine was expelled from the country, based on statements that he had made years earlier as a student, sympathetic to the boycott of Israel for occupation policies.[82]

International democracy indexes took notice. In 2018, after years of stable and robust freedom ratings in Freedom House's annual index (which assesses Israel separately from the West Bank and Gaza), the organization's "Freedom in the World" demoted Israel's civil liberties score slightly, citing pressure on NGOs and the anti-boycott legislation.[83]

Figure 3: Favorability toward human rights in general, Israeli organizations working with Palestinians, 2016–21% favorable (Representative sample of adult Israelis, samples range from n=700–800, Jews and Arabs). Graph created by author. Data source: Surveys commission by B'Tselem, conducted by the author.

Right-Wing and Democracy, Transformed

Interestingly, during the 2010s, certain right-wing groups began to embrace the same concepts and language of civil rights, democracy, and equality. Newly influential research and policy groups began advocating an emerging type of right-wing nationalist, populist agenda that also took on libertarian elements. It appeared that after discrediting concepts of democracy and civil rights when they came from Israel's Left, such actors believed that the language of democracy and rights did hold currency—as long as "rights" applied mainly to Israeli Jews.

In 2015, Jewish Israelis committed an arson attack, killing the parents and a toddler of the Dawabshe family while they slept in their home in Duma, near Hebron. The only survivor was a severely burned four-year-old child. When the suspects were found, an organization called Honenu defended them.[84] Honenu immediately accused security services of committing torture to extract confessions, and eventually filed motions to strike the Jewish suspects' confessions.[85] Back in 1999, the Public Committee against Torture in Israel (PCATI) had finally achieved a landmark Supreme Court ruling placing significant limitations on Shabak's use of interrogation methods that petitioners considered to be torture (once again, the justices had beseeched the Knesset to pass clear legislation, anticipating a backlash against Court intervention).[86]

In 2018, a district court issued a partial victory for the two main Duma suspects (one of them a minor), dismissing some of the confessions. One of the lawyers was the longtime far-right activist, Itamar Ben-Gvir.[87]

PCATI and Physicians for Human Rights approved of the decision regarding the Jewish Israeli terror suspects by reiterating the Supreme Court ruling of 1999 and expressing hopes that Israeli society would reject torture in "less high-profile cases," including against Palestinian suspects.[88] Honenu boasted of the victory but was displeased when the adult defendant was finally convicted in 2020 and sentenced to three life terms. The Supreme Court also rejected Honenu's appeal. "We hoped to find a Supreme Court sympathetic to human rights, justice, and integrity, but we are not surprised to find that the judges are out of touch, working mainly to advance a specific agenda," the organization wrote in response.[89] Honenu's website (2023) states its approach to the judiciary: "In recent decades, the legal system in Israel has undergone an alarming process of blurring identities.... The Jewish national element in the state of Israel is losing its values in legal discourse, and is being replaced permanently by the value of total equality."[90]

Honenu represented an extreme end of the fringe right in Israel at the time. Other right-wing groups in the 2010s were far less radical in tone and focused much more substantively on changes to Israeli policy and institutions in general.

The most important of these was the Kohelet Policy Forum, founded in 2012. The organization's founder, Moshe Koppel, stated that the group aims to strengthen "national sovereignty as well as individual liberty," while advancing free-market principles; to do this, Koppel explained, the group "helps" legislators.[91]

Kohelet became one of the leading groups advancing judicial restraint, introducing draft legislation and public events around the issue, and had close relations with Israel's justice minister, Ayelet Shaked, from 2015 to 2019. Kohelet's researchers have argued that Supreme Court rulings are "an affront to Israeli democracy and sovereignty."[92] The anti-judiciary agenda went well beyond the Supreme Court, criticizing and calling to constrain the roles of the attorney general and the state prosecutor, as well. Figures associated with Kohelet were strong advocates for the nation-state law, which came up for debate throughout the decade; the group sponsored public events advancing Israeli annexation of settlements, where Netanyahu was a speaker, and helped establish an organization aimed directly at advancing and advocating West Bank settlement.[93]

The Israel Law and Liberty Forum was established in 2019 and "inspired" by the Federalist Society, according to the group.[94] The organization "advances a conservative legal worldview based on four core principles: the separation of powers, judicial restraint, individual liberty, and limited government" and accused Israeli academia, media, and intellectuals of an "orthodoxy" promoting judicial supremacy. Another new group was Meshilut: the Movement for Governability and Democracy; the word "governability" was used with increasingly authoritarian overtones, to describe executive power without legal restraints. That group was cofounded by Simcha Rothman, "a leading voice in the fight against judicial activism and for the proper separation of powers in Israel."[95] Within a few years, Rothman would become the head of Israel's Constitution, Law and Justice Committee.

Putting the Nationalism Back into Populism

In 2018, the Israeli government took a leap to legislate the identity of the Jewish state and the exclusive Jewish right to self-determination in Israel. Netanyahu was still prime minister and, since 2015, had led a coalition of all right-wing parties. After years of debate, the Knesset finally passed the Basic Law: Israel as the Nation-State of the Jewish People (informally called the "nation-state law"). The law stated: "The realization of the right to national self-determination in the State of Israel is exclusive to the Jewish People." The remaining citizens—about one-quarter of the population, when it was passed—are not included.[96]

The law commits to preserving Jewish history, culture, identity, and holidays and defining the national symbols—most of which reinforced the long-existing reality. The law commits to Jewish settlement (without specifying where) and gives "special status" to the Arabic language, demoting it from an official language, and commits Israel to working for "the welfare of members of the Jewish People and of its citizens."[97]

As in the past, the word "equality" never appears; nor does "democracy." Analysts at the Israel Democracy Institute were hard-pressed to find any national constitution—in democracies or even many non-democracies—that failed to provide an explicit guarantee of equality to all citizens.[98]

In contrast to the Basic Law on Human Dignity and Liberty, the nation-state law is entrenched and can be changed only by another Basic Law, to be passed by a majority of sixty-one legislators. Its supporters claimed that many normal democratic nation-states, such as Germany, Spain, and Slovakia, define national identity in their constitution. The essential difference was that those constitutions explicitly establish and entrench equality and human rights; moreover, some, such as Spain and Slovakia, explicitly refer to national minorities and ethnicities as equal and integral to the citizen body.[99]

Critics saw the law as a profound blow for democracy, fostered by the extreme Right. But earlier versions of the nation-state bill came from some of Israel's most mainstream politicians from the centrist parties Kadima and Likud. A 2013 draft was cosponsored by Ayelet Shaked of Jewish Home, Yariv Levin of Likud, and a member of Lieberman's Yisrael Beiteinu. Netanyahu had supported the 2013 bill, under certain conditions.[100] That version stated that Israel is "a democratic state, anchored in the foundations of freedom, justice and peace, according to the vision of the prophets of Israel, and maintains the personal rights of all its citizens according to the law."[101]

In March 2018, Betzalel Smotrich—one of the country's most extreme national-religious right-wing legislators, from a faction within the Jewish Home Party—sponsored a version creating the right to establish communities segregated by religion or nation. The opposition submitted 800 challenges to the law.[102] Members from Labor (then the Zionist Union) and Meretz were horrified. "You killed equality, and now you're killing democracy?" asked Revital Sweid, of Labor. Others accused the bill of advancing open apartheid. The left-leaning legislators were particularly stunned that the representative of Kulanu, a short-lived, seemingly center-right party that had broken from Likud, supported the bill. Kulanu representative Roy Folkman insisted that his party was proud to support it.[103]

When the nation-state law finally passed in the summer of 2018, democracy supporters were deeply alarmed, and many Arab citizens were terrified. The move seemed to presage new levels of aggression against them. The ramifications of the law were unknown. Far-right voices had once argued that the Nakba did not exist; a few years after the nation-state law, figures from the *mainstream* right—including Likud—suggested that there ought to be a *new* Nakba.[104] The small, Arab, non-nationalist Druze community in Israel had historically taken an integrationist path, serving in the police and even the army since independence. This group was stunned; they saw the law as a betrayal of their loyalty and as a threat. Druze communities mounted an emotional large-scale demonstration in central Tel Aviv.

Fifteen different petitions against the law were submitted to the Israeli Supreme Court by political parties, civil rights groups, individuals, and a mayor of an Arab town, but in 2021 an expanded panel ruled against all of them, with one dissenting justice out of eleven. Right-wing figures were incensed that the Court agreed to rule at all on a Basic Law, which, they argued, represented a brutal suppression of legislators representing the people.[105] Once again, Freedom House's "Freedom in the World" index demoted Israel's score by one point—this time, in the category of political rights, citing the nation-state law.[106]

Chapter 20: Accelerated Assault on Institutions

The nation-state law represented one of the themes swirling among right-wing circles throughout the decade: anti-left and anti-Arab sentiment, Jewish triumphalism, sentiment against migrants (non-Jewish migrants from African countries), and support for settlement expansion and annexation in the Occupied Territories. The issue of annexation, in particular, was impossible to separate from the rising campaign against the power of the Israeli judiciary.

Right-wing parties seemed to be outbidding one another for more extreme positions. It was becoming fully accepted throughout the decade to advocate for annexation. Ahead of the 2013 elections, the new leader of the Jewish Home Party, Naftali Bennett, proposed annexing Area C—the Oslo-designated land constituting 60 percent of the West Bank, a geographic formation that cut the remaining Palestinian areas into pieces. He wasn't the first to suggest this: Danny Danon of Likud had argued as much in an op-ed in the *New York Times* in 2011.[107] Bennett made annexation his platform and won twelve seats in his first election, and then entered the governing coalition. Once again, parties considered mainstream and far-right were fundamentally aligned on the goal. And as the peace process stagnated to a near-standstill, while Israel fought a series of wars with Hamas, the Jewish population continued to reelect right-wing governments. More and more Israeli Jews self-identified as right-wing in surveys.

In 2017, the Likud Central Committee voted for a resolution supporting the annexation of settlements.[108] Numerous Likud legislators had stated their support, including deputy foreign minister Tzipi Hotovely. Another high-level Likud figure, Yuli Edelstein, declared his support at the conference of the "Sovereignty" movement. The annexation proposals floated at this time varied but were brazen by historical standards, including formal annexation of all settlements; annexation of Area C, the whole West Bank, the Jordan Valley, or key individual settlements such as Ariel, planted halfway between Israel and Jordan.[109]

But more important than the Likud declaration was a law passed earlier that year, in February 2017, to legalize settlements even on privately owned Palestinian land. The law represented annexation by extending the Knesset's jurisdiction over territory, not just people.[110] The Judea and Samaria Settlement Regulation Law would retroactively legitimize such settlements or outposts for Israel, but all settlements remain illegal under Israeli law. The law was also deeply controversial; even right-wing figures such as the president—Reuven Rivlin, a former Likud member—crossed a burning rhetorical line by warning that Israel would look like an apartheid state.[111]

When the law passed, challengers quickly appealed to the Supreme Court. The government's own attorney general sought to freeze its implementation and refused to defend the law in Court.[112] In 2020, the Court struck down the settlement regulation law. Once again, Israel's right wing was furious at the Court, despite the historical legitimization of the vast majority of settlements through Court rulings, or by the Court declining to rule, over the years.

More far-reaching annexation plans and other illiberal policies seemed to depend on one critical change: the Knesset needed formal powers to overrule whatever Court decisions it viewed as an obstacle.

In the second half of the 2010s, the mounting attacks on the Court seemed to reach a new level. In 2015, the right-wing parties won sixty-seven seats; Netanyahu's Likud came in first place by a healthy margin and formed the next coalition. Jewish Home was a key coalition partner and received choice coalition portfolios. Ayelet Shaked became justice minister.

Like Bennett and Lieberman, Shaked began her career as a staff member at the prime minister's office under Netanyahu, before joining Naftali Bennett's Jewish Home Party. She entered the Knesset in 2013 and joined the vocal opposition to the migrants from African countries; when the Court ruled in favor of asylum seekers, she had angrily stated that the Court's verdict "is a blow to the principle of separation of powers and to democracy... . Therefore, I see no option but to legislate an override clause ... even if it contradicts the Supreme Court. The Knesset is sovereign." She repeatedly stressed the insidious erosion of the authority of the Knesset in recent years. When the override bill passed the first approval in a ministerial committee in 2014, she said that "we cannot allow the legislator to be bound and cuffed by the judicial branch, and its status is damaged again and again."[113]

As justice minister under Netanyahu's fully right-wing coalition from 2015, Shaked had a well-developed position on the judiciary that revolved around three aspects: greater control of the governing coalition over the judicial appointment committee; allowing the Knesset by law to override the Supreme Court; and appointing "conservative" judges. In the Israeli context, "conservative" can refer to legal conservatism (meaning opposing judicial activism), or to the right wing in the nationalist sense—or both. Giving greater weight to politicians on the judicial selection committee was intended to allow politicians from the governing coalition to overrule the three justices on the nine-member committee. Critics had long claimed that justices on the committee were prone to appointing colleagues who represented a homogenous, liberal, and activist ideology; the critics claimed that "judges elect themselves." The argument usually included the accusation that historically marginalized groups were not represented on the Supreme Court. The plans became Shaked's signature political program; and party leader Naftali Bennett was no less invested in the mission.

Emerging new right-wing media outlets rallied to the campaign. The online portal Mida was established in 2012, giving voice to far-right and religious perspectives. The free newspaper supporting Netanyahu, *Israel Hayom* (Israel Today), established in 2007 by the American casino magnate Sheldon Adelson, was by now the top-circulating daily paper on weekdays and took a relentlessly anti-judiciary line.[114] A new right-wing television channel targeting religious Jews in Israel began broadcasting in 2014. These and other existing right-wing publications seemed to converge around the increasingly hostile criticism of the Supreme Court.

In 2019, Simcha Rothman, the religious settler and cofounder of the Movement for Governability and Democracy (Meshilut), published a book, *The Ruling Party of Bagatz: How Israel Became a Legalocracy.* Rothman argued that the Court effectively staged a political putsch and clambered over the Knesset and that justices have nearly unlimited power, compared with all other branches of government.[115] His analysis seems to contradict Alexander Hamilton, who argued that the judicial branch "is beyond comparison the weakest of the three departments of power." Hamilton asserted that "the general liberty of the people can never be endangered from that quarter," as long as the judiciary was independent. Rothman accused the Israeli judiciary of destroying the separation of powers by intervening in the Knesset's role of creating law; but Hamilton's view was that the judiciary "can never attack with success either of the other two [branches]; and that all possible care is requisite to enable it to defend itself against their attacks."[116]

Yet Rothman's arguments became increasingly powerful. Separation of powers meant that the Court must not review legislation. Using the legislature to constrain the Court represented a fulfillment of democracy. Failure to stop the Court meant permitting the destruction of the people's will, and the people meant the majority, with no further constraints.

But majority rule raised a problem: the more Israel advanced annexation, the more it risked losing the Jewish majority. One solution was the more selective annexation plans for the West Bank, leaving Gaza out and focusing primarily on Area C, as in Bennett's plan. But to ensure that Jewish identity could be secured, and democratic standards could be suppressed in any scenario, eroding judicial review and delegitimizing the Supreme Court were convenient first steps.[117]

All these processes were in place just as a new factor was emerging that would powerfully tip the scales in favor of the anti-judiciary wave. Netanyahu found himself under investigation, and then indictment, on serious charges of corruption.

Netanyahu Fills His Own Shoes

Despite the rising vitriol against the judiciary throughout the decade, by 2019, the policies to constrain the judiciary (and the most extreme annexation policies) had not materialized. Public criticism in the media provided some normative counterweight. And at critical junctures, Benjamin Netanyahu held his governments back.

Why? Many have struggled to discern whether Netanyahu is motivated by a guiding ideology, or by simple political ambition. He seemed committed to the principle of judicial independence and holding back hotheads at one time. "I believe that in a democracy, a strong and independent Court is what enables the existence of all other democratic institutions," he said in February 2012, following a raft of antidemocratic legislative efforts (during the Eighteenth Knesset). "Just in the last few months, I buried every law that threatens the independence of the system ... and I will continue to do so."[118]

Later, this quote would be revived as a new Netanyahu government sought to dismantle judicial independence entirely, starting in late 2022. Numerous articles cited the same quote, possibly because there were few such statements to choose from.

But Netanyahu also respected Aharon Barak, who reportedly said: "Bibi is committed to the rule of law and will not lend a hand to harming it—among other reasons because of his American education and his demonstrable admiration for the conservative wing of the Republicans who view the Constitution as the rock of ages for the American people."[119] Netanyahu stalled Shaked's efforts to advance an override law, at Barak's urging. In 2019, Barak stated: "Netanyahu has said repeatedly, at every opportunity, that he would not allow harm to the Court."[120]

But Netanyahu was also the unrivaled leader of the Likud that advanced the illiberal bills and sponsored the anti-judiciary legislation, the nation-state law, and the settlement regularization law. He oversaw the withering of prospects for a two-state solution and has maintained Israel's stranglehold policy over Gaza, although he initiated none of these processes. In 2015, he declared that he opposed a Palestinian state while the number of West Bank settlers grew by over 50 percent under his long, consecutive terms.[121] Netanyahu regularly incited against Arab political leadership in Israel, represented Arab voters as a threat to the country, or implied that their political representatives did not count in governing. He dragged out the formation of a new public television corporation to replace the old Israel Broadcast Authority, prompting suspicions that he hoped to undercut public television and critical media.[122] At one point, he held five simultaneous ministries.[123]

Netanyahu forged a series of bold foreign relations with dictator-level authoritarians such as Ilham Aliyev of Azerbaijan and revived diplomatic relations with

Chad, at the time run by the late dictator Idris Déby. From about 2016 onward, Netanyahu accelerated his efforts to forge alliances with illiberal populists around the world who were central to his own political persona. These included Rodrigo Duterte of the Philippines, Jair Bolsonaro of Brazil, Viktor Orbán of Hungary, and Narendra Modi of India, as well as Donald Trump and even Vladimir Putin.

Thus, Netanyahu's own commitment to democratic values was already questionable when, in 2016, police began looking at corruption allegations. There was his shady support for Israel purchasing German submarines that the country might not have needed, which benefited his cronies and possibly his family members.[124] Another file involved accepting luxury items from a businessman crony (often described as the "cigars and champagne" case), possibly in return for help with tax breaks and regulatory favors. There were also two media-related charges—both related to Netanyahu's attempts to orchestrate favorable media coverage by providing regulatory favors or interference in the editorial process. By late 2017, Netanyahu was formally named as a suspect in three cases but not in the submarine purchase, which would have been the most serious.[125]

Netanyahu then made a shift with enormous consequences for the country as a whole. Regardless of what he had thought up to that point about attacks on the judiciary, he now threw the full public weight and rhetorical force of King Bibi behind the attacks—this time, painting himself as the victim.

First, he insisted that the charges would come to naught. He led chants of "nothing will happen, because nothing happened!" (It sounds better in Hebrew.) He portrayed the investigation as political persecution, although he himself had appointed the police chief; he accused the media of hyperinflating the story out of hatred. In late 2017, his party sought to fast-track a bill that would have prevented police from recommending indictment of public figures following their investigation, to be applied retroactively on open investigations; when a massive public street protest erupted, legislators watered down the bill.[126]

In February 2018, the police issued their recommendation to indict Netanyahu in all three cases under investigation. His supporters began to rally: surveys showed that Netanyahu's favorability, which was an unflattering 32 percent positive rate in 2016, had risen to 41 percent by December 2018. Among the Jewish population, support rose 10 points, from 37 to 47 percent. In most surveys since about 2019, Netanyahu's ratings among Jewish Israelis have been remarkably stable: around 45 percent, by various measures.[127] Netanyahu's survey ratings began to decline in 2023, following the attempted judicial overhaul.

In February 2019, Attorney General Avichai Mandelblit conveyed that he was likely to indict Netanyahu; in November, he announced the indictment. In January 2020, Mandelblit formally served the charges: bribery, fraud, and breach of trust.

In response to the February 2019 announcement, Netanyahu gave an impassioned speech that the *New York Times* described as: "angry and choked up, sneering and defiant."[128] He opened by thanking "my friends" Vladimir Putin and Donald Trump on foreign affairs issues, and then issued a full-blown conspiratorial, deep-state screed:

> Now, the left knows that they can't defeat us at the ballot boxes with those kinds of achievements. And that's why for three years they've been engaged in political persecution against us... . They mounted a thuggish, incessant pressure campaign—I'd say almost inhuman—on the attorney general... . Now, since the attorney general is only flesh and blood, the left wing's pressure succeeded... . In this witch hunt against me, they've balked at nothing. They've spilled and continue to spill my wife's blood. They've been persecuting my son. They've put my family for the past three years through seven circles of hell."[129]

The "spilled my blood" language had a long history in Netanyahu's responses to accusations of wrongdoings in earlier years.

In November 2019, when Mandelblit announced the actual indictment, Netanyahu called the charges a full-blown attempted coup. He insisted that the state prosecutor had put pressure on the attorney general that violated all norms (Netanyahu had appointed both the attorney general and the police chief). He accused the investigators of threatening and blackmailing witnesses, forcing them to lie and incriminate him. Then he called to "investigate the investigators," which a veteran commentator called "seditious."[130]

Now under indictment, Netanyahu also faced electoral trouble. He had led a fairly stable, fully right-wing, coalition for nearly four years, and in the April 2019 election, the parties of his outgoing coalition seemed to win a comfortable sixty-five-seat majority. But this time, Avigdor Lieberman refused to join his coalition, leaving him without a majority. The move sparked paralysis and fresh elections. Then other right-wing figures broke with Netanyahu, claiming that they would not support a leader facing indictment (though surely, their own political ambition was not far behind in these considerations).

Netanyahu began firing off accusations of "left-wing" at anyone who crossed him. He continued to harangue key figures of the law; as his trial opened in the Jerusalem District Court in 2020, he gave an infamous speech standing in the halls of the Court, railing against police and the prosecution and carefully, but clearly, also undermining the attorney general, calling the cases "fabricated."[131]

Netanyahu's inability to form a coalition after April 2019 touched off a series of inconclusive elections that paralyzed the country through 2022, while he remained caretaker prime minister but was unable to woo sufficient support even from certain right-wing parties to form a coalition. Neither Netanyahu nor other right-wing anti-judiciary communities paid much attention when the courts ruled in their favor. In 2020, for example, citizens petitioned the Supreme Court to prevent Netanyahu from serving as prime minister because of his corruption cases; the court rejected the petition and allowed him to remain in office.[132] This development did little to disrupt Netanyahu's victim-of-the-court narrative.

The full drama of Israel's five election cycles from 2019 to 2022 could fill its own book. But until 2021, Netanyahu remained prime minister.

The situation raised a democratic conundrum: Was the active trial of a sitting prime minister and the electoral paralysis a sign of democratic collapse, or of institutional resilience? Despite his toxic rhetoric, Netanyahu cooperated with the trial. The country's institutions continued to function throughout unprecedented political instability.

On the other hand, Netanyahu was leading the government in a state that was currently prosecuting him, which many viewed as an intolerable conflict of interest—conceptually, if not legally. What precedent did this set for a generation of young Israelis who had known few other leaders? Some believed Netanyahu: in November 2019, 36 percent agreed with him that the entire legal proceedings against him were "polluted" and trumped up to oust him, while 52 percent disagreed. But among Jewish Israelis, 41 percent agreed with his claims of a political witch hunt.[133]

The same 2019 survey recorded a plunge in optimism in the future of Israeli democracy, from 54 percent that April to 32 percent in November, after the second paralyzed election and the indictment. Center and left-wing respondents were consumed with fears about democracy. Fully 85 percent of left-wingers and more than 60 percent of centrists believed that democracy was in grave danger.[134]

Those respondents probably had the electoral paralysis and Netanyahu's ongoing rule in mind. For his part, Netanyahu forged ahead with actual policies that were undemocratic in themselves, or not conducive to it. In April 2019, Netanyahu openly embraced the annexation agenda, stating, days ahead of the elections, that he supported "extending sovereignty" over all Israeli settlements in the West Bank.[135] In September of that year, again close to the second election in the cycle, Netanyahu unveiled a plan to annex the Jordan Valley.[136] In 2020, President Trump finally released a much-rumored "peace plan" that involved Israel annexing huge swaths of the West Bank, leaving Palestinians with enclaves of land encompassing the mostly urban population centers—disconnected, ungovernable, surrounded by Israel—to be called a Palestinian state.

Netanyahu announced that formal annexation would begin on July 1, 2020, raising international anxiety and a heightened sense of local anticipation. But Netanyahu had a flair for grand surprises and pulled a side move instead, suddenly announcing that Israel had achieved a breakthrough deal to normalize relations with the United Arab Emirates (UAE). Shortly afterward, Bahrain followed; then came two more agreements, with Morocco and a preliminary agreement with Sudan. The US brokered the agreements, calling them the Abraham Accords, which ranked among the flagship foreign policy achievements of the Trump administration. The UAE, for its part, portrayed the August 2020 agreement as a quid pro quo in which Israel had agreed to suspend its declaration of annexation.

The Abraham Accords signaled a major realignment and even a paradigm shift in the Middle East. They strengthened the alliance of countries seeking to block Iranian power in the region, while breaking the leverage of non-normalization as an incentive for Israel to end occupation and resolve the conflict.

But the accords also meant that Israel was deepening its alliances with undemocratic and authoritarian countries. The accords enabled the occupation status quo—along with the death of the peace process, preventing Palestinian self-determination, the ongoing closure and isolation of Gaza, the undemocratic regime in the West Bank, and creeping annexation that violated international law—all of this was increasingly inseparable from Israel's institutions, laws, and identity.

Crises of Constitutional Magnitude

Since about 2020, Israel has experienced unprecedented political, social, and legal crises, including the five rapid-fire election cycles (beginning in 2019) and violent social conflict among Israel's own citizens. But the more dire developments during the same period have been threats to the constitutional order, meaning open conflicts between branches of power, collapsing consensus even at the political level about the sources of authority, and breakdown of the contract between citizens and the state. These structural crises are the manifestation of the weak or missing foundations of democracy, which appeared poised to overwhelm the democratic elements of Israeli society, no matter how robust.

In 2020, Freedom House gave Israel its lowest overall score to date, though still ranking the country squarely in the "free" category, by focusing only on the governance of Israeli citizens. The decline was incremental but steady, as the table below shows.

Historic events—such as the sequence of inconclusive elections, the Covid-19 pandemic, further rounds of Israeli-Palestinian violence on both sides of the Green Line—provided the backdrop for the crises that exposed Israel's democratic vulnerabilities.

Table 2: Decline in Freedom House Scores for Israel, 2017–2022.

Year of Report (based on previous year)	Overall Score (100)	Political Rights (40)	Civil Liberties (60)	Reason for Change
2017	80	36	44	
2018	79	36	43	Anti-boycott & anti-NGO laws
2019	78	35	43	Nation-State Law (2018)
2020	76	33	43	Election paralysis (2019), PM/corruption, delegitimization of law enforcement
2021	76	33	43	
2022	76	34	42	May 2021

[Source: Freedom in the World; table compiled by author][137]

One such constitutional crisis occurred in March 2020, when Israel held its third sequential election, which again proved inconclusive. The pandemic was beginning to ravage the world; still the caretaker prime minister, Netanyahu implemented the early stages of lockdown. Like most people around the world, Israelis were confused by and fearful of the restrictions (which Israel introduced relatively early), in addition to their profound political uncertainty.

After the March elections, the lawmakers were sworn in; normally, the Knesset would at that time elect a new chair (the equivalent of the US Speaker of the House), with little fanfare. But suddenly, the outgoing Likud chair, Yuli Edelstein, blocked the vote, along with the formation of Knesset committees, which the competitor party Blue and White was slated to win. To stop the vote, Edelstein suspended the Knesset. Other parties rushed to the Supreme Court, which ordered Edelstein to hold the vote; instead, Edelstein resigned as chair.[138] The public was shocked by the double blow of the suspension and direct defiance of a Supreme Court order (though clearly, opinions broke down by political leanings). Who was in control? The lines of authority were scrambled just as Israelis were confronting extraordinary restrictions due to Covid-19 and the government most needed the people's trust.

The day after Edelstein resigned, the crisis subsided; the Knesset held the vote and elected the leader of Blue and White temporarily. The arrangement was part of a political bargain that put a Likud lawmaker into the position of speaker once again, and created an ill-fated unity coalition between the two parties that kept Netanyahu in power. The incident was a harbinger of things to come.

The lockdown went into full effect, with severe restrictions on physical movement. Israelis were shaken, and small groups of citizens quickly raised the alarm about government overreach; only a few lone voices wondered why those complaining of movement restrictions hardly considered that Israel had been implementing just such policies against Palestinians for decades.

The next major crisis was the outbreak of political violence among Israel's own citizens, against the backdrop of the Israeli–Palestinian conflict, in May 2021.

The shaky coalition quickly collapsed, and yet another election—the fourth round—was held in March 2021. This time, the parties opposing Netanyahu were on the verge of reaching a coalition deal that would have ousted him as prime minister for the first time since 2009. In May, clashes broke out at the al-Aqsa mosque in Jerusalem, alongside long-running legal battles by Israelis to evict Palestinians from their East Jerusalem homes; these clashes touched off a new round of fighting between Israel and Hamas in Gaza.[139] Arab (Palestinian) citizens around the country demonstrated in solidarity, generating friction with ultranationalist Jewish groups. Finally, Arab and Jewish citizens clashed as mobs attacked members of the other group or their property in various towns; the country braced for full-out ethnic conflict. The violence on all fronts subsided in two weeks, but the trauma and the political consequences lingered. It was not a constitutional crisis but a dark indication that the escalating hostilities of the last decade—sometimes goaded by the political leadership—were fueling a new type of political violence.

Nevertheless, a few weeks later, in June 2021, eight parties that opposed Netanyahu remaining in power established a diverse coalition, with a thin, sixty-one-seat parliamentary majority out of 120. Immediately, the right wing, led by Netanyahu, accused the new coalition of being antidemocratic. One key party that joined the government was the right-wing nationalist party called Yamina, which voters believed would remain loyal to Netanyahu; they now felt betrayed. To cajole Yamina into the coalition with the much larger Yesh Atid Party, Yamina Party leader Naftali Bennett would serve as prime minister first, in a rotation, though Yamina had won less than 6 percent of the vote.[140]

Yet the new government made one major breakthrough for democratic practice. Since 1948, no independent Arab party had ever joined the governing coalition but had served only as legislators. These parties were never invited, and given their own inner conflicts over legitimizing Israel's government or taking part in its policies, it was too sensitive for most to try. Now, with the anti-Netanyahu parties desperate for a majority, they made a deal to include Raam, an Arab party representing the Islamic movement in Israel, in the coalition. The new government thus broke a decades-old psychological and political barrier for both Arabs and Jews in Israel. It was a qualified breakthrough in democratic terms. The coalition parties could tolerate Raam, because the party leader, Mansour Abbas, explicitly set aside the Palestinian issue to prioritize the urgent concerns of Arab citizens in Israel in daily life. To this end, he advocated political partnership, which many Israelis found refreshing. But it was his erstwhile political ally, Ayman Odeh, who had made his national political debut in 2015 as a passionate advocate for Jewish-Arab partnership. Odeh led Hadash, the left-wing party committed to ending the occupation (the party name is an acronym, and the letter 'd' stands for 'democracy'), then forged a combined list of all Arab parties called the Joint List. Raam had left the alliance by 2021. Israeli society could barely tolerate a conservative Islamist Arab party that downplayed the Palestinian issue in its coalition, but it could not countenance an Arab party committed to ending Israel's most undemocratic policy. Nevertheless, many right-wing Israelis were enraged that Raam joined, while the opposition—Netanyahu's camp—insisted that the government was at the mercy of terror supporters.

The new government that had formed in June 2021 promised a new spirit of cooperation and compromise. But it was to fall, precisely over the same issues as previous coalitions: first religion and state, and then the Israeli-Palestinian conflict and—underlying both—the meaning of democratic practice. In the spring of 2022, the health minister from the liberal Meretz told hospitals that they could not prevent visitors from bringing food that was not kosher for Passover, following a Supreme Court ruling that had upheld this position in the previous year. A religious lawmaker quit the coalition over the issue.[141] Unrelated to the first crisis, clashes at the Temple Mount followed shortly afterward, and the already slim coalition teetered.

Finally, the Knesset prepared to vote on the special legislation that extends parts of Israeli laws to settlers in the Occupied Territories. The Knesset had voted every five years since 1967 to extend the "temporary" order (discussed in Chapter 9) before it expired, each time passing the extensions unremarkably—almost unnoticed. But Netanyahu and the opposition were determined to topple the government; to this end, they voted *against* the extension in 2022, hoping to trigger a coalition crisis if it did not pass. Suddenly, Israelis understood how disruptive it would be if whole swaths of Israeli laws governing settler lives were no longer valid. Some raised eyebrows at the fact that the pro-settlement Likud brazenly voted against its own principles—since the law helps settlers. But Netanyahu knew what he was doing: the coalition was unable to extend the law (which was still in force until the expiration date). It was the final crisis; the government fell after one year, sparking fresh elections. Israel's post-1996 average Knesset term was now just 2.4 years, making it the least stable of twenty-one other established democracies, according to the Israel Democracy Institute.[142]

Calling elections also triggered an automatic extension of the 1967 law that applied sections of Israeli law for settlers in the West Bank, until the new Knesset was sworn in. After the 2022 elections were over, the new legislature easily extended the law, a key pillar of the separate, unequal, and undemocratic legal regimes in the West Bank. Israel sacrificed its government for the sake of maintaining the regime.

The 2022 election finally gave Netanyahu a clear victory, with a majority of seats going to Likud and its far-right, ultranationalist, religious and ultra-Orthodox allies. By this time, Likud was transformed. Gone was Jabotinsky's or Begin's right wing, with its tension between the liberal constitutional values and Jewish nationalist territorial maximalism. Likud had become a party of Netanyahu loyalists, largely committed to the illiberal populist agenda that they had promoted for years, trafficking in incitement against Arab citizens, against non-Jewish migrants and asylum seekers, and against left-wing Jewish Israelis. This Likud was committed to annexation, and indulging the ultra-Orthodox, as well as a new kind of extremism.

Israelis once viewed Jewish extremists as bad weeds; but Likud was now openly cultivating the crop. Itamar Ben-Gvir had been a Kahanist agitator in the 1990s, prominent in similar circles as Yigal Amir, Rabin's assassin, who would later tell investigators of a rumor that Ben-Gvir himself talked of killing Rabin. Ben-Gvir had faced dozens of arrests and multiple convictions for supporting terror organizations and incitement prior to becoming a lawyer defending Jewish terrorists, and then a leading figure in the extremist Jewish Power Party. For years, the party was viewed as a fringe, radical right-wing force and failed to cross the electoral threshold to enter the Knesset.

But in 2019, Netanyahu began pushing the religious right-wing factions to bring Jewish Power into their fold. In 2022, he nudged the three most extreme nationalist, militant, theocratic, and homophobic religious parties to run together, including Jewish Power. Netanyahu thereby ensured that the combined list (called Religious Zionism, to the chagrin of many religious Zionists) performed well. The party won third place in the 2022 election, with fourteen seats, and joined Netanyahu's new far-right coalition with top ministerial positions. Party leader Bezalel Smotrich was fanatically anti-Arab, and supported total Jewish victory and sovereignty over all of the land. In 2017, he published a lengthy manifesto for complete subjugation of Palestinians, and he regularly called to stop "chasing mosquitoes, but rather [drain] the swamp." Failure to do so, he repeatedly argued, meant "some mosquitoes will always get away and sting you."[143] Smotrich became finance minister and an "additional minister" in the Ministry of Defense, where he insisted on wresting the Civil Administration in the West Bank away from the control of the military and giving it to a civilian—specifically, him. This gambit represented another bureaucratic form of annexation. Ben-Gvir took the portfolio of internal security, which he promptly renamed "National Security," as if to remove any doubt that his first commitment was to the only national group recognized by Israel's history and laws.

Beyond Religious Zionism and the two ultra-Orthodox parties, Netanyahu had no other coalition allies, since other parties declined to serve under a leader standing trial for corruption. Between the Religious Zionism Party's resentment of the Supreme Court, the Haredi parties with their own historical grievances against the law, and Netanyahu's corruption cases, the stage was set for the most extreme attack on the judiciary in Israel's history.

The coalition's "basic outlines" contained a sworn commitment to prioritize what it called judicial reform above all else, while also declaring exclusive Jewish rights to the entire Land of Israel. The new justice minister—from Likud—immediately announced meticulous plans for a near-total executive takeover of the judiciary. Simcha Rothman, one of the most outspoken anti-judiciary figures (discussed in Chapter 18), became chair of the constitutional committee in the Knesset; he embraced the reforms and advanced even more extreme versions.

The first constitutional crisis followed within weeks: in January 2023 the Supreme Court overruled the appointment of Aryeh Deri to two ministerial posts. Deri had served prison time for his 1999 conviction and later returned to Shas as a stalwart Netanyahu ally, but was convicted once again of tax fraud via a plea deal in 2022. For a second time, the Court ruled that Deri's appointment failed the test of "reasonability." The right wing now viewed the "reasonability" argument as toxic proof of the Court's insidious political overreach.

Netanyahu desperately needed to keep Deri on his side and Shas in the coalition, in order to stay in power. Would the prime minister directly defy a Court order? After days of frenzied speculation Netanyahu managed to remove Deri from his ministerial roles and keep Shas in the coalition.

The government survived, and throughout early 2023, raced ahead with plans to gut judicial independence, stack the judicial appointment committee with coalition figures, and ban judicial review of Basic Laws. The reforms would have effectively ended the Court's ability to strike down legislation violating human rights—while establishing near-automatic powers for the coalition to override such a ruling. Another proposal would have annulled the Court's ability to use the argument of "reasonability"—a move critics saw as "tailor-made to allow future Aryeh Deris to . . . steal and lie without consequence."[144]

The legislative effort now threw the country into turmoil. Street protests swelled immediately after the reforms were announced (there had already been protests against the government for what it represented); the demonstrations snowballed to hundreds of thousands who turned up every Saturday night, in Tel Aviv, Jerusalem, and other cities and towns throughout the country, and often during the week. An unprecedented range of social, economic, professional, and academic groups joined longtime interest groups, such as gender equality, LGBTQ, and anti-occupation activists. Demonstrators called strikes and stopped traffic on highways; reservists threatened not to report for training; major high-tech companies threatened to pull out of the country if judicial independence was destroyed; and medical professionals protested that health care would suffer under what the protesters viewed as regime change.

Yet Israeli–Palestinian violence was rising once again. Three months after the government was formed, in March 2023, the defense minister, from Likud, fearing for the army's morale, called to pause the legislation. Netanyahu promptly fired him and the protests went wild, flooding the highways all night after the announcement, and recruiting the Histadrut to call a general strike the following day. Trains overflowed as citizens poured into Jerusalem for colossal protests at the Knesset, which gave way to a massive demonstration in the evening by right-wingers in favor of the changes. Facing national paralysis and credible fears of a civil war, Netanyahu temporarily suspended the judicial overhaul.

Suddenly, Israelis seemed to converge around the realization that Israeli democracy was not at all well. But after many months of dogged Saturday evening mass protests, it was unclear whether Israelis were prepared for a fundamental reassessment of what had gone wrong. Nearly half a year after the protest began, in mid-2023 the movement remained riven between those who longed to return to a romanticized democratic past, and those who viewed the past as the source of the modern-day undemocratic practices that had become normal and transparent to so many. On the ground, those opposed to occupation were baffled as to why the far larger mainstream of Israeli protesters could not see the connection. "We were silent about occupation," read one sign at the demonstrations, "and we ended up with dictatorship." Right-wing, pro-government figures accused the demonstrations of being a movement to preserve the old Ashkenazi hegemony. Prominent Mizrahim split over the reform, and split over what some viewed as exploitation of their history to advance the government's agenda.

The democracy protests therefore opened some of Israel's deepest wounds. They also generated extraordinary public interest in complex topics of law, constitution, and democracy, like a great national civics class. It felt like a rare opportunity for Israelis who had taken democracy for granted to ask the hardest questions —questions the country had never wanted to confront. But as of this writing, their conclusions and answers are unknown; most likely these answers will evolve only in the years and decades to come.

At present, it is clear that, on its seventy-fifth birthday, Israel is ruled by a populist, militant ethno-nationalist government with authoritarian intentions. The government was legitimately elected by the people. And for all his political influence, Netanyahu is not the source of Israel's democratic deficit. He deftly leveraged the country's profound victim mentality, the zeitgeist pitting masses against elites, and his considerable grasp of global politics, making him the perfect populist. But he did not create the deepest gaps, which were never only circumstantial or fixable flaws in an otherwise robust democracy. Israel's democracy was hewn from crooked timber, and the structure itself can collapse. It is up to Israel to chart a different path for its future.

Conclusion

Throughout the research and writing for this book, I kept casting about for the right metaphor. The options seemed to shift with each new layer of discovery and analysis.

My starting point had been the simple arc: Israel was least democratic in its earliest years, as a heavily controlled and centralized statist society with ersatz freedoms but a reality full of constraints, even for Jews. Elections were coercive, one party ruled, the government faced minimal restraints, and the economy was largely controlled—while a portion of the country's own citizens lived entirely under military rule and formal inequality. Since there cannot be democracy for some citizens and not others, Israel cannot be considered democratic in this phase. The best case for democracy at the start is universal suffrage, but the quality of voter choice was significantly compromised.

In the adolescent decades, the country took some important democratizing steps, ending military rule over citizens and enacting a peaceful transition of power, while the judicial branch, media, and civil society became more assertive and increasingly held the state accountable. Israel also simultaneously embarked on its most undemocratic project ever; but who knew at the start how long the occupation would last? In the 1980s and 1990s, Israel embraced its most liberal democratic side in law, politics, economy, and social values, which even leaned progressive. Not coincidentally, this was the time when Israeli leaders took initiative to end the occupation. But in the 2000s, the arc began its decline, converging with the rise of global populist nationalism and a collapsing peace process. Israel's leaders capitalized on nationalist sentiments that they could dependably ignite due to ongoing conflict, and they sought to roll back liberal progress. To implement undemocratic policies, they began to threaten the institutions that made Israel more democratic over the years. The arc metaphor seemed apt.

But the story could often feel less linear. The roots of the national political project were numerous and tangled. These roots converged sufficiently to establish the trunk of the state, the "crooked timber," as Kant observed, regarding human nature. The branches sometimes grow wild, reflecting the contradictions in their roots; therefore the tree metaphor is also relevant.

During an early conversation, a colleague recommended a thematic, rather than chronological, structure, arguing that there was no coherent linear progress but only changes in certain themes. Another friend opined that Israel has always had a conditional democracy, as long as nothing touches security or settlements. In one reverie, I thought about democracy as a pet that the children love but that the adults keep on a leash to prevent it from entering important rooms of the house.

https://doi.org/10.1515/9783110796582-008

Finally, I imagined a mosaic, because democracy has many little pieces (and big ones) that must come together for the whole democratic system to emerge. Apologists would say that Israeli democracy is a miracle in which all these disparate elements miraculously hold together. But while writing this book, I imagined hands trying to paste tiles of democracy to the wall, while other tiles are constantly falling off. If one sticks, another drops. The picture appears to emerge, and then recedes, each time in different places.

Yet there is some continuity. Law and constitution were on a forward trajectory until the latter stagnated and declined. Governance improved by democratic measures, becoming less centralized, more pluralist, and more transparent, if not more stable. Civil society and citizen engagement evolved to be impressively organized and effective over time, until facing a partisan backlash against one political side of civil society activity. The underlying reasons for each setback in each phase, the limitations on all forward motion, and the recent years of illiberal decline always return to core themes: lack of consensus and social contract about the rule of law; powerful constituencies (mainly the ultra-Orthodox) with wide bargaining power that reject secular, civic sources of state authority; ethno-national-religious identity taking priority over equality (i.e., Jewish-Arab inequality); prioritizing territorial expansion over democratic practice; and indulging religious authority over state, public sphere, society, and private life. Democracy has always been subordinate.

Too many constituencies over time have viewed the law as optional or instrumental, while others have been shortchanged for protection or equality under the law, or pushed out altogether: Arab-Palestinian citizens in the early decades and Palestinians under military occupation. Even after the military regime, the democratic process has never served Arab citizens as it has Jews. In the earliest years, the ultra-Orthodox barely accepted the notion of state authority flowing from the people and stymied the adoption of constitutional principles. Later, the activist, messianic settler community sought to circumvent the law, eventually demonizing its institutions for even the minimal limits on their activity. Mizrahi Jews experienced such institutionalized cultural and class marginalization that some of their political communities came to distrust the law, believing that it persecutes their leadership, or preserves the power of Israel's most privileged groups. Security agencies and the upper political strata have, at times, adopted ambiguous, self-selective, instrumental, and mendacious attitudes toward the law. The all-out assault on the judicial branch in Israel under the government established in late 2022 is the most explicit iteration, designed to protect corrupt politicians and to accelerate annexation and theocratic, even supremacist, Jewish rule. But the foundations go much further back.

To reach these insights, the chapters of this book have walked through Israel's history, albeit with painful omissions. Many developments were necessarily omitted, not only because of length but because of the added complexity that they would bring to an already-tangled story. I have been accused of being too "talmudic" in always seeing yet another counterargument.[1] Nevertheless, the process yielded a number of insights that may have been subsumed under the descriptive detail along the way.

These observations are lost among bromides such as "the only democracy in the Middle East" or a "democratic miracle," or when democracy indexes—essential and valuable as they are—draw a border between Israelis and Palestinians that does not exist, or between Israel's democratic regime and occupation, which is equally artificial.

No Special Treatment for Zionism

The first observation that this book yielded for me is that Zionism is not an obstacle to analyzing democracy. I found it surprisingly easy to write a book about democracy in Israel that was not about Zionism per se; it simply meant treating Israel like other nations, as Israel has asked to be treated. There are democracies with national identities, democratic nation-states, and countries that fought wars for their ethno-national self-determination that are laying the groundwork for democracy. Zionism gets no special dispensation to be less democratic than them. Numerous democratic nation-states have constitutions that recognize a national identity alongside prominent statements of equality, with robust institutional provisions to protect, and sometimes recognize, minority identities and rights. This is true in Spain; in Slovakia; in new countries like Kosovo, which fought a bitter war for the majority Albanians to be independent; in Germany; and in India, born nearly at the same time as Israel. Moreover, Zionism, however one defines it, cannot be predicated on preventing the self-determination of Palestinians and still be democratic. The form Palestinian self-determination might take is a subject for other books.

Many Israelis, but mainly the Jewish citizens, have an everyday experience of sufficiently democratic norms *and* the satisfaction of living in a state that expresses their national identity. Over the generations, these citizens believed that the country is democratic enough, based on a faulty story of what democracy is, defining it broadly as majority rule, with ethno-national identity enjoying superior status to inferior democratic norms of equality. Less consciously, perhaps, these citizens implicitly accept the notion that there can be democracy for some—an oxymoron, by any measure.

Yet for mainstream Jewish Israelis, this undemocratic meaning is what they mean by "Jewish and democratic" or "Zionism" itself. For right-wing Israelis, this is not enough: Zionism should mean that Jewish identity is imposed by law on all of society (many religious right-wingers support imposing Jewish practice, too) and that the country must commit itself to territorial expansion even at the expense of the cherished (even fetishized) majority rule.

Striving for real democracy need not deprive Jews of national identity. The Hebrew language is not going away, and the nation-state law demoting the Arabic language did nothing other than provide a slap in the face to Israel's biggest, and native, minority. The Jewish religion feels much more organic and authentic when not imposed. For much of the time that I worked on this book, I studied in Beit Ariela, the Tel Aviv municipal library. In December 2022, the first night of Hanukkah, a young Haredi man with a French accent held a little spontaneous candle-lighting in the lobby. Most people had left to watch the final match of the World Cup, but a small group of library rats joined, among them a young man holding the waist of a woman in a miniskirt; the man placed his other hand on his head during the blessings in lieu of wearing a kippah. Another woman wore orange flared shorts and high skin-tight boots with chunky white rubber heels. We contributed the occasional scattered "amen," sang a few of the songs, and went back to work. It felt about as coercive as the brightly lit Christmas market on the central road of Haifa or the carnival atmosphere alongside a certain tranquility in Muslim neighborhoods during Ramadan. Naturally, it would feel different for a non-Jewish Israeli for whom even a harmless ritual could symbolize the daily experience of life under an unequal regime. But a stronger democratic culture at all other times would reduce the cumulative pressure on non-Jews, or even non-Orthodox Jews, and possibly reduce their antipathy toward religion itself.

What Israel desperately needs is deeper grounding in democratic principles and reinforcement of the full meaning of democracy. Israelis need to internalize that democratic values are interdependent, as are democratic institutions: an attack on one aspect drags others down with it. By the same logic, the failure to be a democracy for some means that the country is not democratic, full stop. Additionally, failure to be democratic for one community eventually touches other communities that never suspected that they might be next.

Not a Problem of Left and Right

Second, the sources of Israel's democratic failings cannot be attributed to a single side of the political map; nor can its progress and successes. The historical record is remarkably clear: the parties and leaders popularly seen as "left" and "right" have each carried deep responsibility for undemocratic policies. The common thread, not surprisingly, is that Mapai (viewed as "left-wing" in the popular imagination) was at its least democratic when it was most in control. And Likud, whose historical predecessors and constituent parties did a great deal to advance democracy while Mapai/Labor was in power, was at its least democratic when its control was greatest, in the 2010s to the present.

The religious—specifically, the ultra-Orthodox—parties bear the most historical responsibility for preventing a constitution, while advancing theocratic or at least coercive religious practice, rather than freedom of and from religion. They did not sacrifice the primacy of equality; they never accepted it to begin with. Ultra-Orthodox leadership hoped that yeshiva students would be exempt from universal obligations and that women would acquiesce to being subordinate in family and society. The pro-settlement, national-religious parties were among the pioneers driving Israel's most undemocratic project of all, and the settlement project is among the pillars of the occupation today.

But the religious-political leadership is not the only source of Israel's democratic ills. Its parties have disproportionate leverage because left- and right-wing governments alike have given them that power, due to the perennial taboo on normal democratic partnership with Arab parties in government.

The exceptions were two governments, one under a left-wing leader and the other led by a right-winger (in Israeli terms): Yitzhak Rabin arranged "external" support from Arab parties; and the coalition with full participation of an independent Arab party (2021–22) was led by religious nationalist Naftali Bennett and his Yamina Party, meaning "rightward." There have been only three Arab or Druze ministers, two of them under right-wing governments, and the first Arab full minister (there had been a deputy minister earlier) served in what Israelis considered a centrist government led by Kadima, while the minister represented the Labor Party. In other words, Left and Right alike enacted undemocratic policies, but both Left and Right are capable of advancing and improving democracy in Israel, which means that both have the obligation to do so, and neither is off the hook.

As an aside, Israel differs from numerous nation-states regarding minority participation in government. Albanian minority parties have joined governing coalitions in North Macedonia and Montenegro. Hungarian minority parties have commonly joined governments in Romania and Slovakia. Kosovo's constitution requires ministerial positions for the Serb minority in all governments—though relations between Serbs and Kosovo's Albanians are no model for emulation, the wounds of war are still fresh, and the Serb minority, too, balks at recognizing Kosovo's independence. These arrangements certainly do not solve all minority–majority problems, nor do they prevent democratic failings in those countries.

But unlike minorities who have nation-states of their own (Albania, Hungary, Serbia), Palestinians have neither self-determination nor full political decision-making power in Israel. Therefore, their participation can easily become an existential quest for national recognition—which Israel's Jewish majority deems too threatening—perpetuating exclusionary governance. Once again, the fate of the Palestinians is inextricable from the fate of democracy in Israel—a segue to the next main lesson.

No Separate Democracy

The **third** observation has been stated numerous times. Israel is not a double society, a parallel life of democracy alongside an undemocratic occupation. Parallel lines do not touch, but this is one and the same state. Just as the geographic Green Line has disappeared, so has the administrative, executive, and legal border—certainly in the West Bank and (annexed) East Jerusalem. Gaza has been physically isolated, but Israel's near-total control over its perimeters, regulating all population movement into or out of the territory, as well as the movement of goods, and control over most resources, means that life in Gaza effectively flows from the state of Israel, too, managed internally on the ground by Hamas.

All these mechanisms of control are managed from one state—Israel—and by many of the same institutions. And the occupation policies bear no resemblance to democracy.

The non-democracy of occupation has consequences not only for the people under its control but for those who execute the policy. An individual Israeli citizen who lives under democratic governance but also participates in the occupation as a conscript, bureaucrat, career army, or political figure learns to enact undemocratic governance, even if that individual does not *feel* that he or she suffers from it. Routinizing and legitimizing policies that permanently violate democracy weakens the commitment to, or even understanding of, these values among the people enacting the occupation.

To be sure, the Palestinian leadership receives failing grades for democracy. Polls of Palestinians have shown for years that Palestinian society views the Palestinian Authority as corrupt and authoritarian, and national elections have been held only twice since 1993. No society should be complacent about such failures. The lack of genuine sovereign powers and life under a colonial military occupation for six decades are not conducive to good governance anywhere. The argument of this book is that given the lack of genuine separation between the two communities, democracy of each side matters for the other.

Elements of Democracy Exist

Fourth, despite all the deficits, there are clearly numerous elements of democracy in Israel—in some ways, even commendable practices. The electoral institution is one of these. Israel holds mostly free and fair elections at a frantic pace, has never faced serious challenges to the results, and adopted universal suffrage from the start. Yet it should be obvious by now that elections on their own are no measure of democracy—especially when the relevant civil rights required for true competition are threatened.

But Israel has more than elections. It has robust practice, institutions, legislation, and cultural expectations of democracy. A good example is the progress regarding access to information. From the early years of top-down and bottom-up (voluntary) restriction, Israeli media became more independent, Israel passed freedom-of-information laws, moved to e-gov systems, and made vast archives available electronically, for free. The military censor and obstacles to accessing classified archives remain. But a great amount of material in this book—including Knesset protocols, Supreme Court decisions, government guidelines dating back to the start of statehood, and many other records—was available within minutes of searching, for anyone with internet access.

These deepen the irony and bust the excuses. No one can claim lack of knowledge; once again, in this sense, Israel is democratic enough to know just how undemocratic it is.

Tergiversation Nation

The **fifth** observation is that Israel clings to its contradictions and lives in its gray zone. If Israel practices deeply undemocratic rule but also has many democratic elements, what is it? I came to think of Israel's political culture as tergiversation nation. I confess that I only recently learned the word "tergiversate," a form of elusive equivocation, just as I was starting this project. Yet it has not left me since. Levi Eshkol, Israel's prime minister during the 1967 war, was considered indecisive, but that is somewhat unfair. He continued a long tradition of purposeful, even strategic, nondecision, or unwillingness to name de facto decisions. These include the nondecision about a constitution defining either borders or the country's identity; the value of equality; the sources of law and authority; deferral of legislation for years over some of the most sensitive issues; and, of course, refusing to state openly what Israel intended to do with the Occupied Territories. For nearly a decade, from the Camp David negotiations in 2000 to Netanyahu's "Bar Ilan speech" in 2009 outlining a highly qualified vision, Israeli leaders at least formally claimed to support a two-state solution. But by 2015, Netanyahu was openly opposed to a Palestinian state.[2] A decade out of fifty-six years of occupation in which Israel held a clear and explicit position means that, for forty-six years, the country has refused to name its aims while its actions on the ground indicate a very different intention of permanent control over most of the land.

Caution with Comparisons

Sixth, while I have tried to situate Israel within a global context, this book does not provide a comparison, systematic or general, of Israel with other countries. In the propaganda battle, it is fashionable to rank Israel as the "only democracy in the Middle East," or to criticize it with the same phrase in sarcastic air quotes.

In a frank political analysis, Israel is clearly more democratic than other countries of the Middle East for *some* of the people it governs. But the debate comparing Israel with the rest of the Middle East is no more than a polemic, since Israel can just as well be compared with the top-ranked democracies and receive failing grades by comparison. The Middle East trope offers nothing by way of useful analysis in the attempt to make Israel *more* democratic.

Democracy Is Hard to See—but under Threat

Last, the stories herein do not touch all citizens all the time, and some of the threads do not relate to daily life experience. Many processes that are examined here involve legislative debates and policy developments that are tough to untangle. It was a heady privilege for me to read Supreme Court decisions, Knesset protocols, reports of special government commissions, and a civics textbook written in 1958, in the research for this book. But most Israelis are busy trying to get by in a country where life is intense and daily needs are expensive. No one can be faulted for not seeing all the contradictions and threats to democracy all the time. Getting by can be hard enough.

Yet this means that democracy, as Astra Taylor argued, is not always visible or materially felt; nor, as we know, are the injuries to democracy. Neither one is less real for being invisible. We cannot see oxygen, either, or carbon monoxide. That explains why many Israelis cannot see the vulnerabilities and, at least until the extraordinary democracy movement of 2023, did not notice the threat.

On the other side of the visibility equation, however, the reality is that many Israelis are aware and purposeful in their rejection of democratic values and consciously support leaders who will dismantle them. For these citizens, the proverbial frog who fails to notice the water boiling is the wrong metaphor: the public in democracies can also *willingly* choose undemocratic leadership, with open eyes, not with naïveté or indifference.

Finally, I return to the title of this book, recalling Kant's dark view that "out of the crooked timber of humanity no straight thing was ever made."[3] I have argued that Israel will not become democratic until realizing that the problem lies in its very roots. But Isaiah Berlin's transmission of the idea is a better path: lowering the expectation of perfection is the only path forward. A utopian vision of democracy is both unattainable and it lets Israel off the hook. We can only strive to do better—and we *can* do better.

Notes

Section I
Introduction

1 "Ben-Gvir in a Victory Speech: 'We Will Become the Owners of Our State Again,'" *Kipa News*, November 2, 2022 [Hebrew]. Note: Throughout this book, for all sources originally in Hebrew, the translations are my own.

2 "Israel Takes a Troubling Turn toward Illiberal Democracy," Washington Post, November 3, 2022; "The Ideal of Democracy in a Jewish State Is in Jeopardy," New York Times, December 17, 2022.

3 TOI Staff, "Lapid: New Government Not Committed to Democracy, Dismantles Foundations of Society," Times of Israel, December 27, 2022.

4 Bezalel Smotrich and Simcha Rothman, "Law and Justice Program: To Repair the Judiciary and Strengthen Israeli Democracy," Religious Zionism Party, October 18, 2022 https://zionutdatit.org.il/re start [Hebrew].

5 Tamar Hermann and Or Anabi, "Supreme Court Should Retain Power," Israel Democracy Institute, December 6, 2022, https://en.idi.org.il/articles/46635; Tamar Hermann et al., "Israel Democracy Index 2021: Democratic Values," Israel Democracy Institute, January 6, 2022, https://en.idi.org.il/ar ticles/37857.

6 Dahlia Scheindlin, "The Logic behind Israel's Democratic Erosion," Century Foundation, May 29, 2019, https://tcf.org/content/report/logic-behind-israels-democratic-erosion.

7 The Israeli Supreme Court acts as the highest court of appeals and as court for citizen claims against state authorities. In the second role, it is referred to as "sitting as the High Court of Justice," or HCJ. Many issues addressed in this book refer to Court decisions in petitions against the state, which are documented as HCJ and a reference number. However, since the two terms refer to a single body, I will use the more familiar term "Supreme Court" in the text for clarity, unless reproducing a direct quotation.

8 See, e.g., Yeshayahu Leibowitz, "The Territories," in *Judaism, Human Values and the Jewish State*, ed. Eliezer Goldman (Cambridge, MA: Harvard University Press, 1992), 225–26.

9 Data Israel, "Peace Index: P1411," Israel Democracy Institute, November 2014.

10 By "Palestinian areas," I am not implying that Palestinians had historical political control, but this refers to current populations. In the region, the large majority of Palestinians, more than 5 million, live in the West Bank, Gaza, and East Jerusalem. Approximately another 1.5 million live in Israel as citizens.

11 This approach is eloquently captured by Astra Taylor, *Democracy May Not Exist, but We'll Miss It When It's Gone* (London: Verso, 2019), introduction.

12 Joel A. Schlosser, "Herodotean Democracies," *CHS Research Bulletin* 5, no. 1 (2016): 1§3; Josiah Ober, "The Original Meaning of Democracy: Capacity to Do Things, Not Majority Rule," *Constellations* 15, no. 1 (2008): 6.

13 Sara Forsdyke, "Athenian Democratic Ideology and Herodotus' 'Histories,'" *American Journal of Philology* 122, no. 3 (Autumn 2001): 329–58.

14 Mogens Herman Hansen, *Polis: An Introduction to the Ancient Greek City-State* (Oxford: Oxford University Press, 2006), 122–24.

15 John Locke, *Two Treatises of Government and a Letter Concerning Toleration*, ed. Ian Shapiro (New Haven, CT: Yale University Press, 2003), second treatise, 100–210.

https://doi.org/10.1515/9783110796582-009

16 James Madison, Alexander Hamilton, and John Jay, *The Federalist Papers*, ed. Isaac Kramnick (London: Penguin, 1987), 126; originally published 1788.

17 John Stuart Mill, "Considerations on Representative Government," in *Democracy: A Reader*, ed. Ricardo Blaug and John Schwarzmantel (New York: Columbia University Press, 2000), 67; originally published 1861.

18 Francis Fukuyama, "The Future of History: Can Liberal Democracy Survive the Decline of the Middle Class?" *Foreign Affairs* 91, no. 1 (January/February 2012): 54.

19 Summary of T. H. Marshall, in Gershon Shafir and Yoav Peled, *Being Israeli: The Dynamics of Multiple Citizenship* (Cambridge: Cambridge University Press, 2002), 8 – 10.

20 Quoted in Melville B. Nimmer, "The Uses of Judicial Review in Israel's Quest for a Constitution," *Columbia Law Review* 70, no. 7 (November 1970): 1218.

21 Paul Guyer, "The Crooked Timber of Mankind," in *Kant's Idea for a Universal History with a Cosmopolitan Aim*, ed. Amélie Rorty and James Schmidt (Cambridge: Cambridge University Press, 2009), 130 – 32.

22 Madison, Hamilton, and Jay, *The Federalist Papers*, 439 – 40.

23 Alexis de Tocqueville, *Democracy in America: And Two Essays on America*, trans. Gerald E. Bevan (London: Penguin, 2003), 591 – 600.

24 Ibid., 599 – 600.

25 Robert Dahl, *Polyarchy: Participation and Opposition* (New Haven, CT: Yale University Press, 1971).

26 Fareed Zakaria, "The Rise of Illiberal Democracy," *Foreign Affairs* 76, no. 6 (November–December 1997): 22.

27 Daron Acemoglu and James A. Robinson, "Why Did the West Extend the Franchise? Democracy, Inequality, and Growth in Historical Perspective," *Quarterly Journal of Economics* 115, no. 4 (November 2000): 1184.

28 Zakaria, "The Rise of Illiberal Democracy," 26.

29 Summarizing Preston James; see Raymond D. Gastil, *Freedom in the World: Political Rights and Civil Liberties 1978* (Boston: G. K. Hall, 1978), 5.

30 Freedom House (1978), 7. Emphasis in the original.

31 Global State of Democracy Indices.

32 "Democracy Index 2021: The China Challenge," Economist Intelligence Unit (2022), 76.

33 President Franklin D. Roosevelt's Second Bill of Rights Annotated, Bill of Rights Institute, https://www.billofrightsinstitute.org/activities/second-bill-of-rights-annotated#60.

34 Arend Lijphart, *Democracy in Plural Societies: A Comparative Exploration* (New Haven, CT: Yale University Press, 1980).

35 Samuel Huntington, *The Third Wave: Democratization in the Late 20th Century* (Norman: University of Oklahoma Press, 1991), 13 – 16.

36 Zakaria, "The Rise of Illiberal Democracy," 23. The count should not be seen as tripling the number from 1991 (Huntington's book) to 1997, but rather, the different methods of categorization.

37 See ibid., 23 – 26; Larry Diamond, "Is the Third Wave of Democratization Over? The Imperative of Consolidation," Working Paper 237, Helen Kellogg Institute for International Studies, March 1997, 27.

38 Zakaria, "The Rise of Illiberal Democracy," 23.

39 Matt Qvortrup, *Death by a Thousand Cuts: The Slow Demise of Democracy* (Berlin: De Gruyter, 2021).

40 Jan-Werner Mueller, *What Is Populism?* (Philadelphia: University of Pennsylvania Press, 2016), 42. The phenomenon of populism itself has generated a vast literature; for a comprehensive summary, see Cas Mudde and Cristóbal Rovira Kaltwasser, eds., *Populism in Europe and the Americas: Threat or Corrective for Democracy?* (Cambridge: Cambridge University Press, 2012), chap. 1.

41 Mueller, *What Is Populism?*, 55.

42 Asher Arian, *Politics in Israel: The Second Republic* (New York: CQ, 2004), 5; Gal Ariely, *Israel's Regime Untangled: Between Democracy and Apartheid* (Cambridge: Cambridge University Press, 2021), 12.

43 Medding broadly accepts this view, quoting Giovanni Sartori, who called Israel "a most baffling case" and "sui generis"; Peter Y. Medding, *The Founding of Israeli Democracy, 1948–1967* (New York: Oxford University Press, 1990), 4. See also Alexander Yakobson and Amnon Rubinstein, *Israel and the Family of Nations: The Jewish Nation-State and Human Rights*, trans. Ruth Morris and Ruchie Avital (London: Routledge, 2009); Nir Kedar, *Ben-Gurion and the Foundation of Israeli Democracy* (Bloomington: Indiana University Press, 2021).

44 Zeev Sternhell, "Yonatan Shapira: A Pioneer of Critical Research," *Israeli Sociology* 2, no. 1 (1999): 11 [Hebrew].

45 Bernard Avishai, *The Tragedy of Zionism* (New York: Farrar, Straus and Giroux, 1985); Avishai Margalit, "The Birth of a Tragedy," *New York Review of Books*, October 23, 1986.

46 Menachem Mautner, *Liberalism in Israel: Past, Problems, and Future* (Tel Aviv: Tel Aviv University Press, 2019), 19 [Hebrew].

47 Sammy Smooha, "Ethnic Democracy: Israel as an Archetype," *Israel Studies* 2, no. 2 (1997): 198.

48 Asad Ghanem, Nadim Rouhana, and Oren Yiftachel, "Questioning 'Ethnic Democracy': A Response to Sammy Smooha," *Israel Studies* 3, no. 2 (1998).

49 Alan Dowty, "Is Israel Democratic? Substance and Semantics in the 'Ethnic Democracy' Debate," *Israel Studies* 4, no. 2 (Fall 1999): 1–15.

50 Shira Robinson, *Citizen Strangers: Palestinians and the Birth of Israel's Liberal Settler State* (Stanford, CA: Stanford University Press, 2013).

51 Shafir and Peled, *Being Israeli*.

52 Isaiah Berlin, *The Crooked Timber of Humanity: Chapters in the History of Ideas*, ed. Henry Hardy (London: John Murray, 1990), 19.

Section II
Pre-State Zionism and the Tangled Roots of Democracy: Late Nineteenth Century to 1947

1 This experience of Jewish life is eloquently captured in Shachar M. Pinsker, *A Rich Brew* (New York: New York University Press, 2018).

2 Derek Penslar, *Theodor Herzl: The Charismatic Leader* (New Haven, CT: Yale University Press, 2020), 2.

3 Avishai, *The Tragedy of Zionism*, 42–43.

4 Penslar, *Theodor Herzl*, 68–69. Penslar points to evidence that when Herzl originally covered the Dreyfus affair, he did not indicate that it affected him personally. However, the full extent of the cover-up unfolded over years; it seems plausible that Herzl realized the full implications of the case over time, and later attributed his Zionist motivations to the Dreyfus case.

5 Shlomo Avineri, *The Making of Modern Zionism: The Intellectual Origins of the Jewish State* (London: Weidenfeld and Nicolson, 1981), 102.

6 Theodor Herzl, *The Jewish State*, trans. Sylvie D'Avigdor, American Zionist Emergency Council (available on MidEastWeb.org), 1946, 9.

7 Ibid.

8 Quoted in Avineri, *The Making of Modern Zionism*, 103.

9 Ibid.

10 For "ruin the cause," see Penslar, *Theodor Herzl*, 96; for "political nonsense," see Alan Dowty, *The Jewish State: A Century Later* (Berkeley: University of California Press, 1998), 45.

11 Dowty, *The Jewish State*, 45. On the "aristocratic republic," see Penslar, *Theodor Herzl*, 96.

12 Dowty, *The Jewish State*, 45.

13 Ibid., 19.

14 Ibid., 33.

15 Chaim Weizmann, *Trial and Error: The Autobiography of Chaim Weizmann*, bk. 1 (Lexington, MA: Plunkett Lake, Kindle ed., 2013), loc. 764–65/4924. The autobiography was originally published in two volumes, the first in 1941 and the second in 1948.

16 Hillel Halkin, *Jabotinsky: A Life* (New Haven, CT: Yale University Press, 2014), 38.

17 Tom Segev, *A State at Any Cost: The Life of David Ben-Gurion*, trans. Haim Watzman (New York: Farrar, Straus and Giroux, 2019), 161. On the San Remo conference and the relevant resolutions, see "San Remo (1920)," Economic Cooperation Foundation, https://ecf.org.il/issues/issue/251.

18 Segev, *A State at Any Cost*, 49.

19 Anita Shapira, "Labour Zionism and the October Revolution," *Journal of Contemporary History* 24, no. 4 (October 1989): 623–25.

20 Segev, *A State at Any Cost*, 147.

21 On "model to emulate," see Jonathan Shapira, *Democracy in Israel* (Ramat Gan: Masada, 1977), 956 [Hebrew]; on "extreme centralization, see A. Shapira, "Labour Zionism," 628.

22 Segev notes that he and most others referred to him as the secretary-general, in error. Segev, *A State at Any Cost*, 152. Anita Shapira states that he "assumed the post of Histadrut secretary general" in 1921; see Anita Shapira, *Ben-Gurion: Father of Modern Israel*, trans. Anthony Berris (New Haven, CT: Yale University Press, 2014), 65. Since this title appears on official records, it will be used here as well, for consistency. See, e.g., "David Ben-Gurion," Israel Ministry of Foreign Affairs, August 24, 2021.

23 Avishai, *The Tragedy of Zionism*, 114–16.

24 Segev, *A State at Any Cost*, 151–52.

25 Nir Kedar, "Ben-Gurion's *Mamlakhtiyut*: Etymological and Theoretical Roots," *Israel Studies* 7, no. 3 (Fall 2002): 122. Linguists and historians debate the precise origins of the word.

26 Kedar, *Ben-Gurion and the Foundation of Israeli Democracy*, Introduction. On "cult of the military," see Avineri, *The Making of Modern Zionism*, 229.

27 Segev, *A State at Any Cost*, 170–71.

28 Ben-Gurion himself made statements indicating that socialism and Zionism were equally essential; see Anshel Pfeffer, "The Strange Death and Curious Rebirth of the Zionist Left," *Jewish Quarterly* 246 (November 2021): 14. As Segev's title implies, the state was worth any cost, including compromises on pure socialism.

29 On the economic crisis of the late 1920s and development of the private sector, see J. Shapira, *Democracy in Israel*, 26–27.

30 Kedar, *Ben-Gurion and the Foundation of Israeli Democracy*.

31 See Halkin, *Jabotinsky*, 128–29; on reclaiming the Transjordan, 137.

32 Ibid., 165.

33 Jabotinsky articulated the point about Arab migration in Vladimir Jabotinsky, *The Jewish War Front* (Jabotinsky Institute, 1940), 192–94; see also Arye Naor, "Ze'ev Jabotinsky's Constitutional Framework for the Jewish State in the Land of Israel," in *In the Eye of the Storm: Essays on Ze'ev Jabotinsky*, ed. Avi Bareli and Pinhas Ginossar (Sde Boker: Ben-Gurion Institute, 2004), 83 [Hebrew].

34 Avineri, *The Making of Modern Zionism*, 180.

35 See Steven J. Zipperstein, *Pogrom: Kishinev and the Tilt of History* (New York: W. W. Norton, 2018).

36 Quoted in Mark Bruzonsky, "The Mentor Who Shaped Begin's Thinking: Jabotinsky," *Washington Post*, November 16, 1980.

37 Jabotinsky's view of religion and state changed in the 1930s as he supported a particularist Jewish identity for the vision of the future state, but in an abstract form that was "not intended to subjugate law or politics to religion"; see Naor, "Ze'ev Jabotinsky's Constitutional Framework," 70.

38 Mordechai Kremnitzer and Amir Fuchs, *Ze'ev Jabotinsky on Democracy, Equality, and Individual Rights* (Jerusalem: Israel Democracy Institute, 2013), 4–5.

39 Ibid., 8.

40 Ibid., 9.

41 Naor, "Jabotinsky's Constitutional Framework," 86; although Avineri insists that Jabotinsky rejected national rights, the direct quotation on this point is from Jabotinsky's famous work *The Iron Wall* (originally published in 1923), quoted in Kremnitzer and Fuchs, *Ze'ev Jabotinsky*, 8–9.

42 Naor, "Ze'ev Jabotinsky's Constitutional Framework," 85–86. For the English original text, see Vladimir Jabotinsky, *The Jewish War Front*, Jabotinsky Institute (1940), 187.

43 Halkin, *Jabotinsky*, 136.

44 Segev, *A State at Any Cost*, 218 (Jabotinsky and the "Red Swastika"); on Ben-Gurion's accusations, 648; on their similarities, 249.

45 Halkin, *Jabotinsky*, 192–95.

46 Yoel Bin-Nun, "R. Kook's Public Position on Women Voting," *Tradition: A Journal of Orthodox Jewish Thought* 49, no. 1 (2016): 68–71. The term "old Yishuv" refers to the small communities of mostly religious Jews living in Palestine prior to Zionism; Agudath Israel broke with the Zionist community building the new, or Zionist, Yishuv.

47 See Charles Glass, "Jews against Zion: Israeli Jewish Anti-Zionism," *Journal of Palestine Studies* 5, nos. 1–2 (1975): 59; David B. Green, "This Day in Jewish History Zionism's First Political Assassination," *Haaretz*, June 30, 2013.

48 See Shafir and Peled, *Being Israeli*, 137–41.

49 This useful distinction is made by Shafir and Peled, describing the Mizrahi movement's accommodationist approach based on the need for physical protection of the Jews and the theologically derived commitment to the state established by Rabbi Kook. Shafir and Peled, *Being Israeli*, 137–41.

50 Elli Fischer, "The Israeli Rabbinate: The Origin Story," *Moment*, May–June 2015.

51 Avineri, *The Making of Modern Zionism*, 208, 213.

52 Quoted in ibid., 210.

53 Shulamit Eliash, "The Political Role of the Chief Rabbinate of Palestine during the Mandate: Its Character and Nature," *Jewish Social Studies* 47, no. 1 (Winter 1985): 40.

54 John Woodhead, *Palestine Partition Commission Report* (London: His Majesty's Stationery Office, 1938), 165; Economic Cooperation Foundation, https://ecf.org.il/media_items/375.

55 Ibid. This part of the report refers to representatives from Agudath Israel as "orthodox" rather than ultra-Orthodox (Haredi); in general and in this book, "Orthodox" is usually used for religious Zionist communities. The religious Zionist groups were represented at the commission by Mizrahi. See Giora Goldberg, "Religious Zionism and the Framing of a Constitution for Israel," *Israel Studies* 3, no. 1 (Spring 1998): 211–29.

56 Shuki Friedman, Amihai Radzyner, and Yedidia Stern, "Constitution Not Written in the Torah," *Research and Policy* 69 (December 2006): 29.

57 Ibid.

58 Goldberg, "Religious Zionism," 214.

59 Alexander Kaye, *The Invention of Jewish Theocracy: The Struggle for Legal Authority in Modern Israel* (Oxford: Oxford University Press, 2020), 26 – 27.

60 Ibid., chap. 3; on Torah as the ultimate authority, 98.

61 Shafir and Peled, *Being Israeli*, 39 – 40; on Arab exclusion, S. Robinson, *Citizen Strangers*, 12.

62 Avineri, *The Making of Modern Zionism*, 216.

63 Dowty, *The Jewish State*, 50; on the kibbutz, see Shafir and Peled, *Being Israeli*, 47.

64 Segev, *A State at Any Cost*, 73.

65 S. Robinson, *Citizen Strangers*, 16. For background on the Palestine Communist Party and expulsion from Histadrut, see Joel Beinin, "The Palestine Communist Party 1919 – 1948," *MERIP Reports* 55 (March 1977): 6.

66 J. Shapira, *Democracy in Israel*, 98.

67 Ibid.

68 Ibid., 105; for "counterproductive," see Shafir and Peled, *Being Israeli*, 51 (characterizing Shapira's view).

69 Joel Perlmann, "Dissent and Discipline in Ben-Gurion's Labor Party: 1930 – 32," working paper, Levy Institute of Economics at Bard College (2006), 4. This distinction between formalistic democratic procedures and the deeper democratic nature of the institutions also characterizes Jonathan Shapira's treatment of the Histadrut.

70 Segev, *A State at Any Cost,* 226.

71 Pfeffer, "The Strange Death."

72 Segev actually notes that he lacked the power to become an autocrat, suggesting that Ben-Gurion, in fact, had autocratic inclinations; Segev, *A State at Any Cost*, 593.

73 S. Robinson, *Citizen Strangers*, 19.

74 Weizmann, *Trial and Error*, Kindle ed., loc. 4008/4924.

75 Lawrence Davidson, "The Past as Prelude: Zionism and the Betrayal of American Democratic Principles, 1917– 48," *Journal of Palestine Studies* 31, no. 3 (2002): 26.

76 S. Robinson, *Citizen Strangers*, 15.

77 Ibid., 14.

78 Christopher C. Joyner, "The United Nations and Democracy," *Global Governance* 5, no. 3 (July–Sept 1999): 337.

79 To these two founding documents, Joyner adds that in 1960, the UN General Assembly affirmed the right of colonial peoples to independence and self-determination, an affirmation that the UN Secretariat views as part of the UN's overall support for democracy; see ibid., 338.

80 Loeffler explains that Lauterpacht was left out of the UDHR drafting committee, but his work had a strong influence on Robinson and John Humphrey, who directed the UN Division of Human Rights; James Loeffler, *Rooted Cosmopolitans: Jews and Human Rights in the Twentieth Century* (New Haven, CT: Yale University Press, 2018), 147, 152 – 55.

81 "Biltmore Program 1942"; full text of document accessible on the Israeli-Palestinian Conflict: An Interactive Database, Economic Cooperation Foundation. https://ecf.org.il/issues/issue/1426

82 Joseph C. Hutcheson, *Anglo-American Committee of Inquiry*, chap. 8 (Lausanne: Dept. of State, 1946), Avalon Project: Documents in Law, History and Diplomacy, Yale Law School, 2008, https://avalon.law.yale.edu/20th_century/angch08.asp.

83 Quoted in Paul Johnson, "The Miracle," *Commentary*, May 1998, https://www.commentary.org/articles/paul-johnson-3/the-miracle.

84 Uri Milstein, "Without Stalin, Israel Would Not Have Been Established," *News1*, July 3, 2015 [Hebrew], https://www.news1.co.il/Archive/002-D-104013 – 00.html?t=120001.

85 A. Shapira, "Labour Zionism," 636 – 37.

86 Gyoo-hyoung Kahng, "Zionism, Israel, and the Soviet Union: A Study in the Rise and Fall of Brief Soviet–Israeli Friendship from 1945 to 1955," *Global Economic Review* 27, no. 4 (1998): 95–107.

87 Avi Shlaim, "Britain and the Arab–Israeli War of 1948," *Journal of Palestine Studies* 16, no. 4 (1987): 54.

88 Kahng, "Zionism, Israel, and the Soviet Union," 98.

89 Michael Ottolenghi, "Harry Truman's Recognition of Israel," *Historical Journal* 47, no. 4 (2004): 968 – 69.

90 A. Shapira, "Labour Zionism," 637; Segev, *A State at Any Cost*, 494.

91 Hutcheson, *Anglo-American Committee*, chap. 1.

92 Ibid., chap. 6.

93 Ibid., chap. 8.

94 Uri Ben-Eliezer, *The Making of Israeli Militarism* (Bloomington: Indiana University Press, 1998), 35.

95 Asle Sveen, "Ralph Bunche: UN Mediator in the Middle East, 1948 – 1949," https://www.nobelprize. org/prizes/peace/1950/bunche/article; for the UN advancing peace and democracy, see Ralph Bunche, "Democracy: A World Issue," *Journal of Negro Education* 19, no. 4 (1950): 437.

96 Elad Ben-Dror, "Ralph Bunche and the Establishment of Israel," *Israel Affairs* 14, no. 3 (2008): 519. Bunche was named as the special assistant; UNSCOP reports refer to him as part of the "secretariat."

97 Abba Eban, quoted in William Greaves, *Ralph Bunche: An American Odyssey*, Schomburg Center for Research in Black Culture, South Carolina ETV, William Greaves Productions, 2001.

98 Richard Crossman, "The Revolt against Bevin," *McLean's*, February 1, 1947.

99 Britannica, https://www.britannica.com/place/Palestine/The-Arab-Revolt#ref478970.

100 "The Origins and Evolution of the Palestine Problem: Part II (1947– 1977)," UN,<BREAK/>https:// www.un.org/unispal/history2/origins-and-evolution-of-the-palestine-problem/part-ii-1947– 1977.

101 UN Special Committee on Palestine (UNSCOP), "Report to the General Assembly, Vol. II" (1947): 5.

102 UNSCOP, "Report to the General Assembly, Vol. I" (1947), 4.

103 UNSCOP, "Report to the General Assembly, Vol. III" (1947), 243.

104 Ibid.

105 Ihud was the successor group to Brit Shalom, the grouping of humanist intellectuals in the 1930s who advocated a binational vision. The Palestine Communist Party at this time had split along Arab–Jewish lines, largely over the issue of a Jewish state, and reunited only after statehood. Beinin, "The Palestine Communist Party," 11. The UNSCOP report refers to the Jewish group as the Palestine Communist Union, and these representatives referred to themselves as the "Hebrew Communists." See, e. g., UNSCOP, "Report to General Assembly, Vol. III," 234.

106 UNSCOP, "Report to General Assembly, Vol. III," 130.

107 Quoted in Dennis Ross and David Makovsky, *Be Strong and of Good Courage: How Israel's Most Important Leaders Shaped Its Destiny* (New York: Public Affairs, 2019), 37.

108 UNSCOP, "Report to the General Assembly, Vol. III," 149 – 50.

109 Ibid., 159.

110 UNSCOP, "Report to the General Assembly, Vol. I," 45.

111 Ibid.

112 "United Nations General Assembly Resolution 181, November 29, 1947," https://avalon.law.yale.edu/20th_century/res181.asp.

113 The UNSCOP report provides population estimates in the envisioned states, showing that about 45 percent of the Jewish state would be Arab and Bedouin; UN Special Committee on Palestine, *Report to the General Assembly*, vol. 1 (Lake Success, NY, 1947), 54. Robinson states that under the Partition Plan, 49 percent of the population of the Jewish state would have been Arab Palestinians; see S. Robinson, *Citizen Strangers*, 70.

114 Eliav Lieblich and Yoram Shachar, "Cosmopolitanism at a Crossroads: Hersch Lauterpacht and the Israeli Declaration of Independence," *British Yearbook of International Law* 84, no. 1 (2014): 7.
115 Amichai Radzyner, "A Constitution for Israel: The Design of the Leo Kohn Proposal, 1948," *Israel Studies* 15, no. 1 (Spring 2010): 4.

Section III
Independence and the Least Democratic Decades, 1948 – 66

1 Lieblich and Shachar, "Cosmopolitanism," 7.
2 Yoram Shachar, "Israel as a Two-Parent State: The Hebrew Yishuv and the Zionist Movement in the Declaration of Independence," *Zmanim: A Historical Quarterly* 98 (2007): 35 [Hebrew].
3 Lieblich and Shachar, "Cosmopolitanism," 11.
4 On Lauterpacht's student life in Lemberg, see Loeffler, *Rooted Cosmopolitans,* pt. 1; Philippe Sands, *East West Street* (New York: Vintage, 2016), chaps. 29 – 31. See also Hersch Lauterpacht, <BREAK/>*An International Bill of the Rights of Man* (Oxford: Oxford University Press, 2013).
5 Lieblich and Shachar, "Cosmopolitanism," 2; Loeffler, *Rooted Cosmopolitans,* 21.
6 Loeffler, *Rooted Cosmopolitans,* 152 – 55.
7 Lieblich and Shachar, "Cosmopolitanism," 9; Loeffler, *Rooted Cosmopolitans,* 157.
8 Uri Davis and Walter Lehn, "And the Fund Still Lives: The Role of the Jewish National Fund in the Determination of Israel's Land Policies," *Journal of Palestine Studies* 7, no. 4 (Summer): 5 – 6. The formal name is "Declaration of the Establishment of the State of Israel." This will be referred to as the Declaration of Independence, reflecting the common usage.
9 Shachar, "Israel as a Two-Parent State," 35. On the word "democracy" and Shertok's involvement, see Martin Kramer, "Whose Rights Did Israel Recognize in 1948?," *Mosaic,* September 23, 2021.
10 For Lauterpacht's text and references to the "frontiers" of the Partition Plan, see Lieblich and Shachar, "Cosmopolitanism," 46, 49; on Ben-Gurion's resistance, see David Landau, *Ben-Gurion: A Political Life* (New York: Schocken, 2011), 100 – 101; on his response to Rosenblueth/Rosen, see Elyakim Rubinstein, "The Declaration of Independence as a Basic Document of the State of Israel," *Israel Studies* 3, no. 1 (1998): 197.
11 The English text as it appears on the Knesset website states equality of social and political rights to all its inhabitants, while the Hebrew text uses the word *ezraheha*—its citizens. See "Declaration of Independence," https://m.knesset.gov.il/en/about/pages/declaration.aspx.
12 Yair Bauml, "Discriminatory Policy toward Arabs in Israel, 1948–1968," *Iyunim b'Tkumat Israel* 16 (2006): 394 [Hebrew].
13 Central Election Committee, "Elections for the 24th Knesset: Percentage Turnout for Past Elections," Knesset, 2021, https://bechirot24.bechirot.gov.il/election/about/Pages/PercentagePoint.aspx.
14 Shuki Friedman, Amichai Radzyner, and Yedidia Stern, "Constitution Not Written in the Torah," *Research and Policy* 69, Israel Democracy Institute, December 2006, 18 [Hebrew].
15 Radzyner, "A Constitution for Israel," 3.
16 Wireless to the *New York Times,* "Non-Jews Obtain Palestine Pledge," November 10, 1944.
17 Radzyner, "A Constitution for Israel," 6.
18 Yehuda Pinhas Kohn, *Constitution for Israel: Proposal and Explanations, Constitutional Committee, Provisional Council,* Israel National Digital Archive (1948; the Hebrew date is given as Chanukah, 5709).
19 Leo Kohn, "The Constitution of Israel," *Journal of Educational Sociology* 27, no. 8 (April 1954): 371.

20 Philippa Strum, "The Road Not Taken, Constitutional Non–Decision Making in 1948–1950 and Its Impact on Civil Liberties in the Israeli Political Culture," in *Israel: The First Decades of Independence*, ed. S. Ilan Troen and Noah Lucas (Albany: State University of New York, 1995), 85; Radzyner, "A Constitution for Israel," 7–9.

21 L. Kohn, "The Constitution of Israel," 372.

22 On Rosenblueth, see Radzyner, "A Constitution for Israel," 2; on Warhaftig, see Friedman, Radzyner, and Stern, "Constitution Not Written," 10–12.

23 Friedman, Radzyner, and Stern, "Constitution Not Written," 10–12.

24 L. Kohn, "The Constitution of Israel," 369; on the transfer of the legislative powers, see Suzie Navot, *Constitutional Law in Israel* (Alphen aan den Rijn, Netherlands: Kluwer Law International, 2007), 35; Gideon Sapir, "Constitutional Revolutions: Israel as a Case Study," *International Journal of Law in Context* 5, no. 4 (2009): 358.

25 Friedman, Radzyner, and Stern, "Constitution Not Written," 11, 24.

26 This characterization of family law refers to the de facto outcome; the actual letter stated that "matrimony would be dealt with so as 'to eliminate the danger of dividing the House of Israel in two'" —in effect, forcing a single framework based on Jewish law, for Jews; in 1948, Ben-Gurion wrote another letter to the religious leadership, explicitly promising that there would be no civil marriage or divorce. See Strum, "The Road Not Taken," 84–85.

27 "Agudath" is the construct form, as in "Agudath Israel." For brevity, I use the term "Agudah" on its own, where it takes the original form, but these refer to the same group. According to Menachem Friedman, the promises were not sufficient to persuade Agudah to testify to UNSCOP with the Jewish Agency and openly support statehood; its representative testified separately but avoided outright support or rejection. See Menachem Friedman, "The Chronicle of the Status Quo: Religion and State in Israel," in "Transition from Yishuv to State 1947–1949," *Continuity and Change* 47 (1990) [Hebrew].

28 Segev, *A State at Any Cost*, 482–83.

29 For a thorough review, see Kedar, *Ben-Gurion*, chap. 1.

30 Ibid., 35.

31 S. Robinson, *Citizen Strangers*, 69–70, 97.

32 Kedar, *Ben-Gurion*, 34–36.

33 Quoted in Shlomo Aronson, "David Ben-Gurion and the British Constitutional Model," *Israel Studies* 3, no. 2 (Fall 1998): 207.

34 On Ben-Gurion's commitment to democracy as majority rule, see also Medding, *Israeli Democracy*, 39–40.

35 David Ben-Gurion and Neil Rogachevsky, "Against Court and Constitution: A Never-Before-Translated Speech by David Ben-Gurion," *Mosaic*, March 10, 2021.

36 Segev, *A State at Any Cost*, 483.

37 Gideon Doron, "Judges in a Borderless State: Politics Versus the Law in the State of Israel," *Israel Affairs* 14, no. 4 (2008): 594.

38 Ben-Gurion and Rogachevsky, "Against Court and Constitution."

39 United Nations, "Question of Palestine: Admission of Israel to the United Nations—GA Debate—Verbatim Record," Summary Records of Meetings (April 5–May 18, 1949), https://www.un.org/uni spal/document/auto-insert-180950; see also Marte Heian-Engdal, Jørgen Jensehaugen, and Hilde Henriksen Waage, "Finishing the Enterprise: Israel's Admission to the United Nations," *International History Review* 35, no. 3 (June 2013): 471. Israel formally applied the day after declaring independence, but the Admissions Committee and the Security Council did not support the application; thus the applications of December 1948 and March 1949 are the second and the third.

40 Daniel Friedmann, *The End of Innocence: Law and Politics in Israel* (Rishon le'Tzion: Miskal and Yediot Ahronot, 2019), 131 [Hebrew].

41 Itamar Rabinovich and Jehuda Reinharz, eds., *Israel in the Middle East: Documents and Readings on Society, Politics and Foreign Relations, Pre-1948 to the Present*, 2d ed. (Waltham, MA: Brandeis University Press, 2008), 100.

42 Ibid.

43 Ibid., 97.

44 Ibid., 100.

45 Navot, *Constitutional Law in Israel*, 36 – 37.

46 Scholars describe this situation as having "no parallel in any other Western country," while noting efforts to end the state of emergency, with only partial results. For a succinct summary, see Ahaz Ben-Ari and Meir Elran, "States of Emergency: Legal Aspects and Implications for the Corona Crisis in Israel," INSS Insight no. 1292, April 5, 2020.

47 For thorough explanations of this argument, see Gideon Sapir, *The Israeli Constitution: From Evolution to Revolution* (New York: Oxford University Press, 2018), introduction. In 2007, Navot stated: "The State of Israel can now be said to have a formal constitution," though limited and partial; see Navot, *Constitutional Law in Israel*, 48.

48 Friedmann, *The End of Innocence*, 156.

49 Qvortrup, *Death by a Thousand Cuts*, 59.

50 Although formal data about religious practice are not available from the start of statehood, from at least 1962, only 25 – 30 percent of Israeli Jews report keeping "all" or "most" religious practices; see Asher Arian, "Israel: The Challenge of a Democratic and Jewish State," in *Secularism, Women and the State: The Mediterranean World in the 21st Century*, ed. Barry A. Kosmin and Ariella Keysar (Hartford, CT: Institute for the Study of Secularism in Society and Culture, 2009), 79.

51 Inheritance and custody are subject to civil law but can be adjudicated in religious courts under divorce proceedings by choice of the individual parties; see Frances Raday, "Human Rights and the Confrontation between Religious and Constitutional Authority: A Case Study of Israel's Supreme Court," in Kosmin and Keysar, *Secularism, Women and the State*, 222 – 23.

52 Although this group has grown steadily over time, it represents just 13 percent of the total Israeli population in 2021. Lee Cahaner and Gilad Malach, "Statistical Report on Ultra-Orthodox Society in Israel," Israel Democracy Institute, December 28, 2021, https://en.idi.org.il/haredi/2021/?chapter=38439.

53 Raday, "Human Rights," 223 – 24.

54 Gideon Sapir, "Religion and State in Israel: The Case for Reevaluation and Constitutional Entrenchment," *Hastings international and Comparative Law Review* 22 (1999): 617; for a summary of the laws and policies established in the 1950s formalizing the status quo, see Daphne Barak-Erez, "Law and Religion under the Status Quo Model: Between Past Compromises and Constant Change," *Cardozo Law Review* 30, no. 6 (2009): 2496 – 98.

55 Sheneur Zalman Abrahamov, *Perpetual Dilemma: Jewish Religion in the Jewish State* (Cranbury, NJ: Associated University Press, 1976), 193.

56 David Ellenson, "The Supreme Court, Yeshiva Students, and Military Conscription: Judicial Review, the Grunis Dissent, and Its Implications for Israeli Democracy and Law," *Israel Studies* 23, no. 3 (Fall 2018): 198 – 99.

57 Zerach Warhaftig, *Constitution for Israel: Religion and State* (Jerusalem: Ahva, 1988), 233 [Hebrew].

58 Ellenson attributes the rise in the 1970s to the Likud government giving additional concessions to religious coalition partners by removing caps on exemptions; Ellenson, "The Supreme Court," 199.

59 Kaye, *The Invention of Jewish Theocracy*, 138, 140.

60 Ibid., 148.

61 Warhaftig, *Constitution for Israel*, 249; women were included in the mandatory draft for military service already, but the legislation (in effect from 1953) required religious women who had been exempted from the draft to perform national service, although some sources refer to a dispute over military service.

62 Yechiam Weitz, *Israel in the First Decade*, 5, unit 9 (The Open University, 2001), 41 [Hebrew].

63 "Law of Judges—1953 (5703)" and "Basic Law: the Judiciary—1984 (5748)," Knesset. For a thorough history of the evolution of the independent judiciary following statehood, see Kedar, *Ben-Gurion and the Foundation of Israeli Democracy*, chap. 3.

64 Kaye, *The Invention of Jewish Theocracy*, 138.

65 Pnina Lahav, "The Supreme Court of Israel: Formative Years, 1948–1955," *Studies in Zionism* 11, no. 1 (1990): 48–50.

66 Shimon Shetreet, "Forty Years of Constitutional Law: Developments in Constitutional Jurisprudence, Select Issues," *Mishpatim* 19 (1989): 606 [Hebrew].

67 For the property-related petitions, see Friedmann, *The End of Innocence*, 269–70; on administrative detention, see Sapir, *The Israeli Constitution*, 12.

68 Friedmann, *The End of Innocence*, 432.

69 Lahav, "The Supreme Court of Israel," 54.

70 Itzhak Zamir, *The Supreme Court* (Jerusalem: Schocken, 2022), chap. 15.

71 "About the 1949 Elections," Israel Democracy Institute, https://en.idi.org.il/israeli-elections-and-parties/elections/1949.

72 Benjamin Akzin, "The Role of Parties in Israeli Democracy," *Journal of Politics* 17, no. 4 (1955): 517.

73 Ibid.

74 Amichai Cohen has found that Israel is the only democracy with no structural constraints on the legislature, and the Supreme Court is the "almost exclusive" check on the executive branch. Amichai Cohen, "Checks and Balances: The Override Clause and Its Effect on the Three Branches of Government," Book Summary, Israel Democracy Institute, January 23, 2023, https://en.idi.org.il/articles/47482.

75 Eyal Benvenisti, "Party Primaries as Collective Action with Constitutional Ramifications: Israel as a Case Study," *Theoretical Inquiries in Law* 3, no. 1 (2002): 178.

76 Akzin, "The Role of Parties," 511.

77 "Public Service Law (Appointments), 1959 (5719)," Knesset.

78 For "one resolution," see Donna R. Divine, "The Modernization of Israeli Administration," *International Journal of Middle East Studies* 5, no. 3 (June 1974): 295; for "Bolshevik means," see Jonathan Shapira, in Itzhak Galnoor and Dana Blander, *The Handbook of Israel's Political System* (Cambridge: Cambridge University Press, 2018), chap. 9.

79 Ron Tzur and Nissim Cohen, "The Ongoing Israeli Civil Service Reform: Comparing Current Achievements to Past Attempts," Revue française d'administration publique 4, no. 168 (2018): 943–56.

80 Edwin Samuel, "The Histadrut: (The General Federation of Labour in Israel)," *Political Quarterly* 31, no. 2 (1960): 174.

81 Data on Clalit membership from Medding, *Israeli Democracy*, 166–68. Medding uses the term *kupat holim* for the Histadrut health fund, but that term has become generic over time, referring to all health funds; therefore, I use the name of Histadrut's fund, Clalit.

82 Arie Krampf, *The Israeli Path to Neoliberalism: The State, Continuity and Change* (Oxon: Routledge, 2018), 63–64.

83 Avishai, *The Tragedy of Zionism*, 215; Gershon Shafir and Yoav Peled, *The New Israel: Peacemaking and Liberalization* (New York: Taylor and Francis, 2000), 5.

84 Dov Khenin, "From 'Eretz Yisrael Ha'ovedet' to 'Yisrael Hashnia': The Social Discourse and Social Policy of Mapai in the 1950s," in *The New Israel*, ed. Shafir and Peled, 77.

85 Avishai, *The Tragedy of Zionism*, 217. For a full-length book regarding the immigrant medical quarantine that challenges the role of quarantine camps in the Ashkenazi–Mizrahi divide, see Rhona Seidelman, *Under Quarantine: Immigrants and Disease at Israel's Gate* (New Brunswick, NJ: Rutgers University Press, 2020).

86 Arabs were allowed to apply for Histadrut membership starting in 1953. See Jewish Telegraphic Agency, "Histadrut Has 10,000 Arab Members; Doors Open to Arab Work," *JTA News*, July 31, 1953. However, several sources refer to "full" membership from 1959 or 1960. See, e.g., Zachary Brodt, "Histadrut Records, 1956 – 1990," Archives & Special Collections, University of Pittsburgh Library System, August 2010; S. Robinson, *Citizen Strangers*, 190.

87 Yoram Ben-Porath, *The Arab Labor Force in Israel* (Jerusalem: Maurice Falk Institute for Economic Research in Israel, 1966), 50.

88 Khenin, "From 'Eretz Yisrael Ha'ovedet,'" 73 – 76; see also Krampf, *The Israeli Path to Neoliberalism*, chap. 4.

89 Lev Luis Grinberg, *Mo(ve)ments of Resistance: Politics, Economy and Society in Israel/Palestine, 1931 – 2013* (Boston: Academic Studies Press, 2013), 110.

90 Khenin, "From 'Eretz Yisrael Ha'ovedet,'" 84.

91 Mozar Films, *The Red Booklet!* 100 Years of the Histadrut—Full Film, Hot 8, YouTube, February 10, 2021 [Hebrew].

92 Amitai Etzioni, "Alternate Ways to Democracy: The Example of Israel," *Political Science Quarterly* 74, no. 2 (June 1959): 196 – 214, 201.

93 For a short recap, see David B. Green, "1948: The Altalena Arms Ship Reaches Israel, and Is Attacked with Friendly Fire," *Haaretz*, June 22, 2015.

94 Grinberg, *Mo(ve)ments of Resistance*, 98.

95 Etzioni, "Alternate Ways to Democracy," 201.

96 Ibid.

97 Sammy Smooha, "The Mass Immigrations to Israel: A Comparison of the Failure of the Mizrahi Immigrants of the 1950s with the Success of the Russian Immigrants of the 1990s," *Journal of Israeli History* 27, no. 1 (2018): 5.

98 "Settlement of Labor Disputes Law 5717/1957" and "Collective Agreements Law 5717/1957"; English text at International Labor Organization, https://www.ilo.org/dyn/natlex/natlex4.detail?p_lang=&p_isn=36153&p_country=ISR&p_count=173.

99 Dov Khenin and Dani Filc, "The Seamen's Strike," *Theory and Criticism* 12 – 13 (1999): 89 – 98 [Hebrew].

100 William Zukerman, "Israeli Sailors' Strike Broken by Brutality, Slander, Writer Claims," *Sentinel* 178, no. 1 (1952): 10.

101 Khenin and Filc, "The Seamen's Strike," 91; Boaz Garfinkel, "Use of the Army to Break the Locomotive Drivers' and Seamen's Strike in 1951," *Iyunim: Multi-Disciplinary Journal for the Study of Israel* 34 (2020): 152 [Hebrew].

102 National Archive, "Battle at Sea: Mapam against Mapai—the First Political Strike—Seamen's Strike 1951," *Landmarks* (2017), https://catalog.archives.gov.il/chapter/sailors-strike-1951 [Hebrew].

103 Garfinkel, "Use of the Army," 161.

104 Orit Rozin, "Israel and the Right to Travel Abroad, 1948 – 1961," *Israel Studies* 15, no. 1 (Spring 2010): 156.

105 Quoted in ibid., 148.

106 Ibid.

107 Ibid., 149.

108 Ibid., 157.

109 Shraga Makel, "Professor Zamir to Heads of the Treasury: No to Travel Tax through Emergency Regulations," *Maariv,* July 8, 1980 [Hebrew].

110 "Shinui Party and the Democratic Movement Archives, 1/1/1989 – 31/12/1989," *Israel Government Archives,* 15, https://www.archives.gov.il/archives/Archive/0b071706800246ec/File/0b071706805c19fb.

111 "97 Years of Reporting Workers' News," <BREAK/>https://global.histadrut.org.il/news/97-years-of-reporting-workers-news; Davar reopened in 2016 as an online web portal for Histadrut news.

112 Uri Avnery, http://uriavnery.com/en/bio_textual.html.

113 Eli Alon, "An Attack on Uri Avnery's Life," *News1First Class,* August 28, 2018 [Hebrew], https://www.news1.co.il/Archive/0024-D-129591-00.html?t=124313.

114 Oren Meyers, "Expanding the Scope of Paradigmatic Research in Journalism Studies: The Case of Early Mainstream Israeli Journalism and Its Discontents," *Journalism* 12, no. 3 (2011): 270.

115 Quoted in ibid.

116 Quoted in ibid. One source indicates that the Kingdom of Israel underground, discussed below, was convicted of the bombing. See Shimrit Bustan, "1953: Malkhut Israel (Tzrifin Underground), IDF Portal, n.d. [Hebrew].

117 "Uri Avnery: Peace Activist, Journalist, Writer," n.d., https://uriavnery.com/en/bio_textual.html.

118 Meyers, "Expanding the Scope," 271. The agency is known variously as Shin Bet, Shabak, General Security Services (GSS), or Internal Security Agency (ISA). For consistency, I will use the term "Shabak" henceforth.

119 Zvi Lavie, "The Editors' Committee: Myth and Reality," *Kesher* 2, no. 1 (May 1987): 11 – 33 [Hebrew].

120 Amit Schejter, "The End of the Post-Colonial Era: The Transformation in Israeli Media Law on the State's 70th Anniversary," *Publizistik* 67 no. 1 (2022): 113–14. Regarding Ben-Gurion's reluctance, see Tasha G. Oren, *Demon in the Box: Jews, Arabs, Politics and Culture in the Making of Israeli Television* (New Brunswick, NJ: Rutgers University Press, 2004), 42.

121 Yossi Suede, "The Color Revolution: 40 Years after the End of the Anti-Eraser," *Makor Rishon,* October 10, 2021 [Hebrew], https://www.makorrishon.co.il/news/411773.

122 Oren, *Demon in the Box,* 38.

123 Dana Vinkler, "Making Israeli Television—Discussions Leading to the Establishment of Television in Israel, 1948 – 1968," *Kesher* 34 (Spring 2006), 137 [Hebrew].

124 "Regular Survey of Social Problems and Public Opinion," Data Israel G0282, Viterbi Center, Israel Democracy Institute, March 1968.

125 Ben-Gurion lawsuit, Mordechai Naor, "The Ben-Gurion-'Kol Ha'am' Trial," *Kesher* 24 (1998): 34 – 47 [Hebrew]; on suspending distribution in IDF, see Orit Rozin, "Kol Ha'am: Portrait of a Struggle," in *Quiet, [They're] Speaking: Legal Culture of Freedom of Expression in Israel,* ed. Michael Birnhack (Tel Aviv: Ramot, 2006), 94 [Hebrew].

126 Rozin, "Kol Ha'am," 94 – 101. Note, again, that for petitions against state authorities, the Supreme Court sits as the High Court of Justice (HCJ); the term "Supreme Court" is used here for consistency and clarity.

127 HCJ 73/53 and HCJ 87/53, "*Kol Ha'am Corporation, Ltd. and Al-Ittihad Newspaper vs. Minister of the Interior,*" *Versa: Opinions of the Supreme Court of Israel,* Cardozo Law School, October 16, 1953, 6 – 7.

128 Adam Shinar, "Freedom of Expression in Israel: Origins, Evolution, Revolution and Regression," in *Oxford Handbook on the Israeli Constitution,* ed. Aharon Barak, Barak Medina, and Yaniv Roznai (forthcoming, 2023), 4.

129 Ian Black and Benny Morris, *Israel's Secret Wars: A History of Israel's Intelligence Services* (New York: Grove Weidenfeld, 1991), 151.

130 Eyal Pascovich, "Not Above the Law: Shin Bet's (Israel Security Agency) Democratization and Legalization Process," *Journal of Intelligence History* 14, no. 1 (2015): 56–57; see also Black and Morris, *Israel's Secret Wars*, 156.

131 Irene L. Gendzier, "Palestine and Israel: The Binational Idea," *Journal of Palestine Studies* 4, no. 2 (Winter 1975): 12–35; David Green, "This Day in Jewish History: 1933: The Murder of Chaim Arlosoroff," *Haaretz*, June 16, 2013. Revisionist supporters claimed a political frame-up.

132 Benny Morris, *The Birth of the Palestinian Refugee Problem Revisited* (Cambridge: Cambridge University Press, 2014), chap. 5.

133 Cary David Stanger, "A Haunting Legacy: The Assassination of Count Bernadotte," *Middle East Journal* 42, no. 2 (1988): 262.

134 Yinon Roichman, "The Day the Knesset Was (Nearly) Conquered," *Ynet*, September 28, 2006, https://www.ynet.co.il/articles/0,7340,L-3306796,00.html [Hebrew].

135 Ami Pedahzur and Arie Perliger, *Jewish Terrorism in Israel* (New York: Columbia University Press, 2009), 31–32.

136 Bustan, "Malkhut Israel," 2.

137 Pedahzur and Perliger, *Jewish Terrorism*, 31.

138 Quoted in ibid., 35.

139 Friedmann, *The End of Innocence*, 183–84.

140 Ibid., 270.

141 Jewish Telegraphic Agency, "Israel Court Hears More Details on Plot to Bomb Soviet Embassy," August 7, 1957, https://www.jta.org/archive/israel-court-hears-more-details-on-plot-to-bomb-soviet-em bassy.

142 On revelation of the existence of Shabak, see Pascovich, "Not Above the Law," 56; Ofer Aderet, "62 Years On, Why Is Shin Bet Still Hiding Details on Israel Kastner's Murder," *Haaretz*, May 23, 2019, https://www.haaretz.com/israel-news/2019-05-23/ty-article/.premium/62-years-on-why-is-shin-bet-still-hiding-details-on-israel-kastners-murder/0000017f-f5d5-ddde-abff-fdf56a3c0000; on the conviction and early release, see Shabak, "The Kastner Affair," 2020, https://www.shabak.gov.il/english/heritage/affairs/Pages/KastnerAffair.aspx.

143 Segev, *A State at Any Cost*, 588.

144 Grinberg, *Mo(ve)ments of Resistance*, 112.

145 Ibid., 114–15.

146 Segev, *A State at Any Cost*, 502.

147 Many Arab citizens of Israel identify as Palestinians, or see the term "Arab Israelis" as part of Israel's historical mission to create artificial divisions. Despite the continuity of identity, citizens of Israel have a distinct political history that warrants separate analysis; for clarity, this group will be referred to generally as Arab citizens, to distinguish them from Palestinians under occupation following 1967.

148 See Benny Morris, *1948: A History of the First Arab–Israeli War* (New Haven, CT: Yale University Press, 2008).

149 Segev, *A State at Any Cost*, 458.

150 S. Robinson, *Citizen Strangers*, 35.

151 On the six DER laws, see Aviva Halamish, "Mapam's Vacillating Stance on the Military Government: 1955–1966," *Israel Studies Forum* 25, no. 2 (Fall 2010): 31–32.

152 Yair Bauml, "Israel's Military Rule over Its Palestinian Citizens," in *Israel and Its Palestinian Citizens: Ethnic Privileges in the Jewish State*, ed. Nadim N. Rouhana and Sahar S. Huneidi (Cambridge: Cambridge University Press, 2017), 106.

153 S. Robinson, *Citizen Strangers*.

154 Numerous sources cite 418 villages, but an activist group, the Decolonizer, cites more than 600—however, these include cultural destruction as well. See, e. g., Rochelle Davis, *Palestinian Village Histories: Geographies of the Displaced* (Stanford, CA: Stanford University Press, 2011), 9; "Colonialism in Destru(A) ction," Decolonizer, https://www.de-colonizer.org/map.

155 Benny Morris, *The Birth of the Palestinian Refugee Problem Revisited* (Cambridge: Cambridge University Press, 2014), 309.

156 S. Robinson, *Citizen Strangers*, 70.

157 Segev, *A State at Any Cost*, 452; this is extrapolated from Segev's observation that about half the refugees left between the Partition vote and prior to independence.

158 Haim Margalith, "Enactment of a Nationality Law in Israel," *American Journal of Comparative Law* 2, no. 1 (Winter 1953): 64.

159 Tatour and others argue that the Mandate citizenship orders were effectively annulled by independent statehood; Lana Tatour, "Citizenship as Domination: Settler Colonialism and the Making of Palestinian Citizenship in Israel," *Arab Studies Journal* 27, no. 2 (Fall 2019): 18.

160 Ben-Gurion regarding *laissez-passer* documents quoted in S. Robinson, *Citizen Strangers*, 68; eighteen draft bills, ibid., 97.

161 Ibid., 25.

162 Bauml, "Israel's Military Rule," 111.

163 S. Robinson, *Citizen Strangers*, 71; Ben-Gurion in Knesset quoted in Tatour, "Citizenship as Domination," 22.

164 Tatour, "Citizenship as Domination," 23.

165 Knesset, "Law of Return 5710/1950," translation provided by the International Labor Organization, https://www.ilo.org/dyn/natlex/docs/ELECTRONIC/86616/97947/F1439396114/ISR86616.pdf.

166 Knesset, "Nationality Law, 5712/1952," https://www.knesset.gov.il/review/data/eng/law/kns2_na tionality_eng.pdf.

167 Uri Davis, "Jinsiyya versus Muwatana: The Question of Citizenship and the State in the Middle East: The Cases of Israel, Jordan and Palestine," *Arab Studies Quarterly* 17, nos. 1–2 (Winter and Spring 1995): 26.

168 Bauml, "Israel's Military Rule," 111. The remaining 20 percent were defined as internal refugees.

169 Yossi Harpaz and Ben Herzog, "Report on Citizenship Law: Israel," European University Institute (2018), 5.

170 Margalith, "Nationality Law," 66.

171 Ibid., 64. The literal translation of the Hebrew name of the 1952 law is "Citizenship Law," but the author uses the term "nationality law" in this article.

172 Bauml, "Israel's Military Rule," 109.

173 Friedmann, *The End of Innocence*, 271.

174 S. Robinson, *Citizen Strangers*, 39–40.

175 Tom Segev, *1949: The First Israelis*, ed. Arlen Neal Weinstein (New York: Henry Holt, 1986), 51.

176 See Friedmann, *The End of Innocence*, 272–73. The regulation specified that authorities did not have to state the cause; in specific cases, detainees were denied counsel.

177 S. Robinson, *Citizen Strangers*, 42.

178 Friedmann, *The End of Innocence*, 273.

179 Segev, *1949*, 52.

180 S. Robinson, *Citizen Strangers*, 47.

181 Eyal Kafkafi, "Segregation or Integration of the Israeli Arabs: Two Concepts in Mapai," *International Journal of Middle East Studies* 30 (1998): 352. Estimates vary widely—a 1973 article refers to a UN commission concluding that the state had appropriated up to 4 million *dunams* of private land (nearly 100,000 acres), while also observing the large variations in estimates. Sabri Jiryis, "The Legal Structure for the Expropriation and Absorption of Arab Lands in Israel," *Journal of Palestine Studies* 2, no. 4 (Summer 1973): 84.

182 S. Robinson, *Citizen Strangers*, 46; Friedmann, *The End of Innocence*, 272 – 73.

183 Segev, *1949*, 50.

184 Ibid., 51.

185 Neil Caplan, "The 1956 Sinai Campaign Viewed from Asia: Selections from Moshe Sharett's Diaries," *Israel Studies* 7, no. 1 (Spring 2002): 86.

186 Adam Raz, *Kafr Qasim Massacre: A Political Biography* (Jerusalem: Carmel, 2018), loc. 402/959.

187 Danny Orbach, "Black Flag at a Crossroads," *International Journal of Middle East Studies* 45, no. 3 (August 2013): 493 – 97. Orbach notes that military regulations at that time included prohibitions on obeying a manifestly illegal order, but this was not widely known.

188 Ibid., 493.

189 Ofer Aderet, "General's Final Confession Links 1956 Massacre to Israel's Secret Plan to Expel Arabs," *Haaretz*, September 13, 2018; Raz, *Kafr Qasim*.

190 Orbach, "Black Flag," 496.

191 Raz, *Kafr Qasim Massacre*; see chap. 5 for government response; for proceedings against Shadmi and Ben-Gurion telling him to choose the judges, see loc. 528 – 553/959. A *pruta* was one-thousandth of a pound; therefore, ten was equivalent to one-hundredth. A newsletter reporting on the verdict noted that a cup of soda water at the time cost 30 *prutot* (loc. 552/959).

192 Aderet, "General's Final Confession."

193 Yousef Tayseer Jabareen, "The Emergency Regulations," in *The Palestinians in Israel: Readings in History, Politics, Society*, ed. Nadim Rouhana and Areej Sabbagh-Khoury (Haifa: Mada el Carmel—Arab Center for Applied Social Research, 2011), 69.

194 Nir Kedar, "The Rule of Law in Israel," *Israel Studies* 23, no. 3, *Israel at 70; Vision & Reality* (Fall 2018): 165.

195 Tatour, "Citizenship as Domination," 18 – 20.

196 Ian S. Lustick, *Arabs in the Jewish State: Israel's Control of a National Minority* (Austin: University of Texas Press, 1980), 126 – 27; Bauml, "Israel's Military Rule," 120.

197 On the divisions, see Segev, *1949*, 66; on the bureaucratic pressure for political campaigning, see S. Robinson, *Citizen Strangers*, 90.

198 Leena Dallasheh, "Political Mobilization of Palestinians in Israel: The al 'Ard movement," in *Displaced at Home: Ethnicity and Gender among Palestinians in Israel*, ed. Rhoda Ann Kanaaneh and Isis Nusair (Albany: State University of New York Press, 2010), 24.

199 Ibid., 27.

200 Amal Jamal, *The Arab Public Sphere in Israel: Media Space and Cultural Resistance* (Bloomington: Indiana University Press, 2014), 50; for "decontaminate," see Dallasheh, "Political Mobilization," 28.

201 Israel Supreme Court, "Yaakov Yardur v. Chairman of the Central Elections Committee for the Sixth Knesset. At the Supreme Court of Israel: Elections Appeal 1/65," translation commissioned by the Nakba Files, 1965, https://nakbafiles.org.

202 Shulamit Aloni, *Democracy or Ethnocracy* (Tel Aviv: Am Oved, 2008), 173.

203 Bauml, "Israel's Military Rule," 107.

204 Ibid., 108.

205 Segev, *1949*, 62 – 67.

206 Isser Harel, *Security and Democracy* (Tel Aviv: Edanim, Yediot Ahronot, 1989), 441 [Hebrew].

207 S. Robinson, *Citizen Strangers*, 125.

208 Kafkafi, "Segregation or Integration," 360.

209 Bauml, "Israel's Military Rule," 109.

210 Aviva Halamish, "Mapam's Vacillating Stance on the Military Government: 1955–1966," *Israel Studies Forum* 25, no. 2 (Fall 2010): 35.

211 Kafkafi, "Segregation or Integration," 359; Halamish, "Mapam's Vacillating Stance," 35–36.

212 Yair Bauml, "The Military Government and the Process of Its Revocation, 1958–1968," *The New East* 43 (2002): 152 [Hebrew].

213 Yair Bauml, "The Military Government," in *The Palestinians in Israel*, ed. Rouhana and Sabbagh-Khoury, 55; some emergency measures remain in force.

214 Bauml, "The Military Government and the Process of Its Revocation."

215 J. Shapira, *Democracy in Israel*, 192–94.

Section IV
Diverging Paths: Occupation, and Democratic Progress: 1967–77; 1977–92

1 I am grateful to Akiba Cohen for alerting me to this quip. In fact, Eshkol's indecisiveness generated so many jokes that they were collected into a book that included jokes such as "Why didn't he ever take a shower? Because in the bath there were hot and cold water taps and he couldn't decide between them." Zeev Galili, "Levi Eshkol: Jokes and Reality about the Man Who Won the Six-Day War," *Logic to the Madness*, Online Column of Zeev Galili, April 24, 2018, http://www.zeevgalili.com/2018/04/22824 [Hebrew].

2 David Landau, *Ben-Gurion: A Political Life* (New York: Schocken, 2011), 101.

3 Population of the West Bank (including Jerusalem), Gaza, and North Sinai: Joel Perlmann, "The 1967 Census: The 1967 Census of the West Bank and Gaza Strip: A Digitized Version," Annandale-on-Hudson, NY: Levy Economics Institute of Bard College (November 2011–February 2012), https://www.levyinstitute.org/palestinian-census. For information on the nearly 6,500 Druze residents left in the Golan Heights by the end of the war and about 90,000 who fled or were expelled, see Ministry of Defense, IDF, and Defense Establishment Archives, "Population Census 1967 (5727): Golan Heights, Final Data, General Census" and "Displacement in the Heights: How the Population of the Golan Heights Vanished in 1967" (Akevot: Institute for Israeli-Palestinian Conflict Research, n.d.), https://www.akevot.org.il/en/article/displacement-in-the-golan. Gorenberg, however, estimates 1.1 million, based on both CBS and ISA (Shabak) documents, but he also notes that some estimates of Israeli authorities went as high as 1.5 million; Gershom Gorenberg, *The Accidental Empire: The Birth of Israeli Settlements, 1967–1977* (New York: Henry Holt, 2006), loc. 7591/9763.

4 Only Britain, Iraq, and Pakistan recognized Jordan's annexation, and Pakistan's recognition is disputed; Jordan formally renounced its claim to the West Bank in 1988; Economic Cooperation Foundation, "Jordanian Annexation of the West Bank (1950)." The Golan Heights was governed largely by Israeli law, decreed by military command; Neve Gordon, *Israel's Occupation* (Berkeley: University of California Press, 2008), 5.

5 Ben-Gurion made statements almost immediately after the war supporting the return of the territories in exchange for agreements, reiterating the position on several occasions and generally excluding Jerusalem and the Golan. There are historical disagreements on the details of his position. See, e.g., Arthur Hertzberg, "Israel, the Tragedy of Victory," *New York Review of Books*, May 28, 1987; Avi Shilon, "David Ben-Gurion on the Issue of Borders," *Zion* 3, (2015): 431 [Hebrew]; Martin

Kramer, "Israel's Situation Today Looks Much as Ben-Gurion Envisioned It," *Mosaic*, April 30, 2018. Ben-Gurion resigned as prime minister in 1963, as mentioned in Chapter 8.

6 Gorenberg, *The Accidental Empire*, loc. 2280/9763.

7 Viterbi Center for Public Opinion, "Data Israel Survey Archive: G0305, Election Survey 1969—Return Territories," Israel Democracy Institute.

8 David Kretzmer, *The Occupation of Justice: The Supreme Court of Israel and the Occupied Territories* (Albany: State University of New York Press, 2002), 2.

9 Gorenberg's treatment illustrates the gray zone between indecision or elusiveness in Eshkol's thinking, though Eshkol is often portrayed as both dovish and indecisive. On Israel avoiding major decisions prior to 1967, the incrementalist constitution is a good example.

10 On Eshkol's deliberations regarding Gaza and the West Bank, see Gorenberg, *The Accidental Empire*, loc. 933/9763.

11 "Law and Administration Ordinance (Amendment No. 11) Law of 1967," English version, Israel Ministry of Foreign Affairs, https://www.gov.il/en/Departments/General/13-law-and-administration-ordinance-amendment-no-11-law.

12 Occupation may or may not be legal under international law, depending on whether it violates the UN Charter. However, international humanitarian law applies regardless of the nature of the occupation. Annexation and the acquisition of territory through force violate international law, regardless of the previous status of the territory, whether captured from a sovereign power, such the Golan Heights, or an occupying power, such as Egypt or Jordan over Gaza and the West Bank /Jerusalem, respectively (most countries did not recognize Jordan's 1950 annexation of the West Bank). The Fourth Geneva Convention (henceforth, GCIV) defines protection of civilians in war, including occupation.

13 Tom Ginsburg, *Democracies and International Law* (Cambridge: Cambridge University Press, 2021), chap. 2; for a succinct empirical summary, see 101; see also Gregory H. Fox and Brad R. Roth, "Democracy and International Law," *Review of International Studies* 27, no. 3 (2001): 327–52. This is not to suggest that compliance with international humanitarian law is a benchmark of democracy, or that noncompliance proves non-democracy. Rather, I show more generally that tension with international law moves Israel away from its own positioning as part of the family of democracies globally, while violating international humanitarian law generally occurs through undemocratic practice and reinforces it. I am grateful to Yehezkel Lein for probing this issue.

14 Martin Plaut, "Britain's Guantanamo Bay," BBC, August 6, 2002,http://news.bbc.co.uk/1/hi/world/africa/2175882.stm.

15 Quoted in Guy Luria, "The Legacy of Meir Shamgar, Z'L," Israel Democracy Institute, October 14, 2020 [Hebrew], https://www.idi.org.il/articles/32654.

16 Yael Berda, *Living Emergency: Israel's Permit Regime in the Occupied Territories* (Stanford, CA: Stanford University Press, 2018), 18–19; Berda describes how Shamgar's legal team physically cut and pasted the Arabic text of the DER, cutting out references to British colonial figures in order to replace them with Israeli military terms. Both Berda and Neve Gordon find that the occupation is not a replica of the pre-1967 military government, and its immediate aims differed; these are differences of implementation, but the continuity lay in establishing a military regime to govern citizens. See N. Gordon, *Israel's Occupation*, 10–11.

17 Jordan had annexed the West Bank in 1950 but only Britain, Iraq, and Pakistan recognized the annexation; Egypt never annexed Gaza. See "Jordanian Annexation of the West Bank (1950), *The Israeli-Palestinian Conflict, an Interactive Database*, Economic Cooperation Foundation, https://ecf.org.il/issues/issue/134.

18 N. Gordon, *Israel's Occupation*, 26–28.

19 Limor Yehuda et al., *One Rule, Two Legal Systems: Israel's Regime of Laws in the West Bank* (Association for Civil Rights in Israel, October 2014), 6.

20 N. Gordon, *Israel's Occupation*, 27–28.

21 Theodor Meron, "Settlements in the Territories Being Held, Letter to Foreign Ministry, September 18, 1967" [Hebrew]. Special gratitude to Gershom Gorenberg for making this document publicly available. See Gershom Gorenberg, "Kfar Etzion, the Meron Opinion and the Illegality of Settlement," *South Jerusalem blog* (2008), http://southjerusalem.com/2008/09/kfar-etzion-the-meron-opinion-and-the-illegality-of-settlement.

22 Gorenberg, *The Accidental Empire*, loc. 1948/9763.

23 Gorenberg, "Kfar Etzion, the Meron Opinion."

24 David Kretzmer and Yael Ronen, *The Occupation of Justice: The Supreme Court of Israel and the Occupied Territories*, 2d ed. (New York: Oxford University Press, 2021), 189.

25 Berda, *Living Emergency*, 15–20.

26 N. Gordon, *Israel's Occupation*, 33–39. This is only a partial list for illustration; Gordon provides a detailed categorization of the wide range of activities regulated by permits.

27 Ibid.

28 Yizhar Be'er and Saleh 'Abdel-Jawad, *Collaborators in the Occupied Territories: Human Rights Abuses and Violations* (Jerusalem: B'Tselem, 1994).

29 N. Gordon, *Israel's Occupation*, 51.

30 Shlomo Gazit, *Trapped* (Tel Aviv: Zmora-Bitan, 1999), 122.

31 Be'er and 'Abdel-Jawad, *Collaborators*.

32 N. Gordon, *Israel's Occupation*, 31–32; Israel passed a law regulating Shabak activities only in 2002.

33 Ibid., 50–51. Bitton notes that "huge" infrastructure projects were established in the territories; Mary (Miri) Bitton, "Reformist Third Parties: The Rise and Fall of the Progressive Party in the United States and the Democratic Movement for Change in Israel" (diss., City University of New York, 1995), 146.

34 Economic dependency developed in both directions, although it was dependence of Palestinians on Israel that contributed to greater Israeli control; for the nature of this dependence in trade, labor, and finance, as well as infrastructure dependence, see Yusif A. Sayigh, "The Palestinian Economy under Occupation: Dependency and Pauperization," *Journal of Palestine Studies* 15, no. 4 (Summer 1986): 47–51.

35 For "imposed integration," see Mohammed Samhouri, "Fifty Years of Israeli–Palestinian Economic Relations, 1967–2017: What Have We Learned?" *Palestine-Israel Journal* 22, no. 2 (2017). On Palestinians employed in Israel, see Berda, *Living Emergency*, 20–21.

36 Samhouri, "Fifty Years."

37 Yehuda et al., *One Rule, Two Legal Systems*, 13–14.

38 The full name of the July 1967 law applying regular Israeli criminal law to its citizens is: "Emergency Regulations (Judea and Samaria—Adjudication of Offenses and Legal Assistance), 5727/1967," National Legislation Database (the database states that the law was first published in the legal registry on July 4, 1967; full text documents are available only from the first extension published in 1968), https://main.knesset.gov.il/Activity/Legislation/Laws/Pages/LawPrimary.aspx?t=lawlaws&st=lawlaws&lawitemid=2157502.

39 Gazit states that they remained in force as a matter of fact; Kretzmer examines the legal arguments challenging this position in numerous petitions to the Supreme Court; see Gazit, *Trapped*, 39; Kretzmer, *The Occupation of Justice*, chap. 7.

40 Gazit, *Trapped*, 39–40; Shamgar made the decision, and the attorney general at the time, Moshe Ben Zeev, stated that the political leadership fully backed the decision. See Limor Yehuda, "HCJ and the Territories: Judicial Oversight or Legal Stamp for the Occupation," *The Law Film* (2011), https://www.

thelawfilm.com/inside/hebrew/stories/the-opt-and-hcj-landing-page/the-opt-and-the-hcj-introduction. On Shamgar's explanation for the decision, see also Michael Sfard, *The Wall and the Gate: Israel, Palestine and the Legal Battle for Human Rights*, trans. Maya Johnston (New York: Metropolitan, 2018), 38.

41 Sfard, *The Wall and the Gate*, 38; on the earliest petition and "judicial annexation" (quoting Baruch Kimmerling), see N. Gordon, *Israel's Occupation*, 33.

42 On Shamgar's view and the appearance of legitimacy, see Yehuda, "HCJ and the Territories"; Sfard, *The Wall and the Gate*, 39. Sfard posits that the decision was "exceptional" at the time and also suggests that it included "public relations" considerations.

43 Gazit, *Trapped*, 45.

44 Ibid., 53.

45 Ibid., 53–54. On the ministerial committees, see N. Gordon, *Israel's Occupation*, 30.

46 Krampf, *The Israeli Path to Neoliberalism*, 94–96.

47 Ibid., 97–100.

48 Michael Shalev, "Liberalization and the Transformation of the Political Economy," in *The New Israel*, ed. Shafir and Peled, 132.

49 On the evolution of military production as a means of self-reliance from 1967 following the French embargo, and then arms export and emergence of high-technology industries, see Gershon Shafir and Yoav Peled, "Introduction: the Socio-Economic Liberalization of Israel," in *The New Israel*, ed. idem, 5.

50 Yigal Allon, "The Case for Defensible Borders," *Foreign Affairs* 55, no. 1 (October 1976): 38–53.

51 Israel dismantled its Sinai settlements in the early 1980s, following the peace agreement with Egypt; Israel withdrew its Gaza settlements in 2005, along with four West Bank settlements (out of more than 130 West Bank settlements in 2023, according to Peace Now data). In Jerusalem and the Golan Heights, Israel eventually applied civilian law, explored in the following chapters; despite deep inequalities between non-Jews in those areas (who are mostly permanent residents rather than citizens) and Jewish Israelis, the inequality is most formalized between settlers and Palestinians in the West Bank.

52 The name of the law is a shortened version of the full name. Ahead of the expiration in 2022, the Knesset failed to approve the extension of the law for the first time; but elections were soon called, triggering an automatic extension of the law.

53 Yehuda et al., *One Rule, Two Legal Systems*, 15. Note that Israel has no absentee voting for regular citizens.

54 For the "turtle" image, see N. Gordon, *Israel's Occupation*, 29; for "pipelining," see Sfard, *The Wall and the Gate*, 126.

55 Yehuda et al., *One Rule, Two Legal Systems*, 15, 18–19.

56 Ibid., 20–21.

57 Kretzmer and Ronen, *Occupation of Justice*, 222–23.

58 See Adam Raz, "Why Israel Secretly Decided to Erase the Green Line," *Haaretz*, September 9, 2022.

59 Yehuda et al., *One Rule, Two Legal Systems*, 95.

60 From 1981, the Civil Administration was responsible for the planning committee; see Bimkom, *The Prohibited Zone: Israel Planning Policy in Area C* (Jerusalem: Bimkom—Planners for Planning Rights, 2008), 4–5; see also Amir Paz-Fuchs and Alon Cohen-Lifshitz, "The Changing Character of Israel's Occupation: Planning and Civilian Control," *Town Planning Review* 81, no. 6 (2010): 585–97.

61 The term "terror" refers to the standard meaning of violence against civilians for political aims.

62 Ehud Sprinzak, "Extremism and Violence in Israel: The Crisis of Messianic Politics," *Annals of the American Academy of Political and Social Science* 555 (1998): 120; Gazit, *Trapped*, 99.

63 Gazit, *Trapped*, 119–20.

64 Nir Shalev, *The Ofra Settlement: An Unauthorized Outpost* (Jerusalem: B'Tselem, 2008), 7; see also Gorenberg, *The Accidental Empire*, esp. chap. 10.

65 Gorenberg, *The Accidental Empire*, loc. 5328/9763.

66 Ibid., on Sharon and the "immoral order," loc. 5343/9763; on "ethic of illegalism," 5518/9763.

67 HCJ 606/78 and 610/78, full decision scanned/published by Raanan Alexandrovich and Liran Atzmor, *The Law in These Parts: Interactive Journey Following the Film* (2012), 118 [Hebrew].

68 HCJ 606/78 and 610/78, 117. See also Sfard, *The Wall and the Gate*, 189.

69 Kretzmer and Ronen, *The Occupation of Justice*, 201.

70 Ibid., 204. See also HCJ 390/79, "*Dweikat et al. v. State*," *Versa: Opinions of the Supreme Court of Israel*, Cardozo Law School, October 10, 1979. The decision will be referred to as *Elon Moreh*, for clarity.

71 Jewish Telegraphic Agency, "Israel's Supreme Court Rules Elon Moreh in Samaria Must Be Removed," October 23, 1979.

72 The first quote in the sentence comes from Moshe Hanegbi, *Hakvalim shel Tzedek* (Jerusalem: Yavneh, 1981), 11. The second quote comes from Jewish Telegraphic Agency "Government to Seek Alternative Site for Elon Moreh, Special Cabinet Session Thursday to Discuss Issue," October 29, 1979.

73 Sfard, *The Wall and the Gate*, 178.

74 Itzhak Zamir, "Legal Status of Israeli Settlements in Judea and Samaria: Opinion of the Attorney General, Ministry of Justice, February 25, 1980," Alexandrovich and Atzmor, *The Law in These Parts*, 6–7 [Hebrew].

75 Quoted in Yehuda Shaul and Dror Etkes, "The Settlers and the High Court of Justice—Elon Moreh," *Haaretz*, November 27, 2018 [Hebrew].

76 Zamir, "Legal Status," 4–5.

77 Sfard, *The Wall and the Gate*, 186.

78 Ibid., 135, 149 (on "public" and "state" land terminology), 338–339 (on construction on state and private land). Although the term "state land" reflects Israel's approach, the term has become common; it is used henceforth for consistency with much of the literature on the topic. On including settlers as the "local population," see Kretzmer, *The Occupation of Justice*, 187.

79 On the overwhelming consensus on the illegality of settlements based on international law, see Sfard, *The Wall and the Gate*, 132–134.

80 For 1968 and 1976 quotes, see Leibowitz, *Judaism, Human Values, and the Jewish State*, 226, 237; for 1981 quote, see Haim Yavin, "The Elected of '81: Episode 4, Left and Right," Kan Archives, Israel State Broadcasting Corporation, originally broadcast July 30, 1981, https://archive.kan.org.il [Hebrew].

81 Not all Arab citizens lived in areas under military rule, though most sources provide estimates from 1948 (approximately 85 percent, as observed in earlier chapters), rather than from1966.

82 Karin Tamar Schafferman, "Participation, Abstention and Boycott: Trends in Arab Voter Turnout in Israeli Elections," Israel Democracy Institute, April 21, 2009, https://en.idi.org.il/articles/7116.

83 Elie Rekhess, "The Evolvement of an Arab-Palestinian National Minority in Israel," *Israel Studies* 12, no. 3 (Fall 2007): 10.

84 Ibid., 6.

85 Sabri Jiryis, "The Legal Structure for Expropriation and Absorption of Arabs Lands in Israel," *Journal of Palestine Studies* 2, no. 4 (Summer 1973): 84. Estimates of the total amount of confiscated land inside Israel vary; Zayyad cites 6.5 million *dunams* in 1976. See Tawfiq Zayyad, "The Fate of the Arabs in Israel," *Journal of Palestine Studies* 6, no. 1 (1976): 95.

86 See Zayyad, "The Fate of the Arabs in Israel," 97.

87 Rekhess, "The Evolvement of an Arab-Palestinian National Minority," 9–10.

88 Terence Smith, "5 Israeli Arabs Killed in Protest Riots," *New York Times*, March 31, 1976.

89 Quoted in Ehud Ein Gil, "On the Edge of a 'Yod,'" Matzpen: The Socialist Organization in Israel (May 16, 2020), [Hebrew], https://matzpen.org/2020 – 05 – 16/the-supreme-court-of-zionism.

90 Dan Rabinowitz and Khawla Abu Bakr, *The Stand Tall Generation: The Palestinian Citizens of Israel Today* (Jerusalem: Keter, 2002), loc. 80/443.

91 Ibid., loc. 80/443.

92 Schafferman, "Participation, Abstention and Boycott."

93 Shalom Cohen and Kochavi Shemesh, "The Origins and Development of the Israeli Black Panther Movement," *MERIP Reports* 49 (July 1976), and Grinberg, "Mo(ve)ments of Resistance," 171 – 172.

94 Ibid. cite 1.7%. Grinberg reports that the Panthers won 2.2% in the Histadrut; I use the source closer to the time of the events; see Grinberg, "Mo(ve)ments of Resistance," 173.

95 Campaign party platform for Ma'arach, National Library of Israel Archive, posters and signs, https://web.nli.org.il/sites/NLI/Hebrew/collections/treasures/elections/elections_materials/Pages/elect_ephemera_1973.aspx.

96 "Special Session of the Knesset: 480th Meeting of the Seventh Knesset," Knesset, December 25, 1973 [Hebrew].

97 Nahman Uriely and Amnon Barzilay, *The Rise and Fall of the Democratic Movement for Change* (Tel Aviv: Reshafim, 1982), introduction.

98 Israel State Archives (n.d.), "Golda Meir and the Agranat Commission: The Report That Brought Down a Government, November 1973–April 1974," https://catalog.archives.gov.il/en/chapter/golda-meirs-government-agranat-report-april-1974.

99 Eva Etzioni-Halevy and Moshe Livne, "The Response of the Israeli Establishment to the Yom Kippur War Protest," *Middle East Journal* 31, no. 3 (Summer 1977): 284–86.

100 Amichai Cohen, *The Constitutional Revolution and Counter-Revolution* (Jerusalem: Israel Democracy Institute and Kinneret Zmora Dvir, 2020), 39 [Hebrew].

101 Two members opposed it; see Martin Edelman, *Courts, Politics and Culture in Israel* (Charlottesville: University of Virginia Press, 1994), 13.

102 Thomas J. Hamilton, "6 on El Al Plane Wounded in Arab Attack at Zurich," *New York Times*, February 19, 1969; see also Eyal Inon, "1969, Bergman v. Ministry of Finance: Constitutional Revolution in Three Acts," Jerusalem: Ministry of Justice, April 11, 2019 [Hebrew]. Note that the War of Attrition can refer to various phases, including 1967– 70, or 1967– 73; the main fighting with Egypt was from 1969 through 1970.

103 A. Cohen, *The Constitutional Revolution*, 39.

104 Inon, "1969, Bergman."

105 Menachem Hofnung, "The Public Purse and the Private Campaign: Political Finance in Israel," *Journal of Law and Society* 23, no. 1 (March 1996): 132.

106 Knesset, "Basic Law: The Knesset (Originally Adopted in 5718/1958)," trans. Sheila Hattis Rolef. The law stipulates: "The Knesset shall be elected in general, national, direct, equal, [by] secret [ballot], and proportional elections."

107 HJC 98/69, "*A. Bergman v. Minister of Finance and State Comptroller,*" Versa: *Opinions of the Supreme Court of Israel*, Cardozo Law School, July 3, 1969, 4.

108 Inon, "1969, Bergman."

109 Assaf Shapira, "Campaign Financing in Israel," Israel Democracy Institute, January 20, 2016, https://en.idi.org.il/articles/3255.

110 Justice Landau, lead author on the opinion, would become a vocal critic of judicial activism later. See A. Cohen, *The Constitutional Revolution*, 40 – 41.

111 Melville B. Nimmer, "The Uses of Judicial Review in Israel's Quest for a Constitution," *Columbia Law Review* 70, no. 7 (November 1970): 1218.

112 See, e.g., Abraham Bell, "The Counter-Revolutionary Nation-State Law," *Israel Studies* 25, no. 3 (Fall 2020): 242–43.

113 "Arab Accords and Israeli Acrobatics," *Time* magazine, January 3, 1977.

114 Ibid.

115 Ofer Aderet, "Asher Yadlin Dies, among the Top Figures of Labor and the Histadrut in the 1970s," *Haaretz*, June 5, 2016 [Hebrew].

116 Zvi Lavie, "The [Bank of Israel] Governor Who Was Chosen–and at the Last Minute, Arrested," *Ynet/Yediot Ahronot*, August 11, 2013 [Hebrew].

117 Jewish Telegraphic Agency, "Yadlin's Secrets Flushed Out," October 28, 1976, https://www.jta.org/archive/yadlins-secrets-flushed-out.

118 Aderet, "Asher Yadlin."

119 Quoted in Lavie, "The [Bank of Israel] Governor."

120 Ibid.

121 Tomer Avital, "Behind the Scenes of Rabin's Dollar Account Affair," *Shakoof*, August 7, 2019, https://shakuf.co.il/9332 [Hebrew].

122 For Margalit's account, see ibid. On *Ha'olam Hazeh*'s prior investigation, see Sharon Roberts Melzer, "1977, 'Listen, We Have a Problem'—the Dollar Account Affair," Ministry of Justice, April 1, 2019, https://www.gov.il/he/departments/publications/reports/roots_1977#note-3 [Hebrew].

123 Assessment of the total amount varies among different sources; Leah Rabin eventually pled guilty to holding over $21,000, while other reports indicated that the true figure was $32,000. See William E. Farrell, "Mrs. Rabin Is Fined $27,000 in Bank Case," *New York Times*, April 18, 1977.

124 Avital, "Behind the Scenes of Rabin's Dollar Account."

125 Ibid.

126 Friedmann, *The Age of Innocence*, 431.

127 Israel Democracy Institute, "About the 1969 Elections," https://en.idi.org.il/israeli-elections-and-parties/elections/1969.

128 Don Peretz, "Israel's 1969 Election Issues: The Visible and the Invisible," *Middle East Journal* 24, no. 1 (Winter 1970): 34.

129 Bitton, "Reformist Third Parties," 170–71.

130 Ibid., 193–94. Dash mirrored the language of UN Resolution 242, stating that it would be willing to withdraw control of "territories" (without a definite article), but also named the Jordan River as the "defensible border of the country" to the east.

131 Ibid., 196.

132 Amnon Rubinstein, *A Certain Political Experience* (Jerusalem: Eidanim, Yediot Ahronot, 1982), 139 [Hebrew].

133 Uriely and Barzilay, *The Rise and Fall of the Democratic Movement for Change*, 165.

134 Ibid., 11–13.

135 "About the 1977 Elections," Israel Democracy Institute, https://en.idi.org.il/israeli-elections-and-parties/elections/1977.

136 Other sources have listed her birth year as 1928; in a *New York Times* obituary, her son is quoted as stating that she was born in 1927; Jodi Rudoren, "Shulamit Aloni, Outspoken Israeli Lawmaker, Dies at 86," *New York Times*, January 24, 2014.

137 Shulamit Aloni, *Citizen and His State: Foundations of Civics Theory* (Systems—Israel Defense Forces, 1967) [Hebrew]. The Hebrew title does not use the definite article.

138 Shulamit Aloni, *Democracy or Ethnocracy* (Tel Aviv: Am Oved, 2008), 188–89.

139 Ibid.

140 These included Herut, the Liberals, the Free Center, the Mamlakhti List, and the Labor Movement for the Whole Land of Israel, "History of the Likud," Likud, https://www.likud.org.il

141 Segev, *1949*, 170–71.

142 Begin Center, "Upheaval, 1977," Facebook post, May 17, 2016, https://www.facebook.com/watch/?v=1072922082779843.

143 For Likud's campaign material, see "Herut Movement: Elections for the Ninth Knesset," Jabotinsky Institute, 7. For later speeches, see Levi Zini, "Days of Begin: Doing Good for the People," Kan Documentaries, 2019, https://www.youtube.com/watch?v=uRp9un7ixsw [Hebrew].

144 Shelef shows an incremental "de-emphasis" on Herut's "both banks" commitment in the decade prior to 1977, when the balance finally favored those who viewed the Jordan River as the boundary of the historical land of Israel; see Nadav G. Shelef, "From 'Both Banks of the Jordan' to the 'Whole Land of Israel': Ideological Change in Revisionist Zionism," *Israel Studies* 9, no. 1 (2004): 133.

145 "Likud Party Platform, 1973," Israel Democracy Institute [Hebrew], https://www.idi.org.il/media/6995/halikud-8.doc.

146 "1977—Elections for the Ninth Knesset—Further Information," National Library of Israel, https://web.nli.org.il/sites/nli/hebrew/collections/treasures/elections/all_elections/pages/1977-data.aspx.

147 Segev, *A State at Any Cost*, 230 (on Jabotinsky); 648 (on Begin).

148 Quoted in Dennis Ross and David Makovsky, *Be Strong and of Good Courage: How Israel's Most Important Leaders Shaped Its Destiny* (New York: Public Affairs, 2019), 22.

149 Dahlia Scheindlin, "A Family Affair," *Tel Aviv Review of Books* (Spring 2021).

150 Channel 1, "Election Broadcast: Ninth Knesset, May 17, 1977," Kan Archives, August 14, 2021, https://www.youtube.com/watch?v=2vNboq2BiL4 [Hebrew].

151 For a valuable collection of responses to the 1977 elections through 1978, see Herzl and Balfour Hakak, "Racism, Condescension and Hatred: How the Left Reacted to the Upheaval of 1977," *Mida*, January 31, 2016 [Hebrew].

152 Don Peretz and Sammy Smooha, "Israel's Tenth Knesset Elections: Ethnic Upsurgence and Decline of Ideology," *Middle East Journal* 35, no. 4 (August 1981): 506–26.

153 Ibid., 515.

154 Ibid., 512–15.

155 Thomas Friedman, "Economic Crisis in Israel May Remold the Country," *New York Times*, October 29, 1984.

156 Shmuel Tzabag, "Co-operation in the Shadow of a Power Struggle: Israel: The Likud Governments and the Histadrut 1977–84," *Middle Eastern Studies* 31, no. 4 (1995): 853.

157 Ibid.

158 Benjamin Gidron, Michal Bar, and Hagai Katz, *The Israeli Third Sector: Between Welfare State and Civil Society* (New York: Kluwer Academic, 2004), chap. 4; Peretz and Smooha, "Israel's Tenth Knesset Elections."

159 Gidron, Bar, and Katz, *The Israeli Third Sector*, 102.

160 David Kretzmer, interview with author, September 7, 2022.

161 Ibid.

162 This shift of left–right orientation to focus on occupation themes became more prominent in the 1990s, as will be seen. There is an ongoing dilemma in Israel over whether the terms "left" and "right" should refer to economic themes, social values, types of governance, or occupation/conflict-related issues; but broadly and over time, Israelis associate left and right attitudes with dovish and hawkish or nationalist positions toward Arabs (of any nation), respectively. As organizations advancing liberal values often took dovish positions at this time, they were eventually viewed as left-wing in Israeli terms.

163 Amal Jamal et al., "Arab-Palestinian Civil Society Organizations in Israel," Tel Aviv University: Walter Liebach Institute for Jewish Arab Coexistence and Hebrew University (2019), 17 [Hebrew]. The authors note that Arab organizations might have existed under military rule but were probably less formal and not registered, due to fear of restrictions; their data draw on Israel's registrar of nongovernmental agencies.

164 Daphne Tzimhoni, "The Political Configuration of the Christians in the State of Israel," in "The Arabs in Israel: Between Religious Revival and National Awakening," ed. Aharon Layish, special issue, *The New East: Quarterly of the Israel Oriental Society* 32, nos. 125–28 (1989): 157.

165 Jabareen, "The Emergency Regulations," 70.

166 "38 Years Ago This Week," Peace Now, March 8, 2016, https://peacenow.org.il/en/thirty-eight-years-ago-this-week.

167 Nathan Thrall, *The Only Language They Understand* (New York: Metropolitan, 2017), 23.

168 Begin said that "perhaps" the issue of sovereignty could be revisited after five years, and perhaps not. Though he clearly opposed it, he also affirmed to the Americans that Israeli sovereignty ends at the Green Line. See Adam M. Howard, ed., *Foreign Relations of the United States, 1977–80,* vol. 3: *Arab-Israeli Dispute, January 1977–August 1978* (Washington, DC: US Government Printing Office, 2013), 868–70.

169 Thrall, *The Only Language*, 23. See also "Israel and Egypt: Framework for Peace in the Middle East Agreed at Camp David," UN Peacemaker, September 17, 1978, https://peacemaker.un.org/egyptisrael-frameworkforpeace78.

170 "From the Principles and Action Items of the Likud," Israel Democracy Institute, 4 [Hebrew].

171 Thrall, *The Only Language*, 24.

172 For a full analysis of Israel's aims, reflecting the distinctions between Menachem Begin, Ariel Sharon, and other influential figures, contrasted with aims stated either publicly or to the US government, see Zeev Schiff and Ehud Yaar, *Israel's Lebanon War*, trans. Ina Friedman (New York: Simon and Schuster, 1984), esp. chaps. 2, 4.

173 Yishai Menuhin, interview with author, August 11, 2022.

174 William E. Farrell, "Israelis, at Huge Rally In Tel Aviv, Demand Begin and Sharon Resign," *New York Times,* September 26, 1982.

175 Richard Falk, "The Kahan Commission Report on the Beirut Massacre," *Dialectical Anthropology* 8, no. 4 (1984): 319.

176 Eichmann Trial (Channel) "Sessions 41–42," March 7, 2011: 50mn, https://www.youtube.com/watch?v=n9Q65SiAksI [Hebrew].

177 "Deceased Card: Lotte Salzberger," City of David, Ancient Jerusalem/Mount of Olives [Hebrew], https://mountofolives.co.il/he/deceased_card/%D7%9C%D7%95%D7%98%D7%94-%D7%96%D7%9C%D7%A6%D7%91%D7%A8%D7%92%D7%A8/#gsc.tab=0.

178 Uri Ben-Eliezer, "State versus Civil Society? A Non-Binary Model of Domination through the Example of Israel," *Journal of Historical Sociology* 11, no. 3 (September 1998): 383.

179 Krampf, *The Israeli Path to Neoliberalism*, 184–88. The full debate over the causes of the economic crises of the 1980s is beyond the scope of this chapter, which is focused on the government response and its political and social impact.

180 Ibid., 195–96.

181 Lev Luis Grinberg and Gershon Shafir, "Economic Liberalization and the Breakup of the Histadrut's Domain," in *The New Israel*, ed. Shafir and Peled, 109–11, 144.

182 Krampf, *The Israeli Path to Neoliberalism*, 196 (for quarterly inflation); for annual average, see Shafir and Peled, "Introduction: The Socioeconomic Liberalization of Israel."

183 Krampf, *The Israeli Path to Neoliberalism*, 192–93.

184 The Bank of Israel raised interest rates so dramatically that it practically held the economy hostage until the government relented; see ibid., 208.

185 Ibid., 210; M. Shalev, "Liberalization," 138–39.

186 Peter Passell, "Economic Scene; Zionist Dreams, Capitalist Reality," *New York Times,* January 1, 1992.

187 M. Shalev, "Liberalization," 112.

188 Rafael Reuveny, "Democracy, Credibility, and Sound Economics: The Israeli Hyperinflation," *Policy Sciences* 30, no. 2 (1997): 107.

189 Ben-Eliezer, "State versus Civil Society," 386; on the mood ahead of elections, see Marina O. Lowy, "Restructuring a Democracy: An Analysis of the New Proposed Constitution for Israel," *Cornell University Law Journal* 22 no. 1 (Winter 1989): 143–45.

190 Lowy, "Restructuring a Democracy," 116; see also Snir Goldfinger, "The Constitutional Process in Israel: Biography of Power Conflicts and Interests" (thesis, The Open University, 2016), 45.

191 Lowy, "Restructuring a Democracy," 117.

192 In 1978, Freedom House noted that the opposition won the election of 1977; see Gastil, *Freedom in the World,* table 6. For changes of ranking by year, see Freedom House, *Freedom in the World Country Ratings by Region, 1972–2011,* https://freedomhouse.org/sites/default/files/2022–03/Country_and_Territory_Ratings_and_Statuses_FIW_1973–2022%20.xlsx.

193 Peace Now, "West Bank," https://peacenow.org.il/en/settlements-watch/settlements-data/population; for East Jerusalem, see U. O. Schmelz, "The Population of Reunited Jerusalem, 1967–1985," *American Jewish Year Book* 87 (1987): table 22.

194 IDF 1967 Census

195 Thomas Friedman, "A Forecast for Israel: More Arabs than Jews," *New York Times,* Oct. 19, 1987; reporting on Central Bureau of Statistics data, 1985.

196 Yehezkel Lein, *Land Grab: Israel's Settlement Policy in the West Bank* (Jerusalem: Btselem, 2002), 18.

197 IDF 1967 Census 6, Table A.

198 U.O. Schmelz, "The Population of Reunited Jerusalem, 1967–1985," *The American Jewish Year Book* 87 (1987): Table 22.

199 Ibid.

200 Friedman, "A Forecast for Israel."

201 Ibid.

202 Kretzmer and Ronen, *Occupation of Justice,* 206.

203 Ibid., 206–7.

204 Lein, *Land Grab:* 53–54.

205 Raja Shehadeh, "Land and Occupation: A Legal Review," *Palestine-Israel Journal* 4, no. 2 (1997).

206 Lein, *Land Grab,* 54.

207 On land use, see ibid., 51. On 0.25 percent to Palestinians, see Kretzmer and Ronen, *Occupation of Justice,* 209; on 90 percent of settlements, 208.

208 Lein, *Land Grab,* 53–55; 40 percent includes areas that were registered as government lands prior to 1967; see also Kretzmer and Ronen, *Occupation of Justice,* 207. This description of the land-possession mechanisms is a sample of the complexity; each type would be too lengthy to include, but state lands are among the most important such mechanisms.

209 "Law to Extend the Emergency Regulations (Judea and Samaria—Jurisdiction and Legal Aid 5727/1967), Amendment 13 (1984), https://www.nevo.co.il/law_html/law01/319_067.htm#med1 [Hebrew].

210 Knesset, "Law Amending the Income Tax Order (No. 32), 5738/1978," Knesset Legislation Database, September 1, 1978.

211 "The 266th Meeting of the Tenth Knesset," National Legislation Database, January 2–4, 1984.

212 Lein, *Land Grab*, 65. This refers to the "Development Towns and Areas Law, 1988." The term "development town" in Israel refers to areas of lower socioeconomic status, marked for preferential development resources.

213 Quoted in Kretzmer and Ronen, *Occupation of Justice*, 223.

214 I am indebted to David Kretzmer for this insight and for working through these ideas with me, helping with corrections, and providing invaluable feedback on this section.

215 Yardena Schwartz, "Irreconcilable Hebron," *New York Review of Books*, April 21, 2021. Several sources indicate that Begin made the decision to allow Jewish settlement in Hebron specifically following the May attack, but Gazit notes that the government established a yeshiva and a field school in late March; Gazit, *Trapped*, 104.

216 Gazit, *Trapped*, 100.

217 Ibid., 100–101.

218 In an endnote, Gazit added: "In truth, not all the convicts expressed regret"; ibid., 101–2, 108.

219 Oshrat Maimon and Tamar Luster, "Being a Resident of Jerusalem, Not a Citizen," in *Permanent Residency: A Temporary Status Set in Stone* (Jerusalem: Ir Amim, 2012), 38.

220 Dahlia Scheindlin, "The Juggernaut's Achilles Heel," *Cairo Review of Global Affairs: Tahrir Forum*, June 23, 2019.

221 David K. Shipler, "Hijacker's Death: Question in Israel," *New York Times*, April 19, 1986.

222 Saragusti recalled the full details of her role in a Facebook post, with photos of the original magazine cover showing her censored story, September 24, 2022, , https://www.facebook.com/saragusti/posts/pfbid02TezrWzCw35rcV4URp6zS1j5 J5W6Vt1VSoRMokhgTEn6KPMxZuB2qQbu7bjuGg WoBl?__cft__[0]=AZXpyHEnEtUPIFIq697nl-AojPGJOmpvzsBGiwa28xR7 fKHGEXGUwlVdX3_cNgvUGjD KA8QD46bwbErSHYV-kUcAeNVfuron_T_vyUP1aPjvik-2e9kX4XAOQ7 fMtCAqlrhNM6H2yieOdFHgmJEqmy Qy-fDzRaJe1j9uxeuEV6ivBd6iFFGb_wCsRZ9AUBbaX3k&__tn__=%2CO%2CP-R [Hebrew].

223 Ronen Bergman, *Rise and Kill First: The Secret History of Israel's Targeted Assassinations* (New York: Random House, 2018), 291.

224 Gidi Weitz, "How Top Shabak Agents Broke the Conspiracy of Silence around the Bus 300 Affair," *Haaretz*, September 28, 2011 [Hebrew]; see also Michael Bar-Zohar, *Shimon Peres: The Full Biography* (Rishon le'Tzion: Miskal—Yediot Ahronot, Sefer Hemed, 2006), 543 [Hebrew].

225 Bar-Zohar, *Shimon Peres*, 537.

226 Bergman, *Rise and Kill First*, 293–94.

227 For "relieved," see William Claiborne, "Israeli Aide Replace in Dispute," *Washington Post*, June 2, 1986; the *New York Times* reported that he was fired—not technically correct, but this indicates the perception. See Milt Freudenheim and James F. Clarity, "Israeli Cabinet Fires a Zealous Attorney General," *New York Times*, June 8, 1986.

228 Quoted in Lally Weymouth, "Israeli Security and the Rule of Law," *Washington Post*, June 8, 1986.

229 Chezki Baruch, "Justice Zamir Recalls Line 300 Affair," *Arutz 7*, April 4, 2016; video of Zamir from Bar Association conference [Hebrew].

230 Weymouth, "Israeli Security."

231 Sfard, *The Wall and the Gate*, 203.

232 Ze'ev Segal, "End of the Line for Bus 300," *Haaretz*, June 14, 2010.

233 Leon Shelef, "Amnesty Prior to Trial," *Kiryat Mishpat* 3, no. 177 (2003): 182 [Hebrew]. In 2013, despite a lengthy court battle by Israeli journalists, Israel's attorney general and state prosecutor still refused to release all the transcripts of the political figures involved. See Gidi Weitz, "Release the Testimony on the Bus 300 Affair," *Haaretz*, June 20, 2013.

234 Bergman, *Rise and Kill First*, 283.

235 See Moshe Landau, Yacov Maltz, and Itzhak Hoffi, "Commission of Inquiry Report of the Commission of Inquiry into the Methods of Investigation of the General Security Service regarding Hostile Terrorist Activity: Part One," October 1987, 3 – 4.

236 Michal Shaked, *Moshe Landau: Judge* (Tel Aviv: Aliyat Hagag, 2012), 514 [Hebrew].

237 Kretzmer and Ronen, *Occupation of Justice*, 352.

238 Ibid., 354; for reports documenting interrogation practices, see Stanley Cohen and Daphna Golan, "The Interrogation of Palestinians during the Intifada: Ill-Treatment, 'Moderate Physical Pressure' or Torture?," *B'Tselem* (March 1991; March 1992 follow-up report). On Landau, see Shaked, *Moshe Landau*, 12 – 15.

239 Shaul Magid, *Meir Kahane: The Public Life and Political Thought of an American Jewish Radical* (Princeton, NJ: Princeton University Press, 2021), 3.

240 On his arrests in Israel, see ibid.

241 Archive insert in Baruch Kra and Raviv Drucker, " 'Netanyahu Has Poisoned Democracy': Aharon Barak's Battle for the Court," *Reshet* 13, May 30, 2019, https://13tv.co.il/item/news/domestic/crime-and-justice/barak-hamakor-259974 [Hebrew], at 33 minutes.

242 "1977 Elections," Israel Democracy Institute, https://en.idi.org.il/israeli-elections-and-parties/elections/1977.

243 Kach campaign poster from 1984 elections, National Library of Israel Archives, https://web.nli.org.il/sites/nli/english/digitallibrary/pages/viewer.aspx?presentorid=NLI_EDU&docid=NNL03_EDU700275845 [Hebrew].

244 Magid, *Meir Kahane*, 77. On proposed laws against prostitution between Jews and non-Jews, see Robert I. Friedman, "The Sayings of Rabbi Kahane," *New York Review of Books*, February 13, 1986; on expulsion, see Israel Harel, "The Elections in Israel," in *Journal of Palestine Studies* 14, no. 1 (Autumn 1984): 162.

245 Supreme Court verdict, responding to the appeal of both parties against the Central Election Committee for banning them. The original text of the CEC ban appears in the Court's verdict, https://datacheck.co.il/PsakDin.asp?id=411262 [Hebrew].

246 "About the 1984 Elections," Israel Democracy Institute, https://en.idi.org.il/israeli-elections-and-parties/elections/1984.

247 William Claiborne, "Kahane Gains a Following in Israel," *Washington Post*, August 25, 1985.

248 Harel, "The Elections in Israel," 168. Note that Arabs were rarely included in media-commissioned surveys at this time, while academic studies were just beginning to include them.

249 "The One-Hundred and Fifteenth Meeting of the Eleventh Knesset," National Legislation Database, 3256 (p. in file: 32) [Hebrew].

250 Ibid.

251 "The One-Hundred and Eighteenth Meeting of the Eleventh Knesset," National Legislation Database, July 31, 1985, 3898 (pp. in file, 50 – 56) [Hebrew].

252 Ibid.

253 The basic flaw in this argument is that those and other democratic constitutions provide robust provisions for full citizen equality, which Israel lacks. See "The Spanish Constitution, 1978," Agencia Estatal Boletín Oficial del Estado; and Basic Law for the Federal Republic of Germany in the revised version published in the Federal Law Gazette, pt. 3, classification no. 100 – 1, as last amended by the Act of June 28, 2022 (Federal Law Gazette I, p. 968).

254 "The Three-Hundred and Fifteenth Meeting of the Fifteenth Knesset," National Legislation Database, May 15, 2002 [Hebrew].

255 Dana Blander, "The Central Elections Committee: Professional or Political?," *Research and Policy*, Israel Democracy Institute, June 2022.

Section V
The Liberal Potential: 1992–2009

1 Shafir and Peled, "Introduction," in *The New Israel*, 1.

2 For a longitudinal analysis of capitalist or socialist orientation and left–right self-definition, see Dror Walter, "State or Market? On the Meaning(lessness) of the Jewish Israeli Public's Attitudes towards Capitalism or Socialism as the Preferred Economic System," Israel Democracy Institute (2011): 3–4. These polls relate to Jewish Israelis only.

3 Asher Arian and Michal Shamir, "A Decade Later, the World Had Changed, the Cleavage Structure Remained: Israel 1996–2006," *Party Politics* 14 (2008): 689–90, 696. They attribute the synthesis of religious observance with right-wing nationalism to Gush Emunim and the National Religious Party (NRP).

4 The conflict is not the sole ideological division; religion and state remain a firmly divisive topic, as well as progressive-liberal versus conservative values. But these are not as polarizing, and they are also clearly correlated with attitudes toward the occupation.

5 V-Dem Institute, "Democracy for All? V-Dem Annual Report 2018," University of Gothenburg (2018), 17.

6 Larry Diamond, "Democratic Regression in Comparative Perspective: Scope, Methods, and Causes," *Democratization* 28, no. 1 (2021): 36.

7 See Guy Ziv, *Why Hawks Become Doves: Shimon Peres and Foreign Policy Change in Israel* (Albany: State University of New York Press, 2014).

8 Krampf, *The Israeli Path to Neoliberalism*, 219.

9 George Shultz, "Shultz Peace Plan," Economic Cooperation Foundation, March 1988, https://ecf.org.il/issues/issue/160. UNSC Resolution 242 famously avoided the definite article, calling instead for Israel to withdraw from "territories," to avoid defining the scope of withdrawal.

10 See William B. Ries, "Shamir Rejects Shultz Peace Plan," UPI Archives, March 12, 1988; on Shamir's ambiguous rejection, see Yo'el Marcus, "Shamir and the Shultz Plan," *Journal of Palestine Studies* 17, no. 4 (Summer 1988): 153–55.

11 Maureen Dowd and Thomas Friedman, "The Fabulous Bush and Baker Boys," *New York Times*, May 6, 1990.

12 Amnon Rubinstein, "The Story of Basic Laws," *Law and Man—Law and Business/Labor 5772* (September 2012), 12 [Hebrew]; in Israel's political system, the president formally calls on a party leader to form a coalition, usually following elections, based on the likelihood that he/she is capable of forming a coalition. For a description of the intense coalition bargaining and Peres's incentives to the ultra-Orthodox, see Uriel Lynn, *Birth of a Revolution* (Rishon le'Tzion: Miskal—Yediot Ahronot and Chemed, 2017), loc. 438–42/1068 [Hebrew].

13 In colloquial English, the term is usually rendered as "dirty trick," but the literal language illustrates the strength of the sentiment; Nir (Shoko) Cohen, "The Stinking Trick, Original Version," *Ynet*, May 11, 2012, https://www.ynet.co.il/articles/0,7340,L-4227801,00.html [Hebrew].

14 Lynn, *Birth of a Revolution*, loc. 458/1068.

15 Ofer Kenig, "20 Years Later: The 'Dirty Trick' in the Mirror of Time," Israel Democracy Institute (2010), https://www.idi.org.il/articles/1629 [Hebrew]; Rubinstein, "The Story of the Basic Laws," 85 [Hebrew]; *mushchatim* literally means "corrupt people."

16 Lynn, *Birth of a Revolution*, loc. 458/1068.

17 Amir Ben-David, "Kadish Returns to the Battlefield," *Zman Israel*, August 27, 2020 [Hebrew].

18 HCJ 1601/90, "Shalit v. Peres"; and see "Law of the Government, 5761/2001," National Legislation Database.

19 Eyal Benvenisti, "Party Primaries as Collective Action with Constitutional Ramifications: Israel as a Case Study," *Theoretical Inquiries in Law* 3, no. 1 (2002). From 1982, Netanyahu served as deputy chief of mission at the Israeli embassy in Washington, and then as Israel's ambassador to the UN through 1988.

20 The short duration of the reform is the reason that this is mentioned only briefly. There is a rich debate over electoral reform in Israel; and certain proposed reforms, such as regional representation in the Knesset, could have increased checks and balances and accountability, affecting Israeli democracy more significantly. However, the direct election of prime minister was intended to improve coalition instability, and its failure prompted the reversal. See, e.g., Michael Harris and Gidon Doron, "Assessing the Electoral Reform of 1992 and Its Impact on the Elections of 1996 and 1999," *Israel Studies* 4, no. 2 (Fall 1999): 16 – 39.

21 "The Three-Hundred and Twentieth Meeting of the Fifth Knesset," National Legislation Database, January 15, 1964, 10 [Hebrew].

22 Lynn, *Birth of a Revolution*, loc. 151 – 53, 167/1068.

23 Ministry of Justice, "Justices: Benjamin Halevy, z'l," https://judgescv.court.gov.il/c58284ba-645e-e811 – 8105 – 0050568a6817 %D7 %91 %D7 %A0 %D7 %99 %D7 %9E%D7 %99 %D7 %9F-%D7 %94 %D7 %9C%D7 %95 %D7 %99 [Hebrew].

24 Lynn, *Birth of a Revolution*, loc. 194/1068.

25 Ibid., loc. 167– 87/1068. Lynn does note that "freedom of religion" in Halevy's draft is qualified (the draft was produced by the subcommittee for Basic Laws, which he chaired, under the Constitution, Law and Justice Committee). There was no explicit statement of separation of religion and state, or of prohibiting the imposition of religious law on the nonreligious public.

26 Giora Goldberg, "Religious Zionism and the Framing of a Constitution for Israel," *Israel Studies* 3, no. 1 (Spring 1998), 221; Lynn, *Birth of a Revolution*, loc. 194 – 205, 224/1068.

27 Lynn, *Birth of a Revolution*, loc. 203/1068.

28 Ibid., loc. 325/1068. The Hebrew terms used most commonly in this context are *shiryun* or *nokshut*.

29 Dan Meridor, interview with author, September 7, 2022.

30 Minister of Justice and Ministerial Committee for Legislation and Law Enforcement (1990), "Basic Law: Fundamental Human Rights," Ministry of Justice, article 24 (bill prepared and submitted by Minister of Justice Dan Meridor, identical to the bill later submitted by Amnon Rubinstein of Shinui, before the government collapsed) [Hebrew].

31 Ibid., 4; Meridor interview.

32 Meridor interview, 2022.

33 Ibid.; Lynn, *Birth of a Revolution*, loc. 524/1068. See also Rubinstein, "The Story of the Basic Laws," 85.

34 Lynn, *Birth of a Revolution*.

35 Ibid., loc. 810/1068.

36 Rubinstein, "The Story of the Basic Laws," 88.

37 Lynn, *Birth of a Revolution*, loc. 646/1068.

38 Ibid., loc. 590/1068.

39 Ibid., loc. 598/1068.

40 Meridor interview, 2022.

41 Sapir, "Constitutional Revolutions," 368.

42 Rubinstein, "The Story of the Basic Laws," 104.

43 Lynn, *Birth of a Revolution*, loc. 872/1068.

44 Rubinstein, "The Story of the Basic Laws," 97– 98.

45 Ibid., 101; on NRP's concern that future religious legislation could be struck down, see Lynn, *Birth of a Revolution*, loc. 810/1068.

46 Rubinstein, "The Story of the Basic Laws," 102.

47 Ibid., 93.

48 Friedmann, *The Age of Innocence*, 589.

49 Meridor used the term "constitutional revolution" at a judicial swearing-in ceremony; Meridor interview.

50 Menachem Mautner, *Law and the Culture of Israel* (Oxford: Oxford University Press, 2008), 57.

51 Friedmann, e. g., describes Aharon Barak's approach as "everything is justiciable," while noting that Barak denies this. The description is often used critically, although I use it throughout, for lack of a more neutral term. See Friedmann, *The Age of Innocence*, 464. Friedmann asserts that activism accelerated under Shamgar but that Barak took it further. Others credit Shamgar with beginning the change; see Yonah Jeremy Bob, "The Revolutionary Who Changed Israel More than Aharon Barak," *Jerusalem Post*, October 20, 2019.

52 Shoshana Netanyahu, "The Supreme Court of Israel: A Safeguard of the Rule of Law," *Pace International Law Review* 5, no. 1 (1993): 4 – 7.

53 Quoted in ibid., 9 – 10.

54 HCJ 3872/93, "Mitral Ltd. vs. Prime Minister and Minister of Religious Affairs, Yitzhak Rabin," October 22, 1993. This decision applied to actions of the executive, not to legislation.

55 Emmanuel Navon, "Overriding Bagatz Is Essential for Democracy," *Mida*, November 3, 2014 [Hebrew].

56 "One-Hundred and Ninety-Eighth Meeting of the Thirteenth Knesset," National Legislation Database, March 9, 1994, 308 [Hebrew].

57 Ibid., 350.

58 Rubinstein, "The Story of the Basic Laws," 96; see protocol: "One-Hundred and Ninety-Eighth Meeting," 388. The amendment to the Basic Law: Human Dignity and Liberty uses the official name "Declaration of the Establishment of the State of Israel"; the amendments to both Basic Laws were combined and put to a single vote.

59 Amnon Rubinstein, "The Knesset and the Basic Laws Concerning Human Rights," *Mishpat u'Mimshal* 5 (2000): 355 [Hebrew]. The Court struck down just one provision of legislation in 1997, not a complete law.

60 Rubinstein, "The Story of the Basic Laws," 86 – 87.

61 Daniel Elazar, "The Israeli Knesset Elections 1992: A First Analysis," Daniel Elazar Papers Index, Jerusalem Center for Public Affairs (1992), https://www.jcpa.org/dje/articles/elec92-analysis.htm.

62 On Peres, see Ziv, *Why Hawks Become Doves*, chap. 5. For Rabin's campaign promise, see Avi Shlaim, "The Oslo Accord," *Journal of Palestine Studies* 23, no. 3 (Spring 1994): 28.

63 Meretz Party platform, 1992, National Library of Israel, item 25 [Hebrew].

64 Ibid., item 3.

65 "Posters and Notices from the 1992 Elections," National Library of Israel, https://web.nli.org.il/sites/NLI/Hebrew/collections/treasures/elections/elections_materials/Pages/elect_ephemera_1992.aspx. In Israeli elections, many tiny parties compete but do not cross the electoral threshold; these are not considered in the analysis.

66 Nissim Leon, "Rabbi Ovadia Yosef, the Shas Party, and the Arab-Israeli Peace Process," *Middle East Journal* 69, no. 3 (2015): 384 – 85.

67 See "Annexes" to "Coalition Agreements of the 25th Government, Led by Yitzhak Rabin and Approved by the Knesset," Knesset, July 13, 1992 [Hebrew].

68 Janan Bsoul, "Israeli Workers Uniting in Masses? The Numbers Tell a Different Story," *Haaretz*, March 22, 2017.

69 Medding, *The Founding of Israeli Democracy*, 169–71; Bruce Rosen and Gabi Ben Nun, "Legislating the National Health Insurance Law: Why in 1994?," in *Formulating Social Policy in Israel*, ed. Uri Aviram, Johnny Gal, and Yosef Katan (Jerusalem: Taub Center for Social Policy Studies in Israel, 2007), https://www.taubcenter.org.il/en/research/enacting-the-national-health-insurance-law-why-in-1994 [Hebrew].

70 Rosen and Ben Nun, "Legislating the National Health Insurance Law"; Grinberg and Shafir, "Economic Liberalization," 112.

71 Bruce Rosen, "Health Care Systems in Transition: Israel," *European Observatory on Health Care Systems* 5, no. 1 (2003): 15.

72 Grinberg and Shafir, "Economic Liberalization."

73 Quoted in Avishai, *The Tragedy of Zionism*, 137.

74 Yoel Angel, Adi Niv-Yagoda, and Ronni Gamzu, "Adapting the Israeli National Health Insurance Law to the 21st Century: A Report from the 19th Dead Sea Conference," *Israel Journal of Health Policy Research* 10, no. 1 (2021).

75 Yaffa Moskovich, "Transition from the Old to the New: Lessons Learned in the Israeli Histadrut during the Ramon Leadership," *Journal for Labour and Social Affairs in Eastern Europe* 14, no. 4 (2011).

76 See comparative indexes for life expectancy at birth and infant mortality at "Israel," OECD, https://data.oecd.org/israel.htm.

77 Zvi Zameret, "Bar-Ilan Street: The Conflict and How to Solve It," *Democratic Culture* (2000): 215 – 31.

78 HCJ 5016/96, "*Horev v. Minister of Transportation*," *Versa: Opinions of the Supreme Court of Israel*, Cardozo Law School, April 13, 1997.

79 Evelyn Gordon, "Is It Legitimate to Criticize the Supreme Court? Aharon Barak's Revolution," *Azure* 3 (Winter 1998/5758): 57.

80 Shahar Ilan, "Draft Deferment for Yeshiva Students: A Policy Proposal," Floersheimer Institute for Policy Studies 4, no. 10e (December 1995): 15.

81 Lee Hockstader, "Israeli 'Yeshiva Boys' Lose Draft Exemption," *Washington Post*, December 10, 1998.

82 HCJ, "*Rubinstein vs. Minister of Defense*," *Versa: Opinions of the Supreme Court of Israel*, Cardozo Law School, December 9, 1998.

83 Frances Livingstone Raday, "Women's Human Rights: Dichotomy between Religion and Secularism in Israel," *Israel Affairs* 11, no. 1 (January 2005): 81.

84 Itzhak Zamir, *The Supreme Court* (Tel Aviv: Schocken, 2022), 53 [Hebrew].

85 Raday, "Women's Human Rights," 84.

86 For a systematic summary, see Naomi Chazan, "Israel at 70: A Gender Perspective," *Israel Studies* 23, no. 3 (Fall 2018): 141 – 51.

87 "About Israel Women's Network," https://iwn.org.il/english/about-the-israel-womens-network/#:~:text=About%20Israel%20Women's%20Network&text=The%20Israel%20Women's%20Network%20(IWN,judicial%20conditions%20for%20their%20prosperity.

88 Raday, "Women's Human Rights," 82.

89 See "Male and Female Workers (Equal Pay) Law, 5756/1996," International Labor Organization, https://www.ilo.org/dyn/natlex/docs/ELECTRONIC/49589/97926/F585927939/ISR49589.pdf; "Prevention of Sexual Harassment Law, 5758/1998.

90 Chazan, "Israel at 70," 145. Notably, the first adviser on women's affairs for the prime minister's office was appointed in 1978, under the Begin government.

91 Aaron Belkin and Melissa Levitt, "Homosexuality and the Israel Defense Forces: Did Lifting the Gay Ban Undermine Military Performance?," *Armed Forces & Society* 27, no. 4 (Summer 2001): 543.

92 Association for Civil Rights in Israel, "Protecting and Promoting LGBT Rights in Israel," February 15, 2009, https://law.acri.org.il/en/2009/02/15/protecting-and-promoting-lgbt-rights-in-israel.

93 In 2021–22, Uchovsky faced multiple accusations of sexual harassment.

94 "Dana International Visits the Knesset after Winning the Eurovision," Kan Archives, Facebook post, December 26, 2018, https://www.facebook.com/watch/?v=280666355864521.

95 "Law to Prohibit Discrimination 5761/2000," National Legislative Database; Dahlia Scheindlin, "The Woman Trying to Make Israel Equal," +972 Magazine, December 23, 2015; Equal Employment Opportunity Commission, "Annual Report: 2021," Israel Ministry of Industry, Commerce and Trade, 2021, https://www.gov.il/BlobFolder/reports/equal-employment-opportunity-2021-report/he/pirsomim_equal-opportunities-report-2021.pdf [Hebrew].

96 All versions of the law in full text and all amendments, 1953–2018, "Public Education Law, 1953," National Legislation Database, https://main.knesset.gov.il/Activity/Legislation/Laws/Pages/LawPrimary.aspx?t=lawlaws&st=lawlaws&lawitemid=2000665 [Hebrew].

97 Amit M. Schejter, "From a Tool for National Cohesion to a Manifestation of National Conflict: The Evolution of Cable Television Policy in Israel, 1986–98," *Communication Law and Policy* 4, no. 2 (March 1999).

98 Gabriel Weimann, "Cable Comes to the Holy Land: The Impact of Cable TV on Israeli Viewers," *Journal of Broadcast and Electronic Media* 40, no. 2 (1996): 245.

99 HCJ 680/88, *"Schnitzer v. Chief Military Censor,* Decided: January 10, 1989," *Versa: Opinions of the Supreme Court of Israel,* Cardozo Law School, https://versa.cardozo.yu.edu/opinions/schnitzer-v-chief-military-censor.

100 For "culture of secrecy," see International Federation of Library Associations and Institutions, "ILFA/FAIFI World Report: Libraries and Intellectual Freedom: Israel" (January 19, 2001), 1. On the wave of legislation, when fifty-six countries passed such laws within twenty years (the UK passed its Freedom of Information law only in 2000), see John M. Ackerman and Irma E. Sandoval-Ballesteros, "The Global Explosion of Freedom of Information Laws," *Administrative Law Review* 58, no. 1 (2006): 85–130.

101 Zakaria, "The Rise of Illiberal Democracy," 36.

102 Gershon Shafir and Yoav Peled, "Peace and Profits: The Globalization of Israeli Businesses and the Peace Process," in *The New Israel,* ed. idem, 246.

103 "Israel Military Spending/Defense Budget 1960–2022." Macrotrends (based on World Bank data), https://www.macrotrends.net/countries/ISR/israel/military-spending-defense-budget; World Bank, https://data.worldbank.org/indicator/MS.MIL.XPND.GD.ZS?locations=US.

104 Nadav Menuhin, "70 Years of Censorship: The Great Israeli Hits Prohibited from Being Broadcast," *Walla!,* April 15, 2018, https://e.walla.co.il/item/3149851.

105 Zev Nehama, Yosef Lapid, and Ethnix (band),"To Live in New Zealand," *Shironet* (1995), https://shironet.mako.co.il/artist?type=lyrics&lang=1&prfid=176&wrkid=1908.

106 Scott Lasensky, "Underwriting Peace in the Middle East: US Foreign Policy and the Limits of Economic Inducements," *Middle East Review of International Affairs* 6, no. 1 (March 2002): 91.

107 Clyde Haberman, "Rabin Staves Off Collapse of Israeli Coalition, at Least for a Week," *New York Times,* May 12, 1993.

108 For a summary of investigations against Deri in the 1990s, see Ann LoLordo, "At Heart of Israeli Scandal Is Charming, Indicted Rabbi," *Baltimore Sun,* April 19, 1997. The DOP was not a peace agreement but only a preliminary outline for a peace process.

109 For a thorough summary of the events around the High Court ruling on Deri and Pinchasi in 1993, see Haviv Rettig Gur, "How 3 Decades of Deri's Legal Troubles Now See Israeli Judicial Independence at Risk," *Times of Israel,* January 20, 1993.

110 Oren Cohen and Hila Tov, "Knesset Approves the Agreement with PLO by 61 to 50," *Hadashot,* September 24, 1993 [Hebrew].

111 "Enabled": the vote provided normative backing; Rabin was not formally obliged to submit the agreement to a vote; see "The Cairo Agreement: Israel's Negotiations with the PLO, October 1993– May 1994," Israel State Archives, n.d.

112 O. Cohen and Tov, "Knesset Approves."

113 See Dan Ephron, *Killing a King: The Assassination of Yitzhak Rabin and the Remaking of Israel* (New York: W. W. Norton, 2015), 164; "The 376th Meeting of the 13th Knesset, 5 October, 1995," Knesset, full transcript [Hebrew]. On Shas vote, see Friedmann, *The Age of Innocence*, 508 – 9.

114 The assassin, Yigal Amir, assumed that he would be killed in the act by Rabin's security detail; the fact that he was not killed is considered one of the greatest historical failures of Shabak, while Amir saw it as proof of divine intention; see Ephron, *Killing*, chap. 7.

115 Geoffrey Aronson, "Settlement Monitor," *Journal of Palestine Studies* 28, no. 4 (Summer 1999), 144. Figures do not include East Jerusalem, and Aronson describes them as a "conservative approximation," since sources vary.

116 Sfard, *The Wall and the Gate*, 189 – 90.

117 Kretzmer and Ronen, *The Occupation of Justice*, 204.

118 Kiryat Arba settlers and Yigal Amir letter, quoted in Ephron, *Killing*, 192, 232.

119 E. Gordon, "Is It Legitimate," 57.

120 Asad Ghanem, "Founding Elections in a Transitional Period: The First Palestinian General Elections," *Middle East Journal* 50, no. 4 (Autumn 1996): 513 – 28.

121 Edward Said, "The Morning After," *London Review of Books* 15, nos. 20-21 (October 1993).

122 *Freedom in the World: The Annual Survey of Political Rights and Civil Liberties: 1995 – 1996* (New York: Freedom House, 1996), 517 – 18.

123 Khalil Shikaki, "Peace Now, or Hamas Later," *Foreign Affairs* 77, no. 4 (July–August 1998): 32.

124 The original quote was not found; Rabin seems to have repeated it in several forms. The specific quote here appears in the journalist Zeev Galili's blog, in which he cites Rabin's appearance on Channel 1 in March 1994. Zeev Galili, "How the 'New Middle East' Vision Was Realized," *The Logic of the Madness: Online Column of Zeev Galili*, July 20, 2007 [Hebrew]. Galili claims to have heard from Eitan Haber, Rabin's adviser and chief of staff, that Rabin had been impressed when Hosni Mubarak related that he could pave a road by simply expelling residents in the way, and he developed the phrase on this basis. B'Tselem cites his statement with a reference to *Al Hamishmar* newspaper, on September 3, 1993, a few days after the Oslo agreement was announced, prior to the signing of the Declaration of Principles; B'Tselem, "Neither Law nor Justice," August 1995.

125 One of the parties grouped under Barak's "One Israel" was Gesher, headed by David Levy, which split off after the elections; therefore the coalition technically had eight parties.

126 Raday, "Women's Human Rights," 85.

127 Evelyn Gordon, "The Creeping Delegitimization of Peaceful Protest," *Azure* 7 (Spring 5759 / 1999).

128 Youngsters for Tradition (Youtube channel), "He's Innocent: The Song, J'accuse" (originally broadcast in 1999), https://www.youtube.com/watch?v=cYgxKlgn55s.

129 Ethan Bronner, "Sabbath Act Threatens Governing Coalition," *New York Times*, August 15, 1999.

130 Deborah Sontag, "Barak's Coalition Crumbles on Eve of Summit Talks," *New York Times*, July 10, 2000.

131 One demonstrator was from Gaza and was not a citizen. For a detailed version, see Amjad Iraqi, "Thirteen Killed, No One Punished: Remembering October 2000," *+972 Magazine*, October 5, 2015, https://www.972mag.com/thirteen-killed-no-one-punished-remembering-october-2000.

132 The year 2001 was the only time when direct elections were held separately from legislative elections; by 2003, the direct elections for prime minister had been canceled.

133 Sfard, *The Wall and the Gate*, 297 – 98.

134 Suzie Navot, "The Israeli Withdrawal from Gaza: A Constitutional Perspective," *European Public Law* 12, no. 1 (2006): 18. For results of the Likud referendum, see Attila Somfalvy and Diana Bechor-Nir, "Sharon's Defeat: 59.5% against the Disengagement, 39.7%–For," *Ynet*, May 3, 2004 [Hebrew].
135 Navot, "The Israeli Withdrawal," 22.
136 Yair Sheleg, "The Political and Social Meaning of Dismantling Settlements in J.S.G.: The 2005 Disengagement as a Case Study," *Policy Research* 72, Israel Democracy Institute (August 2007): 79–80 [Hebrew; J.S.G. refers to Judea, Samaria, and Gaza, often referred to by their Hebrew initials].
137 I use the term "pro-settlement" to indicate settlement supporters, regardless of where they live. Note that many settlers do not consider themselves far right-wing and a portion are not religious, although Jewish settlements generally vote for right-wing parties that support the positions described here. For example, in Israel's 2022 elections, nearly 85 percent of voters from West Bank settlements supported right-wing pro-settlement parties, including: Religious Zionism, Likud, Torah Judaism, Shas, Jewish Home. "Data on Results of Elections for 25th Knesset from Judea, Samaria and Jordan Valley," Yesha Council, December 18, 2022. http://myesha.org.il/?CategoryID=251&ArticleID=10295
138 "Netanyahu in 2008: A Prime Minister under Investigation Lacks the Mandate to Decide," *Walla!*, February 14, 2018 [Hebrew].
139 Netanyahu had voted four times in favor of the disengagement, in the government and in the Knesset votes, but eventually publicly opposed the plan and resigned as finance minister in August 2005, just before the implementation. David Makovsky, "Sharon, Netanyahu, Disengagement, and Likud Leadership," PolicyWatch 511, Washington Institute for Near East Policy, August 17, 2005.
140 Anshel Pfeffer, *Bibi: The Turbulent Life and Times of Benjamin Netanyahu* (London: Hurst, 2018), 428; on Netanyahu's relationship with ultra-Orthodox parties, see Yair Ettinger, "Netanyahu Defends Child Allowance Cuts at Haredi Meet," *Haaretz*, January 3, 2007.
141 Likud won second place in terms of parliamentary seats but was the only party capable of forming a government. Olmert was indicted in August 2009 and convicted in 2014, with a second conviction in 2015.
142 Yuval Yoaz, "Whoever Raises His Hand against the Court, I'll Knock It Back," *Haaretz*, February 7, 2007 [Hebrew].
143 Friedmann, *The End of Innocense*, chap. 47
144 Ibid., 737–39. Friedmann explained that he was uncomfortable expanding the power of rabbinic courts because women cannot serve on the ultra-Orthodox-dominated institutions, which directly affect their lives.

Section VI
Backlash: 2009 – present

1 Larry Diamond, "Is the Third Wave of Democratization Over? The Imperative of Consolidation," Working Paper 237, Helen Kellogg Institute of International Affairs, March 1997.
2 Zakaria, "The Rise of Illiberal Democracy," 42.
3 Diamond, "Democratic Regression," 24.
4 In the 2022 runoff vote, Le Pen won over 41 percent, while her father won just below 18 percent in 2002. Le Monde with AP and AFP, "Macron wins French Presidential Election," Le Monde, April 24, 2022. See also Tim Boersma, "The Netherlands' Complicated Election Result, Explained," *A Guide to Europe's 2017 Elections*, Brookings Institution, March 20, 2017.

5 Leslie D. Susser, "Avigdor Lieberman," *Britannica,* June 1, 2022, https://www.britannica.com/contrib utor/Leslie-D-Susser/6695.

6 Total former Soviet Union immigration, 1989–96, calculated based on Mark Tolts, "A Half Century of Jewish Emigration from the Former Soviet Union: Demographic Aspects," paper presented at the Project for Russian and Eurasian Jewry, Davis Center for Russian and Eurasian Studies, Harvard University, November 20, 2019, 2. Total Israeli population data, Central Bureau of Statistics (CBS), "Population Data of Israel, 1990–2009" (2010), 2.

7 Tamar Horowitz, "The Increasing Political Power of Immigrants from the Former Soviet Union in Israel: From Passive Citizenship to Active Citizenship," *International Migration* 41 no. 1 (March 20013): 47–73.

8 Ilan Marciano, "Lieberman: Judge Arab MK's Like at Nuremberg," *Ynet,* May 4, 2006 [Hebrew].

9 Lily Galili, "Exposé: Avigdor Lieberman Was a Member of the 'Kach' Movement," *Haaretz,* February 4, 2009 [Hebrew].

10 "Election Broadcasts 2009," National Library of Israel, https://web.nli.org.il/sites/nli/hebrew/collec tions/treasures/elections/elections_materials/pages/elec_videos_2009.aspx; on Finkelstein's role, told by his consulting partner George Birnbaum, see Lily Galili, "I Explain—I Don't Apologize," *Haaretz,* February 12, 2009.

11 For 2009 results, see "About the 2009 Elections," Israel Democracy Institute, https://en.idi.org.il/ israeli-elections-and-parties/elections/2009. Parties included in the right-wing tally: Likud, Yisrael Beiteinu, Shas, Torah Judaism, National Union, and Jewish Home. For analysis of polling dynamics between Yisrael Beiteinu and Likud, see Galili, "I Explain," and author conversation with Rafi Barzilay, Yisrael Beiteinu 2009 campaign strategist. For a collection of public polls prior to 2009 elections, see "Opinion Polling for the 2009 Israeli Legislative Election," Wikipedia https://en.wikipe dia.org/wiki/Opinion_polling_for_the_2009_Israeli_legislative_election.

12 Sammy Smooha, *Index of Arab–Jewish Relations in Israel: 2003–2009,* Arab-Jewish Center, University of Haifa (2009), 10.

13 Ibid.; on socioeconomic gaps, 12.

14 Ibid., 18.

15 The plan was first partially reported in May 2004; Lily Galili, "Lieberman Presents His National Separation Plan to Putin's Representative," *Haaretz,* May 30, 2004, https://www.haaretz.co.il/misc/ 2004-05-30/ty-article/0000017f-e325-d7b2-a77f-e3272b330000 [Hebrew].

16 "Disengagement from Umm-el-Fahm," *Walla!,* June 15, 2005, https://news.walla.co.il/item/731700 [Hebrew].

17 Rekhess notes that Maki (Israel Communist Party) approved a resolution supporting self-determination for Palestinian Arabs "to the point of separation" in its 1953 and 1957 conventions but had dropped this item by 1960. See Rekhess, "Arab-Palestinian National Minority," 6.

18 Shibley Telhami, "2010 Israeli Arab/Palestinian Public Opinion Survey," Saban Center for Middle East Policy (2010), slides 30–31, https://www.brookings.edu/wp-content/uploads/2016/06/israeli_arab_ powerpoint.pdf. "Political transfer" refers to moving geopolitical borders, in contrast to far-right versions of physical "transfer," or deportation/expulsion.

19 Telhami, "Public Opinion Survey," 31. The study asked all those who opposed transfering Arab towns to a Palestinian state to choose one of five reasons offered in a multiple-choice list. In 2009, the top response was "better living standards" (51 percent), while 12 percent chose "Israel is likely to be more democratic than a Palestinian state" (ranked third place).

20 Secessionist wars include those in Georgia, Armenia, Azerbaijan, Chechnya, and the dissolution of the former Yugoslavia; national minorities seeking peaceful secession through referendums include those of Quebec, Catalonia, and Iraqi Kurdistan. These movements were all within the 1990s and 2000s and continued into the 2010s, approximately the phase that is under consideration here.

21 In 2021, just 8.3 percent of Arabs lived in mixed areas. See Nasreen Haddad Haj-Yahya et al., "Statistical Report on Arab Society in Israel: 2021," Israel Democracy Institute, March 17, 2022, https://en.idi.org.il/articles/38540.

22 Amal Jamal, "The Political Ethos of Palestinian Citizens of Israel: Critical Reading in the Future Vision Documents," *Israel Studies Forum* 23, no. 2 (Winter 2008): 5. I use the term "Palestinian" for the leaders, many of whom consider themselves "Palestinian." Yet overall, I continue using the term "Arab citizens," for consistency, while recognizing that "Palestinian" remains a strong aspect of the community's identity.

23 Jamal, "The Political Ethos," 21. The article provides a systematic comparison of the three main documents.

24 Ibid., 9–10.

25 Scheindlin, "A Family Affair."

26 Uri Levy, "'They Are Afraid': Netanyahu Head to Head with the Media: A Look at the Past, May 10, 2018," Kan News, Israel Broadcast Corporation, YouTube, May 12, 2018, https://www.youtube.com/watch?v=Nywa2wQt9-M [Hebrew].

27 Lawrence Joffe, "Obituary: Rabbi Yitzhak Kaduri," *The Guardian*, January 31, 2006.

28 See Ishaan Tharoor, "Cover Story: Why Bibi Netanyahu Is King of Israel," *Time* magazine, May 17, 2009; the actual cover story was written by Richard Stengel.

29 "Law to Amend Orders for Cooperative Associations 8 (2011/5771)," National Legislation Database, March 30, 2011, https://main.knesset.gov.il/Activity/Legislation/Laws/Pages/LawBill.aspx?t=law suggestionssearch&lawitemid=322702 [Hebrew].

30 HCJ 6698/95, *"Ka'adan v. Israel Land Administration,"* Versa: *Opinions of the Supreme Court of Israel,* Cardozo Law School. "Israel Land Administration" is called the "Israel Land Authority" in Israeli government English sources, or "Israel Lands Administration" in other sources; the term here reflects Versa's translation. On IDF exemption for Arabs: this has never been as controversial as the Haredi exemption. Both the government and Arab citizens have historically preferred that Arabs do not serve in an army that is fighting Palestinians or Arab countries. The issue has, however, raised significant social and political questions, including questions of an alternate national service, over the years.

31 Joel Greenberg, "Israeli Court Rules Arab Couple Can Live in Jewish Area," *New York Times*, March 9, 2000.

32 Simcha Rothman, *The Ruling Party of Bagatz: How Israel Became a Legalocracy* (Tel Aviv: Sella-Meir, 2019), 249.

33 Qvortrup, *Death by a Thousand Cuts*, 19–20.

34 Krampf, *The Israeli Path to Neoliberalism*, 227.

35 "Israeli Supreme Court Upholds 'Admissions Committees Law' That Allows Israeli Jewish Communities to Exclude Palestinian Arab Citizens," press release, Adalah: The Legal Center for Arab Minority Rights in Israel, September 17, 2014, https://www.adalah.org/en/content/view/8327.

36 Qvortrup, *Death by a Thousand Cuts*, chap. 7.

37 On the draconian early versions, see Roy Konfino and Mordechai Kremnitzer, "Implications of the Nakba Law on Israeli Democracy," Israel Democracy Institute, June 22, 2009, https://en.idi.org.il/ar ticles/10132.

38 As seen, freedom of expression—specifically, media freedoms—are inherently constrained by the military censor, archives classification rules, gag orders, and the lack of primary legislation for freedom of speech. However, the new legislation explicitly constrained speech and expression regarding a political topic. On the Supreme Court ruling, see *"HCJ 3429/11 Alumni Association v. Minister of Finance," Versa*, Cardozo Law School, January 5, 2012.

39 On the cultural context, note that the bill stipulated that boycott activity against Israel would include areas under its control; see Amir Fuchs, Dana Blander, and Mordechai Kremnitzer, *Anti-Democratic Legislation in the 18th Knesset (2009–2013)* (Jerusalem: Israel Democracy Institute, 2015), 59–60. This type of bill therefore targeted external pressures but also implicitly identified the cultural community as an internal enemy.

40 "Law Preventing Harm to the State of Israel by Means of Boycott – 2011," English version, ACRI https://law.acri.org.il/en/wp-content/uploads/2011/07/Boycott-Law-Final-Version-ENG-120711.pdf.

41 HCJ 5239/11, *"Avneri v. the Knesset," Versa*, Cardozo Law School, April 15, 2015,<BREAK/>https://versa.cardozo.yu.edu/opinions/avneri-v-knesset-summary; Dahlia Scheindlin, "Boycott Goes on Trial in Israel's High Court," *+972 Magazine*, February 16, 2014, https://www.972mag.com/boycott-goes-on-trial-in-israels-high-court.

42 "Most Ministers Oppose Muezzin Bill: 'A Provocation and a Disgrace,'" *Ynet*, December 11, 2011, [Hebrew].

43 Allyn Fisher-Ilan, "Israel Party Proposes Loyalty Oath to Jewish State," Reuters, May 25, 2009.

44 Daniel Bernstein, "Two Brothers Sent to Prison for Torching Jewish-Arab School," *Times of Israel*, July 22, 2015.

45 "Temporary Citizenship Law Is Extended for a Tenth Year," ACRI, April 23, 2013, https://law.acri.org.il/en/2013/04/23/temp-citizenship-law.

46 Dahlia Scheindlin, "Wedding Crashers: Do Anti-Miscegenation Protesters Hate or Love Judaism?" *+972 Magazine*, August 18, 2014.

47 The Knesset, "Protocol No. 78: Meeting of the Committee for Advancement of the Status of Women," Knesset: Committees and Protocols, February 8, 2011.

48 Fuchs, Blander, and Kremnitzer, *Anti-Democratic Legislation*, 16–17.

49 Ruth Levush, "Israel: Supreme Court Decision Invalidating the Law on Haredi Military Draft Postponement," Law Library of Congress, Global Legal Research Directorate, March 2012, 5–6.

50 Ibid., 9.

51 Quoted in HCJ 8300/02, *"Gadban vs. Government of Israel,"* May 22, 2012 [Hebrew], 6.

52 Tal Dahan, "The State of Human Rights in Israel 2009," ACRI, 2009, 67–68.

53 For laws (or articles) struck down by the High Court, see Amir Fuchs, "How Many Laws Were Struck Down by the Supreme Court in Israel?" Israel Democracy Institute, November 8, 2022, https://www.idi.org.il/articles/22273 [Hebrew].

54 Basic Law: Judiciary (Amendment to Public Petitioners)," National Legislation Database, 2011, https://fs.knesset.gov.il/18/law/18_lst%20%20_167223..doc. The bill was proposed by Likud MKs Danny Danon and Yariv Levin. See also Dahlia Scheindlin, "The Assault on Israel's Judiciary," Century Foundation, July 7, 2021, https://tcf.org/content/report/assault-israels-judiciary.

55 Fuchs, Blander, and Kremnitzer, *Anti-Democratic Legislation*, 115.

56 Ibid., 16–17.

57 Merav Michaeli, interview with author, June 9, 2021. The comment was not made during the Eighteenth Knesset (2009–13) but following the more extreme phase of his later terms. Still, the same dynamic is seen in the Eighteenth Knesset, and the characterization applies.

58 Data from Peace Now, based on the Central Bureau of Statistics, https://peacenow.org.il/en/settlements-watch/settlements-data/population.

59 For founding dates, see "About Us," Yesh Din, https://www.yesh-din.org/en/about-us/#:~:text=Yesh%20Din%20was%20established%20in,therefore%20seek%20to%20end%20it. "About Gisha," https://gisha.org/en/about-gisha; "Home," Bimkom, https://bimkom.org/eng/home-mobile.

60 Some contest the use of the term "war" for these rounds of fighting, since they involve a state and a nonstate actor. The Israeli government refers to "operations." I use "war" not in the formal sense but to indicate the severity of the fighting, compared with more routine violence.

61 Gisha notes that the army's policy permitted hummus but not hummus with pine nuts or mushrooms, for example. "A Guide to the Gaza Closure: In Israel's Own Words," Gisha–Legal Center for Freedom of Movement, September 2011, https://www.gisha.org/UserFiles/File/publications/gisha_closure/gisha_brief_docs_eng_sep_2011.pdf.

62 "Gaza: 1.5 Million People Trapped in Despair," International Committee of the Red Cross, June 2009, 6.

63 Human Rights Watch, "'I Lost Everything': Israel's Unlawful Destruction of Property during Operation Cast Lead," Human Rights Watch, May 13, 2010,

64 Israeli and Palestinian casualties in this paragraph: Fatalities during Cast Lead," B'Tselem, https://www.btselem.org/statistics/fatalities/during-cast-lead/by-date-of-event; Palestinian sources reported more than 1,400 killed, including nearly 1,000 civilians. "Human Rights Centers: More than 1,400 Palestinians Killed in Cast Lead," WAFA Palestine News and Info Agency, December 27, 2011, https://english.wafa.ps/Pages/Details/113430.

65 Haviv Rettig-Gur, "Goldstone: Israel Should Cooperate," *Jerusalem Post*, July 16, 2009.

66 "Finance Minister: UN Backing of Goldstone Report Is Anti-Semitic," *Haaretz*, October. 18, 2009.

67 See, e. g., ACRI, Gisha, the Public Committee Against Torture in Israel, HaMoked: Center for the Defence of the Individual, Yesh Din, Adalah, and Physicians for Human Rights–Israel, "Submission of Human Rights Organizations Based in Israel to the Goldstone Inquiry Delegation June 2009," *Adalah's Newsletter* 61, June 2009, https://www.adalah.org/uploads/oldfiles/newsletter/eng/jun09/goldstone%20report_and_appendix%5B1%5D.pdf.

68 "Initial Response to Report of the Fact-Finding Mission on Gaza," Ministry of Foreign Affairs, September 24, 2009, updated August 19, 2021, https://www.gov.il/en/Departments/General/initial-response-to-report-of-the-fact-finding-mission-on-gaza.

69 Emily Alinikoff and Ted Piccone, "The Goldstone Report: Behind the Uproar," Brookings Institution op-ed, April 19, 2011. In 2011, Richard Goldstone qualified some of the commission's findings, particularly regarding Israel targeting civilians, reigniting the controversy.

70 "Israeli NGOs," NGO Monitor, https://www.ngo-monitor.org/report-category/israeli-ngos.

71 Disclosure: The author has conducted consulting projects and public-opinion surveys for the NIF and a number of its grantees, including the human rights organizations involved.

72 Ron Kampeas, "Breaking Down the Im Tirtzu Report on New Israel Fund," *Cleveland Jewish News*, February 12, 2010.

73 The author appeared on one such list by Israel Academic Monitor, while teaching as an adjunct lecturer at Ben-Gurion University in 2011.

74 See, e. g., Ziv Goldfisher, "Leftists Out. Lecturer Dr. Mordechai Kedar Goes on the Attack," NRG/Makor Rishon, November 8, 2010 [Hebrew].

75 Nir Hasson, "Supreme Court Dismisses Fascism Ruling against Im Tirzu," *Haaretz*, July 15, 2015. The original trial heard testimony from experts on fascism, and the Court concluded in 2013 that the similarities outweighed the claim of libel. In 2015, the Supreme Court dismissed the ruling, finding that the issue should not be adjudicated in court.

76 Roni Sofer, "Knesset Supports: Investigative Committee for Left-Wing Groups," *Ynet*, January 5, 2011 [Hebrew].

77 Full text of bill reproduced in Fuchs, Blander, and Kremnitzer, *Anti-Democratic Legislation*, 73–74.

78 New amendments in Israel are often commonly referred to as laws. For an English summary of the NGO transparency law of 2016, see "Law Requiring Disclosure by NGOs Supported by Foreign

Governmental Entities (Amended)—2016"; and the explanation: "Update–NGO Law Approved by the Knesset," ACRI, https://law.acri.org.il/en/2016/07/11/update-ngo-law-passed.

79 Rozin's and Herzog's quotes from the Knesset, "NGO Transparency Law Approved in Final Reading," Knesset News, July 12, 2016, https://main.knesset.gov.il/News/PressReleases/pages/press120716.aspx [Hebrew]. Herzog formally led the Zionist Union Party at the time, a combined list including the Labor Party, led by Herzog, and Tzipi Livni's smaller party, called The Movement. Disclosure: the author provided public-opinion research and consulting for the Zionist Union Party during the 2015 electoral campaign.

80 Surveys commissioned by B'Tselem, conducted by the author; data collection: New Wave Research. The 2011 survey was commissioned by a consortium of human rights organizations and conducted by the author. All data cited with permission of the commissioning groups.

81 Raoul Wootliff and TOI Staff, "Israel Passes Law Limiting Activities, Funding for Get-Out-the-vote Groups," *Times of Israel*, March 21, 2017.

82 "Israel Expels Human Rights Watch Director Today," Human Rights Watch, November 25, 2019, https://www.hrw.org/news/2019/11/25/israel-expels-human-rights-watch-director-today.

83 Freedom House, "Freedom in the World 2018: Israel," https://freedomhouse.org/country/israel/freedom-world/2018.

84 Chaim Levinson, "'I Saw the Bottle Explode and Then I Fled': Dawabshe Family Killer's Reenactment," *Haaretz*, May 18, 2020 [Hebrew].

85 For an extensive list of developments in the case and Honenu's activities, in English, see Uri DeYoung, "Kfar Duma Arson Case," https://www.honenu.org/kfar-duma-arson-case.

86 HCJ, 5100/94, *"Public Committee against Torture in Israel v. the State of Israel, the General Security Service," Versa: Opinions of the Supreme Court of Israel*, Cardozo Law School, September 6, 1999.

87 For an explanation of the ruling on admissibility, see Mordechai Kremnitzer and Yuval Shany, "'Special Interrogations,' Confessions and the Duma Arson Attack," *Lawfare*, July 9, 2018; for Ben-Gvir's involvement, see TOI Staff and JTA, "Foreign Report Says American-Israeli Teen Held in Duma Case," *Times of Israel*, December 23, 2015.

88 Avishai Grinzweig, "Duma Case: Court Dismisses Confessions Attained under Torture," *Maariv*, June 19, 2018 [Hebrew].

89 "Honenu: In the State of Israel It Takes a Miracle for Justice to Come to Light–and That Miracle Didn't Happen Today–the Struggle Is Not Over" (n.d.; response to March 2021 Supreme Court rejection of appeal against conviction), https://www.honenu.org.il/%d7%90%d7%a8%d7%92%d7%95%d7%9f-%d7%97%d7%95%d7%a0%d7%a0%d7%95-%d7%91%d7%9e%d7%93%d7%99%d7%a0%d7%aa-%d7%99%d7%a9%d7%a8%d7%90%d7%9c-%d7%a6%d7%a8%d7%99%d7%9a-%d7%9c%d7%94%d7%aa%d7%a8%d7%97%d7%a9-%d7%a0 [Hebrew]; see also Yonah J. Bob, "Duma Terrorist Tries to Put Shin Bet on Trial before Supreme Court," *Jerusalem Post*, March 21, 2021.

90 "About Us," Honenu, https://www.honenu.org.il/%d7%90%d7%95%d7%93%d7%95%d7%aa/%d7%90%d7%95%d7%93%d7%95%d7%aa-%d7%97%d7%a0%d7%a0%d7%95 [Hebrew].

91 Kohelet Policy Forum, https://en.kohelet.org.il.

92 Emmanuel Navon, "Israel's High Court of Justice Undermines Democracy and Sovereignty," Kohelet Policy Forum, October 5, 2014, https://en.kohelet.org.il/publication/israels-high-court-of-justice-undermines-democracy-and-sovereignty.

93 On the settlement organization, see Shuki Sadeh and Shomrim, "The Kohelet Tentacles: Inside the Web Surrounding the Right-Wing Think Tank," *Haaretz*, February 12, 2023. On the conference, "Live: Conference on the Pompeo Doctrine," Kohelet Policy Forum, January 7, 2020,<BREAK/>https://en.kohelet.org.il/event/conference-on-the-pompeo-doctrine.

94 All quotes from Israel Law and Liberty Forum, https://lawforum.org.il/about-the-law-and-liberty-forum/?lang=en; and Nettanel Slyomovics, "The U.S. Right-Wing Group behind a Conservative Legal Revolution in Israel," *Haaretz*, January 30, 2023.

95 "Simcha D. Rothman," Tikvah Fund, https://tikvahfund.org/faculty/simcha-d-rothman.

96 "Basic Law: Israel as the Nation-State of the Jewish People (originally adopted in 5778/2018)," unofficial trans. Sheila Hattis-Rolef, National Legislation Database, 2022.

97 Ibid.

98 Mordechai Kremnitzer and Amir Fuchs, "Regarding: The Bill for the Nation State of the Jewish People," Israel Democracy Institute, September 17, 2017, https://fs.knesset.gov.il//20/Committees/20_cs_bg_391027.pdf [Hebrew].

99 Dahlia Scheindlin, "Israel's Nation-State Law," Zentrum Liberale Moderne, September 8, 2018,<BREAK/>https://libmod.de/dahlia-scheindlin-israels-nationalstaatsgesetz-warum-spaltet-netanjahu-sein-land [German].

100 "Bill for Basic Law: Israel—The Nation-State of the Jewish People, by MK Zev Elkin, Ayelet Shaked, Yariv Levin, and Robert Ilatov," Knesset, July 22, 2013. On Netanyahu's view, see Government Secretariat, "The 33rd Government, Benjamin Netanyahu, Decision Number 2227," November 23, 2014, https://www.gov.il/he/departments/policies/2014_dec2227 [Hebrew].

101 Ibid.

102 Joint Committee of the Knesset and the Constitution, Law and Justice Committee, "Protocol on Nation-State Law," National Legislation Database, July 18, 2018 [Hebrew].

103 "Protocol Number 11, Meeting of Joint Committee of Knesset and Constitution, Law and Justice Committee, Discussion of Bill: Israel—the Nation-State of the Jewish People," National Legislation Database, March 13, 2018, 13 [Hebrew].

104 Meron Rapaport and Ameer Fakhoury, "How Threats of a Second Nakba Went Mainstream," *+972 Magazine*, June 23, 2022.

105 Amy Spiro and TOI Staff, "High Court Rejects Petitions Seeking to Strike Down Nation-State Law," *Times of Israel*, July 8, 2021.

106 "Freedom in the World 2019: Israel," Freedom House, https://freedomhouse.org/country/israel/freedom-world/2019. The political rights rating declined from 36 (out of 40) to 35, citing the nation-state law as the main reason.

107 Danny Danon, "Making the Land of Israel Whole," *New York Times*, May 18, 2011.

108 Rami Amichay, "Likud Party Calls for De Facto Annexation of Israeli Settlements," Reuters, December 31, 2017.

109 Dahlia Scheindlin, "The Right-Wing Solution for the Violence," *+972 Magazine*, October 10, 2015; "Sovereignty" movement, https://www.ribonut.co.il/BlogCategories.aspx?pageIDU=10&lang=1.

110 Yesh Din, "Regulation of Settlement in Judea and Samaria Law 5777/2017," Annexation Legislation Database, April 1, 2019.

111 Yossi Verter, "Israel's President on Land-Grab Law: We Will Look Like an Apartheid State," *Haaretz*, February 12, 2017.

112 Elena Chachko, "Israel's Settlement Regularization Law: The Attorney General's Extraordinary Brief and What It Means for Israel's Legal Stance on Illegal Settlements," *Lawfare*, December 8, 2017.

113 "Blow to the principle of separations of power": quote from "Domestic Affairs Committee Reveals: The Attorney General Will Oppose an Override Clause," *Knesset News*, October 6, 2014 [Hebrew]; second quote, Zeev Kam, "Ministerial Committee Approved Law to Circumvent HCJ," Makor Rishon/NRG, October 26, 2014 [Hebrew].

114 Hadas Rivak, "TGI Survey: Israel Hayom Gets 30% Stronger and Passes Yediot," *Walla!*, July 28, 2010 [Hebrew].

115 Rothman, *The Ruling Party*, 183 – 84.

116 Madison, Hamilton, and Jay, "The Federalist Papers: LXXVIII," 437.

117 This section reviewing the assault on the judiciary and connecting the general illiberal trends with annexationist expansionism in the West Bank draws significantly on my research that was originally published by the Century Foundation: see Scheindlin, "The Assault on Israel's Judiciary"; idem, "The Logic behind Israel's Democratic Erosion."

118 Mordechai Kremnitzer and Amir Fuchs, "Basic Law: Legislation—A Lethal Blow to the Supreme Court," Israel Democracy Institute, April 30, 2012, https://en.idi.org.il/articles/10280.

119 Tova Tzimuki, "The Radical Change in Netanyahu's Relationship with the Judicial System," *Ynet*, June 18, 2021 [Hebrew]. (The source of the quote is not stated and could be a paraphrase.)

120 Aharon Barak interview, in Kra and Drucker, "'Netanyahu Poisoned Democracy': The Battle of Aharon Barak for the Court," *Reshet 13*, May 30, 2019, 46mn, https://13tv.co.il/item/news/domestic/crime-and-justice/barak-hamakor-259974.

121 On new settlements, see Isabel Kirshner, "Israel Approves First New Settlement in Decades," *New York Times*, March 30, 2017; for data on outposts and settler growth, see "Settler Population," Peace Now, https://a/peacenow.org.il/en/settlements-watch/settlements-data/population.

122 On Netanyahu's 2015 demonization of Arab voters, see, e. g., Pfeffer, *Bibi*, 530. On public television, the corporation was eventually established to replace the old Israel Broadcast Authority, and the news channel Kan 11 retains significant critical independence. However, suspicion of the broadcaster remained; in 2023, Netanyahu's minister of communications threatened to close the corporation entirely.

123 Dahlia Scheindlin, "Ten Years with Netanyahu: Maintaining Israel, the Conflict—and Himself," Friedrich Ebert Stiftung International Policy Analysis, January 2017, http://library.fes.de/pdf-files/iez/13126.pdf.

124 TOI Staff, "AG Says Won't Investigate Netanyahu over Lucrative Stock Sales, Submarine Case," *Times of Israel*, October 15, 2020.

125 For a summary of these and several more police investigations regarding Netanyahu and his wife, Sara, some of which did not lead to charges, see Pfeffer, *Bibi*, 562 – 68.

126 Dahlia Scheindlin, "Legal Bullying in the Service of the Prime Minister," *+972 Magazine*, December 1, 2017.

127 Data on Netanyahu's personal favorability arefrom 2016 – 18 surveys conducted by the author for B'Tselem. The stable 45 percent support refers mainly to publicly available surveys testing job approval ratings, overall favorability, preference for prime minister, or agreement with Netanyahu's stated positions on key issues.

128 David Halbfinger, "Netanyahu Responds to Attempts to Indict Him: What He Said and What He Meant," *New York Times*, February 28, 2019 (translations of original speech by *New York Times*).

129 Ibid.

130 Summary of Netanyahu's full speech and videos embedded, Moran Azoulay and Itamar Eichner, "Netanyahu Responds: Attempted Coup, Investigate the Investigators," *Ynet*, November 21, 2019 [Hebrew]; for "seditious," see Chemi Shalev, "Netanyahu Reacts to Criminal Indictment with Seditious Call to Arms," *Haaretz*, November 22, 2019.

131 TOI Staff, "Full text: In Pre-trial Speech, Netanyahu Assails the Justice System and Media," *Times of Israel*, May 24, 2020.

132 David Halbfinger and Adam Rasgon, "Israeli High Court Lets Netanyahu Form Government, despite Indictments," *New York Times*, May 6, 2020.

133 Tamar Hermann and Or Anabi, "The Israel Voice Index," Israel Democracy Institute, November 2019, https://en.idi.org.il/articles/28984.

134 Tamar Hermann et al., *Israel Democracy Index 2020* (Jerusalem: Israel Democracy Institute, 2020), 44.

135 TOI Staff, "Netanyahu: If I'm Re-elected, I'll extend Sovereignty to West Bank Settlements," *Times of Israel*, April 6, 2019.

136 BBC News, "Israel PM Netanyahu Vows to Annex Occupied Jordan Valley," BBC, September 10, 2019.

137 Freedom House, "Freedom in the World: Israel," multiple years available on Freedom House website.

138 Raoul Wootliff and Michael Bachner, "In Defiance of High Court Order, Edelstein Refuses to Hold Vote for New Speaker," *Times of Israel*, March 25, 2020.

139 Rami Ayyub, Zainah El-Haround, and Stephen Farrell, "East Jerusalem's Sheikh Jarrah Becomes Emblem of Palestinian Struggle," Reuters, May 10, 2021.

140 Yamina won seven seats, but one lawmaker rejected the defection from Netanyahu's bloc and refused to join the new government.

141 Jewish dietary laws for Passover are distinct from regular laws, prohibiting leavened products such as bread, and certain grains.

142 Ofer Kenig, "Five (Elections) in Less than Four (Years)," *Communique*, Israel Democracy Institute, June 20, 2022.

143 Bezalel Smotrich, "Israel's Decisive Plan," *Hashiloach*, September 7, 2017.

144 Haviv Rettig Gur, "How 3 Decades of Deri's Legal Troubles Now See Israeli Judicial Independence at Risk," *Times of Israel*, January 20, 2023.

Conclusion

1 Numerous author conversations with Anshel Pfeffer.

2 "Israeli PM Netanyahu's Bar Ilan Speech (2009), ECF: The Israeli-Palestinian Conflict Interactive Database (n.d.), https://ecf.org.il/issues/issue/70; on his 2015 rejection of a Palestinian state, see Pfeffer, *Bibi*, 529.

3 Quoted in Berlin, *Crooked Timber*, 19.

Bibliography

Secondary Sources

Acemoglu, Daron, and James A. Robinson. "Why Did the West Extend the Franchise? Democracy, Inequality, and Growth in Historical Perspective." *Quarterly Journal of Economics* 115, no. 4 (November 2000): 1167–99.

Abramov, S. Zalman. *Perpetual Dilemma: Jewish Religion in the Jewish State.* Cranbury, NJ: Associated University Press, 1976.

Ackerman, John M., and Irma E. Sandoval-Ballesteros. "The Global Explosion of Freedom of Information Laws." *Administrative Law Review* 58, no. 1 (2006): 85–130.

Aderet, Ofer. "General's Final Confession Links 1956 Massacre to Israel's Secret Plan to Expel Arabs." *Haaretz*, September 13, 2018.

Akzin, Benjamin. "The Role of Parties in Israeli Democracy." *Journal of Politics* 17, no. 4 (1955): 507–45.

Allon, Yigal. "The Case for Defensible Borders." *Foreign Affairs* 55, no. 1 (October 1976): 38–53.

Aloni, Shulamit. *Citizen and His State: Foundations of Civics Theory.* Systems–Israel Defense Forces, 1967. [Hebrew].

Aloni, Shulamit. *Democracy or Ethnocracy.* Tel Aviv: Am Oved, 2008.

Angel, Yoel, Adi Niv-Yagoda, and Ronni Gamzu. "Adapting the Israeli National Health Insurance Law to the 21st Century: A Report from the 19th Dead Sea Conference." *Israel Journal of Health Policy Research* 10, no. 1 (2021).

Arian, Asher. "Israel: The Challenge of a Democratic and Jewish State." In *Secularism, Women and the State: The Mediterranean World in the 21st Century.* Ed. Barry A. Kosmin and Ariella Keysar, 77–90. Hartford: Institute for the Study of Secularism in Society and Culture, 2009.

Arian, Asher. *Politics in Israel: The Second Republic.* New York: CQ, 2004.

Arian, Asher, and Michael Shamir. "A Decade Later, the World Had Changed, the Cleavage Structure Remained: Israel 1996–2006." *Party Politics* 14 (2008): 685–705.

Ariely, Gal. *Israel's Regime Untangled: Between Democracy and Apartheid.* Cambridge, Cambridge University Press, 2021.

Aronson, Geoffrey. "Settlement Monitor." *Journal of Palestine Studies* 28, no. 4 (Summer 1999): 135–44.

Aronson, Shlomo. "David Ben-Gurion and the British Constitutional Model." *Israel Studies* 3, no. 2 (Fall 1998): 193–214.

Avineri, Shlomo. *The Making of Modern Zionism: The Intellectual Origins of the Jewish State.* London: Weidenfeld and Nicolson, 1981.

Avishai, Bernard. *The Tragedy of Zionism.* New York: Farrar, Straus and Giroux, 1985.

Avital, Tomer. "Behind the Scenes of Rabin's Dollar Account Affair." *Shakoof*, August 7, 2019. [Hebrew].

Bar-Joseph, Uri. "The 'Special Means of Collection': The Missing Link in the Surprise of the Yom Kippur War." *Middle East Journal* 67, no. 4 (Autumn 2013): 531–46.

Bar-Zohar, Michael. *Shimon Peres: The Complete Biography.* Rishon le'Tzion: Yediot Ahronot, 2005 [Hebrew].

Barak-Erez, Daphne. "Law and Religion under the Status Quo Model: Between Past Compromises and Constant Change." *Cardozo Law Review* 30, no. 6. (2009): 2495–2507.

https://doi.org/10.1515/9783110796582-010

Bauml, Yair. "Discriminatory Policy toward Arabs in Israel, 1948–1968." *Iyunim b'Tkumat Israel* 16 (2006): 391–413. [Hebrew].

Bauml, Yair. "Israel's Military Rule over Its Palestinian Citizens." In *Israel and Its Palestinian Citizens: Ethnic Privileges in the Jewish State.* Ed. Nadim N. Rouhana and Sahar S. Huneidi, 103–36. Cambridge: Cambridge University Press, 2017.

Bauml, Yair. "The Military Government." In *The Palestinians in Israel: Readings in History, Politics, Society.* Ed. Nadim Rouhana and Areej Sabbagh–Khoury, 47–57. Haifa: Mada el Carmel—Arab Center for Applied Social Research, 2011.

Bauml, Yair. "The Military Government and the Process of Its Revocation, 1958–1968." *The New East* 43 (2002): 133–56. [Hebrew].

Beinen, Joel. "The Palestine Communist Party 1919–1948." *MERIP Reports* 55 (1977): 3–17.

Belkin, Aaron, and Melissa Levitt. "Homosexuality and the Israel Defense Forces: Did Lifting the Gay Ban Undermine Military Performance?" *Armed Forces & Society* 27, no. 4 (2001): 541–65.

Ben-Ari, Ahaz, and Meir Elran. "States of Emergency: Legal Aspects and Implications for the Corona Crisis in Israel," *INSS Insight* 1292 (April 5, 2020).

Ben-Dror, Elad. "Ralph Bunche and the Establishment of Israel." *Israel Affairs* 14, no. 3 (2008): 519–37.

Ben-Eliezer, Uri. "Is Civil Society Emerging in Israel? Politics and Identity in the New Associations." *Israeli Sociology* 2, no. 1 (1999): 51–97. [Hebrew].

Ben-Eliezer, Uri. *The Making of Israeli Militarism.* Bloomington: Indiana University Press, 1998.

Ben-Eliezer, Uri. "State versus Civil Society? A Non-Binary Model of Domination through the Example of Israel." *Journal of Historical Sociology* 11, no. 3 (Sept. 1998): 370–96.

Ben-Gurion, David, and Neil Rogachevsky. "Against Court and Constitution: A Never-Before-Translated Speech by David Ben-Gurion." *Mosaic*, March 10, 2021.

Ben-Porath, Yoram. *The Arab Labor Force in Israel.* Jerusalem: Maurice Falk Institute for Economic Research in Israel, 1966.

Benvenisti, Eyal. "Party Primaries as Collective Action with Constitutional Ramifications: Israel as a Case Study." *Theoretical Inquiries in Law* 3, no. 1 (2002): 175–95.

Berda, Yael. *Living Emergency: Israel's Permit Regime in the Occupied Territories.* Stanford, CA: Stanford University Press, 2018.

Be'er, Yizhar, and Saleh 'Abdel-Jawad. *Collaborators in the Occupied Territories: Human Rights Abuses and Violations.* Jerusalem: B'Tselem, January 1994.

Bell, Abraham. "The Counter-Revolutionary Nation-State Law." *Israel Studies* 25, no. 3 (Fall 2020): 240–55.

Bergman, Ronen. *Rise and Kill First: The Secret History of Israel's Targeted Assassinations.* New York: Random House, 2018.

Berlin, Isaiah. *The Crooked Timber of Humanity: Chapters in the History of Ideas.* Ed. Henry Hardy. London: John Murray, 1990.

"Biltmore Program 1942." The Israeli–Palestinian Conflict: An Interactive Database. Economic Cooperation Foundation.

Bin-Nun, Yoel. "R. Kook's Public Position on Women Voting." *Tradition: A Journal of Orthodox Jewish Thought* 49, no. 1 (2016): 68–71.

Bitton, Mary (Miri). "Reformist Third Parties: The Rise and Fall of the Progressive Party in the United States and the Democratic Movement for Change in Israel." Diss., City University of New York, 1995.

Black, Ian, and Benny Morris. *Israel's Secret Wars: A History of Israel's Intelligence Services.* New York: Grove Weidenfeld, 1991.

Blander, Dana. "The Central Elections Committee: Professional or Political?" *Research and Policy,* Israel Democracy Institute, June 2022.

Brodt, Zachary. "Histadrut Records, 1956–1990." Archives & Special Collections, University of Pittsburgh Library System, August 2010.

Bunche, Ralph. "Democracy: A World Issue." *Journal of Negro Education* 19, no. 4, (1950): 431–38.

Bustan, Shimrit. "1953: Malkot Israel (Tzriffin Underground). Prosecutor of the Military Advocate General, n.d. [Hebrew].

Cahaner, Lee, and Gilad Malach. "Statistical Report on Ultra-Orthodox Society in Israel." Israel Democracy Institute, December 28, 2021.

Caplan, Neil. "The 1956 Sinai Campaign Viewed from Asia: Selections from Moshe Sharrett's Diaries." *Israel Studies* 7, no. 1 (Spring 2002): 81–103.

Chachko, Elena., "Israel's Settlement Regularization Law: The Attorney General's Extraordinary Brief and What It Means for Israel's Legal Stance on Illegal Settlements." *Lawfare*, December 8, 2017.

Chazan, Naomi. "Israel at 70: A Gender Perspective." *Israel Studies* 23, no. 3 (Fall 2018): 141–51.

Clark, Melissa L. "Israel's High Court of Justice Ruling on the General Security Service Use of 'Moderate Physical Pressure': An End to the Sanctioned Use of Torture?" *Indiana International and Comparative Law Review* 11, no. 1 (2000): 145–82.

Cohen, Amichai. *The Constitutional Revolution and Counterrevolution.* Jerusalem: Israel Democracy Institute and Kinneret Zmora Dvir, 2020. [Hebrew].

Cohen, Mitchell, and Nicole Fermon, eds. *Princeton Readings in Political Thought: Essential Readings since Plato.* Princeton, NJ: Princeton University Press, 1996.

Cohen, Shalom, and Kochavi Shemesh. "The Origins and Development of the Israeli Black Panther Movement." *MERIP Reports* 49, July 1976.

Cohen, Stanley, and Daphna Golan, "The Interrogation of Palestinians during the Intifada: Ill-Treatment, 'Moderate Physical Pressure,' or Torture?" B'Tselem, March 1991 and March 1992.

Crossman, Richard. "The Revolt against Bevin." *McLean's*, February 1, 1947.

Dahan, Tal. "The State of Human Rights in Israel 2009." *Association for Civil Rights in Israel* 2009.

Dahl, Robert. *Polyarchy: Participation and Opposition.* New Haven, CT: Yale University Press, 1971.

Dallasheh, Leena. "Political Mobilization of Palestinians in Israel: The al 'Ard movement." In *Displaced at Home: Ethnicity and Gender among Palestinians in Israel.* Ed. Rhoda Ann Kanaaneh and Isis Nusair, 21–38. Albany: State University of New York Press, 2010.

Data Israel: Eliyahu (Louis) Guttman Survey Data Resource, Israel Democracy Institute.

"Peace Index: P1411—Democracy." November 2014.

"Regular Survey of Social Problems and Public Opinion: G0282—Influence of Television." March 1968.

"Election Survey 1969," G0305, Election Survey 1969—Return Territories." 1969.

Davidson, Lawrence. "The Past as Prelude: Zionism and the Betrayal of American Democratic Principles, 1917–48." *Journal of Palestine Studies* 31, no. 3 (2002): 21–35.

Davis, Rochelle. *Palestinian Village Histories: Geographies of the Displaced.* Stanford, CA: Stanford University Press, 2011.

Davis, Uri. "Jinsiyya versus Muwatana: The Question of Citizenship and the State in the Middle East: The Cases of Israel, Jordan and Palestine." *Arab Studies Quarterly* 17, nos. 1–2 (Winter–Spring 1995): 19–50.

Davis, Uri, and Walter Lehn. "And the Fund Still Lives: The Role of the Jewish National Fund in the Determination of Israel's Land Policies." *Journal of Palestine Studies* 7, no. 4 (Summer 1978): 3–33.

Diamond, Larry. "Democratic Regression in Comparative Perspective: Scope, Methods, and Causes." *Democratization* 28, no. 1 (2020): 22–42.

Diamond, Larry. "Is the Third Wave of Democratization Over? The Imperative of Consolidation." Working Paper no. 237, Helen Kellogg Institute for International Studies, March 1997.

Divine, Donna R. "The Modernization of Israeli Administration." *International Journal of Middle East Studies* 5, no. 3 (June 1974): 295–313.

Doron, Gideon. "Judges in a Borderless State: Politics versus the Law in the State of Israel." *Israel Affairs* 14, no. 4 (2008): 587–601.

Dowty, Alan. "Is Israel Democratic? Substance and Semantics in the 'Ethnic Democracy' Debate." *Israel Studies* 4, no. 2 (Fall 1999): 1–15.

Dowty, Alan. *The Jewish State: A Century Later, Updated with a New Preface.* Berkeley: University of California Press, 1998.

Edelman, Martin. *Courts, Politics and Culture in Israel.* Charlottesville: University of Virginia Press, 1994.

Ein Gil, Ehud. "On the Edge of a 'Yod.'" *Matzpen: The Socialist Organization in Israel*, May 16, 2020. [Hebrew].

Elazar, Daniel. "The Israeli Knesset Elections 1992: A First Analysis." *Daniel Elazar Papers Index*, Jerusalem Center for Public Affairs, 1992. https://www.jcpa.org/dje/articles/elec92-analysis.htm.

"The Elections in Israel," *Journal of Palestine Studies* 14, no. 1 (Autumn 1984): 162–74.

Eliash, Shulamit. "The Political Role of the Chief Rabbinate of Palestine during the Mandate: Its Character and Nature." *Jewish Social Studies* 47, no. 1 (Winter 1985): 33–50.

Ellenson, David. "The Supreme Court, Yeshiva Students, and Military Conscription: Judicial Review, the Grunis Dissent, and Its Implications for Israeli Democracy and Law." *Israel Studies* 23, no. 3 (Fall 2018): 197–206.

Etzioni, Amitai. "Alternate Ways to Democracy: The Example of Israel." *Political Science Quarterly* 74, no. 2 (June 1959): 196–214.

Etzioni-Halevy, Eva, and Moshe Livne. "The Response of the Israeli Establishment to the Yom Kippur War Protest." *Middle East Journal* 31, no. 3 (Summer 1977): 284–85.

Falk, Richard. "The Kahan Commission Report on the Beirut Massacre." *Dialectical Anthropology* 8, no. 4 (1984): 319–24.

Farsakh, Leila H., ed. *Rethinking Statehood in Palestine.* Oakland: University of California Press, 2021.

Fischer, Elli. "The Israeli Rabbinate: The Origin Story," *Moment*, May–June 2015.

Freedom House:

Freedom in the World: Country Ratings by Region, 1972–2011.

Freedom in the World: The Annual Survey of Political Rights and Civil Liberties: 1995–1996. New York: Freedom House, 1996.

"Freedom in the World 2019: Israel," Freedom House, https://freedomhouse.org/country/israel/freedom-world/2019.

Forsdyke, Sara. "Athenian Democratic Ideology and Herodotus' 'Histories.' " *American Journal of Philology* 122, no. 3 (Autumn 2001): 329–58.

Fox, Gregory H., and Brad R. Roth. "Democracy and International Law." *Review of International Studies* 27, no. 3 (2001): 327–52.

Friedman, Menachem. "The Chronicle of the Status Quo: Religion and State in Israel." *Continuity and Change* 47 (1990). [Hebrew].

Friedman, Robert I. "The Sayings of Rabbi Kahane." *New York Review of Books*, February 13, 1986.

Friedman, Shuki, Amichai Radzyner, and Yedidia Stern. "Constitution Not Written in the Torah." *Research and Policy* 69, Israel Democracy Institute, December 2006.

Friedmann, Daniel. *The End of Innocence: Law and Politics in Israel.* Rishon le'Tzion: Yediot Ahronot, 2019. [Hebrew].

Fuchs, Amir, Dana Blander, and Mordechai Kremnitzer. *Anti-Democratic Legislation in the 18th Knesset (2009 – 2013).* Israel Democracy Institute, 2015.

Fukuyama, Francis. "The Future of History: Can Liberal Democracy Survive the Decline of the Middle Class?" *Foreign Affairs* 91, no. 1 (January–February 2012): 53 – 61.

Galili, Zeev. "How the 'New Middle East' Vision Was Realized." The Logic of the Madness: Online Column of Zeev Galili, July 20, 2007. http://www.zeevgalili.com/2007/07/446.

Galnoor, Itzhak, and Dana Blander. *The Handbook of Israel's Political System.* Cambridge: Cambridge University Press, 2018.

Garfinkel, Boaz. "Use of the Army to Break the Locomotive Drivers' and Seamen's Strike in 1951." *Iyunim* 34 (2020): 147 – 71.

Gastil, Raymond D. *Freedom in the World: Political Rights and Civil Liberties 1978.* Freedom House. Boston: G. K. Hall, 1978.

Gazit, Shlomo. *Trapped.* Tel Aviv: Zmora-Bitan, 1999.

Gendzier, Irene L. "Palestine and Israel: The Binational Idea," *Journal of Palestine Studies* 4, no. 2 (Winter 1975): 12 – 35.

Ghanem, Asad. "Founding Elections in a Transitional Period: The First Palestinian General Elections." *Middle East Journal* 50, no. 4 (Autumn 1996): 513 – 28.

Ghanem, Asad, Nadim Rouhana, and Oren Yiftachel. "Questioning 'Ethnic Democracy': A Response to Sammy Smooha." *Israel Studies* 3, no. 2 (1998): 253 – 67.

Gidron, Benjamin, Michal Bar, and Hagai Katz. *The Israeli Third Sector: Between Welfare State and Civil Society.* New York: Kluwer Academic, 2004.

Ginsburg, Tom. *Democracies and International Law.* Cambridge: Cambridge University Press, 2021.

Glass, Charles. "Jews against Zion: Israeli Jewish Anti-Zionism." *Journal of Palestine Studies* 5, nos. 1 – 2 (1975): 56 – 81.

Goldberg, Giora. "Religious Zionism and the Framing of a Constitution for Israel." *Israel Studies* 3, no. 1 (Spring 1998): 211 – 29.

Gordon, Evelyn. "Is It Legitimate to Criticize the Supreme Court? Aharon Barak's Revolution." *Azure* 3 (Winter 1998): 50 – 89.

Gordon, Evelyn. "The Creeping Delegitimization of Peaceful Protest." *Azure* 7 (Spring 1999): 30 – 46.

Gorenberg, Gershom. *The Accidental Empire: Israel and the Birth of Settlements, 1967 – 1977.* New York: Henry Holt, 2006.

Greaves, William. *Ralph Bunche: An American Odyssey.* Schomburg Center for Research in Black Culture, South Carolina ETV. William Greaves Productions, 2001 [film].

Grinberg, Lev Luis. *Mo(ve)ments of Resistance: Politics, Economy and Society in Israel/Palestine, 1931 – 2013.* Boston: Academic Studies Press, 2013.

Guyer, Paul. "The Crooked Timber of Mankind." In *Kant's Idea for a Universal History with a Cosmopolitan Aim.* Ed. Amélie Rorty and James Schmidt, 129 – 49. Cambridge: Cambridge University Press, 2009.

Haj-Yahya, Nasreen Haddad, et al. "Statistical Report on Arab Society in Israel: 2021." Israel Democracy Institute, March 17, 2022.

Halamish, Aviva. "Mapam's Vacillating Stance on the Military Government: 1955–1966." *Israel Studies Forum* 25, no. 2 (Fall 2010): 26–53.

Halkin, Hillel. *Jabotinsky: A Life.* New Haven, CT: Yale University Press, 2014.

Hanegbi, Moshe. *Hakvalim shel Tzedek.* Jerusalem: Yavneh, 1981.

Harel, Isser. *Security and Democracy.* Tel Aviv: Edanim, 1989. [Hebrew].

Harris, Michael. "Assessing the Electoral Reform of 1992 and Its Impact on the Elections of 1996 and 1999." *Israel Studies* 4, no. 2 (Fall 1999): 16–39.

Harris, William W. "Israel's West Bank Settlement Policy in the Early 1980s: Strategy, Impact and Implications." *SAIS Review* 5, no. 2 (1985): 233–48.

Heian–Engdal, Marte, Jørgen Jensehaugen, and Hilde Henriksen Waage. " 'Finishing the Enterprise': Israel's Admission to the United Nations." *International History Review* 35, no. 3 (June 2013): 465–85.

Herman Hansen, Mogens. *Polis: An Introduction to the Ancient Greek City-State.* Oxford: Oxford University Press, 2006.

Hermann, Tamar, et al. "Israel Democracy Index 2021: Democratic Values," Israel Democracy Institute, January 6, 2022. https://en.idi.org.il/articles/37857.

Hermann, Tamar, Or Anabi. "The Israel Voice Index," Israel Democracy Institute, November 2019. https://en.idi.org.il/articles/28984.

Hermann, Tamar, et al. *Israel Democracy Index 2020.* Viterbi Family Center for Public Opinion and Policy Research, Israel Democracy Institute, 2020.

Hertzberg, Arthur. "Israel, the Tragedy of Victory." *New York Review of Books,* May 28, 1987.

Herzl, Theodor. *The Jewish State.* Trans. Sylvie D'Avigdor. American Zionist Emergency Council, 1946.

Hofnung, Menachem. "The Public Purse and the Private Campaign: Political Finance in Israel." *Journal of Law and Society* 23, no. 1 (March 1996): 132–48.

Horowitz, Tamar. "The Increasing Political Power of Immigrants from the Former Soviet Union in Israel: From Passive Citizenship to Active Citizenship." *International Migration* 41, no. 1 (March 2013): 47–73.

Howard, Adam M., ed. *Foreign Relations of the United States, 1977–80,* vol. 8: *Arab- Israeli Dispute, January 1977–August 1978.* Washington, DC: US Government Printing Office, 2013.

Huntington, Samuel. *The Third Wave: Democratization in the Late 20th Century.* Norman: University of Oklahoma Press, 1991.

Hutcheson, Joseph C. *Anglo-American Committee of Inquiry.* Lausanne: Department of State, 1946. Avalon Project: Documents in Law, History and Diplomacy, Yale Law School, 2008.

Ilan, Shahar. "Draft Deferment for Yeshiva Students: A Policy Proposal." Floersheimer Institute for Policy Studies 4, no. 10e (December 1995).

Inon, Eyal. "1969, Bergman v. Ministry of Finance: Constitutional Revolution in Three Acts." Jerusalem: Ministry of Justice, April 11, 2019. [Hebrew].

"About the Elections." All years available at "About Elections and Parties," Israel Democracy Institute. https://en.idi.org.il/israeli-elections-and-parties.

Jabareen, Yousef Tayseer. "The Emergency Regulations." In *The Palestinians in Israel: Readings in History, Politics, Society.* Ed. Nadim Rouhana and Areej Sabbagh-Khoury, 67–73. Haifa: Mada el Carmel—Arab Center for Applied Social Research, 2011.

Jabotinsky, Vladimir. *The Jewish War Front.* Jabotinsky Institute, 1940.

Jamal, Amal. *The Arab Public Sphere in Israel: Media Space and Cultural Resistance.* Bloomington: Indiana University Press, 2014.

Jamal, Amal. "The Political Ethos of Palestinian Citizens of Israel: Critical Reading in the Future Vision Documents." *Israel Studies Forum* 23, no. 2 (Winter 2008): 3–28.

Jamal, Amal, et al. "Arab-Palestinian Civil Society Organizations in Israel." Tel Aviv University: Walter Liebach Institute for Jewish Arab Coexistence and Hebrew University: Center for the Study of Civil Society and Philanthropy in Israel, 2019.

Jiryis, Sabri. "The Legal Structure for the Expropriation and Absorption of Arab Lands in Israel." *Journal of Palestine Studies* 2, no. 4 (Summer 1973): 82–104.

Johnson, Paul. "The Miracle." *Commentary,* May 1998.

"Jordanian Annexation of the West Bank (1950)." The Israeli–Palestinian Conflict: An Interactive Database, Economic Cooperation Foundation.

Joyner, Christopher C. "The United Nations and Democracy." *Global Governance* 5, no. 3 (July–Sept 1999): 333–57.

Kabha, Mustafa. "The Life of Jewish Immigrants from Muslim Countries in the Transit Camps as Reflected in the Arabic Journalistic Discourse in Israel, 1950–1967." *Israel Studies* 23, no. 3 (2018): 123–31.

Kafkafi, Eyal. "Segregation or Integration of the Israeli Arabs: Two Concepts in Mapai." *International Journal of Middle East Studies* 30, no. 3 (August 1998): 347–67.

Kahng, Gyoo-hyoung. "Zionism, Israel, and the Soviet Union: A Study in the Rise and Fall of Brief Soviet–Israeli Friendship from 1945 to 1955." *Global Economic Review* 27, no. 4 (1998): 95–107.

Kaye, Alexander. *The Invention of Jewish Theocracy: The Struggle for Legal Authority in Modern Israel.* Oxford: Oxford University Press, 2020.

Kedar, Nir. *Ben-Gurion and the Foundation of Israeli Democracy.* Bloomington: Indiana University Press, 2021.

Kedar, Nir. "Ben-Gurion's *Mamlakhtiyut:* Etymological and Theoretical Roots." *Israel Studies* 7, no. 3 (Fall 2002): 117–33.

Kedar, Nir. "The Rule of Law in Israel." *Israel Studies* 23, no. 3 (Fall 2018): 164–71.

Khenin, Dov. "From 'Eretz Yisrael Ha'ovedet' to 'Yisrael Hashnia': The Social Discourse and Social Policy of Mapai in the 1950s." In *The New Israel: Peacemaking and Liberalization.* Ed. Gershon Shafir and Yoav Peled, 71–100. New York: Taylor and Francis, 2000.

Khenin, Dov, and Dani Filc. "The Seamen's Strike." *Theory and Criticism,* 12–13 (1999): 89–98. [Hebrew].

Kohn, Leo. "The Constitution of Israel." *Journal of Educational Sociology* 27, no. 8 (April 1954): 369–79.

Kohn, Yehuda Pinchas [Leo]. *Constitution for Israel: Proposal and Explanations, Constitutional Committee, Provisional Council.* Israel National Digital Archive, 1948 (Hebrew date given as Chanukah, 5709).

Kramer, Martin. "Israel's Situation Today Looks Much as Ben-Gurion Envisioned It." *Mosaic,* April 30, 2018.

Kramer, Martin. "Who Saved Israel in 1947?" *Mosaic,* November 6, 2017.

Krampf, Arie. *The Israeli Path to Neoliberalism: The State, Continuity and Change.* Oxon: Routledge, 2018.

Kremnitzer, Mordechai, and Amir Fuchs. *Ze'ev Jabotinsky on Democracy, Equality, and Individual Rights.* Jerusalem: Israel Democracy Institute, 2013.

Kremnitzer, Mordechai, and Yuval Shany. " 'Special Interrogations,' Confessions and the Duma Arson Attack." *Lawfare,* July 9, 2018.

Kretzmer, David. *The Occupation of Justice: The Supreme Court of Israel and the Ocupied Territories.* Albany: State University of New York Press, 2002.

Kretzmer, David, and Yael Ronen. *The Occupation of Justice: The Supreme Court of Israel and the Occupied Territories.* 2d ed. New York: Oxford University Press, 2021.

Lahav, Pnina. "The Supreme Court of Israel: Formative Years, 1948 – 1955." *Studies in Zionism* 11, no. 1 (1990): 45 – 66.

Landau, David. *Ben-Gurion: A Political Life.* New York: Schocken, 2011.

Landau, Moshe, Yacov Maltz, and Itzhak Hoffi. "Commission of Inquiry Report of the Commission of Inquiry into the Methods of Investigation of the General Security Service regarding Hostile Terrorist Activity: Part 1." Jerusalem: Government Press, October 1987.

Lasensky, Scott. "Underwriting Peace in the Middle East: US Foreign Policy and the Limits of Economic Inducements." *Middle East Review of International Affairs* 6, no. 1 (March 2002): 89 – 105.

Lauterpacht, Hersch. *An International Bill of the Rights of Man.* Oxford: Oxford University Press, 2013.

Lavie, Zvi. "The Editors' Committee: Myth and Reality." *Kesher* 2, no. 1 (May 1987): 11 – 33. [Hebrew].

Leibowitz, Yeshayahu. *Judaism, Human Values and the Jewish State.* Ed. Eliezer Goldman. Cambridge, MA: Harvard University Press, 1992.

Lein, Yehezkel. *Land Grab: Israel's Settlement Policy in the West Bank.* Jerusalem: B'Tselem, 2002.

Leon, Nissim. "Rabbi 'Ovadia Yosef, the Shas Party, and the Arab–Israeli Peace Process." *Middle East Journal* 69, no. 3 (2015): 379 – 95.

Levush, Ruth. "Israel: Supreme Court Decision Invalidating the Law on Haredi Military Draft Postponement." Law Library of Congress, Global Legal Research Directorate, March 2012.

Lieblich, Eliav, and Yoram Shachar. "Cosmopolitanism at a Crossroads: Hersch Lauterpacht and the Israeli Declaration of Independence." *British Yearbook of International Law* 84, no. 1 (2014): 1 – 51.

Lijphart, Arend. *Democracy in Plural Societies: A Comparative Exploration.* New Haven, CT: Yale University Press, 1980.

Likhovski, Assaf. "Legal Education in Mandatory Palestine." *Tel Aviv University Law Review* 25, no. 2 (November 2001): 291 – 342. [Hebrew].

Loeffler, James. *Rooted Cosmopolitans: Jews and Human Rights in the Twentieth Century.* New Haven, CT: Yale University Press, 2018.

Lustick, Ian S. *Arabs in the Jewish State: Israel's Control of a National Minority.* Austin: University of Texas, 1980.

Lynn, Uriel. *The Birth of a Revolution.* Rishon le'Tzion: Yediot Ahronot, 2017. [Hebrew].

Madison, James, Alexander Hamilton, and John Jay. *The Federalist Papers.* Ed. Isaac Kramnick. New York: Penguin, 1987.

Magid, Shaul. *Meir Kahane: The Public Life and Political Thought of an American Jewish Radical.* Princeton, NJ: Princeton University Press, 2021.

Maimon, Oshrat, and Tamar Luster. "Being a Resident of Jerusalem, Not a Citizen." In *Permanent Residency: A Temporary Status Set in Stone.* Jerusalem: Ir Amim, 2012.

Marcus, Yo'el. "Shamir and the Shultz Plan." *Journal of Palestine Studies* 17, no. 4 (Summer 1988): 153 – 55.

Margalit, Avishai. "The Birth of a Tragedy." *New York Review of Books*, October 23, 1986.

Margalith, Haim. "Enactment of a Nationality Law in Israel." *American Journal of Comparative Law* 2, no. 1 (Winter 1953): 63 – 66.

Mautner, Menachem. *Law and the Culture of Israel.* Oxford: Oxford University Press, 2008.

Mautner, Menachem. *Liberalism in Israel: Past, Problems and Future.* Tel Aviv: Tel Aviv University Press, 2019. [Hebrew].

Medding, Peter Y. *The Founding of Israeli Democracy, 1948–1967.* New York: Oxford University Press, 1990.

Meron, Theodor. "Settlements in the Territories Being Held, Letter to Foreign Ministry, September 18, 1967." [Hebrew]. Available at Gershom Gorenberg, "Kfar Etzion, the Meron Opinion and the Illegality of Settlement," *South Jerusalem blog* (2008). http://southjerusalem.com/2008/09/kfar-et zion-the-meron-opinion-and-the-illegality-of-settlement.

Meyers, Oren. "Expanding the Scope of Paradigmatic Research in Journalism Studies: The Case of Early Mainstream Israeli Journalism and Its Discontents," *Journalism* 12, no. 3 (2011): 261–78.

Mill, John Stuart. "Considerations on Representative Government." In *Democracy: A Reader.* Ed. Ricardo Blaug and John Schwarzmantel, 59–67. New York: Columbia University Press, 2000.

Ministry of Defense, IDF, and Defense Establishment Archives. "Population Census 1967 (5727): Golan Heights, Final Data, General Census." "Displacement in the Heights: How the Population of the Golan Heights Vanished in 1967." Akevot: Institute for Israeli Palestinian Conflict Research, n.d.

Morris, Benny. *The Birth of the Palestinian Refugee Problem Revisited.* Cambridge: Cambridge University Press, 2014.

Morris, Benny. *1948: A History of the First Arab–Israeli War.* New Haven, CT: Yale University Press, 2008.

Morris, Benny. "Operation Dani and the Palestinian Exodus from Lydda and Ramle in 1948." *Middle East Journal* 40, no. 1 (Winter 1986): 82–109.

Moskovich, Yaffa. "Transition from the Old to the New: Lessons Learned in the Israeli Histadrut during the Ramon Leadership." *Journal for Labour and Social Affairs in Eastern Europe* 14, no. 4 (2011): 571–88.

Mudde, Cas, and Cristóbal Rovira Kaltwasser, eds. *Populism in Europe and the Americas: Threat or Corrective for Democracy?* Cambridge: Cambridge University Press, 2012.

Mueller, Jan-Werner. *What Is Populism?* Philadelphia: University of Pennsylvania Press, 2016.

Naor, Arye. "Ze'ev Jabotinsky's Constitutional Framework for the Jewish State in the Land of Israel." In *In the Eye of the Storm: Essays on Ze'ev Jabotinsky.* Ed. Avi Bareli and Pinhas Ginossar, 51–92. Sde Boker: Ben-Gurion Institute, 2004. [Hebrew].

Naor, Mordechai. "The Ben-Gurion 'Kol Ha'am' Trial." *Kesher* 24 (1998): 34–47. [Hebrew].

Navot, Suzie. *Constitutional Law in Israel.* Alphen aan den Rijn, Netherlands: Kluwer Law International, 2007.

Navot, Suzie. "The Israeli Withdrawal from Gaza—A Constitutional Perspective." *European Public Law* 12, no. 1 (2006): 17–33.

Netanyahu, Shoshana. "The Supreme Court of Israel: A Safeguard of the Rule of Law," *Pace International Law Review* 5, no. 1 (1993): 1–24.

Nimmer, Melville. "The Uses of Judicial Review in Israel's Quest for a Constitution." *Columbia Law Review* 70, no. 7 (November 1970): 1217–60.

Ober, Josiah. "The Original Meaning of Democracy: Capacity to Do Things, Not Majority Rule." *Constellations* 15, no. 1 (2008): 3–9.

Orbach, Danny. "Black Flag at a Crossroads." *International Journal of Middle East Studies* 45, no. 3 (Aug. 2013): 491–511.

"The Origins and Evolution of the Palestine Problem: Part II (1947–1977)." *The United Nations.* https://www.un.org/unispal/history2/origins-and-evolution-of-the-palestine-problem/ part-ii-1947-1977.

Ottolenghi, Michael. "Harry Truman's Recognition of Israel." *Historical Journal* 47, no. 4 (2004): 963 – 88.

Pascovich, Eyal. "Not above the law: Shin Bet's (Israel Security Agency) Democratization and Legalization Process." *Journal of Intelligence History* 14, no. 1 (2015): 54 – 69.

Paz-Fuchs, Amir, and Alon Cohen-Lifshitz. "The Changing Character of Israel's Occupation: Planning and Civilian Control." *Town Planning Review* 81, no. 6 (2010): 585 – 97.

Pedahzur, Ami, and Arie Perliger. *Jewish Terrorism in Israel.* New York: Columbia University Press, 2009.

Penslar, Derek. *Theodor Herzl: The Charismatic Leader.* New Haven, CT: Yale University Press, 2020.

Peretz, Don. "Israel's 1969 Election Issues: The Visible and the Invisible." *Middle East Journal* 24, no. 1 (Winter 1970): 31 – 46.

Peretz, Don, and Sammy Smooha. "Israel's Tenth Knesset Elections: Ethnic Upsurgence and Decline of Ideology." *Middle East Journal* 35, no. 4 (August 1981): 506 – 26.

Perlmann, Joel. "Dissent and Discipline in Ben-Gurion's Labor Party: 1930 – 32." Working Paper no. 458, Levy Institute of Economics at Bard College, 2006.

Perlmann, Joel. "The 1967 Census of the West Bank and Gaza Strip: A Digitized Version." Annandale-on-Hudson, NY: Levy Economics Institute of Bard College (November 2011–February 2012). https://www.levyinstitute.org/palestinian-census.

Pfeffer, Anshel. *Bibi: The Turbulent Life and Times of Benjamin Netanyahu.* London: Hurst, 2018.

Pfeffer, Anshel. "The Strange Death and Curious Rebirth of the Zionist Left." *Jewish Quarterly* 246 (November 2021): 1 – 47.

Pinsker, Shachar M. *A Rich Brew.* New York: New York University Press, 2018.

"Question of Palestine: Admission of Israel to the United Nations–GA Debate–Verbatim Record," Summary Records of Meetings, April 5–May 18, 1949. https://www.un.org/unispal/document/auto-insert-180950.

Qvortrup, Matt. *Death by a Thousand Cuts: The Slow Demise of Democracy.* Berlin: De Gruyter, 2021.

Rabinovich, Itamar, and Jehuda Reinharz, eds. *Israel in the Middle East: Documents and Readings on Society, Politics and Foreign Relations, Pre-1948 to the Present,* 2d ed. Waltham, MA: Brandeis University Press, 2008.

Rabinowitz, Dan, and Khawla Abu Bakr. *The Stand Tall Generation: The Palestinian Citizens of Israel Today.* Jerusalem: Keter, 2002. [Hebrew].

Raday, Frances. "Human Rights and the Confrontation between Religious and Constitutional Authority: A Case Study of Israel's Supreme Court." In *Secularism, Women and the State.* Ed. Barry A. Kosmin and Ariella Keysar, 213 – 40. Hartford: Institute for the Study of Secularism in Society and Culture, 2009.

Raday, Frances Livingstone. "Women's Human Rights: Dichotomy between Religion and Secularism in Israel." *Israel Affairs* 11, no. 1 (January 2005): 78 – 94.

Radzyner, Amichai. "A Constitution for Israel: The Design of the Leo Kohn Proposal, 1948." *Israel Studies* 15, no. 1 (Spring 2010): 1 – 24.

Raz, Adam. *Kafr Qasim Massacre: A Political Biography.* Jerusalem: Carmel, 2018.

Reuveny, Rafael. "Democracy, Credibility, and Sound Economics: The Israeli Hyperinflation." *Policy Sciences* 30, no. 2 (1997): 91 – 111.

Rekhess, Elie. "The Evolvement of an Arab–Palestinian National Minority in Israel." *Israel Studies* 12, no. 3 (Fall 2007): 1 – 28.

Robinson, Shira. *Citizen Strangers: Palestinians and the Birth of Israel's Liberal Settler State.* Stanford, CA: Stanford University Press, 2013.

Rosen, Bruce. "Health Care Systems in Transition: Israel." *European Observatory on Health Care Systems* 5, no. 1 (2003).

Rosen, Bruce, and Gabi Ben Nun. "Legislating the National Health Insurance Law: Why in 1994?" In *Formulating Social Policy in Israel*. Ed. Uri Aviram, Johnny Gal, and Yosef Katan. Jerusalem: Taub Center for Social Policy Studies in Israel, 2007.

Ross, Dennis, and David Makovsky. *Be Strong and of Good Courage: How Israel's Most Important Leaders Shaped Its Destiny*. New York: Public Affairs, 2019.

Rothman, Simcha. *The Ruling Party of Bagatz: How Israel Became a Legalocracy*. Tel Aviv: Sella-Meir, 2019.

Rozin, Orit. "Israel and the Right to Travel Abroad, 1948–1961." *Israel Studies* 15, no. 1 (Spring 2010): 147–76.

Rozin, Orit. "Kol Ha'am: Portrait of a Struggle." In *Quiet, [They're] Speaking: Legal Culture of Freedom of Expression in Israel*. Ed. Michael Birnhack, 71–128. Tel Aviv: Ramot, 2006. [Hebrew].

Rubenstein, Amnon. *A Certain Political Experience*. Jerusalem: Eidanim, 1982. [Hebrew]

Rubenstein, Amnon. "The Knesset and the Basic Laws Concerning Human Rights." *Mishpat u'Mimshal* 5 (2000), 339–58. [Hebrew].

Rubenstein, Amnon. "The Story of the Basic Laws." *Law and Man–Law and Business/Labor 5772* (September 2012): 79–109. [Hebrew].

Rubinstein, Elyakim. "The Declaration of Independence as a Basic Document of the State of Israel." *Israel Studies* 3, no. 1 (1998): 195–210.

Samhouri, Mohammed. "Fifty Years of Israeli-Palestinian Economic Relations, 1967–2017: What Have We Learned?" *Palestine-Israel Journal* 22, no. 2 (2017).

Samuel, Edwin. "The Histadrut: (The General Federation of Labour in Israel)." *Political Quarterly* 31, no. 2 (1960): 174–84.

Sands, Philippe. *East West Street*. New York: Vintage, 2016.

"San Remo (1920)." The Israeli–Palestinian Conflict: An Interactive Database, Economic Cooperation Foundation.

Sapir, Gideon. "Constitutional Revolutions: Israel as a Case Study." *International Journal of Law in Context* 5, no. 4 (2009): 355–78.

Sapir, Gideon. *The Israeli Constitution: From Evolution to Revolution*. New York: Oxford University Press, 2018.

Sapir, Gideon. "Religion and State in Israel: The Case for Reevaluation and Constitutional Entrenchment." *Hastings international and Comparative Law Review* 22, no. 4 (1999): 617–66.

Sayigh, Yusif A. "The Palestinian Economy under Occupation: Dependency and Pauperization." *Journal of Palestine Studies* 15, no. 4 (Summer 1986): 46–67.

Schafferman, Karin Tamar. "Participation, Abstention and Boycott: Trends in Arab Voter Turnout in Israeli Elections." Israel Democracy Institute, April 21, 2009.

Scheindlin, Dahlia. "A Family Affair." *Tel Aviv Review of Books*, Spring 2021.

Scheindlin, Dahlia. "Israel's Judicial Assault." *Century Foundation*, July 2021. https://tcf.org/content/report/assault-israels-judiciary/

Scheindlin, Dahlia. "The Logic behind Israel's Democratic Erosion." *Century Foundation*, May 29, 2019. https://tcf.org/content/report/logic-behind-israels-democratic-erosion.

Schejter, Amit. "The End of the Post-Colonial Era: The Transformation in Israeli Media Law on the State's 70th Anniversary." *Publizistik* 67, no. 1 (2022): 109–26.

Schejter, Amit. "From a Tool for National Cohesion to a Manifestation of National Conflict: The Evolution of Cable Television Policy in Israel, 1986–98." *Communication Law and Policy* 4, no. 2 (1999): 177–200.

Schiff, Zeev, and Ehud Yaari. *Israel's Lebanon War.* Trans. Ina Friedman. New York: Simon and Schuster, 1984.

Schlosser, Joel. A. "Herodotean Democracies." *CHS Research Bulletin* 5, no. 1 (2016): 183.

Schmelz, U. O. "The Population of Reunited Jerusalem, 1967–1985." *American Jewish Year Book* 87 (1987): 39–113.

Segev, Tom. *1949: The First Israelis.* Jerusalem: Keter, 1984; English ed., Arlen Neal Weinstein. New York: Henry Holt, 1986.

Segev, Tom. *A State at Any Cost: The Life of David Ben-Gurion.* Trans. Haim Watzman. New York: Farrar, Straus and Giroux, 2019.

Seidelman, Rhona. *Under Quarantine: Immigrants and Disease at Israel's Gate.* New Brunswick, NJ: Rutgers University Press, 2020.

Sfard, Michael. *The Wall and the Gate: Israel, Palestine and the Legal Battle for Human Rights.* Trans. Maya Johnston. New York: Metropolitan, 2018.

Shafir, Gershon, and Yoav Peled, eds. *Being Israeli: The Dynamics of Multiple Citizenship.* Cambridge: Cambridge University Press, 2002.

Shafir, Gershon, and Yoav Peled, eds. *The New Israel: Peacemaking and Liberalization.* Oxon: Taylor and Francis, 2000.

Shaked, Michal. *Moshe Landau: Judge.* Tel Aviv: Aliyat Hagag, 2012.

Shalev, Michael."Liberalization and the Transformation of the Political Economy." In *The New Israel: Peacemaking and Liberalization.* Ed. Gershon Shafir and Yoav Peled, 129–60. Oxon: Taylor and Francis, 2000.

Shapira, Anita. *Ben-Gurion: Father of Modern Israel.* Trans. Anthony Berris. New Haven, CT: Yale University Press, 2014.

Shapira, Anita. "Labour Zionism and the October Revolution." *Journal of Contemporary History* 24, no. 4 (October, 1989): 623–56.

Shapira, Jonathan. *Democracy in Israel.* Ramat Gan: Masada, 1977. [Hebrew]

Shelef, Leon. "Amnesty Prior to Trial." *Kiryat Mishpat* 3, no. 177 (2003). [Hebrew]

Shelef, Nadav G. "From 'Both Banks of the Jordan' to the 'Whole Land of Israel': Ideological Change in Revisionist Zionism." *Israel Studies* 9, no. 1 (2004): 125–48.

Sheleg, Yair. "The Political and Social Meaning of Dismantling Settlements in J.S.G.: The 2005 Disengagement as a Case Study." *Policy Research* 72, Israel Democracy Institute, August 2007.

Shetreet, Shimon. "Forty Years of Constitutional Law: Developments in Constitutional Jurisprudence, Select Issues." *Mishpatim* 19 (1989): 573–615. [Hebrew].

Shikaki, Khalil. "Peace Now, or Hamas Later." *Foreign Affairs* 77, no. 4 (July–August 1998): 29–43.

Shilon, Avi. "David Ben-Gurion on the Issue of Borders." *Zion* 3, 2015). [Hebrew].

Shinar, Adam. "Freedom of Expression in Israel: Origins, Evolution, Revolution and Regression." In *Oxford Handbook on the Israeli Constitution.* Ed. Aharon Barak, Barak Medina, and Yaniv Roznai. Forthcoming, 2023.

Shlaim, Avi. "Britain and the Arab–Israeli War of 1948." *Journal of Palestine Studies* 16, no. 4 (1987): 50–76.

Shlaim, Avi. "The Oslo Accord." *Journal of Palestine Studies* 24, no. 3 (Spring, 1994): 24–40.

"Shultz Peace Plan, March 1988." The Israeli–Palestinian Conflict: An Interactive Database, Economic Cooperation Foundation.

Smith, Pamela Ann. "The Palestinian Diaspora, 1948–1985." *Journal of Palestine Studies* 15, no. 3 (1986): 90–108.

Smooha, Sammy. "Ethnic Democracy: Israel as an Archetype." *Israel Studies* 2, no. 2 (1997): 198–241.

Smooha, Sammy. *Index of Arab-Jewish Relations in Israel: 2003–2009.* Arab-Jewish Center, University of Haifa, 2009.

Smooha, Sammy. "The Mass Immigrations to Israel: A Comparison of the Failure of the Mizrahi Immigrants of the 1950s with the Success of the Russian Immigrants of the 1990s." *Journal of Israeli History* 27, no. 1 (2018): 1–27.

Smotrich, Bezalel, and Simcha Rothman, "Law and Justice Program: To Repair the Judiciary and Strengthen Israeli Democracy." Religious Zionism Party, October 18, 2022. https://zionutdatit.org.il/restart. [Hebrew].

Sprinzak, Ehud. "Extremism and Violence in Israel: The Crisis of Messianic Politics." *Annals of the American Academy of Political and Social Science* 555 (1998): 114–26.

Stanger, Cary David. "A Haunting Legacy: The Assassination of Count Bernadotte." *Middle East Journal* 42, no. 2 (1988): 260–72.

Sternhell, Zeev. "Yonathan Shapiro: A Pioneer of Critical Research," *Israeli Sociology* 2 no. 1 (1999): 11–21. [Hebrew].

Strum, Philippa. "The Road Not Taken, Constitutional Non–Decision Making in 1948–1950 and Its Impact on Civil Liberties in the Israeli Political Culture." In *Israel: The First Decades of Independence.* Ed. S. Ilan Troen and Noah Lucas, 83–104. Albany: State University of New York, 1995.

Subotic, Jelena. "Narrative, Ontological Security, and Foreign Policy Change." *Foreign Policy Analysis* 12 (2016): 610–27.

Sveen, Asle. "Ralph Bunche: UN Mediator in the Middle East, 1948–1949." Nobel Prize, 2006. https://www.nobelprize.org/prizes/peace/1950/bunche/article.

Tatour, Lana. "Citizenship as Domination: Settler Colonialism and the Making of Palestinian Citizenship in Israel." *Arab Studies Journal* 27, no. 2 (2019): 8–39.

Taylor, Astra. *Democracy May Not Exist, but We'll Miss It When It's Gone.* London: Verso, 2019.

Telhami, Shibley. "2010 Israeli Arab/Palestinian Public Opinion Survey." Saban Center for Middle East Policy, 2010.

Thrall, Nathan. *The Only Language They Understand.* New York: Metropolitan, 2017.

Tocqueville, Alexis de. *Democracy in America: And Two Essays on America.* Trans. Gerald E. Bevan. London: Penguin, 2003.

Tolts, Mark. "A Half Century of Jewish Emigration from the Former Soviet Union: Demographic Aspects." Paper presented at the Project for Russian and Eurasian Jewry, Davis Center for Russian and Eurasian Studies, Harvard University, November 20, 2019.

Tzabag, Shmuel. "Co-operation in the Shadow of a Power Struggle: Israel: The Likud Governments and the Histadrut 1977–84." *Middle Eastern Studies* 31, no. 4 (1995): 849–88.

Tzimhoni, Daphne. "The Political Configuration of the Christians in the State of Israel." Special issue, *The New East: Quarterly of the Israel Oriental Society* 32, nos. 125–28 (1989): 139–64.

Tzur, Ron, and Nissim Cohen. "The Ongoing Israeli Civil Service Reform: Comparing Current Achievements to Past Attempts." *Revue française d'administration publique* 4, no. 168 (2018): 943–56.

"United Nations General Assembly Resolution 181, November 29, 1947." https://avalon.law.yale.edu/20th_century/res181.asp.

United Nations Special Committee on Palestine (UNSCOP). "Report to the General Assembly," 1947. Vols. 1, 2, and 3.

Uriely, Nahman, and Amnon Barzilay. *The Rise and Fall of the Democratic Movement for Change*. Tel Aviv: Reshafim, 1982.

V-Dem Institute. "Democracy for All? V-Dem Annual Report 2018." University of Gothenburg, 2018.

Vinkler, Dana. "Making Israeli Television—Discussions Leading to the Establishment of Television in Israel, 1948–1968." *Kesher* 34 (Spring 2006): 130–41. [Hebrew].

Walter, Dror. "State or Market? On the Meaning(lessness) of the Jewish Israeli Public's Attitudes towards Capitalism or Socialism as the Preferred Economic System." Israel Democracy Institute, 2011.

Warhaftig, Zerach. *Constitution for Israel: Religion and State*. Jerusalem: Ahva, 1988. [Hebrew].

Weimann, Gabriel. "Cable Comes to the Holy Land: The Impact of Cable TV on Israeli Viewers." *Journal of Broadcasting & Electronic Media* 40, no. 2 (1996): 243–57.

Weitz, Yechiam. *Israel in the First Decade*, Unit 5: On the Reparations Agreement. Open University, 2020. [Hebrew].

Weizmann, Chaim. *Trial and Error: The Autobiography of Chaim Weizmann*, bk. 1. Lexington, MA: Plunkett Lake. Kindle ed., 2013.

Woodhead, John. *Palestine Partition Commission Report*. London: His Majesty's Stationery Office, 1938, 165. Economic Cooperation Foundation. https://ecf.org.il/media_items/375.

Yakobson, Alexander, and Amnon Rubenstein. *Israel and the Family of Nations: The Jewish Nation-State and Human Rights*. Trans. Ruth Morris and Ruchie Avital. London: Routledge, 2009.

Yaron, Zvi. "The Teachings of Rabbi Kook, Jerusalem, 5734." Virtual Library: Herzog College, 1974.

Yavin, Haim. "The Elected '81: Episode 4, Left and Right," Kan Archives, Israel State Broadcasting Corporation. Originally broadcast July 30, 1981. https://archive.kan.org.il. [Hebrew].

Yehuda, Limor, et al. *Two Legal Systems: Israel's Regime of Laws in the West Bank*. Association for Civil Rights in Israel, 2014.

Zakaria, Fareed. "The Rise of Illiberal Democracy." *Foreign Affairs* 76, no. 6 (November–December 1997): 22–43.

Zameret, Zvi. "Bar-Ilan Street: The Conflict and How to Solve It." *Democratic Culture* 3 (2000): 215–31.

Zamir, Itzhak. "Legal Status of Israeli Settlements in Judea and Samaria: Opinion of the Attorney General, Ministry of Justice, Feb. 25, 1980." Scanned/published by Alexandrovich and Atzmor, *The Law in These Parts*, 2012.

Zamir, Itzhak. *The Supreme Court*. Jerusalem: Schocken, 2022.

Zayyad, Tawfiq. "The Fate of the Arabs in Israel." *Journal of Palestine Studies 6, no. 1* (1976): 92–103.

Zini, Levi. "Days of Begin: Doing Good for the People." Kan Documentaries, 2019. YouTube. https://www.youtube.com/watch?v=uRp9un7ixsw. [Hebrew].

Zipperstein, Steven J. *Pogrom: Kishinev and the Tilt of History*. New York: W. W. Norton, 2018.

Ziv, Guy. *Why Hawks Become Doves: Shimon Peres and Foreign Policy Change in Israel*. Albany: State University of New York Press, 2014.

Zukerman, William. "Israeli Sailors' Strike Broken by Brutality, Slander, Writer Claims." *Sentinel* 178, no. 1 (1952).

Selected Primary Sources

Israel State Archives

Defense Establishment Archives, "Population Census 1967 (5727): Golan Heights, Final Data, General Census." In "Displacement in the Heights: How the Population of the Golan Heights Vanished in 1967." Akevot: Institute for Israeli Palestinian Conflict Research, n.d.

"Golda Meir and the Agranat Commission: The Report That Brought Down a Government, November 1973–April 1974." N.d. https://catalog.archives.gov.il/en/chapter/golda-meirs-government-agranat-report-april-1974.

"Battle at Sea: Mapam against Mapai—the First Political Strike—Seaman's Strike 1951." *Landmarks*, 2017. https://catalog.archives.gov.il/chapter/sailors-strike-1951. [Hebrew].

Minister of Justice and Ministerial Committee for Legislation and Law Enforcement. "Basic Law: Fundamental Human Rights." *Ministry of Justice*, 1990.

Selected Israeli Legislation and Ordinances

Source: National Legislation Database, unless otherwise specified. Hebrew, unless otherwise specified. Protocols are available in endnotes.

Basic Law: Israel as the Nation-State of the Jewish People (originally adopted in 5778/2018). Unofficial trans. Sheila Hattis-Rolef. National Legislation Database, 2022.

Basic Law: Judiciary (amendment to public petitioners), 2011.

Basic Law: The Knesset (originally adopted in 5718/1958). Trans. Sheila Hattis Rolef.

(Emergency) Regulations (Judea and Samaria—Adjudication of Offenses and Legal Assistance), 5727–1967.

Law and Administration Ordinance (Amendment no. 11) Law of 1967. English version: Ministry of Foreign Affairs. https://www.gov.il/en/Departments/General/13-law-and-administration-ordinance-amendment-no-11-law.

Law to Amend Orders for Cooperative Associations (Amendment no. 8) 2011 (5771).

Law Preventing Harm to the State of Israel by Means of Boycott–2011." English version: ACRI. https://law.acri.org.il/en/wp-content/uploads/2011/07/Boycott-Law-Final-Version-ENG-120711.pdf.

Law of the Government, 5761–2001.

Law of Return, 5710–1950. English version: International Labor Organization. https://www.ilo.org/dyn/natlex/docs/ELECTRONIC/86616/97947/F1439396114/ ISR86616.pdf.

Nationality Law, 5712–1952.

Public Service Law (Appointments), 1959 (5719).

Settlement of Labor Disputes Law 5717/1957 and Collective Agreements Law 5717/1957. English text: International Labor Organization.

Supreme Court—High Court of Justice Rulings (HCJ)

All sources in English from *Versa: Opinions of the Supreme Court of Israel*, Cardozo Law School, unless otherwise specified.

HCJ 73/53 and HCJ 87/53. *Kol Ha'am Corporation, Ltd. and Al-Ittihad Newspaper v. Minister of the Interior.* October 16, 1953.

HJC 98/69. *A. Bergman v. Minister of Finance and State Comptroller.* July 3, 1969.

HCJ 390/79. *Dweikat et al. v. State.* October 10, 1979.

HCJ 606/78 and 610/78. *Ayub v. Defense Minister* ("Beit El"). Raanan Alexandrovich and Liran Atzmor, *The Law in These Parts: Interactive Journey Following the Film* (2012), March 15, 1979. [Hebrew].

HCJ 1601/90. *Shalit v. Peres.* May 8, 1990.

HCJ 3872/93. *Mitral Ltd. v. Prime Minister and Minister of Religious Affairs, Yitzhak Rabin.* October 22, 1993.

HCJ 6698/95. *Ka'adan v. Israel Land Administration.* March 8, 2000.

HCJ 5100/94. *Public Committee against Torture in Israel v. the State of Israel, the General Security Service.* September 6, 1999.

HCJ 8300/02. *Gadban v. Government of Israel.* May 22, 2012. [Hebrew].

HCJ 5239/11. *Avneri v. The Knesset.* April 15, 2015.

HCJ 3429/11. *Alumni Association v. Minister of Finance.* January 5, 2012.

Index

https://doi.org/10.1515/9783110796582-011

Printed in the USA
CPSIA information can be obtained
at www.ICGtesting.com
JSHW010953251123
52008JS00016B/9

9 783110 796452